the INTEGRATING GOSPEL & the CHRISTIAN: FIJI 1835-67

Titles in The Missiology of Alan R. Tippett Series

The Jesus Documents (2012)

The Ways of the People: A Reader in Missionary Anthropology (2013)

The Road to Bau and *The Autobiography of Joeli Bulu* (2013)

No Continuing City (2013)

Fullness of Time (2014)

Slippery Paths in the Darkness (2014)

the INTEGRATING GOSPEL

THE MISSIOLOGY OF ALAN R. TIPPETT SERIES
DOUG PRIEST, SERIES EDITOR
DOUG PRIEST, EDITOR

The Integrating Gospel and The Christian: Fiji 1835–67
Copyright © 2015 by Fuller Theological Seminary
All rights reserved.

No part of this book may be reproduced, stored in a retrieval system, or transmitted in any form or by any means—electronic, mechanical, photocopy, recording, or otherwise— without prior written permission of the publisher, except brief quotations used in connection with reviews in magazines or newspapers.

Most Scripture quotations are from The Authorized (King James) Version. Rights in the Authorized Version in the United Kingdom are vested in the Crown. Reproduced by permission of the Crown's patentee, Cambridge University Press.

Scripture quotations marked (ASV) are from the American Standard Version, Thomas Nelson and Sons, 1901. Public domain in the United States.

Scripture quotations that have been paraphrased or that are from unknown versions have been indicated in the text.

Published by William Carey Library
1605 E. Elizabeth St.
Pasadena, CA 91104 | www.missionbooks.org

Brad Koenig, copyeditor
Mel Hughes, editor
Rose Lee-Norman, indexer
Josie Leung, graphic design

William Carey Library is a ministry of
Frontier Ventures
Pasadena, CA | www.frontierventures.org

Printed in the United States of America

19 18 17 16 15   5 4 3 2 1 BP100

Library of Congress Cataloging-in-Publication Data
Tippett, Alan R. (Alan Richard), 1911-1988.
  [Works. Selections]
  The integrating gospel and the Christian, Fiji 1835-67.
     pages cm. -- (The missiology of Alan R. Tippett series)
  Includes bibliographical references and index.
  ISBN 978-0-87808-480-7 -- ISBN 0-87808-480-0 1. Missions--Fiji. 2. Christianity--Fiji. 3. Missions--Anthropological aspects. 4. Fiji--Church history--19th century. I. Tippett, Alan R. (Alan Richard), 1911-1988. Integrating gospel. II. Tippett, Alan R. (Alan Richard), 1911-1988. Christian, Fiji 1835-67. III. Title.
  BV3680.F5T575 2015
  266.0099611--dc23
                              2015005044

CONTENTS

The Integrating Gospel

Series Foreword vii

Foreword ix

Personal Note 1970. xi

Preface xiii

PART ONE

CHAPTER 1 Introductory Statement. 3

CHAPTER 2 The Field for Investigation: The Church in the Fiji Islands 7

CHAPTER 3 General Concluding Statement. 29

PART TWO

CHAPTER 4 Introductory Statement: The Field and the Nature of Research Material. . . . 35

CHAPTER 5 The Impact of Culture on Christian Practice 39

CHAPTER 6 The Impact of Culture on Christian Belief. 71

PART THREE

CHAPTER 7 Introductory Statement: Breaking *Down* or Breaking *Through* Cultural Barriers 105

CHAPTER 8 Reception 107

CHAPTER 9 Transmission 129

CHAPTER 10 Discovery. 143

References Consulted or Discussed 153

Index 271

SERIES FOREWORD

Always the creative thinker, Alan Tippett, transplanted to the United States from Australia (never really integrated), is the originator of the concept of cultural fatigue which continues after culture shock has passed. One afternoon he walked the entire midtown business district of Pasadena seeking "a reel of cotton." Returning in despair, what was he asking for? Well, of course, a spool of thread. However, in the field of anthropology, he didn't miss a thing and had a compendious knowledge, especially of the Southern Pacific sphere.

His alert mind took him in many directions, some complete surprises, and from volume to volume in this series you will find very little overlap and much that is rich for contemplation. Thanks to Doug Priest as well as Darrell Whiteman, Charles Kraft, and Greg Parsons for making sure these gems of thought are still available.

Ralph D. Winter
Pasadena, California
May 2009

FOREWORD

When studying for my master's in missiology at the Fuller School of Theology School of World Mission in 1979, the newly retired Dr. Alan Tippett returned from Australia to teach a class on the Development of Missionary Anthropology. Glenn Schwartz, our international student advisor, had noticed how deliberate I was in my choice of classes, so he asked me if I was particularly interested in that topic. My reply was, "From my reading of Alan Tippett, I really don't mind if the topic is 'ethnic diversity in toenails,' I will still take it in order to have a class with Dr. Tippett." As it turns out, Tippett's encyclopedic knowledge of the world of missions meant that even his frequent diversions from the topic at hand were wonderfully productive for me. And being a fellow Australian I was informally appointed as an "interpreter" of his Aussie brogue by the other students. Reading *The Integrating Gospel* later, I came to appreciate the depth of Tippett's research that backed up his classroom diversions.

Having just completed his master's degree at the American University in 1956, Alan Tippett returned to Fiji enthused with his discovery of interdisciplinary research techniques such as ethnolingistics, ethnopsychology, etc.[1] His utilisation of those techniques resulted in him completing *The Integrating Gospel* in 1958 with the subtitle *An Ethnolinguistic Study in the Communication of the Gospel in the Fiji Islands*. The volume has three main parts: Part One—The Impact of the Gospel on Language; Part Two—The Impact of the Culture Pattern on the Practice and Belief of the Christian Church; Part Three—Communicating the Gospel beyond Cultural Barriers.

Late 1960, Victor Hayward of the World Council of Churches' International Missionary Council's Department of Missionary Studies, the person who subsequently arranged for Tippett to do the research that led to Tippett's best-known *Solomon Islands Christianity*, had correspondence with Tippett about finding a publisher for *The Integrating Gospel*. But knowing Lutterworth Press had declined the manuscript, Hayward asked that if a publisher was

---

[1] Interestingly enough, he wrote *The Integrating Gospel* before he discovered ethnohistory, which subsequently proved to be his favourite research tool, although he utilised it informally in the writing of Alan R. Tippett, *No Continuing City: The Story of a Missiologist from Colonial to Postcolonial Times* (Pasadena: William Carey Library, 2013), 239.

not found, would Tippett give him permission to publish the third section of the book as one of the IMC Research Pamphlets.[2]

Tippett's response included the statement, "Young missionaries need to know this sort of thing when they go out in the full bloom of youth." His point was that it takes decades to gain these sorts of insights on one's own, and by then that missionary is often in a leadership/administrative position rather than in frontline service. Implied in this statement is the likelihood that this is a self-perpetuating problem. He didn't warm to the suggestion that only the third section be published because, to him, findings such as these should never be separated from their database.[3]

With that as background, it is exciting that at last this whole volume is being published by William Carey Library. Missiologists and missionary practitioners will be thankful to William Carey Library's foresight in making this available as part of *The Missiology of Alan R. Tippett Series*.

It is doubly good news to see it going to print, in that by 1970 Tippett seemed to have given up seeing it published when he wrote, "I have decided to bind this manuscript and keep it as a library item rather than publish it as a book." He gave his self-deprecating reasons, but also pointed out that he had changed a lot since writing it due to the subsequent influence of other scholars. However, that is one aspect that makes it so valuable in getting to know Alan Tippett and his journey in missiology. While it is true that the Fiji being described in this volume no longer exists and will never be reconstructed, the publication of this volume contributes much more to missiology and the study of missions than a historical record.

In the detail of this book Tippett addresses many issues that provide guidance for contemporary missions. One simply needs to see past the intricate detail to extract the gold for missions today.

Kevin Hovey
department head, Pastoral and Cross Cultural Ministry
Alphacrucis, Sydney

---

2   Hayward to Tippett, 28 October 1960, St. Mark's Library, Canberra, TIP 70-38, vol. 1-10.
3   Tippett to Hayward, 2 November 1960, St. Mark's Library, Canberra, TIP 70-38, vol. 1-10.

PERSONAL NOTE 1970

I have decided to bind this manuscript and keep it as a library item rather than publish it as a book. It represents my thinking during 1956-58 which I was still on the field in Fiji. I was registered as a citizen of the colony and was of a mind to spend the rest of my days with the Fijian people. Two things interfered with this intention. A sickness made it essential for me to get away to a milder climate at least for a year; 1959 was a rough year physically and emotionally. I came to the conclusion that permanent settlement in Fiji would not be good for the emerging indigenous church; that my work was finished. The new day had arrived. I belonged to old Fiji, but I knew I was leaving a team of men (men who had passed through my hands in the Bible school or the theological institution or as ministers on probation) in whom I had the greatest confidence. The hardest truth I ever had to accept in my life was to admit that my service to Fiji was finished.

This manuscript belongs to a day that has gone, both for Fiji and for me. Yet I believe it speaks to all pioneer missionaries trying to penetrate animistic society. I wrote it in the nineteenth year of my missionary service. As I look back on it now I realise what Fiji and the Fijians did to me as a man and a Christian. This was written before I met Donald McGavran. The manuscript represents the raw material of my cross-cultural experience. It also predates my contact with Homer Barnett. I am sure that I could not write this manuscript the same way today, leaving McGavran and Barnett out of it—or Malinowski either, or Linton, or Kroeber, or Wallace to mention only a few. This manuscript is intensely Fijian. It represents perceptions that have become dim over my decade of absence. This is why I want to keep it as it is. To publish it now would require rewriting from my present position, quite apart from the fact that Fiji has changed out of all recognition (both country and people) during that decade.

Quite apart from scores of articles, I think my pilgrimage is reflected in my books. The monograph *The Christian: Fiji 1835-67* came before this manuscript. I had taught wider than Fiji in Pacific Church History at Davuilevu, but Polynesian people movement studies at Eugene drew me out of Fiji into the wider Pacific. Although my fellowship research, *People Movements of Southern Polynesia* (1971), was entirely my own material, the tools and orientation were strongly influenced by Barnett and McGavran. My last flutter in depth with Fiji was *Fiji Material Culture: A Study of Cultural Context, Function, and Change* (1968), a secular study in anthropology. It goes with a series of papers presented before the Fiji Society and published in their *Transactions*.

I look back on this now with some degree of nostalgia. I now came to look at myself as an anthropologist and found myself frequently standing with Malinowski, although I am not aware that I consciously borrowed from him. My new missiological dimensions were brought to bear on *Solomon Islands Christianity* (1967), the hardest thing I have had to write as I had so many critical things that were difficult to say to put on paper. More recently I have swung away into missiological theory and theology—not by my choice but because of trends in the philosophy of mission today. *Verdict Theology in Missionary Theory* (1973) and *Church Growth and the Word of God* (1970) reflect this. If I rewrote *The Integrating Gospel* now it would be clearly a different book. Therefore I have decided to keep it as a library item reflecting my mental struggles with the missionary problems at the peak of that phase of my life.

Furthermore, as a critical study it would have shortcomings. I was out in mid-Pacific entirely limited to my own library. I had only minored in anthropology for my master's degree. I had no friends with anthropological knowledge with whom I could engage in dialogue. When I wrote it, publishers had no market for this type of material. When the market broke it was opened to *Missionary Go Home!* type of writing rather than the empathetic approach with which I was trying to deal with the same problems. So I bind the manuscript merely as a matter of record.

PREFACE

An encouraging feature of modern study in the humanities and social sciences is the manner in which specialists, hitherto almost isolationists in their respective fields, have been coming together for the exploration of the new fields opening for interdisciplinary research.

New fields have thus been found between psychology and linguistics, culture and personality, ethnology and linguistics, history and anthropology, and so on. This trend away from the isolation of research fields shows that man is learning to see himself as an integrated whole.

This book, *The Integrating Gospel*, is an interdisciplinary study. It lies in a hitherto undefined field somewhere between linguistics, anthropology, comparative religion, theology, and the technique of missions. I have given it the subtitle *An Ethnolingistic Study in the Communication of the Gospel in the Fiji Islands*.

Missionary literature has not produced a great deal on the church as a factor in semantic change, and good missionary linguists have not contributed a great deal to ethnolinguistics as a science. Most anthropologists working on Pacific Island studies have confined their studies from a recent point of time, without proper relation to a century or more of Western cultural impact, which could have been studied had they also been more familiar with methods of historical research, and this has sometimes led them to findings which are not supported by island archives.

This book is a humble attempt at studying the church in a South Pacific setting, of studying it historically, its impact on island language, and its own modification under the influence of the island culture pattern. It has been a longtime piece of original research covering almost two decades and is research *in identification*.

It will probably have many critics. I am not alarmed if they prove me wrong and their criticisms lead on to truth. On the other hand, I venture to suggest there is much for missionaries, students, and critics of missions, and members of mission boards in its pages; possibly much that will disturb some of them.

I have presented here three studies, each in itself complete, yet each related to the others. They seem to indicate three aspects which lend themselves as focal points for specific research.

The first, "The Impact of the Gospel on Language," is a straightforward statement on historical ethnolinguistics, and has actually involved as much historical research as linguistic. The second, "The Impact of the Culture Pattern on the Practice and Belief of the Christian Church," is a missionary study of a young church integrating itself within an island community. This is really the reverse process of the first, but in reality many of the factors studied in each reveal more interaction than impact. By classifying them as impacts, however, I have been forced to examine them carefully with a view to taking a stand that the balance of influence is one way or the other. It has its value as such. These two cultural studies demand the third, "Communicating the Gospel beyond Cultural Barriers," and is an attempt at stating my own missionary experience in relating this original research to the practical ends for which I first came to the islands.

An underlying aim of this book is to convince any Westerner who should chance to read it that we Westerners are on the whole extremely egocentric. We have our own ideas of ethics, of progress, of worship and theology, and are always ready to argue that we are right, often to force our concepts on people of other cultures, we are so certain about it. "Nothing is easier," wrote Dr. Ryder Smith, "than to ridicule other people's ritual; few things harder than to enter sympathetically into it" (Smith 1946, 64). The kind of research found in this book cannot be done from the outside or by an observer. One must "enter sympathetically into it." It is research *in identification.*

For this reason there are not a great many quotations in this book. The research has been done in villages, churches, homes, vernacular songs, psalms, chants (many oral only), and material written by islanders. Dictionaries have only been used for verification when necessary or when points in doubt have been raised. All this is firsthand, and little has ever been published before.

Here and there comparisons are made with things in other lands. There are points gleaned from reading; they must stand on their own merits—out here in mid-Pacific I have no library resources for adequate verification. They should therefore be received as illustrations only and are all acknowledged.

The field of special research throughout is the Fiji Islands, where I have worshipped in the island pattern for much of the last two decades. The thesis is built round this field, although I feel certain that many of my particular findings would be safe generalisations for world missions.

In *The Integrating Gospel* we are studying the manner in which the gospel breaks *through* cultural barriers without breaking them *down*, and integrates itself in the society. This study warns against breaking *down* policies on missions, and explores methods of breaking *through.* To all who are concerned with the communication of the gospel, at home or abroad, I offer this small contribution to thought born out of my own missionary experience.

Alan R. Tippett
Davuilevu, Fiji
1958

PART ONE

The Impact of the Gospel on Language

1
INTRODUCTORY STATEMENT

Words are pictures that reflect scenes and episodes. They are more than this, for they represent ethnolinguistic fusion (i.e., in words we may pinpoint cultural elements, reflections of ways of living, relationships, attitudes, philosophy, historical changes, and even the development of theological concepts). Thus we may take a word with a long and interesting history, and study its use at any given point of time, and find therein a reflection of cultural elements of that precise period in the history of its users. Therefore words are important evidence in the science of historical reconstruction.

This operates both ways, so that sometimes a word will reveal new light on a cultural idea or custom, and at other times cultural studies will throw light on the use of a word; this in turn illuminating the context in which it is used. Again by means of the comparative method, a word used in different contexts of the same date may bring to light much important information. Ultimately this may be used for dating other texts, or for the investigation of questionable texts, as to whether they are genuine or spurious. There is no end to the study of ethnolinguistics, and no knowing where it may lead one. Its value in biblical exegesis has been tremendous, and especially in the reconstruction and verification of biblical history, and in the tracing of the development of religious concepts.

Some Scripture Examples

Let us take an example. Following Robert I. Kahn, we consider the attributes of God and wonder, perhaps, how to reconcile the paradoxical ideas of justice (*mishpat*) and mercy (*chesed*). The question arises as to how these ideas stand in the Talmud, and how the sages viewed them. Immediately our current theological problem has become an ethnolinguistic one. They were not concerned with the documentary theory of J and E, where J showed, perhaps, the Merciful One and E the Just One, and JE the two attributes in one Being. The dualism did not trouble them, so much so that they even visualised two thrones in the heavenly throne room, and God sat on one in justice and moved to the other in mercy, thereby delaying or suspending the judgement of the former (Kahn 1956, 581),[1] and we begin to appreciate a bold anthropomorphism as part of the cultural ethos, which is not so easy for philosophic moderns. Thus ethnolinguistics enables us to pinpoint concepts in time, place, and cultural setting.

As an example of the use of this science in historical reconstruction, let us take the word *ecclesia*. Here we have the lawful assembly of a Greek city-state, comprised of those with full citizenship rights, but excluding foreigners and slaves. They met to deal with the business of the state. We find the word used secularly thus three times in Acts 19, where we are concerned with the faith making its impact or encounter within the Greek world. This is the assembly fixed by law as opposed to the illegal concourse (*sustrophe*), and in those days, it met three or four times monthly in Greek cities (Webster and Wilkinson 1855, 1:664). The word was taken over by the translators of the Septuagint for the Greek-speaking Hebrews of the Dispersion, for the rendering of the Hebrew *quahal*, as for example in 2 Chronicles 30:23.[2] The emphasis is on the assembly having been *summoned* to meet with God, and the word is chosen to differentiate from another (*synagogue*), which is assembled like a congregation,[3] of its own volition, so the background of the word is Greek in form but Hebrew in meaning.

The word becomes of immediate interest to us when we discover that it is common in the Acts of the Apostles and in the Epistles but appears only twice in the Gospels, and both those times on the lips of our Lord (Matt 16:18; 18:17 twice). Thus in anticipation He describes His church and falls in line with other utterances wherein He stresses the *call* (John 15:16). Our Lord is the one who calls. It is *His* church.

How then was the word used later on, after He had departed from their midst? If we take the first letter to Corinth as an example, we will find already differentiations of use. The greeting is addressed to the local church at Corinth (1:2); further on the word has a wider sense as of the church universal (10:32); and in the closing verses greetings are sent from one of the household churches (16:19), which were springing up throughout the Graeco-Roman world, especially in places of pioneering and heavy persecution.

The word *ecclesia* is used throughout, but we have a sequence of reflections of a changing pattern, which can be pinpointed in time and place as an operator stops a filmstrip.

---

1   The writer holds no particular brief for Kahn's views but uses his facts merely as an illustration to show how a modern biblical theological problem may find its explanation in an ethnolinguistic pinpoint. For the reader desiring to study further the words *mishpat* and *chesed*, the writer recommends Snaith (1944), where the origins of these two words are discussed in a most scholarly manner, though strangely without mention of the dual thrones.
2   It has been suggested that there are etymological affinities between *quahal* and the Greek, *kalein*; the Latin, *calare*; and the English "to call" (Trench 1865, 3).
3   The Alexandrian translators were not entirely consistent in this, and Trench (1865, 1:2–4) points out the inconsistencies while admitting this seems to have been their general plan. Another authority claims the former summons men from the whole world to become its members, the latter brought together members of an existing society; and that this differentiation reveals the ultimate distinction between the Christian church and the Jewish synagogue (Bullinger 1924, 72–73). See also the chapter on "The Church of God" in Barclay (1955).

Introductory Statement

The words of the Bible capture the changes of formative days for the church of God. Today we have a basic doctrine of the church, and our theological colleges provide a course of lectures about it; but in the Scriptures we may study its development—we have a filmstrip which reflects the cultural ethos at different points of time. The word and the culture pattern are mutually confirmatory, and therefore either one is valid evidence for suggesting the other where light on one is not clear. The whole must integrate. Therefore whenever a text reveals a peculiar use of a well-known word, we are justified in asking why, and likewise whenever a word suddenly changes its meaning.

There must be a reason, which calls for investigation. Take, for instance, the use of the term *Lord* for Jesus in the gospel narrative. You may, according to Durell, find it used in three ways, and these uses are found to fall into historic periods (1910, 33–34). Something happened at a specific point of time, and from then a known word had a new meaning and indicates a new attitude on the part of the disciples towards Jesus. The pattern must integrate as a whole, and we are compelled to pinpoint the Caesarea Philippi incident and the Resurrection as being vital experiences leading to the changes concerned.

One of the many examples which might be taken from Paul is the word *tapeinophrosune*, "with a lowly mind." *Tapeinos*, to heathen writers, had a bad meaning—groveling, abject—but the full word is a Jewish seed brought to maturity in the Christian church. It was used in the Septuagint (e.g., Prov 29:23) but is not found in classical Greek before the Christian era. A common word in the New Testament, it reveals how Christ's teaching and life raised the idea of humility to a new level (Phil 2:3) (Lightfoot 1913, 109).

Some Examples from Church History

Many volumes have been written on key words of the Bible, but that is not the theme of this study. The purpose of this preamble has been to use well-known data to illustrate a point of view or an attitude towards the relationship of words and culture pattern, of words and events, of words and changing society, of words and the development of theological and ethical concepts. What has been said of the days of the early church—that they were formative days—applies also of the church throughout history. Its days are never anything but formative, and semantic change when it has bearing on the church (either its organisation or its thought) is valid evidence for historical investigation. We are interested in the experience of the saints. This is our tradition, as Bishop Moore said—the cumulative heritage of actual experience, the faith of past generations, through which God has helped to create ours, as ours in time will help create that of the next (Edwards 1951, 41).

Thus, throughout the history of the church, the experiences of men especially in times of crisis, have led to the reading of some new meaning into old words, and this very change is evidence of both the event and the experience of the saints. Just as the meaning of the words *bread* and *wine* received a new significance because of a certain act, in a certain room, at the time of the Last Supper, so all through history where events and personalities have come together, words have been left as evidence. Was there not a time when men spoke of "the Eternal City" and thought of Rome? Then came the fall of Rome, and this event reacted on Augustine, leading him to write his *City of God*; and did not this change forever the meaning of the proud term—"the Eternal City"? And are there not words which belong to church history, which, though we claim them ours, we can never completely separate from certain names and events and a particular religious background? Would any of us preach on *justification by faith* without thanking God in our hearts for Martin Luther? It was in the Bible, of course, and we might have found it without Luther, but it would not have been quite the same meaning. *Justification by faith*, consciously or unconsciously, for every one of us, involves something conceived against a background of sixteenth-century Roman Catholicism. Nor will it ever be easy for an expositor to speak of *predestination* without reference to Calvin. There are other words like *perfect love*, which have similar significance for Methodists. This is a "cumulative heritage of actual experience." We cannot ponder these theological terms without reference to the past, and even in concepts which we reject, we still feel the drag of those focal points where the concept was changed or charged with new meaning, or a long-forgotten meaning rediscovered with power.

Now, the cardinal fact of this study is that what has applied for the people of God in biblical times, and down through history, is also applying today for the young churches. I want to take you now from the known to the unknown, and show you how the church is a causative factor in semantic change, and how these very changes in word meanings are evidence of new and vital Christian experiences, of developing organisation, and a growing theology—indigenous growth reflecting a struggle with racism, Western money economy, and social forces of disintegration that have invaded from without. My examples come from the Fiji Islands, the field where I labour.

2

THE FIELD FOR INVESTIGATION: THE CHURCH IN THE FIJI ISLANDS

The church has been in the Fiji Islands for a little over a century, and one of the outstanding features of this mission was the number of excellent linguists who were among the earliest missionaries. A great deal of their work remains extant for study. In their journals they explain their reasons for many of the decisions they made, and those of us who follow know they laid a good foundation. They were sound in their judgements, and we can find little fault with their techniques.[4] Proof of this may be had in the way in which their innovations have been received and become thoroughly indigenous. Their system for Fijianising English names was remarkable and has stood the test of time.[5]

Problems of the Communicator

But things are never easy for the pioneer missionary evangelist and translator. Difficulties of communication, even to the missionary who has the work of his predecessors on which to build, seem to me to involve the translator in one of two problems—either he translates his own linguistic thought forms, which are imperfectly understood by the new Christian, or he has to escape his own thought forms altogether and try to reduce everything to basic experience, and then seek out some native thought form which can be used to express the concept. Both of these have their dangers. Theological courses and Bible studies in English to island people, whose English is limited and colloquial, run into the former danger. They are often justified on the score that sooner or later the words will acquire their intended meaning, even though it be delayed a generation or two. The chances are that, by the time they do acquire such intended meaning (if ever), Western Christian ideas will have been modified, and thus often when the islander does eventually catch up with the ideas involved, they are some thirty years out of date. This criticism is justly made against many sects that are at present pouring into the Pacific Islands with their peculiar gospels in theological jargon with which Westerners are familiar. Their real appeal is an ability to

---

4 There has been some criticism of the Fijian orthography, mostly from people who have been unready to learn to use it. For those of us who use it day by day it is excellent.
5 By comparing the notes of Messrs. Hunt and Lyth in this matter the situation can be completely reconstructed. The principles involved may be studied in Lyth's *Journal* in the Mitchell Library, Sydney, Australia.

cite Scripture from all sorts of contexts to suit their ends. Their converts likewise learn to cite the same passages, but the significance is temporally delayed. Their acceptance is blind on the simple authority that they are the word of God.

The second alternative has its danger in its boldness. A missionary certainly takes a responsibility on his shoulders when he selects a concept from some element of pagan life, for building up Christian understanding. This is what the early Fijian missionaries did in many respects, and it was just here that their daring scored the greatest triumphs for the gospel. And this, it seems to me, is more in line with the tradition behind the word *ecclesia* and many other cherished possessions, as, for example, the transforming of the birthday of the sun (25 December) into our festival of Christmas. The seeds of the desired concept were there awaiting the rain of Christianity for them to burst forth into new life.

Therefore, as we pass on to the detailed study of these word changes, it would be well for the reader to take cognisance of this basic assumption at the outset. The selection of words for biblical translation and catechetical exercises by the early Fijian missionaries was deliberate and thoroughly considered. Wherever possible they used native thought forms—some very daring.

Because they were willing to take this risk in faith, the language of the church was immediately thoroughly indigenous, and this, more than any other fact, gave the much divided Fijian people their unity and their *lingua franca*. Although the missionaries were extremely critical of the pagan religion and disgusting social practices of the people, and wrote at length on this subject, they were never blind to the fact that there were, here and there, same glimmers of light, even in the darkness. Wherever such a glimmer was evident, they tried to preserve it in a sanctified form. These are the basic facts for the reader to remember as we proceed.

Types of Semantic Change Observed

There were many types of semantic change. Some were deliberately made and explained. Some came slowly over the years and reflect the changing culture. There were, as with every language, some foreign borrowings. There were combinations of old words which gave new ideas by their association. There were similar words which demanded reflection and selection, as we have already seen with *ecclesia* and *synagogue*. The growing church required a unique terminology. There were spiritual experiences which required description, and a new ethic to be explained. Perhaps no one word proves anything, but let it be observed that we are dealing with cumulative evidence. These tremendous changes reveal something of the terrific impact the church was making on Fiji and its people, and the cumulative evidence of semantic change is real and valid evidence of this.

Foreign Borrowings

Now it suits our purpose to deal quickly with the foreign borrowings and dismiss them. There are, however, two significant things that must be said: (1) Where a completely new idea was to be introduced, that had no island counterpart, an English word was borrowed and Fijianised. (2) Where possible the word was fitted into the Fijian linguistic pattern and used as a root with normal prefixes and suffixes. Let us consider a few examples of each of these facts.

COMPLETELY NEW IDEAS

Secular vocabulary has made hundreds of borrowings—*sitoa* (store), *retio* (radio), *wavu* (wharf), *simede* (cement), *ki* (key), *idini* (engine), *etita* (editor), *poudi* (pound), *silini* (shilling), and *peni* (penny), to give a few examples, which are enough to show how Western culture has been imposing itself on the islands over the last century and a half. This was inevitable, but there are documentary references to the early missionaries' conscious efforts to avoid it, and they confined the practice to items which were environmental or cultural but extra-Fijian. For instance, there were things in the biblical and ecclesiastical environments which had no Fijian counterparts.

Thus, the fauna of the Bible sometimes presented problems, for though Fijian had its *gata* (snakes) and *vuaka* (pigs),[6] there were no sheep or horses. As these animals were actually introduced by the missionaries, the English names were brought with them and Fijianised as *sipi* and *ose*.

In the matter of flora they usually found some related tree or plant in Fiji and used this name, but sometimes, when they felt the similarities were not close, they borrowed a foreign environmental word (e.g., *sita*; cedar).[7]

Names of foreign places and people were borrowed and Fijianised according to set rules, depending on whether they were of Hebrew or Greek origin.

In the organisation of the church completely new cultural elements were introduced, some with theological significance of great importance to the missionaries. Thus they used a few words like *sakaramede* (sacrament) and *papitaiso* (baptism). There are not many such words.

ABSORBING WORDS IN THE INDIGENOUS PATTERN

These foreign words had to conform to the Fijian linguistic pattern. The name for the church itself, or for the Christian religion, as distinct from the pre-Christian practices,

---

6 *Vuaka* is really an English word, "porker," but it is of pre-Christian origin in Fiji. It exists as *puaka* in Tonga and *vua'a* in Samoa, and was an early trade word. Even so there is an earlier native word for "pig," which survives in *vore* in the Kadavan dialect (Fiji). The writer knows a documentary reference to pigs in the islands over three hundred years ago.

7 Also used of the timber of the tree, which was introduced to the islands in the furnishings of the vessel *John Wesley* in 1847.

was a foreign word borrowed from Tonga, *lotu*. There were also a few words borrowed for ecclesiastical purposes but which subsequently became used for secular purposes—*same* (psalm) and *tevoro* (devil), for instance. Let us examine these three interesting words.

The original use of *lotu* was as a verb and a noun, the former being used to describe the act of decision when a heathen "bowed the knee" to God, and the second *na Lotu* referring to the Christian religion, an all-inclusive word. Christianity came via Tonga, and there were many Tongans in Fiji, so the use of a Tongan word was natural. In these two senses the word was used by pagan and Christian alike to describe the phenomena which was appearing in their midst. Decision was a ritual act and described by a simple statement (*Sa lotu ko Ratu Nagatalevu*; Chief Big Snake has *lotu*-ed). This was a perfectly meaningful act to any Fijian, both regarding its performance and its consequences. The word was absorbed into the Fijian linguistic pattern almost immediately, so that we get *vale ni lotu* (church house); *vakakoso lewe ni lotu* (congregation), thus avoiding the confusion of the many meanings of the English word "church"; *vakalotutaka* (convert)—the regular pattern for a causative verb (i.e., "to cause to lotu"); and a secondary use, at first within the church and then outside, *lotutaka* (to pray for)—literally, to make something an object, in the interests of which an act of worship is employed.⁸

Much the same thing may be said of *same* (psalm), although the Fijian word *meke* was often used instead. There were many real affinities between the two, but as there were many unsavoury forms of *meke*, the church gradually dropped the use of the native word in this connection. *Same* is a good example of how perfectly natural borrowings may be fitted into the linguistic form of the borrowing language. From the noun *same* a verb was formed, *samea* (to sing psalms or to praise). In the process of time the secondary meaning became uppermost, and the word was used to praise in other ways, as we would say, "I am singing his praises today," a form of metaphoric use. When a speaker uses numerous complimentary epithets about the womenfolk of a tribe who have entertained him, as in a speech of thanks, these are termed *yaca ni vakasasamei* (names of much praising). A visitor desiring to depart with all fitting decorum will engage in this form of what we would consider extravagance. Yet, even to the Fijian there is a point where such extravagance brings forth retorts from those praised, and the decorum is lost. This is a regular form of Fijian humour—praises and words of endearment pass from one to the other, growing more and more extravagant, and rousing laughter among those present. This form of patter is known as *veisamei* (singing each other's praises), a reciprocal action noun formed in the regular pattern by prefixing *vei-* to the passive form of the verb. This example serves

---

8   Actually in pre-Christian Tongan the word was found for an act of worship and was so recorded by Mariner in 1817. However, when it came to Fiji it was used as the word for the Tonga religion only (i.e., Christianity). So the secondary Tongan meaning was the primary Fijian meaning of this borrowed word. The modern tendency to use the word of religion (e.g., *Na Lotu Mahomet;* The Muslim Religion) is good pre-Christian Tongan usage but is much resented by the older Fijians.

to show how completely indigenous an English word may become when its thought fits the cultural pattern, and its form lends itself to use as a verbal root.

The history of the word *tevoro* (devil) is not so easily reconstructed. It is easier to recognise in the form *tevolo*, but its wide distribution among the islands prior to the arrival of the church, more or less forces us to attribute it to the English-speaking navigators, sandalwood traders, and whalers of fifty years earlier. It is certainly a word of modern introduction, and in Fiji, at least, was seized on for description of the later forms of magic and spiritual evil which were infiltrating just before the historic arrival of Christianity. This is a highly significant fact which the anthropologist cannot afford to miss, that the Fijian clearly differentiates between the sympathetic magic of the tribal medicine man and the hostile foreign magic of the sorcerer. Yet Europeans persistently miss this and speak of *ka vakatevoro* (things of the devil) as all-inclusive. This display of ignorance has often caused a Fijian to say that it only shows how little the foreigner knows about this. Except where under considerable Western influence, or where he adapts his speech to the Westerner, the Fijian differentiates clearly. My personal experience has been that an antidote for black magic is sought from the tribal medicine man, not the Fijian minister. They do not confuse *ka ni Vu* and *ka vakatevoro*, or *na veiqaravi makawa* and the *ka vakatevoro*. That is, they speak with respect of "the things of the Ancestor" or "the old practices" but with fear of "things of the devil." In the meantime "the devil" has taken his place in Fijian ideas. The phrase *tiko vakatevoro* (to live together in the way of the devil) has been accepted as the term for living together in an unmarried state. This problem has arisen since the acceptance of Christianity, and the church scored a strong moral victory in securing the use of this term. The very term is a judgement.[9]

For all this the term *tevoro* has always been an elusive one when it comes to actual definition. Like the devil himself, it seems to take on many forms, and may be used of a man who is in a devil's service, during the time he is "possessed." There is a proverb, the origin of which must be in historic times surely—*Sa vuka na tevoro ka sa tu na tamata* (the devil has flown and the man remains). This proverb is used of a person who, having done evil, now comes again to his senses. It suggests strong affinities between biblical and Fijian demonology. It seems that the proverb could almost be traced to the influence of the Scripture itself.[10] Here we must leave our examples of borrowed words. Perhaps we have seen enough to realise that, although the church did not introduce a great number of borrowed words,

---

9 The earliest reference I have been able to locate is a resolution of the district meeting of 1857. It was used as the opposite of *vakalotu*, at a time when the polygamy issue was being fought out. Converts were accepted as adherents and were admitted to instruction but were not baptised unless they became truly *vakalotu* and abandoned living *vakatevoro* (*Fiji District Miscellaneous Resolutions Book*, 1854—67, resolution 45). It is highly significant that this public use of the term dates just a few months after the abandonment of polygamy by the paramount chief, Ratu Cakobau.

10 For example, see Matthew 9:32,33; Mark 1:23–27; 5:1–20; 7:29,30; 9:20–27; Luke 4:33–36; Acts 16:16–18; 19:11–16. This type of Scripture narrative was highly acceptable to the Fijian mind at a period in their history when this was a grim problem to them.

except for the names of people, places, animals, etc., the new words she did introduce were significant words which have either been fitted naturally into Fijian life and culture or have molded them. In all cases they have become Fijian in form and followed the rules of grammar.

Retentions from the Pre-Christian Religion

We now turn to a highly significant group of words—those selected from the pre-Christian ritual and religion for use in the church. The ancient religious practices were highly ritualistic and left a rich selection of words like *ai soro* (sacrifice), *cabora* (present in a liturgical or sacrificial manner), *masu* (pray or prayer), *cuva* (bow down in respect), and many more, all highly significant words, and clearly understood by the people, and which would be used in their original sense for Scripture translation with little, if any, modification of meaning. It is a matter of great satisfaction to us that the early missionaries penetrated deeply enough into heathen worship to realise the rich heritage of ceremonial and sacrificial terminology the Fijian people possessed, and were sufficiently bold to retain it for Christian use. Without this, neither Christianity nor the Scriptures could have become meaningful so quickly to the Fijian people.

Out of these words has come the Fijian concept of worship. It is not Western, but truly Fijian. These are revealing words. Take *cuva* for instance. In the New Testament we meet the concept of "bowing down." In Romans 11:10 we have a word which means "to bend the knee joint" and is metaphorically used as "to humble oneself." But it is quite a different word that is used in Luke 24:5 of the visitors to the sepulcher on Resurrection Day, who "bowed down their faces to the earth." The "every knee" that should bow before the Christ in Philippians 2:10 is still another word. So the New Testament offers three concepts—humiliation, reverence, and worship in the word "bow" or "bow down."

It seems to me that the word *cuva* used by itself can be used in any of these three senses, but it is never used flippantly, and is a word of spiritual quality. For a man to kneel down to bale water out of a canoe, an entirely different word is used. There are times when *cuva* signifies shame or sorrow, but here again the word has a spiritual significance; it is far from a mere physical act. The Fijians call it a "word of deep significance" (*vosa bibi*). The root is used in a transitive form as *cuvata* (to conceal oneself behind). We have here a clue to the concept. It is a bowing down which hides the subject's face before some great sorrow or before a divine manifestation. It involves a feeling of pain or unworthiness. A man walking, with his head bent in sorrow, is said to *lako cuvacuva*; or for one walking erect to bow humbly as he passes a great chief, is *cuva tutu*. For a man who has committed some grievous error to fly from judgement, but to know all the time that he cannot escape, is *cuva vudi*. Is it any wonder that the church took over this word which so perfectly expressed the emotional ideas behind Peter falling down before Christ (Luke 5:8) and similar passages?

In the period of the great mass movements into the faith, which commenced under John Hunt in the 1840s at Viwa, when scores fell on their faces weeping bitterly in repentance, and with one accord the folk who had already passed through the experience would kneel with elbows and foreheads touching the floor, in worship before this outpouring of the Spirit (a custom still observed in churches without seats and in private home devotions), do we wonder that a new phrase came into use, *cuva vakalotulotu*, to describe this particular form of worship?[11]

A similar word to *cuva* is *cabe*, which literally means to go up a steep place, such as the ascent on land after the canoe has returned from a journey at sea. This also is a significant word, with Fijian associations. When a stranger arrives in a village, he reports first to the chief. This is simple island courtesy. He is said to *cabeta* (ascend) to the chief's house, even though in point of fact he may have descended from the mountains into the valley. As far back as the records go, one always ascended to the house of the chief or to a heathen temple, whatever the topography of the land, and *cabeta* is therefore found to be a word with more than a mere physical significance.

This truth is further illuminated by its derivatives. *Cabetaka* is to ascend with a gift or some special thing for presentation, yet the word is merely the root plus the verbal suffix. There is not so much as a phoneme to suggest the presentation or gift, and this can only mean that it is lexically implied in *cabe* itself. *Caberaka* means to raise a stepchild, and the stepfather is sometimes called *tamana vakacabecabe* (his father who brings about his ascent). That such ideas can be expressed in a single patterned adjective is itself an index to Fijian thinking.

Ai vakacabe (the place of ascent) in use signifies the place where the god first appeared to the people, and this therefore becomes a "high place," whether it is in a valley or on a mountain top. Thus *ai Vakacabe ni Lotu* is *Bucainabua* (the valley of the Bua). Rev. Paula Seru wrote me an account of the conversion of Kadavu. He entitled the account: "*Cabe na Lotu ki Kadavu*" ("The Ascent of the Church to Kadavu"). When the psalmist asks, "*Ko cei ena cabe cake ki na ulunivanua i, Jiova?*" ("Who shall ascend into the hill of the Lord?"), we have an idea of deep spiritual significance to the Fijian, even before the Christian plan of salvation was understood. This was the kind of thought which led so many heathen Fijians to attend Christian services and listen respectfully. The Spirit was surely working through their own culture patterns.

Another word of this same group is *masu* (pray and prayer) with its combinations—*masumasu* (cumulative prayers), *masulaka* (to pray for), *masuta* (to pray to), and *vakamamasu* (intransitive form). These words were in use when the first missionaries arrived. The idea of prayer was not foreign. There are two important things to note here. (1) The existence of

---

11   A more detailed evaluation of these mass movements may be read in Tippett (1954, 27ff.).

these words proves a concept of prayer existed: that there were forces and fortunes somewhere beyond themselves which could be theirs if the right mode of approach and offering were presented, and this implied a realisation of human limitations and shortcomings, and a will somewhere that was stronger than their own. At the very least the existing vocabulary involves this belief. Prayer was more than a mere acquisitive device, it was also protective. The greatest things in the life of the heathen were matters of prayer—supply of food, control of the weather, victory in war, security of the tribe, increase of population, and the skill of the craftsmen. (2) The words involving root duplication are interesting. They imply something continuous and cumulative—regular assemblies when the group gathered together and the priest prayed on their behalf. Here is the basic element of the ancient religious system, which the church took over and stressed. Corporate worship was not a foreign idea. Although these gatherings were usually confined to men of certain status, they were regular and corporate and had definite purpose.

The early missionaries kept all they could. The biggest change they accomplished was to bring the men and women together in a common gathering, but still to this day they are kept in their respective portions of the building.

The greatest linguistic change was the creation of a new word, according to a pattern we have already met in this paper: *veimasulaki* is a reciprocal action noun indicating intercessions—the praying of each for the other. It is one of the words created for the translation of the Bible and is a direct Christian contribution to Fijian vocabulary. The Fijian language always had the potentiality of discovering this concept, but it took the Christian gospel to make it an actuality. The Fijians had learned some ways of praying, but not to pray for each other.

Before we leave this group of words taken over from the old religion, we must look at the sacrificial system itself. The generic word for sacrifice is *soro* (verb), from which *ai soro* (noun) is derived, and also *sorova* (to *soro* to; i.e., worship) and *sorovaka* (to *soro* on behalf of). *Soro* is translated in various ways—"to make an offering," "to sacrifice," "to sue for peace," "to humble oneself," and so on—but basic to them all is the idea that this is a ritual act, or a symbolic act, the presentation of a symbol of one's willing submission.[12] The best translation of *ai soro* is "atonement," and in this sense the church has used the term with capitals: *Ai Soro*, or *na lodai Soro* (Our Atonement) as a title for Christ. A traditional termination for prayer is in the name of Jesus Christ, "Our Atonement and Saviour."

Many of the ancient acts of atonement have been retained in the Fijian culture pattern, but since the coming of Christianity those which were purely religious have been Christianised, and the others have been secularised, and supported by Christianity. Thus

---

12 The more common secondary meaning of the English word "sacrifice," to give something valuable away for very little, is a meaning the English-speaking Fijian finds difficult to comprehend, and which he associates with a completely different word picture.

we have *ai soro wale*, a private atonement made by an offender to the offended, the symbol of which is a whale's tooth; *ai soro matanigasau*, symbol, a reed, is a confession of laxness in one's official responsibilities; and if this is a serious shortcoming, it will be a spear that is presented, and known as *ai soro matanimoto*. These have been shorn of their religious significance, but as they are moral corrections of existing causes for discord, though secular acts, they have the blessing of the church, and are even performed within the church at times.

There are also other types of offering, the names of which are not connected with the root *soro*. Of these the most significant is *ai bulubulu* (the burying), which is also an atonement or a peace offering by which an offence is "buried." The Christian missionaries took this term for "propitiation," for which it was a very good equivalent. There is still preserved a celebrated sermon preached by a Fijian minister[13] many years ago in which he listed side by side the virtues of the ancient Fijian propitiation, which was used as the "type," and the more perfect offering of Christ. It is excellent typology after the pattern of the letter to the Hebrews.

Another of these offerings is *ai madrali* (thank offering) and its forms like *madralitaka* (to offer thank offerings for). The reader will thus see that the sacrificial system of old Fiji was a highly diversified one, and this indicates a long period of development. There was much good in it which Christianity did not destroy.

Offerings had to be ceremonially presented. The root used for this act is *caho*, usually in a compound form *vakacabora* (causative form). Actually this is rendered "to set apart," "to dedicate," or "to present" to the gods or to a chief. This is another of those spiritual quality words, like *cuva*, *cabe*, and *masu*. The common word is *solia*, the tone-word *vakacabora*. From the root *cabo* we have some useful derivatives, like *ai cabocabo* (that which is presented in this way; i.e., the sacrifice or offering) and *ai cabocabo ni soro* (that on which the *soro* is presented; i.e., the altar).[14] By means of this terminology, Christianity captivated the highest tonal level of the Fijian cultural ethos, and this I believe is the reason why so many of the prominent priests of old Fiji came over to the Christian side, while others became so bitterly opposed to it.

Words Transferred to New Contexts

We now turn to a number of words which show how semantic change takes place by an ever-widening of context, or a shifting from one context to another. Again Christianity was a causative factor in these changes. She discovered a number of secular words and charged them with a wider and then a religious meaning. Some of this was inevitable in Bible translation. For example, *sova* (to pour out), was used of liquids only, but it is not the

---

13   Samuela Nowesita, reported in Heighway's diary, 19 July 1891, and cited in Heighway (1932).
14   See Tippett (1944, 285–86) for the function of the altar in early Fiji.

only word with this meaning (e.g., *talo*, *daqi*, and *livi*), yet it was *sova* that was selected to speak of the pouring out of the Holy Spirit on all flesh, and has become a concept common in Fijian prayer to this day.[15]

The missionaries had trouble finding a word for "forgive." The concept itself was quite foreign. When Ratu Cakobau proved that he had become a Christian by releasing his war prisoners, Fiji was amazed. Such a thing was unheard of. In translating the Lord's Prayer, the translators had to say, "*Kakua ni cudruvi keimami e na vuku ni neimami valavala oa*" ("Do not be angry with us on account of our sins"), but they were never satisfied with it, quite apart from the change from a positive to a negative statement.

However, there existed a word, *boko*, which was used to express the fact that a fire was extinguished; or actively, *bokoca* (to extinguish). The use of this was expanded in the early days of the first schools in Fiji, for "to wipe out" or "rub out," and secondary to this we got *ai bokoboko* for either a blackboard duster or an eraser. So in time through this new widened use of an old word, a suitable word was discovered to express the concept of forgiveness, the blotting out of sin. It was not until about twenty years ago that the preparation of a new hymnbook reprinted the Lord's Prayer, substituting the positive *bokoca* for the negative *kakua ni cudruvi keimami*. So the literal meaning now is "erase our sins," although this itself is an extended meaning. A dictionary entry today will therefore read—*bokoca*: extinguish (a fire), erase, forgive. They represent a sequence of semantic change.[16]

One could cite many words that have retained their basic meaning but shifted from one context to another, and many of these reflect the moral and spiritual changes that have come with Christianity. *Bokola* once meant the highly prized food—human flesh. The word still means much the same, but it is no longer desirable, and its only common use is as an offensive term said by a person who wants to abuse another, even though it may be in friendly backchat.

With this are other words, like *kusikusima*, which originally signified "a desire to eat human flesh," but today means a "desire to eat fish." This is an interesting shift. The word has retained its meaning of a desire to eat flesh, but that flesh once prized is now repulsive, and fish has taken its place. Words like these indicate the cultural changes that have come with the faith, and there are scores of words still used from time to time of pagan customs, but Christianity has placed them in an entirely remote ethical category from that in which they were originally set, and their use is retained mainly for purposes of ethical contrast.

---

15 Of these two words both *talo* and *sova* had ceremonial uses and were therefore tonal words, but *talo* meant a thin stream, whereas *sova* implied large quantities; it seemed therefore the more suitable word for the pouring out of the Spirit.

16 John Hunt anticipated such a possible use in one of his early hymns, but his fellow missionaries did not see fit to use it in the Lord's Prayer.

A Significant Choice

We have already seen how translators were at times forced to make choices between several possible words. One of these concerned the word for "missionary" or "minister." The natural word was *bete* (priest), and the use of this word would certainly have given them many advantages. There may have been some anti–Roman Catholic feeling in the choice, a natural antipathy to the word "priest," but these were not the main reasons for their rejection of this word.

Bete is used for "priest" throughout the Scriptures, but the missionaries were particular to see that they were in no way linked up themselves with the Jewish priesthood but rather with the apostolic movement. Their mind was on the word *apostolos*, from the verb *apostelo*. They thought of themselves as sent forth to Fiji, and chose to use *Ai Talatala*, from the verb (to send), meaning the one sent forth with an important message. By making this selection, they not only captivated the apostolic concept, which the Roman Catholics, by the choice of *bete* have missed, but they also have avoided certain problems and dangers that *bete* would have posed for them.

Firstly the priests represented a clan section in the tribe, involving certain relationships and status, and responsibilities under the chiefs. The priest revealed the mind of the god by going into ecstatic tremblings, during which times he was often spoken of as the god himself. There would have been serious theological problems with the choice of this word. As it was they had been sent from without, and had an authority from without, and a message to proclaim, or the good news (*ai tukutuku vinaka*). Furthermore by using *ai talatala* they distinguished themselves from *ai talaki* (inferior messengers). They were sent with authority. It all ties up perfectly with the apostolic scene.

Decades later when, under British administration, the word *ai talatala* was required for a civil administrative officer, it had become so firmly associated with the Christian minister that another word had to be found, and the normal passive verb was used as a noun—*na Talai* (the Sent), and the authority going with it has been by implication. In the same way the captivating of *ai Tukutuku vinaka* for the gospel has been of tremendous importance in revealing the "good news" concept, and has served to distinguish it from *ai tukuni* (tales or oral traditions), like their own mythology. From the very start this was great news brought by men with authority.

New Ideas by Word Combination

Another device used by the early missionaries for expressing non-Fijian ideas was by creating compound Fijian words, and thereby assisting semantic change. In this they were not original. Coverdale introduced into his translation of the Bible combination words like "loving-kindness" and "tender-mercy." Tyndale in the same manner gave us "long-suffering."

The outstanding example of this technique in Fijian is the expression of the idea of sin as active and continuing evil (i.e., the state of sin), by means of *ai valavala ca* (the bad habits or customs). This combination was necessitated by the wide range of uses of the word *ca* in those days. It was an adjective meaning bad or evil, and had had as wide a range as it has with us and could be used to describe fruit or fish as well as people. It also meant ruined, in the sense of something destroyed by fire, war, hurricane, or famine; but used as a noun it signified war, and from this a common phrase was used—*sa ca na vanua* (the land is at war, or the land is in a state of war). Today the same words would signify that the land is evil. Christianity has changed an era of internal wars into an era of peace, and the meanings no longer needed have dropped out of use; and *ca* stands simply as "bad" (adjective) and "evil" or "badness" (noun), and the combination *ai valavala ca* signifies the state of sin or a habitual disposition.

The derivatives of *ca* ramify throughout the language and provide a tremendously interesting theological potential. We have *cata* (hate), an old derivative, together with *veicati* (reciprocal hatred, or hating one another), and *vakacacana* (to injure or to cause a thing to go bad), and from this *vosavakacacataka* (to make someone or something bad by ones words; i.e., to slander), and from *ai valavala ca*, the biblical translators created a new verb *vakaivalavalacataka* for "to cause another to sin."[17] The etymological study of the uses of the root *ca* illustrates the theological potential of the Fijian language, and the simplicity with which the concept of sin, with its ramifications, causes, and effect, can be presented to the common people by the preacher.

Scores of illustrations of this theological potential could be cited, but let us be satisfied with one more: *dina* (true). *Dina* itself may be interpreted in terms of genuineness, reality, worthiness, or sincerity. The seeds of all these aspects were in pre-Christian Fijian, but in each case there has been an ethical shift in the personal judgement of what is genuine, real, sincere, or worthy. From these qualities, refined under Christian influence, we now have the concept of truth itself (*na dina*). *Vakadinata* is to recognise a thing as true, and therefore to believe; *vakadinadina* and *vakadinadinataka* mean to testify to the truth of something, to bear witness—the former in a commonplace manner, the latter as a legal testimony. *Ai vakadinadina* is a witness (one who testifies to the truth) or evidence (that which reveals the truth). *Dinadina* is an intensified assertion of truth (i.e., certainly true); *rokodinadina* describes the person who regards it a matter of honour to be true to his word. In the Fijian marriage proposals, presentations made and accepted are spoken of as *ai vakadinadina*, the mutual promise to carry out the marriage.

This is an interesting use of the concept of truth in symbolic cultural ceremonial, and shows how basic concepts like evil (*ca*) and true or truth (*dina*) charge all aspects of daily

---

17 Required for passages like 1 Kings 15:34, where three different *ca* root derivatives are used in one verse—a truly Fijian passage.

life with significance. It therefore follows that a shift in meaning or depth or tone in one of these key root words will ratify throughout all private and social life. Truly then it may be said that the church—by giving new meaning to words like sin, truth, right, honour, and many others—has charged a secular vocabulary with a spiritual quality. Even nontonal words have received tonal qualities by being taken for religious work. For instance, when the earliest missionaries to Fiji wanted to translate the word "cross" to describe the death of Christ, they found the Fijians had no noun, or even a concept of such an object. In their houses and canoes and for taboo signs they had made crosses, but their thinking had never isolated a cross as an object. The missionaries felt that the cross was a real object in itself. It was a symbol of deep significance, and they determined to create a word within the linguistic pattern. The word was *kauveilatai*, used with *na*, the definite article. *Kau* is tree or a piece of timber. *Vei-latai* indicates two pieces crossing each other in different directions. The term was clear, and the first Fijian Christians were able to visualise the construction of the instrument on which Christ was put to death.

To subsequent generations it ceased to be a phrase-construct and became an object. Now the hymn writer or preacher can speak of the cross, and it has literally become an object which appears in church furnishings and architecture as a significant symbol. The innovation was meaningful within the culture and language and therefore acceptable, and in time it assumed the desired meaning and use.

New Theological Significance for Old Words

Perhaps the time has now come for us to take note of a few words from the old way of life, which were taken by the church and deliberately changed for use in a new way. They represent a most significant semantic change.

Let us start with God Himself. God represents a category of beings to the old Fijian, not a name, and even to this day he never says, "O God," as we do; it is the God (*na Kalou*), or Our God (*na noda Kalou*), or the God our Father (*na Kalou na Tamada*), or Jehovah the God (*O Jiova na Kalou*).[18] In other words, primitive usage from a polytheistic period is still in use, although they have long considered themselves monotheistic people.

Kalou used as a verb means to fear, in the sense of the fear of God rather than of moral cowardice. *Vakalou* as a verb means to deify, and reflects the manner in which the hierarchy of old Fijian gods developed; as an adjective it means godlike, divine, or supernatural, or that appertaining to God. These words have had little modification in meaning. The important word is *vakalougatataka* (to bless), *kalougata* (blessed or happy), and its other derivative *vosa ni veivakalougatataki* (blessing).

---

18   *Ko na Kalou* is a form used in some Roman Catholic documents and also by William Moore (1867) in his translation of *Pilgrim's Progress*, but it has never become indigenous.

Now the literal meaning of this phrase for blessing is "words of snake-god-ising," if I may create the English word which would be its counterpart. This word is said to come direct from Degei worship, or an ancient snake worship. Originally there was a form of worship of this deity which was supposed to bless the worshipper with great happiness. This was supposed to be the sublime happiness; we need to remember that Degei worship had sadly declined before the historic arrival of Christianity. He was a high god, but the local gods were of much more significance in that period. Yet the word *kalougata* was widely accepted for the happy state, or the blessed state, and had been more or less divorced from the Degei cult. It expressed the happiness brought through the fear of the god, and so Christianity took it over.

About that time a secondary meaning had been given it by some who knew not Degei. They claimed the root was *gata* (sharp), and that *kalongata* meant the *mana* of the deity was sharp, and this meant blessing or happiness. The word has assumed the normal meaning of blessed, and in a modern colloquial sense "lucky." As the blessing of Christian happiness it assumed an entirely different significance from its original meaning, the happiness being measured in different tone, quality, and desires.

The same may be said of *so kalou*, which phrase I believe to have been retained by Fijian usage rather than by missionary approval. The *so kalou* was an assembly of priests and others for the partaking of a ritual drink together as a symbolic act of preparation for war. On this occasion a priest approached the war god, and was possessed by him, for some pronouncement on the outcome. The missionaries were familiar with the ceremony, several of them having left descriptions of the performance. They had no admiration for it, and I am sure they had nothing to do with the preservation of the term. There is little doubt that its survival and use in public prayer have been caused by the native preachers, who developed vigorous ideas about the church militant and the war with Satan.

Another word taken over with a changed meaning is *laga*. This was a demonstration in which the leader of a war dance brandished his club as a threat or challenge (*vakalaga*) as he set the pitch of the rhythm or tune (*ai lagalaga*) of the dance. He cried "*Laga*" at the commencement of each unit of the dance. The person pitching the chant was also called the *laga*. *Ai vakalaga* was associated with the dance before going to war, especially on a war of revenge. Upon return a similar dance was performed with the ceremony *ai laga*, when fire was set to the cords of any prisoners taken as torture before killing them. Eventually their cooked bodies were divided out among the relations of those whose deaths were thereby avenged, and this was *ai laga ni mate*.

Now nothing surely could be more remote from Christianity than this grim set of customs, and yet over the process of a very short period of time this word *laga* (transitive *lagata*) became accepted as the word for "sing," and the people of the cry of war and death and torture became the singing Wesleyans of the islands. In its older form the word survives in *laga same* (chant psalms) and newer in *laga sere* (sing hymns); *ai lagalaga ni sere* becomes a hymn tune, and *kabakaba* (instrument for climbing; i.e., ladder or scale) becomes the written score. The dramatic change in the meaning of this word reveals something of the dramatic changes brought about by the faith.

Another word, perhaps less dramatic, but equally significant is *loloma*. This was the only word that could be found to express a host of ideas which represent the shades and tones of Christian love, and really it was a long way off. It meant pity. It was used when a powerful chief was willing to relax his hardness, and spare the life of a victim, even though his victim thereby became a slave. This faint glimmer of mercy was the only word that could be found for love and for grace. It has, over the years, acquired the meaning of love, but it has done so from the use of the word in Scripture, from the teachings of John the Apostle, from the life and works of Christ Jesus and in particular his death on the Cross. Its shades and tones have to be obtained by means of adjectives like *loloma tawayalani* (boundless love), *loloma vakaveitamani* (fatherly love), *loloma cecekia* (astonishing love), *loloma tauwale* (love given freely), and from the verbal form *lomana veilomani* (loving one another). How far the church has taken this word from the thoughtless glimmer of mercy in the cannibal chief! The gospel does to a language much the same as it does to men.

The Unique Terminology of the Church

These words show the church was not merely a borrower, it was a transformer. Perhaps the time has now come for us to ask what completely new terminology (not mere foreign words) the church has given Fiji. I find these words fall into three categories: (1) terminology of its organisational basis, (2) that which is the outgrowth of its own religious experience, and (3) the terminology demanded by its new ethical atmosphere.

TERMINOLOGY OF ORGANISATIONAL BASIS

We shall pass very quickly over the first. We have already spoken of *ai Talatala*, the minister who is sent with a message and with his Lord's authority. *Ai Vakatawa*, for catechist and for shepherd; *ai vakavuvuli*, for a village teacher; *na Qase ni Vuli*, for schoolmaster; *na Tuirara*, for the lay officer; *na Dauvanau*, for the preacher; the *Qase ni Sigat*, for the class leader; the titles in the stages of advancing membership; the whole terminology of the law book and its discipline; the terminology of business meetings; the basic terms of the school and the hospital; and many others have been given to the Fijian people by the church and were understood and used when British administration took over. I might well have made this paragraph the theme of the whole study.

OUTGROWTH OF RELIGIOUS EXPERIENCE

Much that has been explained above grows out of the church's experience rather than her organisation, but there are many poignant words I could add still. The root *taro* (question) has been given. I shall never forget the first time after a service a young couple I had married only that afternoon came to me and said they desired to *tarobula*. I had not heard the word before, but I had no doubt of its meaning. They desired life (*bula*)—they wanted to start their married life right; they felt challenged in the service and came to me afterwards to enquire (*taro*) about the way of life. They wanted to meet *Ai Vakabula* (the Giver of Life). The word *tarobula* isn't in the dictionary, but it is in every Methodist congregation. It is a perfect word for its purpose, and it came with the gospel.

We also have the word *masu* (pray). Once the prayers were the business of the priests alone, but now they are the priceless heritage of the common people. There are always some people who value their heritage more than others. When it became apparent that this man and that woman engaged frequently in prayer, it was said that they were *daumasu* (habitually at prayer), and as this refining habit bore fruit in their daily lives, this epithet *daumasu* gave them a new concept which we might translate by calling them "pious." There was no such thing as piety in Fiji until men learned to pray their own prayers and to form regular habits of prayer.

I selected those two examples of many because they are the two aspects of faith most dear to our hearts—the seeking and finding of the Saviour and fruits worthy of our repentance. Perhaps I may add a third to tie up with the Christian obligation to communicate the gospel to others. There is a little word *caca*, which means to tell or expound a thing. It implies the element of surprise, and springs from an interjection or series of interjections of surprise: "This is so astonishing that it simply must be told abroad." There was nothing that ever hit Fiji which brought forth more of the interjections of surprise than the gospel narrative of grace. Its very wonder demanded the telling, and there was no place in Fiji from which it spread faster than Viwa. Thus from experience there arose a proverb—*Tukutuku e rogo maluat rogo ki Viwa caca vakabuka* (A report normally spreads slowly, but once heard at Viwa it is told abroad spreading like fire). Theirs was the concept that the good news was exciting; it had to be expounded far and wide, to be shared, to be communicated. Thus the church made a word of interjection into a word of action. Viwa has had its day, but the experience of Viwa goes on, and the proverb reflects the experience still for the benefit of others.

TERMINOLOGY OF THE NEW ETHIC

The third outcrop of new words developed by the church represents the terminology of a new ethic. The main device used for the creation of these words was a word combination after an existing pattern by the appending of an adjective to a noun to create a compound, which in turn could be used either as a noun or an adjective. The key word for these compounds is *yalo* (soul or spirit), from which we get *yalo-ca* (evil-spirited or angry), *yalo-kocokoco* (spirit that continually covets; i.e., covetousness or covetous), *yalo-dina* (true-spirited, genuine), *yalo-dodonu* (right-spirited or righteous or righteousness), *yalo-savasava* (clean-spirited, pure, purity, holy, holiness), *yalo-vinaka* (good-hearted, generous, well-disposed towards the other person), *yalo-batabata* (cool-spirited, without enthusiasm), *yalo-katakata* (hot-spirited, enthusiastic), *yalo-loloma* (spirit which pities or [now] loves; i.e., merciful), *yalo-balavu* (long-spirited, of one who takes a long time to act), and *yalo-lailai* (little-spirited; i.e., discouraged). It must be apparent that this device has unending possibilities for purposes of theology and ethics. *Yaloca* and *yalovinaka* are certainly pre-Christian words, and also *yalo-leyu* (big spirit, meaning possessed by a spirit; i.e., mad), so that the construction is endemic; but Christian ethics demanded its expansion, and at the same time threw a new emphasis on the human spirit and its force in human behaviour. This was quite new, and the word *vakayalo* (spiritual; i.e., apart from the body) hitherto came to mean spiritual, also in the sense of the spiritual qualities within the nature of man. Reciprocal forms also exist; e.g., *veiyaloni* (being of one spirit or mind) and *yalovata*, which means much the same (together-spirited). All these words can by their particular use in a sentence be used either as the noun or the adjective.

The tone or quality of the spirit of a man is reflected in his behaviour, and the set of *yalo* words has its counterpart in words of human action or habitual behaviour. In this connection the same adjectives are compounded with *tovo* (behaviour, custom, manner). The difference between these two basic words, therefore, is the same as that between cause and effect, the *tovo* of a man is the visible proof or fruit of his *yalo*. So we have *tovo-ca*, *tovo-vinaka*, *tovo-dina*, *tovo-dodonu*, and so on. Once again the concept lay in old Fijian but was exploited and developed by the church, and today patterns of *yalo* and *tovo* words, which originally contained three or four words in each group, have been subjected to enough diversification by new combinations to provide the basic potential for the Christian ethic.

These are not the only words of this type. A similar list could be prepared of *loma* words, with which the identical principle operates. We have here a stress on the "mind" or attitude as distinct from the *spirit* or *behaviour*. *Lomavinaka* (to be of a good mind), *lomadina* (of true mind), *lomasavasava* (of a pure mind), *lomadei* (of steadfast mind), *lomalialia* (of foolish mind), *lomasoli* (of a mind to give), and many others are in daily use today. Christian ethics has demanded these terms, and the development of this vocabulary in the Fijian language since the coming of Christianity illustrates how when the gospel, with its new ethic, is hard pressed for moral terms in the pagan language the missionary should look around for the inherent potential of the language rather than introduce foreign words *ad lib*. There are references not intended for publication, in private journals of some of the early missionaries, to the effect that Bro. So-and-so spoilt the effectiveness of his translations by introducing too many foreign words. What concept in either theoretical or applied Christian ethics cannot be expressed in a language which approves the creation of new compound words by adding any adjective to prefixes which distinguish between spirit, mind, and activity?

This potential is widespread in the South Seas if the communicator of the gospel is capable of forgetting his English terms and thinking them in the linguistic pattern of the islands.

Mariner, a castaway in Tonga a century and a half ago, was able to produce a list of words which falls in the same category as the Fiji *loma* words. The Tongan form was *loto*, which he defined as "mind, sentiment or disposition." Retaining the form of spelling he used, he gave us *lotoboto* (wise), *lotohee* (insane), *lotolahi* (ambitious or haughty), *lotolille* (good-natured), *lotomahalo* (jealous), *lototaha* (of one mind), *loto-oo'a* (of two minds), *lototow* (brave), *lotovale* (ignorant), *lotomow* (fixed mind), *loto ita* (quarrelsome), and so on (Martin 1817).

Dr. Bromilow's polyglot vocabulary indicates the same phenomena in Samoa, also using the *loto* form but without the differentiation of *loma* and *yalo* as in Fiji. This practice has counterparts much more far distant in time and place than the present-day Pacific.

In the Scriptures themselves we find it used with effect in the Pastoral Epistles, for example:

philautoi	lovers of self (2 Tim 3:2)
philarguroi	lovers of money
philoxenos	given to hospitality (1 Tim 3:2; Titus 1:7)
philandros	husband-loving (Titus 2:2)
philoteknoi	children-loving

In English we are familiar with the use of negative prefixes and suffixes for word expansion—*im-, in-, un-, anti-, -less*, and so on. The islands have their counterparts. There is no difficulty in expressing thoughts like "unrighteousness" or "sinlessness" by the use of *tawa*, or *sega ni-tawadodonu*, or *tawacala*. The existence of positive and negative words is invaluable in the communication of the gospel.

We are now beginning to realise the expansion potential of a primitive language. Take the Fijian word *tawayalovinaka*. It breaks down into *tawa* (negative) *yalo* (spirit) *vinaka* (good) and is used of a person whose spirit is not well-disposed. The same idea is found in Dobuan by the combination *nuana nigea 'ida bobo'ana* (not of good disposition), and is a regular pattern phrase. *Nigea* combinations correspond with the *tawa* or *sega* in Fijian words (e.g., imperishable, *sega ni rusa rawa* and *nigea 'ida to'umalina*). They are thought of as units, and are thoroughly indigenous. The nearest approach we have to it in English is in phrases like "forever and ever," and "once upon a time," which we think of as unit. Other examples include *lototele* (Samoan), *yaloqaqa* (Fijian) (courageous); *lotovaivai* (Samoan), *yalolailai* (Fijian) (discouraged); *lotoalofa* (Samoan), *yalovinaka* or *lomasoli* (Fijian) (generous); *lotogatasi* (Samoan), *lomavata* or *yalovata* (Fijian) (of one mind) (Bromilow 1904).

The process is not confined to the Polynesian islands, for as far away as Dobu, off Papua, although there is no similarity of the words, the constructional form is found, as will be seen by the following selection of words, which could have been much longer.

Fijian	Samoan	Dobuan
yaloca	*lotolenga*	*nuana 'i to'umalina*
yalodei	*lototumau*	*nuana 'i pa'aranuaiaina*
yalovinaka	*lotolelei*	*nuana 'i bobo'ana*

Compare also:

lomalomarua   lotolotoua   enuanarua

In *bubuna* the Dobuan has a counterpart of the Fijian *valavala* or *tovo*. Here are a few comparisons:

Fijian	Dobuan	
valavala vinaka	*bubuna bobo'ana*	good conduct
tovovinaka		
valavala deivaki	*bubuna 'ebweuna*	consistent
tovo-deivaki		
valavala dodonu	*bubuna paruparuna*	integrity
tovo-dodonu		

Although these are compounds of two words, each example is really a single concept. Provided the missionary keeps to the linguistic pattern, the expandability of its thought forms is tremendous. Certain grammatical constructions within the Fijian language also proved useful in establishing the Christian ethic. We have several times mentioned reciprocals formed by prefixing *vei-* to the passive form of the verb to produce a reciprocal verb or an action noun. *Veivinakati* (to be of the same good disposition towards one another), *veilomani* (to love one another), *veikilai* (to know one another), *veicati* (to hate one another), *veivukei* (to help one another) are a few examples. The construction of the sentence reveals whether these words are used as verbs or nouns. As nouns they are the gerund form—knowing one another, loving one another, helping one another, hating one another, and so on. A similarly useful construction, much used in Christian ethics is the use of *vata* (together, or "of the same kind"). Thus we have *yalo vata, loma vata, tovo vata* (of the same spirit, of the same mind, of the same nature or behaviour), or if written with a verb, *masu vata, tagi vata, laga sere vata* (pray together, weep together, sing hymns together).

By means of such constructions Christianity was able to develop a sense of Christian relationships and also fortify her demands for the corporateness of the church, and for this reason the number of combinations was greatly increased and the language enriched. Some of these combinations became new words. Thus, for instance, we have already met *veimasulaki* (praying for one another; i.e., intercession). There was also *veivinakati* (being well-disposed towards each other), used as a church word for "peace." The old word was *sautu*, which emphasised the time of plenty, war being associated with food shortage. Old Fijian had *veivuke* for "help." Christianity differentiated between kinds of help by adding *veivukei* (mutual help). There are other similar constructions which could be developed in the same fashion,[19] but they all illustrate the same thing—that the Fijian language had a great potential, and that in the development of this the church greatly enlarged its vocabulary from within itself (i.e., realised the natural potential) for theological and ethical purposes.

Summary of Findings

What then is the finding of this study regarding the church as a causative factor in semantic change in the Fiji Islands? May we tabulate these?

1. The church took over the linguistic forms of the native people and found her doctrine and ethic expressable in the constructions and thought forms of the people, and there followed great semantic development within the indigenous heart of the language.
2. Foreign borrowings were restricted deliberately to (a) names of people and places; (b) new words required by cultural innovations; (c) elements of the world environment, which could someday be introduced to Fiji (e.g., animals, trees, etc.); and (d) unique terminology required within the church, like "baptism," "sacrament," "church," "psalm," etc. All these foreign words were made to conform to the native pattern in sound, syllable, and grammatical use; and from these, many new semantic developments were achieved.
3. Many words from the pre-Christian liturgies and sacrificial ritual were preserved because they contained basic elements of worship, not confined to one religion, but these were charged with new meaning as the indigenous theology was developed in the light of Scripture translation and Christian experience. Many new combinations were developed. The semantic change here is ethnolinguistic and reflects the cultural impact of the coming of Christianity.

---

19 *Veiyaki* is another, for instance, a construction expressing movement to and fro, useful for describing restlessness, busyness, or instability.

4. In some cases these words were reinterpreted in the light of the new religion, but in others they were given completely new meaning.
5. Some significant choices had to be made between old words for use in the new. The choice between *bete* and *ai talatala*, for instance, is seen to involve the nature of the church and ministry—was it to be priestly or apostolic? The semantic study shows the Fijian church captured the true apostolic concept, and this had social implications.
6. The church widened the Fijian lexicography by means of word combination, and thereby assisted the development of an indigenous ethic and theology. The doctrinal potential of the language was discovered and exploited.
7. Both morphological devices and endemic thought forms were used for the development of this potential, and words were found for concepts like incarnation and transfiguration, but are nevertheless conditioned by the Scripture narrative. There is real semantic development here.
8. The church is found to have developed her own original and unique terminology in three respects: (a) arising from her constitution and organisational pattern, (b) growing from her ever-widening religious experience, and (c) arising from the demand for a terminology of Christian ethics.
9. By the reduction of the spoken language to written form, the translation of the Scriptures, composition of hymns, preparation of a catechism, and the writing and printing of other books, the church has standardised the language, and expanded its vocabulary so that it is quite adequate for the Christian experience of its members. Secular vocabulary has been charged with spiritual significance, and the moral quality of many acts is indicated by the word root and morphology much more obviously than in English.

3

GENERAL CONCLUDING STATEMENT

For the writer, the study of the island church as a causative factor in semantic change is perhaps an end in itself, but the general reader will require a general conclusion. We began our introductory preamble by asserting that words represent ethnolinguistic fusion, that in their forms we may pinpoint cultural elements, reflections of ways of living, relationships, attitudes, philosophy, historical changes, and the development of theological and ethical concepts. This statement is well-illustrated in the examples cited in connection with the church in the Fiji Islands.

We took the word *ecclesia* as an example of semantic change to show a sequence of reflections of changing pattern—something borrowed from one society by another, something inherited, but something newly developed or added. Here was a word with a potential which had to be realised or worked out. Again we took the word "Lord," and we saw how its meaning developed at Caesarea Philippi, but the full significance of its potential required the Resurrection to make it a reality. We saw how it required the fall of Rome and Augustine's experience to bring out the full significance of the term, "the Eternal City." We find it hard to think of "justification by faith" without remembering Luther and the background against which he lived.

God's Method: To Discover the Dormant Potential

A Method of God's Work with Man

So much there is to glorify Him, which lies dormant in life, awaiting discovery, awaiting the right time and the right set of circumstances, and the right mind to discover it and give it to mankind. Nothing brings home this truth better than the study of biblical and ecclesiastical ethnolinguistics—largely (but by no means entirely), religio-linguistics. Our excursion in the Pacific Islands is but another example of this truth, and in this connection there are two other things that have to be said.

Our Identification with the Apostolic Church

In the first place we have here a continuity of the forces and factors that operated in the apostolic church. I make it a fixed rule of my personal pattern of evangelism that when I kneel to pray with a convert I begin by thanking God that the book of the Acts of the Apostles is still unfinished, that the spiritual forces that called men and women to him in those days are still doing the same today. In this way I strive to impress my new friend in Christ that the "cumulative heritage" of the church even from apostolic times is his own. Once that connection is forged in the mind of a young convert, his experience must expand, and common words will swell with new significance. Surely this is valid too for the home church. Where this vital continuity has been lost sight of, there is no further expansion of an apostolic character.

The Operation of the Apostolic Mission in Our Time

Arising out of this, there is a second point to be made. There is something in the young churches that perhaps does not wholly apply at home. These are apostolic in the sense that they are pioneering and not yet fully developed. They are still in the testing period—they have not yet fully developed their theological and ethical potential; there are spiritual and linguistic resources they have yet to discover and exploit; there are experiments of faith going on that have yet to be consolidated and interpreted; and there are experiences being worked out which will ultimately be reflected in new terminology. In the young churches (I speak generally, not of Fiji in particular) we are today able to observe the apostolic mission in action, and the faith that is being forged today in one place in the face of communism, and in another in the face of commercialism, will be no less vital than that which was forged in the face of Caesar worship and Roman persecution, because it is both experiential and apostolic. The home church is fortunate in being able to observe these movements in our time, and might well question herself about the nature of her theology (Is it mere accumulated tradition, or growing from a vital experience?) and whether or not she has a clear concept of her apostolic mission, and again whether or not her ministry is a commission or a career. She may be able to answer herself satisfactorily, but the questions should be asked and answered nevertheless. Again, looking forward, she should ask whether the old world of Westernism has a sufficiently apostolic religion to face and explore and control the coming atomic age.

The persecutions of Rome were overcome only in an apostolic faith, and likewise the forces of Druidism, and the same applies to the cannibalism and widow strangling and patricide of Fiji. It would seem that only a church with apostolic faith and commission is likely to survive communism, and surely nothing less will be required for the control of, or survival in, the atomic era.

History reveals how churches have developed and been sorely tested. Some have survived, and some have been exterminated. Their experiences have been reflected in the literary records they have left, not merely in narrative but in the very words they selected to use. Historic periods of spiritual growth have always been likewise periods of semantic growth. We see this in the words of Jesus, of Paul, of Augustine, of Coverdale and Tyndale, of Luther and Calvin, of Wesley, and of Hunt and Hazlewood in Fiji. Furthermore, periods of real religious strength growing in experience are reflected in semantic growth in the indigenous vocabulary, by the discovery and development of terminology with strong apostolic affinities.

PART TWO

*The Impact of the Culture Pattern on the Practice
and Belief of the Christian Church*

INTRODUCTORY STATEMENT: THE FIELD AND THE NATURE OF RESEARCH MATERIAL

To what extent has the Fijian culture pattern influenced the belief and practice of the Christian church?

The Gospel Integrating in the Culture Pattern

This is the reverse process of that which we have already considered, but both processes have one thing in common. They reveal that the Christian gospel is one which integrates; that it can find its expression in a culture quite different from that of the Graeco-Roman world in which it was born or from that of the Western culture through which it has been transmitted. The Christian gospel is not limited by mere cultural elements.

We have already seen how it sometimes modifies a cultural element, but even when Christianity sets itself firmly in opposition to some cultural feature, it had to obliterate by some process of substitution rather than suppression. If Christianity is to stand and grow in that culture pattern, its introduction must be by integration—by positive sublimation—there must be no mere negative destruction and no empty void must remain. There are mission fields where this very thing has happened, and Christianity has been accepted as the white man's religion and has never become indigenous.

It was echoed in the words of Pip in *Moby Dick* during the nasty squall which left him thoroughly afraid: "Oh! Thou big white God aloft there somewhere in yon darkness, have mercy on this small black boy down here" (Melville 1892, 169). Yet there have been other places where Christianity has found its place within the culture pattern, and I think Fiji is a good example of such a case. There are many Christian workers on the mission fields whose Christianity is so Western that they are unable to appreciate the reality of cultural adaptations. Quite often to them the past is entirely dark and Western Christianity alone is light. When these are in the majority on any mission field, the flock tends to think of the "big white God aloft there somewhere in yon darkness."

Autonomous Drift through a Combination of Factors

That great linguist Edward Sapir has set out clearly for us the principles of linguistic drift and phonetic law. He says there is a "sort of shifting about without loss of pattern, or with a minimum loss of it" (Sapir 1949, 182). He says it is the most important tendency in the history of speech sounds. Change is acceptable as long as it fits the pattern, but if it upsets the morphological balance there is a resistance.

The scientific principles worked out by Hunt and Lyth for Fijianising Greek and Hebrew names in Scripture translation was so thoroughly made to fit the linguistic pattern that there has been a 99 percent acceptance of form with no resistance whatever. Even in the field of cultural borrowing the native drift is a basic and active factor, and, except perhaps when cultural impositions are made by war and conquest, the modifications come mainly from within, from the autonomous drift.

Now, while this is probably true of language more than of any other cultural phenomena, we must remember that language has a cultural background—an environment. As Sapir put it: "Language does not exist apart from culture" (ibid., 207). Culture, as well as language, has its pattern. The culture pattern as well as the linguistic pattern has its autonomous drift.

The speed of change varies at different points of history. When a people raises *the right man for leadership* when *the public need* is felt, and the *right circumstances* arise for the leader to appropriate for use, there will be rapid change within the culture pattern. Writers tend to evaluate this by saying that "the influence of A on B led to a period of rapid change," whereas it would have been usually more correct to have said that "culturally B felt a *public need*, and the *right set of circumstances* and the *right personalities* came together at the right point of time, and the result was a cultural development, not a cultural imposition."

Religion is one configuration of the culture pattern. Cargo cults and other nativistic movements spread like wildfire because the need (in this case, desire), the circumstances, and the personality meet at a given point of time.

Herein we are facing one of the greatest issues in the communication of the gospel among non-Western people, if only we would realise it. No matter how vigorous a personality a missionary may be, unless the need and the circumstances are brought together in his message and method, he will be driving into the proverbial "brick wall." Our message has to be culturalised. We have to see a *need* that is *indigenous* through a culture pattern that is not our own.

The tendency of the missionary is to preach the ideas which his Western Christianity finds missing in his flock. He is puzzled by what he considers contradictory traits in the characters who comprise his flock, without realising that these inconsistencies are only inconsistencies in Western Christianity. Quite often the adjustment of some abnormality in a primitive community cannot be effected until the pattern itself has reached a point ready for change.[20]

Field of Research; Nature and Use of Indigenous Evidence

We shall now return to our special field for investigation, the Fiji Islands, and ask the question: to what extent has the culture pattern influenced the practice and belief of the Christian church? Again our evidence will contain considerable linguistic material, partly because the subject has to be sufficiently confined for concentrated investigation, and partly because linguistic evidence is a positive form of data which suits our purpose.

Our linguistic evidence more often than not will be further confined to original material actually written by Fijians. This is necessary because the Fiji missionaries have been particularly active in writing hymns, sermons, religious and other textbooks and journal articles; and their writing naturally enough is an attempt to put Western concepts, beliefs, and practice into a Fijian form. This is the very thing which must be avoided in a study of this kind. We must be able to differentiate and state definitely that what data is now to be used is direct from Fijian minds. The source material used therefore comprises mainly hymns known to be the composition of Fijians, *polotu* (chants), original literary works of Fijians (mostly in manuscripts only), early correspondence, and sermons.

---

20 A good study of how certain abnormalities may function with ease and honour in certain primitive societies may be read in Benedict (1949, 175–94).

5

THE IMPACT OF CULTURE ON CHRISTIAN PRACTICE

Communal Entity and Corporate Participation

To some observers the Fijian church in the villages has long seemed dead or at least very sick. Others interpret the feeling differently. Is it a sense of something lost, a heart crying out for something it once had, but now finds beyond its reach? Is it the natural effect of a transition from the "primitive" to the West, from exchange to money economy, from communalism to individualism, from the contentment of social solidarity to the recklessness of "progress"? Whatever may be the cause, something passed out of the Fijian worship service not so long ago, and in passing it has left a void for a large portion of the congregation.

I will not have it that the church is sick or dead. In my day I have seen it bound forward dramatically in many respects. Its youth is possessed of tremendous potential and is pressing its claim with the utmost vigour. Its vision has been widened by youth camps. The war has brought money, private possessions, and new opportunities. The new day has given young Fijians the hope of travel for sport, or study, or war; and thousands have broken with the ties of the tribe and flocked to the industrial areas and the city. In those places where they have remained in the villages, they have taken over the choirs and often have forced the older women and their ancient chanting into the background. Missionaries, to aid the indigenous church, have supported this break with custom and urged on their venturesomeness. Well, the future is rightly theirs!

The peril of the enthusiasm of youth is that its eagerness for "progress," social reform, and action leaves it little time or inclination for worship. Choir competitions and other functions spring up like mushrooms, there is much going and coming, much spending and good fellowship. And to what end, we may ask? Is it not that the excitement but enables them to carry on until the next similar event? Or is it that they really return home to put life into the local village worship week by week? I feel that more often it is the former. What is the value of religion unless it is down to earth in the home village, and where is this better reflected than in the worship service?

Age usually finds it hard to hand things over to youth, but when the handing over is contemporaneous with a cultural breakdown, it is an extremely bitter experience, and for many it seems that the very bottom is falling out of life. Either age has to pipe the tune for the dance of youth, or bury itself in a sense of loss and loneliness.

This is exactly what you find in Fiji. At any Christian youth camp you will find a goodly number of grey heads who are willing to pipe the tune. On the other hand, along the coasts and back in the mountain villages you sense this feeling of loss and loneliness. It reminds me of Kendall's character, *The Last of His Tribe*:

> He crouches, and buries his face in his knees,
> And hides in the dark of his hair;
> For he cannot look up at the storm-stricken trees,
> Or think of the loneliness there:
> Of the loss and the loneliness there. (Kendall 1869, 60)

Now clearly we have here the natural emotional differences of youth and age, accentuated and aggravated by rapid and dramatic culture change. Certainly in neither the case of youth nor age can we say it is dead. The enthusiasm of youth and the cravings of age are themselves both religious.

Let us then turn to investigate just what has been lost and whether or not it was necessary. This question is valid because we are dealing with the communication of the gospel, and we have run into an issue where something is being denied instead of communicated. Yet within the living memory of these folk it was being effectively and satisfyingly communicated.

For my own part I have no doubt that this was somehow tied up with the liturgy which gave every member of the congregation an active part in the worship service.

The history of this subject has not been written. It can only be reconstructed by studying the records and the survivals of printed material published over the last century or so.

The early missionaries established a clear liturgy in the Fijian church from the very beginning. Although little of this remains in our hands for study, there are references in the journals and records, and there is absolutely no room for doubt that these were highly acceptable to the first converts.

The ritual for the morning and evening worship were among the first things translated into Fijian, and also the Lord's Prayer, the Confession, prayer for entrance to church, and prayer for dismissal, all of which were recited or chanted by the whole congregation in unison or with the elderly women leading parts after the endemic pattern. These were printed in thousands for the use of the people who learned to read in a very short time, and were committed to memory. The congregational chanting of the *Te Deum* became a feature of worship at Viwa and was used in every service at which heathen "bowed the knee" (*cuva vei Jiova*), which was itself a ritual act of submission to God.

In May 1845 John Hunt visited Vanua Levu, a remote and new area for evangelism, where there had as yet been no white missionary stationed. Joeli Bulu had been at work there and had prepared converts for reception into the church. This is what he wrote at the time of a service at Muanaicake:

> We had a regular service here also, consisting of singing, prayer, chanting the Confession and Lord's Prayer, a lesson and chanting the Te Deum. Then I explained "Go ye out into all the world" and etc. This done, 37 candidates for baptism stood up, and chanted the Creed; after which I baptised them in the name of the Holy Trinity. (*Wesleyan Magazine* 1846, 936)

The following day they partook of the Lord's Supper for the first time and Hunt's impression was that they "felt the solemnity of the occasion."

On the same journey he describes a first Love Feast in a certain village:

> The love feast was a new thing to them yet they entered into it. Many spoke very short, mostly about their lost state as sinners, and the love of Christ to them. They expressed the obligation they now felt to be faithful to God, having eaten the bread and drunk the wine. They evidently regarded this solemn act as an act of entire consecration to God. (Ibid.)

In another village he said of the candidates for baptism, that they

> were very intimate with that admirable summary of scriptural truth, contained in what is called the Apostles' Creed, which they chanted in the presence of the congregation. No music is equal to the sound of so many Fijian voices, chanting with evident sincerity, "I believe in God, the Father Almighty" and etc. (Ibid.)

After this he explained the ordinance and they knelt for baptism. He added that "it was a time of refreshment in the presence of the Lord." These are typical references relative to the very beginning of the church in Vanua Levu.

Perhaps it would not be out of place to set beside these references from the notes of a pioneer missionary the comment of a sea captain, who visited the same area in the midst of the persecution period which followed within a few years. There was a white missionary stationed there by the time.

> Some parts of the service, such as the Te Deum were chanted in the regular Fijian manner, a most judicious arrangement, not only as assimilating the worship to their old customs, but as attracting many heathen listeners, who, standing outside the door, seemed, with respect and attention, to enjoy the music going on within. (Erskine 1853, 223–24)

To a great extent the pre-Christian religion was a congregational act, led by a priest, but including chants and responses from the assembled gathering. The early missionaries realised this, and finding a natural capacity for congregational response allowed its use to the full, so much so that I am including this in the section of my study on the cultural impact on Fijian Christianity. Unfortunately some of their successors were not so wise. They belonged to a day when the service was more centred on the minister, and he depended on the "moving of the Spirit" (i.e., of extemporary preaching and prayer). The native ministry followed the white missionary, and congregational participation became less and less, until it almost disappeared and left a tragic void and a shallow foreignness in the worship service. It is reflected in our printed books. For instance, until this present hymnbook, the Ten Commandments were read by the minister with a congregational response after each commandment. Today the response is excluded, and as a result the Ten Commandments are seldom read at all.

From time to time during my ministry in Fiji I have composed plays in Fijian for educating the people in Bible background, an active form of communicating the gospel about which I have more to say elsewhere, but I have found no more inspiring a conclusion than to work the theme round in the last few minutes to a dramatic climax in which the whole company is brought onto the stage and to recite the *Te Deum* in unison and with uniformity of gesture. The effect is terrific—there is empathy everywhere throughout the audience. Most of all to me on these occasions is the realisation that these are moments when the youngbloods and the greyheads are completely one in worship.

There is only one possible conclusion to this section of our subject. Whatever new forms of religious exercise are developed in these most formative years, we must safeguard the Fijian capacity for congregational participation and response so there is no further cleavage when the present day youngbloods themselves become the greyheads.

The Concept of Status and Its Effect on the Young Church

The missionary who uproots himself from the rights and privileges of democratic society never finds it easy to settle down to his task of evangelism in a status society—yet it is imperative that he do so. His message will never really break through unless he does. One important question before us is: can the Christian gospel break through into status society? We can (and I fear often do) impose a Western Christianity upon the people whom we seek to evangelise, but this will never break through until the country has been thoroughly Westernised. It will always be regarded as a foreign imposition.

Yet there can be a real and experiential Christianity within a status society, and should the status society break down slowly over a period of years, as is happening in many parts of the world today, there is no reason why its form of Christianity need not be perfectly adaptable to each respective stage of the change. Let it not be forgotten that it is the core of belief which remains unchanged; the forms and practices of Christianity are infinitely varied. They vary even within a single congregation from generation to generation.

The Fijian people accepted Christianity and set it squarely in their chiefly system. The problem before us then is, what was the influence of their system on the young church?

The basic fact is that in status society every person has a place, a status, a prescribed duty, for which he was born. The Pauline picture of the parts of the Christian body is dear to the heart of the Fijian. Just as the eye does not attempt the work of the hand, so it is irrational to imagine the man born into the clan of fishermen or carpenters, say, usurping the position of a great chief. Even when the services of an incompetent chief were dispensed with, his successor would have to be born of the correct rank.

The present day tendency of the youngbloods of low birth to seek positions of wealth and influence especially in the administration of the country is viewed most bitterly by the rank and file in the villages.

Opetaia Dreketirua writes, "The people of the land are arranged in divisions for the different duties of the land, according to the will of God who created us."[21]

He is eloquent against the lowborn fellow who covets his neighbour's status, and cites the tenth commandment as an example of the word of God against it (Ex 20:17). He uses the strongest of terms against this practice that is growing among the young men of today.[22]

Dreketirua considers it *an act of rebellion against the will of God*, and this has been a note of status society ethics—let every man know his status. Of old, both in the war and the peacetime councils, a man had to know his status before he could speak. A person with too much to say could be challenged—"Disclose yourself!"—and if the declaration he made revealed the required status, the answer was "*Tagane!*" (True man). If the speaker had not the required status, he was rebuked with the formula "*Tiko lo yani ko iko, sega ni dau vosa eke ko tamamu*"—"You keep quiet, your father was not accustomed to speak in this assembly" (Drekitirua 8:60).

The missionary from the Western world does not always realise that this concept is essentially religious, and has continuity with the pre-Christian past. The arrival of the church was a change of direction rather than a break with the past, in this respect.

The chiefs of old Fiji, Dreketirua explains, were not entirely dark but were appointed by God and represented Him according to their light, in the same way as the Greeks worshipped the Unknown God. They represented the Great Chief who was still to come. Their light and their *mana* were adequate only for their particular periods of rule. Imperfect though they were, they were yet instructors until the arrival of Christ—like the *paidagogos* (law, Gal 3:24)—instructors leading to Christ (Drekitirua 4:19-20).

Now clearly this is a modification of belief. In ancient times these chiefs died and were deified. Dreketirua does not say they were gods, but that they were teachers until the arrival of the Great Chief, Christ.

He resents the habit of some to designate the old deified chiefs as *tevoro* (devils), and asserts that when Christ comes and calls all men to give an account of themselves, many of these will undoubtedly reach heaven, for they will be judged according to the light given them.[23]

---

21 *Era dui cakava nai wasewase tamata i Taukei na dui nodra cakacaka vakavanua, me vaka na lewa nei Koya ka buli keda* (Dreketirua 3).
22 *Na noda yato seva tiko vakaoqo e nai tubu eda sega ni eucu kaya. Yato* is to acquire something by stealth, *seva* is in the wrong way.
23 *Na yalodra ga sa bula tiko, ka na lewai ira na nodrai Liuliu e na rarama a solia ko Kova me basa nodra gauna* (Their souls live, and the Master will judge them according to the light He gave them in their respective times).

Whatever we ourselves might think of this, it must be admitted that at least it is a Christian attempt at interpreting their history in the light of New Testament passages. On the other hand, it shows a considerable cultural impact on Christian belief.

Then what of the chief of today, now that Christ has come? This seems to provide no difficulty. The chiefly system having been ordained of God in the past is still His instrument, and the chief is God's representative or appointee for certain specific tasks.

The regular phrase is *nai sosomi ni Kalou*, God's representative (ibid., 7:88). Each chief takes his place in the hierarchy of chiefs under the Great Chief, Christ (ibid., 4:20). The service rendered to the chief is therefore part of service rendered to God; and to despise the chief is to despise the order of society which God Himself has set up for the people's security as a tribe. To seek status other than that which God determined for a person by his birth is to rebel against God's will. This is a most serious offence in Fijian Christian ethics.

An expression of respect which sometimes irritates foreigners is the use of the *Tama* when people arrive in a village and approach the house of the chief. It is a call and a response.

> Visitor (outside): *Duo—O!*
> Chief (inside): *O!*

The call is an expression of humble obedience and respect to the chief, whom God has appointed. Dreketirua claims the responsive *O!* represents the clouds, or heaven, where God is ("O" being cloud), and means the respect is accepted as offered to God above.

The women also have a similar act of respect, the cry being: *Mai na Vakadua, Dua!*, which suggests that there is only one God, and He has appointed the chiefs, and the honour paid to them is not on their own account but to God, whose representatives they are (ibid., 9:104). These interpretations, however, being monotheistic, must date from Christian times.

The concept may be sheer heresy to a lover of democratic liberty, but many a would-be missionary evangelist has lost the ear of his people through being outspoken on this matter.

Ask the Fijian how he justifies his point of view, and he can cite Scripture at length, and you will be a good man if you can convince him that he is wrong.

"Let every soul be subject unto the higher powers," he begins. "For there is no power but of God: the powers that be are ordained of God. Whosoever therefore resisteth the power, resisteth the ordinance of God: and they that resist shall receive to themselves damnation . . . Render therefore to all their dues: tribute to whom tribute is due; custom to whom custom; fear to whom fear; honour to whom honour" (Rom 13:1,2,7).

"I have learned, in whatsoever state I am, therewith to be content" (Phil 4:11).

"I exhort therefore, that, first of all, supplications, prayers, intercessions, and giving of thanks, be made for all men; for kings, and for all that are in authority; that we may lead a quiet and peaceable life in all godliness and honesty. For this is good and acceptable in the sight of God our Saviour" (1 Tim 2:1-3).

"Servants, be subject to your masters with all fear" (1 Pet 2:18).

"Be subject to every ordinance of man for the Lord's sake" (1 Pet 2:13 ASV).

"Do honour to all, love the brotherhood, reverence God, honour the emperor" (1 Pet 2:17, paraphrase).

All these passages and many others I have known the Fijians to quote in defence of a Christian status society, and be it noted that they are all from the New Testament and from the life of the apostolic church.

Foreign criticism, however, has been mostly unfortunate because it implies that the chiefs simply bleed the commoners and virtually make slaves of them.[24] Nothing could be further from the truth. The chief has his responsibility, and the security of society is dependent on a system of interaction and interrelationships.

Nor has the Fijian overlooked the Pauline teaching that while the servant has his duties to the master, the reverse is equally true. The dependence of a tribe on its chief is apparent to any observer, who ponders the people of two nearby villages; in one case, well-housed and prosperous, and in the other, badly housed and miserable. More often than not the reason lies in the spirit and character of the chief and nothing else. Without a natural leader a tribe loses its personality. They call him the *ulu i keitou*, the head of their body.

Epeli Rokowaqa insists that every man is in his status by divine appointment, and we observe with much interest the three strong terms he uses to state his case. They are:

ai solisoli	the gift
ai votavota	the portion, or inheritance
ai tavi cakacaka	the responsibility

Of the chiefs, he says that they are divinely appointed to control and administer the life of the tribe to assure its prosperity and comfort. The security of the whole depends on their effectiveness.

This *tavi cakacaka* (responsibility) is a *solisoli* (gift) from God and, according to the degree of appointed responsibility, so is the Holy Spirit appropriately given as *nai votavota ni Yalo Tabu* (the portion of the Holy Spirit). This is a divine (*Vakalou*) matter and not human (*vakatamata*). It is all a categorical statement (Rokowaqa n.d., 78).

He insists that the strength and power of the chief is itself a God-given quality. It is right, then, that the rank and file should fear this power as from God, coming through the Holy Spirit, so the chief's work may be effective for the sake of the tribe (ibid., 76).

In the same way there is a strong tendency to feel that a Christian minister has also his share of the power of God, according to the needs of his task, and acquired through the Holy Spirit. Thus he lays great stress on any power-transmitting rites, like ordination, for

---

24 An example of this is found in a South Pacific Regional Commission publication (Hayden 1954, 4), although that author does not appear to have realized the reaction of Ratu Sir Lala Sukuna, whom he had write an introduction to the book. The latter goes to some trouble in pp. x–xi to show that subject Moturiki drew much from her Bauan overlords.

instance. Paul's words to Timothy, "Stir up the gift of God that is within you by the putting on of my hands" (2 Tim 1:6, paraphrase), and similar passages of Scripture have strengthened the status theology of the Fijian Christian.

A good example of the manner in which these cultural elements can influence the forms and practices of the church may be seen in some aspects of church architecture. Take the classic example of the Cakobau Memorial Church at Bau, the chiefly island of the Group. This huge building, the stone walls of which are three feet in thickness, was built from the foundations of seventeen heathen temples, the services of which were dispensed with when Christianity came to Bau. The seating is arranged according to the pattern of status society; the males sitting right and women left, facing the pulpit. (The places for children and choir are innovations.) Proximity to the pulpit indicates height of status, and the highest chiefs are on the side of the pulpit area. Those with status in the work of God—ministers, catechists, and missionaries—who might be attending, have the corresponding position on the women's side.

From a raised platform between these two groups, where a reading desk is also provided, chiefs or other persons of status will stand to make speeches of welcome or farewell, give reports, or make announcements; but central in this platform and much higher is the pulpit, from which no ordinary message is given—only the preaching of the Word. The highest chief of the land has a special pew, and the people would not have it otherwise.

The building stands as a fine example of its type, but is in great contrast with the beautiful Centenary Church in Suva, a cruciform building more adapted to the life and economy of a Westernised city, and ornamented with Christian symbols from a different world.

Many foreigners have expressed grave concern at the use of a dais for the chiefs in a Christian church, but again the Fijian will justify the custom because he believes the chiefly office is a divinely appointed one and accepts the dais as he accepts the will of God, and thereby honours Him who has appointed all men to their different stations in life. The Fijian attitude to this is changing at a fairly rapid rate in commercial, industrial, and educational centres, and was speeded up by the impact of the war but remains fixed for the majority of people living in the village pattern.

The Methodist pattern of church membership brought from Britain and Australia was acceptable to the Fijians. In providing for members, adherents, prayer leaders, class leaders, preachers, and so on, every person could find himself a place or status, a corner where he could work, a status to be recognised, an obligation for him to carry out. Such status was not a matter of mere personal pride, but a certain knowledge that each person knew his place and responsibility in the society and the fellowship. In private life he knew himself as a fisherman, a warrior, a farmer, or a carpenter; and he approved the church which offered him something definite in the way of status, even though he be a layman—a status wherein he felt he could render a service to the whole.

The placing of certain taboos on persons in status in the church did not seriously worry him, for that was so in secular life, and a church without some taboos would not have been meaningful to him.

We have, in the last few pages, stated something of the configuration of status in island society and have shown some of its influence on the life of the young church. These influences cover a wide field, ranging from church architecture to the concept of membership, and grow from a firm conviction that status itself is a matter of divine election, and that it is unethical to rebel against the will of God.

Its weakness lies in its rigid enclosure. There is little scope for progress among the rank and file. A man with natural capacity for leadership gets little opportunity for it unless he is born into the right group. When the young church needs indigenous leadership as it does today and the status pattern is so rigid, the weakness is serious indeed; and for this reason many a missionary has turned his back on the system, and some have been actively hostile to it.

On the other hand, its strength lies in its fine communal integration and system of interrelationships and interresponsibilities, now being rapidly undermined by encroaching commercialism and materialism. The system was, in its earlier form, a model of what ecumenicity is trying to achieve on a world scale. One's duty to the whole, and therefore to one's neighbour, was more highly developed under this system than I have ever heard of in the West.

The cutthroat standards of commercialism, the wild hope of quick fortune, prospects for regular pay week by week, and facilities for spending it, are causing a rapid drift to the city and the industrial areas. As the body becomes impotent when deprived of hands and feet, so the village system is slowly but surely being wrecked of its own accord.

Present-day missions have a grim problem before them as they watch this transition. Such social changes must inevitably change the pattern of the church, but the issue of immediate significance is, to what extent should the church speed up this process? If she does so, can she cope with the ever-widening rift between village conservatism and city radicalism? Already indeed there are two completely different Fijis, and the missionary must seek to understand them both if he is to communicate the gospel to them both.

The Pattern of Rhythm and Its Effect on Worship

One of the finest examples of the way in which a truly pre-Christian cultural element can remain and impress itself on a young church is the custom known as *polotu*. Culturally (i.e., in form) it is thoroughly endemic; religiously it is thoroughly Christian and therefore new. Here is an example, not of a Christian imposition on an ancient culture, but an ancient culture's steadfast refusal to disintegrate, in spite of dramatic religious change. Here is an element of cultural stability. How and why could it be so?

There were strong natural similarities (I hesitate to say affinities) between the ancient Fijian culture pattern and the Hebraic roots of Christianity. Christianity in its modifications of method and practice throughout the centuries has continually adapted itself to fit the changing world needs and outlook, but the essential roots are still there for twentieth-century folk to seek out if they so desire. When the gospel, together with the Old Testament, was given to the Fijian people a century or so ago, they were quick enough to recognise these similarities (though they have often taken them as true affinities) and to seize them for use in their own familiar mechanisms. In many parts of Fiji they are still used. The parts where they are not greatly used are the commercial and industrial centres where the culture has gone to pieces under the impact of materialism and the West. But no one who has lived in these islands away from such centres and has learned to worship in the real island church can fail to feel the pulse of this kind of worship. This, of course, involves leaving the West and letting one's heart go in sympathetic identification. Their worship must be accepted as sincere and deep and real, for only thus can religious experience be shared. Without this, it will never be any more to the observer (however skilled an anthropologist he may be) than a wild cry of primitive man. As Dr. Ryder Smith said, few things are harder than to enter sympathetically into other people's ritual (1946, 64).

For one prolonged period I lived on an outer island, seldom hearing my own language beyond the confines of my own compound, and I was at worship week in and week out in this island environment. I feel I came near enough to its soul to find my own way of drawing a deep spiritual satisfaction from its form of worship. Of one thing I am quite certain—this culture has received both the Bible and its message as its own. To me, a white man of the twentieth century, there is suddenly transmitted a feeling, an atmosphere, a deep reality of the Semite firesides, when under the stars of the great, spacious East the humble folk were trained in the way of faith by means of oral tradition.

As we turn now to consider some of the island chants, let it be clearly understood at the outset that these are no ecclesiastical chants borrowed from our own society or imposed on the islanders by missionaries. These are ancient lyrics, composed in the measures and with the techniques that were once used for the hero stories of Fijian mythology. It was in these rhythms that islanders of generations of the pre-Christian era heard tales of the jealous ancestor who stole the mountaintop from his neighbour so his own would be the higher, of the brothers who shot the sacred bird and thereby brought on Fiji the calamity of the deluge, of ancestors who exchanged mosquitoes for shellfish, and so on.

With the acceptance of Christianity, these tales became no longer reasonable as objects of faith, and those which have survived have done so only for their entertainment value, for storytelling and dancing. The technique, however, has been transferred to the new faith.

Frequently the Bible itself has supplied the basic narrative. Let us take an example.

Kalou sa bula mai liu sara	God Himself lived at first
Sa ia tiko nona cakacaka;	And carried on His work;
Vakarautaki vuravura lala	He prepared the empty earth
E butobuto na wasawasa,	And the sea was darkness,
Yalo ni Kalou sa yavala,	The Spirit of God moved,
Yavala ga e na dela ni wasa.	Moved on the surface of the sea.
Rai na Kalou ka sa vinaka	God saw, and it was good
Ka sa yakavi ka sa bogibogi;	And it was evening and it was morning;
Nai matai ni siga ko ya.[25]	That was the first day.

And here is the story of Joseph:

Ko Josefa, gone sa dina,	Joseph was a good child,
Tuakana era vuvutakina;	But his brothers were jealous;
Nai keliwai ra biuta kina,	They cast him in the well,
Ka lutu ka mani maca na waia.	He fell in but it was dry.
Isa, oi lei! na ka rarawa.	Alas, Alas! What sorrow!
Isa, oi lei! na ka rarawa.	Alas, Alas! What sorrow!
Tuakana era sega ni lomana.	His brothers have no mercy.
Luve i Isireli ra lako yania	The sons of Israel went away
Ra veivosaki, ra la'ki raica	Discussed it and went to find
E dua na dali era viritakina	A rope to throw to him.
Ra tukuca sobu ra sa yavia.	They let it down and drew him up.

This has all the rhythm and atmosphere of an ancient dirge of a particular type—a narrative verse with a lament chorus. It also contains two rhythmic constructions not used in normal speech: viz., the terminal *a* (as in *yania* and *waia* for *yani* and *wai*), and the infixed -*ta*- as in *vuvutakina* and *viritakina*. We are here faced with a significant configuration of the culture pattern. It is not a matter merely of translation. We are dealing with thought rhythms foreign to English.

The *polotu* of Rahab provides us with still another example of such rhythmic elements that are purely cultural.

Isireli ra sa lako yani.	Israel set off.
Ko ira na bete era liu yani,	The priests set off in front.
Kato ni Kalou ra colata yani,	They carried the ark of God,
Na Joritani ra vavaca yani.	Their feet touched the Jordan.
Ai valu! Ai valu! Ai valu i Jisu!	The army, the army, the army of Jesus!
Ai valu! Ai valu! Ai valu i Jisu!	The army, the army, the army of Jesus!
Jeriko sa rusa yani.	Jericho is destroyed.
Ka sa vakabulai ko Reapi,	Rahab is saved,
Na yalewa ga ka dautagane,	The prostitute,
Vunitaki rau ha yamatari.	Who hid the spies.

---

[25] The narrative is close to the essentials of the Scripture narrative, but there are peculiarities in the construction. Some of the words are poetic in form. *Wasa* is not normally used without an adjective. The dropping of verbal signs and articles is also poetic licence.

There is no such word as *yamatari*. It is *yamata*. The terminal *-ri* is demanded however by the rhythm. This construction is used for poetic purposes in dances, but has been largely eliminated from the hymnbook and substituted by regular rhyme. Rhyme means nothing to the Fijian. He is unaware of the need of it and seems at loss to understand just what it is. When he ends several lines with the same word, it is for the sake of rhythm, not rhyme. It is the writer's opinion that quite often when old hymns have been recast into our rhyming pattern so that they are more euphonious to our ears, that the same may not apply to the Fijians, especially the more elderly ones, who have never taken kindly to such changes.

The above *polotu* is a traditional chant which carries a type of chorus (*na kenai kau*), which is entirely independent of the main theme song. The army of Jesus has nothing whatever to do with the wars of Joshua. Actually it is not part of the song at all but is a purely functional instrument for dividing off the scenes of the drama. Usually the independent chorus is a couplet of an entirely different rhythm, and its function demands it stand out in obvious contrast. This is a technique more known to the Hebrews than the English. In secular music the intruding couplet is often a sensual thought. In the pre-Christian days it was always so, and its repetition would bring forth a wild laughter even though the main theme should be a perfectly harmless narrative.

Other themes which have been featured in the *polotu* chants suggest that the Bible has been thoroughly combed for the type of material which will fit the cultural machinery. All the biblical laments, many of the hero stories, dramatic social episodes like the building of Solomon's temple, incidents from the life of our Lord like the storm on Galilee, and his death on the Cross, and others from the life of Paul like his conversion on the way to Damascus, and dramatic descriptions like that of the New Jerusalem, are all well known.

What is probably an original Christian development of the *polotu* is its use in a few cases for abstract teaching. The writer has the words of two or three of these, one for example on faith and another on Christ's teaching on the way to life eternal.

To this interesting repertoire the young church has added a few of a historical nature, telling of the growth of the Fijian church. The tradition is being preserved by the composition of special chants (sometimes nowadays anthems) for the opening of new buildings and for centenaries. "The Psalm of the Hundred Years" (1835–1935) was a good example which is still chanted in almost every part of Fiji. Another was composed by the people of Daku for the centenary of Ratu Cakobau's conversion. This was tape recorded at the time and used over the radio, and sent to Malaya for the Fijian troops who were there.

In many churches in the interior, along the coasts, and in the outer islands, the system of chanting is used by the women members of the church for their catechism. There is a form in which every syllable is emphasised so that they can fit the words to any rhythm. A call to worship is also used fairly widely still today and is based on the same principle.

This, then, is one realm in which the island church has an endemic configuration in its pattern, which is quite strange to the Westerner, but which has a tremendous value in impressing on any Westerner, who will trouble himself to investigate it, the great power and reliability of oral tradition as an instrument for the transmission of the faith.

Very few hymns and chants composed by foreigners have really captivated this rhythm and tone of the islands, and from what Parrinder writes of Africa, the same would seem to apply there (1946, 190). He raises the question, "Are African hymns tonal as the language is?" He was influenced by the clash of rising inflections and descending notes, advocated the wider use of native lyrics with local instruments in public worship, and thought that missionaries were so forced to give time to administrative work that they had little time for these things and, indeed, were often found to teach that African music was bad.

His point about rising inflections and descending notes has some similarities with a view expressed by David Hazlewood in Fiji a century ago on the matter of rhythm and stress. He found it impossible to put English iambic hymns into Fijian, which is dominantly trochaic (1872, 59–60).

It seems to the writer that *translation* is not a matter of finding suitable words to convey ideas which may be foreign, but rather the discovery of an indigenous rhythm to serve as the instrument for their expression. Communication is as much rhythmic as lexical.

We have seen how, in the *polotu*, an endemic rhythm has been preserved for use in Christian worship. Fiji is by no means the only place where this has happened. A most illuminating article appeared a decade or so ago relative to certain hymns of China. Some fifty original hymns were printed and sent out to persons capable of suggesting or composing suitable tunes, and in response some 512 tunes were sent in for consideration. Sixty-seven of these were found to be of real Chinese character. Nineteen were compositions of missionaries who had a deep appreciation of the local culture pattern. Thirty-three were by Chinese and quite original. The remaining fifteen are of great interest to us as they all reflect some aspect of cultural borrowing—eight were old folk tunes, one a Confucian chant, another a Buddhist chant, three were tunes for chanting indigenous poetry, and two came from a repertoire that belongs to the seven-stringed Chinese psaltery from a two-thousand-year-old tradition (Wiant 1946).

The same article cited various examples of how two important collections of Chinese hymns have borrowed both thought and form as well as music from the local culture. Some of these are particularly apt. There is the "Boatman's Song," a chant used by boatmen when pulling their craft along the Yangtze and other rivers, as they struggled through all sorts of weather and temperature, handling coal and lumber—dangerous work—over slippery rocks and along the edge of many a precipice. Many had lost their lives in this work, which still had to be continued in the service of mankind. In the rhythmic beat of this tune the Chinese sing:

> Deeply I believe
> That the Lamb was slain:
> He, on the cross, bled
> And love subdued pain. (Ibid., 432)

Another popular song, well known to farmers and students, is "The Song of the Hoe," which has been taken by Dr. T. C. Chao and given a Christian counterpart.

> Dig out the wild weeds, man the hoe, wah!
> Dig out the weeds, and let the good seed grow, wah!
> 	Ye yah hey! Ye yah hey!
> Dig weeds and man the hoe,
> Let the good seeds grow! (Ibid.)

Dr. Chao's Christian hymn preserves the rhythm, although some is lost in its translation into English.

> Great are Thy mercies Heavenly Father,
> All our food and shelter come from Thee.
> 	Serving Thee every day. Humbly we would live.
> I am a tender blade of grass,
> Breathe on me. (Ibid.)

In discussing a collection, *Hymns of Universal Praise*, Wiant shows how the committee responsible considered the possibility of Christianising cultural ideals, ceremonies, and festivals. Thus, for instance, there are hymns for the following occasions in the collection—the celebration of the first birthday, remembrance of ancestors, the sixtieth birthday, a grave-sweeping ceremony, weddings, funerals, the establishment and dedication of a home, the midautumn harvest festival, the Chinese new year, in honour of one's parents, and the dedication of friendship when friends are about to part (ibid., 430–31).

To realise the significance of such a statement, let us take one element—say, the occasion of farewell. The traditional English hymn of farewell is, "God Be with You till We Meet Again." This hymn, Bliss Wiant tells us, has been substituted by a song and chorus modeled on a "Song of Farewell" by a Christian poet, Y. L. Yang. This song has a Chinese tradition dating back to the eighth century. Here are the two choruses set side by side for comparison:

Springtime in Wei Ch'eng	Merciful good Lord,
Early rains refresh the earth,	Lead on, lead on,
'Round the inn, willow's tender green	O'er mountain and o'er sea.
Pledge me just another cup,	All adored Lord.
West from Yang Kuan	One with Thee; won by Thee,
No friends are seen.	Fellowship shall ever be. (Ibid., 433)

I have cited these refreshing examples of a young church at work from the writing of one who has studied the hymnology of China as I have that of the Fiji Islands, and I do so because of the remarkable similarities. It would seem that any young church is bound to seek out the indigenous rhythm and pattern and captivate it for Christianity. Mostly this has to be done by the people themselves, although now and again some foreigner does produce a hymn which really fits the pattern and thought forms. Such hymns become quickly adopted and are soon thoroughly indigenous. Joseph Nettleton, who followed up John Hunt's work at Viwa, Fiji, was able to write confidently of the latter's translation of "Jesu, Lover of My Soul" as "an exquisite native poem, more tender, if possible, than the original" (1906, 84). This version, which was composed to fit a native lyric, has been lost, like most of Hunt's hymns, through subsequent generations of missionaries who wanted Fijian hymns to fit the English music.

Even among the more modern hymns by Europeans, however, there are a few which have made themselves thoroughly at home. One of these, a translation of "Now Praise We Great and Famous Men," will serve as a good example. The thought, of course, has Hebrew origins, coming from the Apocrypha (Sir 44:1–15), but it expresses at least two ideas common among Fijian Christians; the first, to treasure the traditions of their fathers; and the second, to moralise for the present day. The last verse advises us to follow the faithful who have gone before and to be true to the heavenly Father, whom they also served. Technically, the remarkable thing about this hymn is that it reveals a device by means of which an English iambic hymn may be put into Fijian.

Every line begins with a single-syllabled word, a verbal sign, the article, a conjunction, or a three-syllabled word with the stress on the second syllable. This must be a considerable limitation to the poet, but in this hymn we observe than it can be quite naturally done. It is also assisted by the fact that the tune used, a Welsh melody, begins each line with a long note with a gentle emphasis that permits the real stress to fall on the second syllable or note. It could well be argued that the hymn is still trochaic, the opening long vowel being a double syllable. It is really:

Mai sé/re tá/ki í/ra gá
Sa ró/go ná/ ya-cá/dra

or is it

Má-i /sé-re/ tá-ki/ í-ra / gá
Sá-a /ró-go/ ná ya/cá-dra?

A thoroughly characteristic aspect of Fijian breathing is to commence a sentence with a long, drawn-out monosyllable—like *Sa*, *E*, or *I* (although *Mai* is actually two syllables)—followed by a thought-pause, and then to continue with a normal accented syllable. By the use of this linguistic characteristic an English trochaic verse may be translated into Fijian and be made to fit an iambic tune. Here is another example of why the communicator of the gospel should set out to make himself thoroughly familiar with the language of the people among whom he works. Language has an amazing capacity for adjustment, and some remarkably foreign ideas can be communicated. Mere vocabulary is not enough. One must set out with patience to study linguistic devices for expression.

A communicator of the gospel with a small but select vocabulary can achieve much if he has an ear for stress and inflection, rhythm and idiom—much more indeed than the man with a wide vocabulary, but who builds his sentences after the fashion of his English grammar book. After all, a missionary may have a regular alphabet of academic distinctions, but unless he can get his gospel through the mental and cultural barriers of his flock, he is a failure. Where there is no reception, there is no communication. This is one reason why some succeed and others fail.

Life Close to the Soil and the Christian Festivals

The two great factors which have led to the development of man's concepts of time have been the movements of the heavenly bodies and the cycle of seasons and harvests. Both factors have applied everywhere, but the more society has concentrated on the former (i.e., through the priest class), the more mathematical was the concept of time evolved, and the more man became a slave of the hours, minutes, and seconds, by which he now regulates his life. On the other hand, the more man has concentrated on the harvests, the more he has discovered time regularity which is not so mathematical but which nevertheless fits his way of life.

The Pacific Islander had no concept of hours and minutes. Mariner, a castaway in Tonga a century and a half ago, prepared the first copious dictionary of Tongan, and found no time classifications more refined than *day* and *night.* Now those words, in Mariner's orthography (*a'ho* and *bo'ooli*), like those for month (*mahi'na*) and year (*tow*), are probably not time classifications at all, but rather the terms for certain natural phenomena that was regularly observed, for these four terms resolve themselves into—*day,* being literally *daylight; night darkness; month moon;* and *year harvest.*

The same situation is met with in Fijian, where *vula* is both *moon* and *month,* and *yabaki* (year) is really the cultivating season,[26] and *siga* (day) is also *daylight.*[27] The Fijian people named the recurring moons by association with other natural phenomena or with seasonal cultural factors, so that when the white men brought the calendar the native people were able to use these names for the months of the year. The growth of commerce, however, has now led to the substitution of Fijianised English month names. One reason, however, for the loss of this cultural element was that it belonged to the coastal people and

---

26   The *yabaki* is the whole process, including the cultivating and the cropping. Its divisions are not temporal but functional. *Sa bulu koto na yabaki* (the planting has been done). *Sa matua na yabaki* (the harvest is ready). *Sa cava na yabaki* (the harvest is ingathered). It more particularly refers to the yam season.
27   *Siga* is primarily *daylight; matanisiga* (face of the day) is used for *sun* but is secondary. Daylight exists before and after the appearance of the sun, and continues when the sun is hidden by cloud.

did not fit the total environment of the group, especially the mountain areas. It must not be forgotten that there was no such thing as unity in Fiji before the coming of the church.

On the authority of Epeli Rokowaqa (n.d., 3), the moons were named by the pre-Christian Fijians, but as his list is by no means identical with other lists which exist, one is inclined to think there were strong local variations, and thus it would be much easier for them to accept the foreign calendar than to resolve their own differences.

Rokowaqa's arrangement will bear some close examination, for he thinks of the year in three quite unequal divisions, functional not temporal—six moons, two moons, and four moons—and classified as follows.

Period[28] of Flowering and Fruiting of Trees and Birth of Fish

1. *Ko Sakalo*, which means to eat but not to be satisfied, and approximates to our month of September.
2. *Ko Tui Naoco* signifies the period when fruit from the gardens is given in repayment for the labour put into it. This is October and in other lists is known as the *Moon of the Small Balolo Rising*. Rokowaqa insists this is a secondary name, however. The *balolo* is a sea worm, considered a great delicacy by the Fijians.
3. *Namaravu*, meaning the period of calms (November), and has the secondary title, the *Moon of the Great Balolo Rising*.
4. *Suva Lala*, meaning empty mounds, the yams as yet having developed no roots (December). Several other names are supplied: the *Moon of the Small Nuqa*, when the *nuqa* fish are about but not yet plentiful and also the time when the *nuqa* tree, a Fijian myrtle, is in flower; the *Moon of Tudravu* (from *dravusa*, ashes), the *tudravu* being a series of entertainment contests held at the time of the clearing out of the ashes from the priests' ceremonial fires at the pre-Christian temple. It was accompanied by an offering (*ai tudravu*) made to the deity after the yam planting was completed but when the yam mounds were still empty.
5. *Suva Tawa*, signifying the mounds are full of developing yam roots. January is known also as the *Moon of the Great Nuqa*, when the *nuqa* fish are plentiful and the *nuqa* trees are in full bloom.
6. *Ko Tui Nacovu*, from *covuta* (to cut up one's food for use) or as Rokowaqa put it, "when the mounds are full of roots and the mouths are full of food." It is also known as the *Moon of the Firstfruits*, when the first fruit of the yam harvest are presented to the priest of the deity of the yam harvest at his temple. After this, yams are presented to the other gods and the chiefs of the people, after which any may eat of them.

---

28   I use the term "Period" for the translation of *Gauna*, rather than "Time." The word refers to an age or season rather than a specific point of time (cf. Eccl 3). The old Fijian never asks, "What is the time?" but "How much by your clock?"

Thus the month of February ends a period of time or season, and the offering of the firstfruits is the climax of a process of activity which has lasted for six months or moons. This period is sometimes designated the *Vula i Lawana (Vula i lala)* (the Empty Moons) or the *Vula i Sotaki* or *Vula i Tubutubu* (the Moons of Growth). The food available throughout the period is confined to that stored from the previous crops and wild forest foods.

Period of Harvesting or Moons of Ingathering (Vula i Matua)

1. *Vula i Kelikeli* (March)—the *Moon for Digging* up the crop.
2. *Vula i Gasau* (April)—the *Moon of Reeds*.[29]
3. Although these terms mainly concern the yam cropping, many of the fruit-bearing trees are also harvested in these months, and with much rejoicing the ingathering is terminated with a ceremonial thank offering to the deity, *Ratu mai Bulu*, and this offering is designated *ai solisoli ni sautu* (gifts presented because of the abundant harvest).

Period of Garden Preparation

1. *Vula i Doi.* This is the month, says Rokowaqa, when the biggest rooted *dalo* (taro) is planted. It is known as *doidoi*. The last of the hurricanes (*cagi ni doi*) blow, and the *doi* tree is in flower (May).
2. *Vula i Werewere*—Moon for Clearing the land (June). The sign is the flowering of the large reeds and grasses (*co-kau* or tree grasses).
3. *Vula i Vakamakama*, or *Vula i Samaki* (*Moon for Burning Off*, or cleaning up). In July nature again provides a natural sign for activity—the *drala* tree flowers and thereafter there must be no delay.
4. *Vula i Cukicuki* (*Moon for Digging* to plant). It was the duty of the priests to point out that the *drala* was in flower and that the yam planting should be commenced immediately. The whole of what we know as August was devoted to this occupation.

Rokowaqa's year began with the month of September, the translation of the name meaning to eat but not to be satisfied. Another table used the title *Vula i Vavakada*, but Rokowaqa makes no mention of this, even as an alternative or secondary title. Yet the term comes also from the yam culture and could have been fitted into his scheme, had he known it. It indicates the period when the long reeds were placed in the mounds to provide the young yam creepers with a vehicle for climbing. This is to *vakada* the yam vines.

---

29 Epeli Rokowaqa makes no attempt to explain the meaning of the term *Moon of Reeds*. We can offer the following suggestions. It certainly was a month when reeds were required in great numbers. The yams were dug and stored in small storage houses (*lololo*) that were constructed from reeds. Reeds were also used for making the darts used for the game of *veitiqa*, the traditional entertainment for the month when the harvesting was completed. These are well established facts and may account for the name, *Moon of Reeds*.

Rokowaqa's notes, especially those with reference to December and January, strongly suggest he has a highly composite picture in his mind, and it seems to me he is trying to reconcile two entirely different patterns of the seasons from two environments. However, be that as it may, in his picture of the cycle of the yam season we have some remarkable parallels with those of the Palestinian barley harvest and the Hebrew sacred year, but it must be remembered that these parallels represent cultural convergence rather than affinities.[30]

Comparison becomes relevant to this study when we remember that the Hebrew Bible was part of the religious equipment brought to Fiji with the gospel. With this book in his hands to read, the Fijian discovered that the Jew and himself had much in common. They both lived close to the soil, and both viewed their cultivation of the soil as tied up in some way with their service to God. Seasons of harvests determined their actions, rites, and celebrations. The Hebrew year fell into four periods of not exactly equal length—harvest, summer, seedtime, and winter. The former and latter rains had to be awaited, and their arrival called for action. Plowing and sowing followed the former. The work had to be done when the *sign* of nature so decreed. The barley, the wheat, the wine, and the oil each followed its respective cycle; and the firstfruits were presented at the beginning of each harvest, and always according to the ceremonial procedure. The firstfruits of the barley harvest fell in with the festival of the Passover, and the firstfruits of the wheat and all the ground with Pentecost. When all was gathered in, the whole pattern was brought to a close with the Feast of Tabernacles, and the firstfruits of the wine and oil (manufactured products) were presented.[31]

The Pacific Islander had no great problem in accepting this kind of picture from the Old Testament, for it was also his own, and his language has the natural idiom for such a description. He can say, for example, that the Hebrews cultivated their land, and in doing so they made each respective phase of their agriculture an act of worship to God, by means of a single phrase—*Era qarava vata na Kalou kei nai teitei*. This is far removed from the Graeco-Roman world of New Testament times, and this sympathy with the Old Testament cultural ethos has conditioned the nature of preaching in the islands.

The Christian church lost a great opportunity when it failed to present the island people with a Christian counterpart of all these aspects of worship through agriculture and cultivation of the soil, which was, from pre-Christian days, so close to their hearts.

The only serious attempt that has been made is the Harvest Festival, and in this case we have confused their minds by not knowing the significance of the festival ourselves.

---

30 This also applies to the poetic parallels mentioned earlier.
31 Harvest (Ex 12:1–51; 13:3–10; 23:19; Lev 23:10–12,17,20; Deut 26:2,10; see also Deut 11:14; Josh 3:15; Ruth 1:22; 1 Sam 12:17); summer (Lev 26:5; Num 13:23; 2 Kgs 4:18–20); seedtime (Lev 16; 23:34; Num 29:1; Deut 16:13; Joel 2:23); winter (Josh 10:11).

As I look back over the days of my youth, when I sat in the pew and listened to scores of sermons, I try to recall what the harvest festival preachers really taught me about the occasion. To some it was a thanksgiving for the harvest, to others the emphasis was on the community effort in the display of fruit and vegetables; others used it as an occasion for preaching on providence or the goodness of God, sometimes it was the firstfruits, and frequently the sermon was about bread, and often it was on anything about nature. The popularity of the occasion with us was because it was something out of the usual run of services.

This confused thinking has been transmitted to the mission field, so that, in Fiji for instance, the Harvest Festival is called *Ai Sevu* (firstfruits), whereas, unless I am greatly mistaken, the Harvest Festival is really the Feast of the Ingathering. Many preachers preach on one thing, giving it the name of another.

At some point during the history of the church in Fiji, the festival became associated with Pentecost, on which occasion the Jews were wont to present the firstfruits of the wheat and general harvest. This was at least an attempt to give some real meaning to the term in current use, but it had unfortunate results. In the first place it came into competition with the Christian occasion of Pentecost, and when the writer came down to Fiji he was always faced by the need for deciding which of the meanings he would give to the day. About that time a successful attempt was made by the Ba delegates to Synod to separate them and give each its place in the Christian year. Both gained some benefit thereby, but the firstfruits again became the ingathering in significance but not in name.

The Bauan delegates could never reconcile themselves to such an abuse of their language (Bauan being the *lingua franca*) and pressed for the dropping of the name "firstfruits," recommending *ai sigani*. They insisted that this was at least a thank offering at the end of the harvest and therefore more truly reflected the present intention. The resolution failed on account of the pagan associations of the term, showing that the present generation of church leaders is much more narrow-minded than the first. Personally I have always regretted that the church did not select the Old Testament terra *Solevu ni Kumi-kumuni* (Feast of the Ingathering [Ex 34:22]), which would have solved the problem and removed the confusion. I regret still more that the church did not work into its Christian calendar the whole pattern of agricultural festivals in the Old Testament life. Why not? Was it not part of the pattern of life followed by Jesus himself?

There is a tendency on the part of many communicators of the gospel to segregate this kind of thing from the gospel. To many it is Old Testament and therefore inferior and could well be done away with. But let me assure this person that a race of people living close to the soil, and coming suddenly out of a pagan world into an experience of God, is faced with a situation very similar to that which existed between Hebrew and Canaanite and needs rite and rubric as we have learned to use the creed. It is worthwhile noting how the

Hebrew constantly reiterated certain phrases like "Yahweh thy God" in connection with the firstfruits rite (Welch 1953, 112–19). We are therefore not at all surprised at the Fijian using certain set terminology in his cultural ritual. Phrases like *Na Kalou Cecere Sara* (the Most High God) are thoroughly typical in prayers at all levels. Nor has he any difficulty in turning his daily labour into an act of worship.

When associated with a tree-planting project in one part of Fiji, the writer had no hesitation in approving an act of worship to be associated with the labour involved, and again I have been asked by a team of builders to lead them in an act of worship before they began their task. They rise responsively to services of investiture, induction, or dedication. All these things satisfy a sense of need that lies deep within them and, where such a need exists but is neglected, one invariably discovers them resorting to non-Christian rites.

On one occasion I passed by a field of rice ready for reaping. It was, alas, completely overgrown with sensitive grass and thereby rendered practically impossible to reap by hand. I commented on this to my Fijian companion. His reply was that he expected as much, for the cultivators had made oblations to their ancestor at the time of planting. The incident is not mentioned for its own sake, but to illustrate how people not long won from paganism may need ritual forms or rubrics to strengthen them in a way in which a Christian from a Western city may find hard to understand. It is part of the task of the communicator of the gospel to study how best he may achieve his communications even though it mean communicating a New Testament message by means of an Old Testament form or method.

Or maybe it will mean taking over some pagan cult and superinducing Christianity on it. At the time of writing this particular paragraph, we have been celebrating Christmas. Originally, we know, it was a pagan festival of the winter solstice, but that meaning is seldom thought of today. A nature festival associated with the return of the sun now commemorates the advent of the Redeemer. A one-time act of nature worship is now the symbol of a historic event of worldwide significance and redemptive character, as Welch describes it (ibid., 92).

The same writer has also given us a good modern example of Christianity superinduced on a pagan cult. A young Bechuanaland chief, having become a Christian, was faced with a problem. The spring plowing of his tribe had always been accompanied by a religious ritual that was supposed to protect the grain from evil spirits and promote growth. As a Christian, what should he do? With this question he faced missionary John Mackenzie.

Mackenzie pointed out that this custom (*letsemma*) had real social value for the people, for it was their public acknowledgement that the life of the tribe depended on more than human skill and industry. He seized the opportunity and there and then prepared a Christian *letsemma*, retaining throughout the normal form of the rite, but stripping it of pagan ideas, adding a new rubric based largely on the Psalms as he was unable to find a model in the New Testament (ibid., 113–14).

Two significant matters in this incident should not be missed. First, it recognises the spiritual need of the tribe concerned and makes a positive effort to satisfy it. Second, it represents a problem that was more Old Testament than New, and the missionary had no hesitation in going to the Old for his model.

The pioneering Christian missionary may thus superinduce Christianity on a pagan cult form to keep his communication of the gospel within a culture pattern and win the form for Christ. The Hebrews seem to have done this long ago. Dr. Snaith has suggested that Hosea's use of the marriage allegory was actually a chief element of Canaanite fertility cults, and the use of such a figure was aimed at transforming with new significance the central theme of popular religion. This is not to appropriate the pagan teaching, but rather to use a familiar literary form as a means of communicating a new message. Snaith offers his suggestion with the comment that it is sound missionary method (1944, 111).

The Concept of Mediation

Mediation is a form of intercommunication which takes place between an authoritative being and his subjects or between two authorities. It operates on two levels—between man and man, or between man and his gods or God. In either case the custom of segregating a special class of persons for such mediation is almost universal. On the lower level we have representatives, heralds, agents, spokesmen, and ambassadors; and on the higher level, priests, prophets, and ministers.

The coming of Christianity to the islands created no serious problem in the concept of mediation.

Dreketirua writing of his homeland, Fiji, describes the heralds as those "who hold a significant status in the land, whose responsibility is to see that things are done in the correct manner. They stand in a central social position. They are the mouthpiece of the chiefs to the people, and the mouthpiece of the people to the chiefs" (1:57). Elsewhere, he expands his description, elucidating something of their peacemaking function, peacemaking being essential to the tribe's security.

> The heralds (*matanivanua*, eye of the land) are the cords of the land (*wa ni vanua*) binding together the people and their leaders. They press down (*bika*) and hide within their own hearts the angry words of the chiefs about the people, and they hide also in their hearts the angry words of the people about their chiefs; and for this reason they are called the Stomach of Evil (*Kete ni Ka Ca*) for their first responsibility is to preserve the land from weakness or destruction through dissention. (ibid., 2:10)

They have free access to the house of the highest chief, kept him informed on problems, and have the special task of preparing agendas prior to discussions at the various council meetings, and are entitled to draw on the chiefly reserves for food and clothing. There is a further differentiation within their clan.

In pre-Christian days identical work was carried out on the other level by the priests. They too had to maintain the stability of the tribe by keeping the relations with the gods correct.

Both heralds and priests had set ceremonial, which it was their duty to know thoroughly and to perform without error. The priests would enquire of and receive information from the god. Sometimes the god would inspire or possess the priest. This was a highly emotional state accompanied by extreme muscular tension, which left the priest thoroughly exhausted after the "departure" of the god. During this period of possession the priest was said to be the god's shrine or boat or envelope (*waqawaqa* or *waca ni kalou*).

To some extent this is the background of the Fijian's thinking on mediatorial work, even of the Christian minister, who is possessed by God's Holy Spirit.

The translator of the New Testament chose to use *waqa qele* for "earthen vessels" in the Corinthian passage (2 Cor 4:7), and thus he has culturally conditioned the translation. It was not the normal way of translating the idea. The light shining in the heart is the power of God Himself "possessing" the earthly shrine. The choice of this one phrase colours the whole of the Fijian of the passage. I have heard a Fijian preacher develop the chapter along these cultural lines.

At the ordination service held in Suva in 1957, the Rev. S. A. Tuilovoni, Secretary of Synod and a Fijian, although he has travelled and lectured much outside his own culture, in his dedication prayer for young ministers, prayed that they might be *Kemuni waqawaqa* (Thy shrines). Quite often one hears foreigners say that ideas like "the indwelling God" or "God in us" cannot be translated into Fijian. They can be translated alright if one is daring enough to use the pre-Christian concept of god-possession. One seldom hears it from a foreigner, but the island evangelists use it.

In the very same Synod as that mentioned immediately above, the Rev. Setareki Rika addressed the delegates on the subject of their responsibility as mediators. He made an attempt to interpret Jacob's dream and fixed his exposition on the ladder which, he claimed, represented the link or contact between man and God, between earth and heaven. In spite of sin and separation the ladder was there, showing the divine desire to restore the broken fellowship. He then fixed his attention on the angels, whom he described as *lewe ni kabakaba* or "inhabitants of the ladder," those whose appointed place was between God and man, who go up and down as mediators, interceding for man and bringing down God's blessing. This, Setareki pressed to his fellow ministers, is the job of the Christian ministry.

This fine Christian minister was not indebted to any commentary for this concept. It was his native reaction to the biblical narrative, and few ministers I know of any race carry out more diligently in their practical pastoral work this concept of ministerial mediation.

The translators of the Fijian New Testament (perhaps unconsciously) have forced an interesting truth upon us. The word translated as "mediator" in the English New Testament appears half a dozen times in the noun form. They all have one common word also in the Greek, yet in the Fijian the translators have been forced to use two different words. They are entirely different and unrelated. The Fijian has required a differentiation of civil and sacrificial mediating.[32] Thus the description of Christ as "Mediator of the new covenant" has required the civil term, it being a civil act to mediate a covenant (Heb 8:6; 9:15; 12:24); but the "Mediator between God and men" (1 Tim 2:5) implies a sacrificial mediatorship, although the same word is used in the Greek. So often we find ourselves pressed to find the English or Fijian words for the Greek differentiations, that it comes as a shock when we meet with the reverse wherein the translator into Fijian has to differentiate.[33]

The last point reminds us that we must consider the mediatorial instrument of *sacrifice* also under this head, although we have already discussed this in the linguistic study. The gospel communicator and the translator are in difficulties when faced with the English word "sacrifice" and are driven back on to the context itself before they can select the word for use. A moment's examination of the categories of sacrifice in the Fijian New Testament should be of some value to us at this juncture. The ideas fall into two categories—*ai madrali* and *ai soro*.

"Present your bodies a living sacrifice" (Rom 12:1); *ai madrali*, a thank offering, an offering and a sacrifice (Eph 5:2); *ai soro*, a remedial sacrifice. For general purposes that is sufficient, but the translator must first determine whether the sacrifice is (a) an offering, presentation, or gift (these cover thank offerings, gifts of honour, or of freewill—meat offered to idols and so on); or (b) a remedial sacrifice to solve a problem, relieve a tension, correct a fault, or cover a sin.

Having determined this, the communicator is faced with a further refinement of the breakdown. If it be a sacrifice for sin, it must be qualified. *Ai soro ni valavala ca* (a sacrifice for sin) is commonly used in the Bible (Heb 5:1,27), although *ai bulubulu* most certainly could have been used.

Ai madrali may be described as *ai madrali vakayalo* (a spiritual sacrifice; 1 Pet 2:5) or *ai madrali ni vakavinavinaka* (a sacrifice of thanksgiving; Heb 13:15) and so on.

The translators of the New Testament religiously preserved the word *ai bulubulu* for the Greek word *hilasmos* (as distinct from *thusia*), which is rendered "propitiation" in English (Rom 3:25; 1 John 2:2; 4:10).

---

32 *Dautataro*, from *tataro*, to intercede; and *Dauveisorovaki*, from *sorovaka*, to make a *soro* (sacrifice) on behalf of someone.
33 In some aspects of secular life this is even more so. Take for instance the word *war-club*. In Fijian one is faced with a great differentiation of perhaps over a score of different types. Elaborate refinement indicates a highly developed cultural element.

The interesting verse in Hebrews (10:8) which refers to various forms of sacrifice should test any language as a means of communication in this respect—"Sacrifice and offering and burnt offerings and offering for sin."

The Fijian uses *nai soro*, *nai madrali*, and *nai soro kama*; and instead of *nai bulubulu*, we read *nai soro sa soroyaki kina nai valayala ca* (the sacrifice in which atonement is made for sin). This is the most obvious refusal to use the word *ai bulubulu* that one could ever hope to meet. It virtually proves that the translators set the word aside for "propitiation" and refused to use it for any other word.

Yet the parallels are not perfect. It would be easy to assume that as the Greek uses *prosphora* and *thusia*, and the English uses "offerings" and "sacrifices," and the Fijian, *nai madrali* and *nai soro*, that these are identical categories. As this contains the clue to the Fijian concept of sacrifice, we must examine it more thoroughly.

In the first place let us ask if the average English-speaking Christian can distinguish between *offerings* and *sacrifices* made to God. Can the words for "offering" and "sacrifice" be used interchangeably in, say, narrating the story of Cain and Abel? The muddled thinking of the West on this issue is reflected in the *Oxford Dictionary* on my desk. An offering is an act of worship or a sacrifice and could refer to firstfruits, prayer, or a victim. A sacrifice is an offering to a deity, prayer, thanksgiving, penitence, propitiation, offering of a victim. This is truly vague. In the Greek an offering is an oblation without blood, and a sacrifice, either by slaughter or burning, is yet the shedding of blood or taking of a life. Although this allows for many types, the distinction is clear-cut.

Many English speakers define an offering as something freely given but which involves no really great cost, and retain sacrifice for such as involve great personal cost. If the average Westerner differentiates between these two words at all, it would probably be on the degree of cost involved. The New Testament differentiation is one of nature—was the taking of a life involved or not? In Fijian society the differentiation is functional and springs from the intention of the person making the offering or sacrifice.

If the offering is to praise or honour or give thanks, either with or without blood, either large or small, and irrespective of cost, it is *ai madrali*. It can be used of an act of favour, a good turn, or service rendered. The gifts and service Paul received from Philippi through Epaphroditus were described as a sacrifice of sweet smell (Phil 4:18), and although *thusia* in the Greek, it is *ai madrali* and not *ai soro* in the Fijian. It was a service rendered to God through Paul, a generous act, not asked for, and it is the attitude of the offerers that determines which word should be used (i.e., to which category it belongs).

Paul's request to the Roman Christians to present their bodies a living sacrifice (Rom 12:1) is another case where the Greek uses the blood-shedding word, *thusia*, but yet the Fijian uses *nai madrali*. The significance of this passage to the Fijian who hears it read is not so much whether or not he has to be ready to give his life (although this could be involved), but that his attitude to God should be such that he desired to honour Him or give thanks. He can honour Him by a life that is "good, and acceptable, and perfect" (Rom 12:2) and show thankfulness for the greatness of his salvation. This is quite different from the attitude of a person presenting an atonement, for instance.

The firstfruits (*ai sevu*) belong to neither of these categories for the simple reason that their function is entirely different. These are obligatory rites rather than mediatorial ceremonies and so do not concern us at this point.

The concept of a priest clan or class for the work of mediation is a worldwide notion. Mariner found them in Tonga a century ago and in his orthography (1820) wrote *fahegehe* as a composite name comprising *fahe* (class) and *gehe* (separate). Taboos and prohibitions, places and things made a mediator a fundamental necessity in those days.

The Christian ministry in the Fijian islands, although it took the place of the priest class, refrained from using the priestly designation. The use of *ai talatala* has been explained elsewhere (ibid., 36–37); namely, that it throws the emphasis on the apostolic commission of being sent with a message, rather than on the nature of the ritual performed. Although there is still a definite cultus in island Christianity, the office of priest has been transferred and modified. Biblical characters like Samuel, in whom the work of both priest and prophet were combined, have strengthened their concept of the Christian ministry, so that a minister both performs their religious ritual and receives his commission direct from God by inspiration.

The Rev. Iliesa Vatanitawaita, addressing the Methodist Synod in 1959, preached on the mediatorial office of Moses between God and Israel, comparing it with that of Christian ministry today. His designation was "*a dua na mataqali tamata*" (a certain type of person), who operates between God and man, and though he built his sermon round the priestly note, it was quite clear that he also viewed the work of Moses as prophetic. The two concepts seemed to integrate perfectly and to be indispensible to each other. Their mutual interdependence creates no intellectual problem for the Fijian.

To pass now from lower-level mediatorship to that of Christ, the Fijian has no problem in visualising Christ as Mediator. He is the Chief Shepherd, as His ministers are the lesser shepherds. He is the Mediator, as His servants are lesser mediators. As He took up His cross, so do His ministers. Here is an identity of spirit and mission. The differences are of quality and perfection. He has His mediatorship by His perfect identification both with God and man. He is Mediator on His own merits.

The human minister cannot say this. He has his mediatorship by a divine call and the seal of Christ, and the strength and comfort of the Mediator is transmitted through the lesser mediators under His power and guidance. Christ, the Mediator, sends the Spirit to those whom He calls and appoints. The communication of power from the Mediator to his mediators is a strong doctrine in the island church. So also is the whole pattern of representation—the Mediator intercedes before God on man's behalf and before man on God's behalf.

There is nothing new in this particular doctrine, but the point we are pressing is not the doctrine in itself but the fact that it so perfectly synchronises with the Pacific Islanders' cultural concepts. From time immemorial for them, life, social security, comfort, peace, and happiness (insofar as they have known these things) have come from effective mediation either on the man-to-man level or on the divine–human level. We are therefore not a bit surprised that the worldwide wave of Christian humanism or the social gospel of the last fifty years has left the island church untouched and unimpressed. In fact we may go so far as to say that those who have tried to explain away the mediatorial work of Christ by interfering with His true identification on the Godward side have completely failed to break through the cultural barrier, even to the extent of being understood. The mediatorial work of Christ for the Fijian is neither philosophical nor metaphorical. It is real. To think of a world without a Mediator between God and man would be inconceivable. From the very beginning, when John Hunt and those who built on his foundations prepared the *Christian Confession* (*A Vakatusa ni Lotu*), with 280 very closely printed pages, mostly in summary form with numbered points and scores of proof texts, a whole chapter was devoted to the priestly mediatorial work of Christ (Hunt and Calvert 1908). This is quite apart from the other sections on His sacrificial work.

What, then, may we say happened in Fijian religious thinking when the old religion gave way to Christianity? The old priesthood disappeared, although it is amazing how, throughout the years, so many who have been *kawa ni bete* (descendants of the priest unit in the tribe) have entered the Christian ministry. The priestly hierarchy has been modified and developed in the Christian ministry, which has also to some extent assumed the prophetic role of the seers. This raised no serious problems, as often the priest and seer were united in pre-Christian Fiji, and to this extent the Christian ministry was a perfectly natural thing in Fiji.

Two new and significant changes were made, however, which were immediately acceptable to the new Fijian Christians because they so synchronised with their natural thought forms. One was the tie-up with the New Testament concept of a call to apostleship—a being sent to a people to mediate a special message from Christ. This made the itinerant ministry possible, whereas the native priesthood had been a local fixture. The natural desire for some local expression was satisfied by the approval of class meetings, lay preaching, and lay stewardship.

The second concept which Christianity brought is the unique place of Christ, who, seen theologically as the Mediator between God and man, Himself both true God and true man, created neither offence nor problem in Fijian thinking, but even gave a definite doctrinal form to feelings which were inherent, if rudimentary. The doctrine provided the answer to that goal which Fijian ideas seem to have been blindly seeking. They had certainly felt both the separation from and the affinities with the divine. They felt there were divine presences among them, and even at times within certain inspired persons, but the vagueness of it all had, with its uncertainty, led to an involved system of taboos which warned the unwary to tread carefully. The doctrine of the Mediatorship of Christ, who was both true God and true man, who came to reveal God to man and represent man to God, satisfied the secret cravings of the Fijian heart and, therefore, despite his strong Old Testament atmosphere, he developed this strong new Testament doctrine.

Many Westerners have been puzzled by the apparently anomalous combinations of Old and New Testament faith in these island people. In reality they are not anomalies, but cultural conditioning, or examples of how culture influences belief.

The Offering as a Communal Act of Worship

Presenting offerings is a custom probably as old as religion itself, and we may well argue that it is one of the universal features of religion. The animist and the Christian alike feel the claim of religion and the rightness of making material contributions to their deity. The motives behind these offerings may vary considerably, but ritual acts of living are a universal means of expressing religious feeling.

Over a century ago Thomas Williams described in detail a ceremonial presentation of offerings in Fiji. It comprised forty whale's teeth of solid ivory, ten thousand yams, thirty turtles, and forty roots of *yaqona*,[34] hundreds of native puddings, weighing two tons in all, 150 giant clams, watermelons, coconuts, landcrabs, *dalo* (taro), and bananas (1860, 148–49). This offering was presented to a Fijian deity, and, in this particular case, the motive was for support and victory in war, but it might well have been an appeal for rain in a period of drought, or for a good harvest at the time of the planting of the crop.

Such presentations may be individual or communal. Communal ceremonial offerings were fluent in pre-Christian times and followed a regular culture pattern, which was subsequently taken over by Christianity and has remained the traditional method right through to the present day.

The only thing which Christianity really changed, apart from the character of some of the objects offered (e.g., human bodies), was the motive. The Christian missionaries pressed the biblical view of a covenant with God. He would be their God and they would be His people. They urged the Christians to present offerings, not to achieve some immediate end thereby, but because it was right and fitting to do so, and strongly resisted the idea that God dispensed His blessings in proportion to the size and frequency of the offerings presented.

---

34   The plant from which the *kava* drink is made.

This error was a strong pre-Christian belief inspired by the principal beneficiaries, the priest class, and the early records show that they alone resisted the missionary attitude. Actually the country was more than ready for change in this respect.[35] Now and again a trace of the old pre-Christian feeling of making an offering for some immediate end does still reappear, more particularly after some natural calamity has roused a feeling of fear. After the earthquake tremblings of 1953, there was a noticeable increase both in church attendance and activity. Scores of people, who for long had been quite indifferent to religion, became suddenly devout and generous. However, we must remember that these were not the rank and file of the church, but only those on the fringe.

On the whole the island Christians have a high sense of responsibility to God. If analysed on a statistical basis, their contributions far outweigh those of the home church.

Furthermore, their giving is cheerful, even to the point of group rivalry in giving. Public collections or offerings are culturally conditioned acts of worship and, in spite of the intergroup rivalry, to which many Europeans most strongly object, they are truly gatherings to glorify God.

The bone of contention is that this rivalry is an unworthy motive, which tends to the praise of man instead of God. Especially have these critics objected to the system of calling the names of the families present, who then come forward and make their family offering, knowing full well that the totals will be subsequently announced. This, it is claimed, is shaming people into giving more than is in their hearts to give.

But let it not be overlooked that this rivalry is a cultural feature of the giving process in communal society. In Fiji it is known as *veiqati*, and although it often reaches a great pitch of excitement, it is universally accepted as a good thing because the whole offering is thereby more successful—and this is the deepest motive. This society is much better integrated than that of the West, the sense of communal responsibility is infinitely higher and more sensitive, and there is a strong belief that for an individual or household to fail to carry its share of the load in any respect whatever is to jeopardise the stability of the whole society. There is no shame whatsoever attached to the smallest giver if he has carried his share. Usually some sort of an estimate is made beforehand, and a kind of quota system is used. The rivalry arises at a point somewhere above the quota, and once the quota is reached, no one is shamed.

The regular mode of presenting offerings, whether of goods or money, is for the contributors to advance to the front of the gathering with a good deal of show. Some may go forward many times before the offering is complete, and the spectators express their approval vocally with thanks and maybe with applause. It is, above all, an occasion of joy, and the island folk have much to teach us about the joy of giving.

---

35 The land was overburdened with gods and temples, and the rapid changeover from polytheism to monotheism shows that the place and people were ready for such a change.

The foreign observer is often distressed by the apparent ostentation of the giving, but this is because he sees it as a display from a number of individuals, whereas in reality it is a communal act of worship, for which there has been considerable preparation, and it is a festival of joy.

This traditional pattern applies to both secular and religious presentations. Even the food to be eaten by visitors to a village is brought in this way and ceremonially presented *as a whole* before being divided up for eating. Sometimes when a gathering of some considerable size has come together, maybe for a conference of some sort, the line of people making the offering of food will stretch to the end of the village and beyond. When the huge heap of food is ready, the proper person comes forward and presents it as a whole to the highest person of the visiting party, and it is ceremonially received. The symbolism of the ceremony is at a high level throughout. The line of persons signifies that though each individual person has had his part to play in the preparation of the offering, yet the offering is that of the group as a whole. Presentations for church purposes are made on the same pattern, and usually the performance ends with an act of dedicatory prayer.

From the early days the missionaries endeavoured to preserve the communal sense of responsibility or duty towards God. On each station and in selected villages, annual school examinations were held and each Christian, adult and child, brought his offering, usually his own handcraft, which was given to the church, either for use or sale to provide for the native catechists. These offerings included mats, baskets, fans, mosquito curtains, and other similar handcraft goods; and often a converted warrior would present his weapons of war.

Right down to the beginning of this century these offerings were comprised of goods, but the last fifty years has seen a slow but steady change over to the money economy.[36]

Some of the sea captains who visited the islands in the middle of the last century did much mischief against the missions by circulating accounts of the church making much profit out of the islanders. These reports were deliberately distorted to discredit those who were liable to expose some of their own nefarious trades on moral grounds. Later on in the plantation period the claim was pressed again, because church building and other Christian enterprises were being financed by the cultivation of cotton and manufacture of oil. The simplest reply to this is that none of the Fijian churches belong to the Mission. They always have been and still are owned by the people. Very little island revenue left the Pacific.

The mischief makers roused the ire of men like Dr. Fison of Fiji, for pressing overseas that the island people were forced to raise more money than their islands could fairly carry. Fison, defending the Tonga Mission, pointed out that the offerings were "gifts . . . of natural

---

36 Standard forms were printed for tabulating offerings, the names at the heads of the respective columns being of produce and handcraft. The forms were still used into this century and may be seen preserved in the Methodist Church Archives at Davuilevu, Fiji.

productions" which they possessed in abundance beyond their needs with very little labour. He wrote of them as *tribal offerings*, which signifies a coordinated communal effort.[37]

Sometimes these communal offerings were made on principle of the Fijian *solevu*,[38] in which craft goods were ceremonially presented to the church for use or sale, and in return for which imported goods—especially printed books, hymnbooks, catechisms, and testaments—were ceremonially exchanged.

Thomas Williams records such a *solevu* at the mission house when yams and handcrafts were presented in exchange for books and printed tracts.[39] In 1847 a *solevu* was held at Viwa in which mats, pots, and clubs were presented to assist the building of a chapel at Auckland. New Zealand was a mission district in those days, and the Fijians had heard much of the Maoris. This was a commendable act of generosity at an early date and for which there would be no return expected.[40]

Sometimes the whole presentation would comprise a single kind of gift. Williams recorded a whole offering of combs in 1852.[41] It was the offering of a women's group. Even to this day it is not uncommon to find the womenfolk engaged in some such project of their own, perhaps cutting copra over a period of time and collecting the returns from it for establishing an electric light plant for their church or some other worthy cause. Their savings having reached the required amount, there would then be a ceremonial presentation, and if it was something for the church, most probably there would be a service of dedication.

Another occasion for such an offering is the opening of a new church, a school, or some other building. Here is a description of such an event at Tiliva, Bua, in 1850, although it might well have happened this very year:

> As soon as the congregation broke up the strangers took off their mats and upper cloth dresses and petticoats, throwing them into a heap, to which Messrs. Hazlewood and Moore added a wedge axe each.
>
> The Tiliva people meantime were bringing the food from Zion to the open space in front of the chapel, with Tongan singing. There was more food than I expected, a large quantity of yams, taro and breadfruit, several hundred puddings, a quantity of crabs and fish, one hog and five turtles. Then they built a pile of nuts and cast about it a quantity of cloth and petticoats …
>
> The food was then presented to the strangers, which done, the Dama chief in the name of his friends and those from Nandy approached our chief with 10 or 12 whale's teeth.

The question now arises—to what extent are these ceremonial presentations relevant to the communication of the gospel?

---

37 Recorded in Fison's unpublished manuscript, "Tonga Note Book," p. 21.
38 A great assembly for exchange of goods and social intercourse to mutual benefit of guests and hosts. See Roth (1953, 47).
39 Unpublished "Journals of Thomas Williams," entry dated 3 May 1849 and also 18 October 1848.
40 Ibid., entry dated 31 Oct 1847.
41 Ibid., entry dated 12 Mar 1852.

The gospel certainly demands real and practical evidence of the spiritual experience of the group as well as of the individual. These acts of generosity are not motivated by a desire to win merit thereby. The act of giving, whether individual or communal, should be an act of worship. Man is thereby drawing near to God and realising the image of God within himself. Our God is a giving God. He gives freely, abundantly, and without thought of return. It becomes his worshippers to do likewise. As Francis Ridley Havergal put it: "Thou gavest Thyself for me. I give myself for Thee."[42]

All man has to give is already God's, for "the earth is the Lord's, and the fulness thereof" (Ps 24:1). The heart warmed by the gospel recognises God as Creator and Provider, and feels also that the blessings dispensed to him by God are more than adequate for all his needs. The gospel reveals that eternal life is freely given far beyond what we deserve, and the mind of Him who gave Himself for us should be "in [us]" also (Phil 2:5). The gospel demands our self-giving. The Christian is called to live a giving life, and the Lord loves a "cheerful giver" (2 Cor 9:7).

In the island ceremonial presentations, one sees spontaneous and bounding joy in giving. The mutual rivalry, so frowned on by some foreigners, is locally a strong virtue, and these occasions are joyful acts of worship within the culture pattern of the people.

The gospel was won for mankind because *a life was given away*. The gospel of the self-given life breaks through the cultural barriers of island society and inspires the *worship of giving*.

The most unsuccessful method of collecting gifts from Fijians is to solicit them from individuals one by one, but to organise a service or gathering where an offering is made on the basis of the group is quite another matter. In the West we may find individual giving easier than the islander does, but we have much we can learn from him regarding giving as a communal act of worship and joy.

---

42 From hymn number 391 in the current *Australian Methodist Hymnbook*.

6

THE IMPACT OF CULTURE ON CHRISTIAN BELIEF

Pagan Thought Forms Transferred to Christianity

We find it appropriate to commence this unit of our investigation of the impact of culture on Christian belief by first establishing the fact that in the early stages of a mission, the young church does actually take over pagan thought forms and terminology, and for better or for worse these initial choices tend to become permanent. That is why it is foolish for missionaries to rush into print with Scripture translation in their first two or three years with the language. They would be better advised to confine themselves to plain paraphrases of gospel narrative until they have mastered the idiom and atmosphere of their area.

Let me give a Fijian example of a bad choice, which to this day has created serious misunderstanding and has led to a view of plurality in the Godhead.

The term for "God in Three Persons" is *Lewe Tolu Vakalou*, which means precisely what "three persons" means in colloquial English today, and is far removed from persona, the three masks of a single actor in a classical play. A questionnaire, initiated some time ago by one of the missionaries, revealed a shockingly large percentage of educated Fijians, whose sense of the unity of the Godhead was the weakest tenet of their faith.

Unfortunately the Fijian way of saying "Almighty God" (*Na Kalou Kaukauwa Duadua*), although it does mean this, also means "the most almighty of gods." "King of kings, and Lord of lords" is often supplemented in Fijian religious jargon with "God of gods." I do not see how these phrases could have been avoided, the grammatical construction for degrees of adjectives being what they are, but there was no need for the transmission of all our trinitarian problems to the island people.

If the native thought forms, even in their paganism, contain the germinal ideas of the Christian gospel, then it is good and right that these concepts should be captivated for Christ. Some of these thought forms, which were transferred to Christianity in Fiji, will bear examination. There was already there, as we saw in the linguistic study, the terminology for the concepts of catechetical fellowship, the idea of incarnation, the indwelling Spirit, and salvation. And to these cultural transfers from the past we may add the Christian concept of *mana*.

The Fijian pattern of question and answer was taken over by the church. It has been stated that the early missionaries imposed a Western catechetical system on their converts. They did nothing of the kind. They took over an existing pre-Christian system with its significant distinction—in the West the catechetical method was a means of instruction (and to most school boys who have had to learn the answers, an uninspiring one at that), but in the islands the system of question and answer is a form of corporate worship or fellowship. The instructional value is there as oral law or narrative law, but primarily it was an experience of mutual or responsive fellowship. It was not an individual but a communal act. The impact of this cultural element, then, was that with the coming of Christianity it changed the Christian catechism into a liturgy.

Many of the pre-Christian sacrificial ceremonies had liturgies, with responsive arrangements, and many of the ballads of their dances were patterned with questions and answers. The arrangement of the Song of Solomon with its self-contained chorus intrusions between the songs is thoroughly Fijian. Sometimes these choruses in Fijian were either questions or answers. The Psalms in which choir, psalmist, and God engaged in question and answer might well have been composed in the islands.

The evolution of Fijian idiomatic or metaphoric speech reached its highest point not in the proverbs, but in the pastime of riddle making (*vatavatairalago*), a reciprocal contest of the evenings round the friendly bowl.

The Fijian word *taro* (question) is highly developed, with *taroga* (to ask a question); *vakataroga* (to ask about or enquire into); *veitarogi* (enquiry or investigation, originally a pastime as well as a serious enquiry); *tarotaro* (much questioning). *Taro* itself is either the noun or verb. The church took this word *Na Taro* (the questions) for use as "Catechism," by which name it is still known. The idea of the catechism was so indigenous that when the first catechisms were printed, the missionaries thought thereby to occupy the folk for some time to come, but returning to one place a few weeks later they found the whole catechism entirely memorised, and being chanted by the women, a privilege which the senior women still claim in church liturgy to this day.

Another thought form taken over by the church in early Fiji is found in the root *liā* and its derivatives. *Liā* really suggests one thing changing its form into another and is a strong tonal word of pagan religious significance, and as such was used of a god who made his appearance as an animal or human being. A common phrase of the time was *Sa liāgata ko Degei*—Degei (the god) has changed himself into a snake. He made his manifestations to man in this manner. The word is also used in purely secular contexts. A fossilised bivalve is said to be *liavatu* (changed into stone).

It was a somewhat daring act of translation when the missionaries, for instructional purposes, applied this term to the incarnation of the Son of God. It was daring in the first place because of its strong pagan religious associations. It is not usual scriptural usage, the Scriptures speaking of his "being man" or "becoming man" or "taking upon himself the form," and these English phrases are reflected in the Fijian translation, although the translators worked from the biblical languages.

It is not easy for us to date the first use of the phrase, *na nona liātamata mai* (his being changed into man), as a theological term for the Incarnation, but it certainly expresses the idea of *in carnis*, and was also far nearer to native idiom than "became man."

Its greatest virtue is its greatest danger—it put a definite theology into current native terminology. In the process of time the doctrine of the Incarnation has been firmly established on biblical truth, if not on biblical terms, and a speaker can use this term today without worrying about its cultural background.[43] But what lay behind its first use?

One thing is clear to the student of pre-Christian religion in Fiji: that there were two ways of viewing the earthly aspect of divine manifestations or activities. A god could reveal himself through some independent form or shrine (i.e., by inhabiting the animal or tree or rock) or, on the other hand, he could transform himself into an animal or some other creature. They are two completely different forms of divine manifestation, and the Fijian never confused one for the other. This is clearly demonstrated in Fijian vocabulary:

> *Sa liātamata mai ko Tuidelaigau.*
> Tuidelaigau has changed himself into a man.
>
> *Na waqawaqa i, Dakuwaqa na qio.*
> The shark is the shrine of Dakuwaqa.

Or as it was in some places:

> *Ha bete ni yavusa sa waqawaqa ni nodra kalou.*
> The priest of the tribe is the shrine of their god.

The word *waqawaqa* (shrine, boat, or envelope) has been discussed already. It is the physical or material object which enshrines the spirit of the god, and through whom or which he may be approached in a ceremonial way. The one god may have more than one shrine.[44]

When the god is *liātamata*, however, he has become man for the time being. He is still a god but has subjected himself to certain human limitations, and has confined himself to one place and form for the purpose of some revelation or investigation.

Both concepts were well known in old Fiji, although in the case of *waqawaqa* different dialect words were used. Old Epeli Rokowaqa, who died a decade ago at a great age, used *ai yakatakilakila* (the instrument of revelation or manifestation).

The problem of the Gnostics, as to how physical form or matter could be related to spirit, was thus not unknown in the islands on its own level. The missionaries anticipated problems in interpreting Christ's Person. They did not want it thought He was a mere

---

43   Yet many Europeans use it with reluctance. Not so native preachers.
44   *Digo* appears in the stone *Mataidigo*, but there are three such stones situated at Bau, Taikobau, and Viwa.

apparition. They did not want it believed that Jesus of Nazareth was a mere *waqawaqa*, a person inhabited by the Spirit of God. Therefore they took the bold step and used the term which had heathen associations but left no doubt about its meaning. As a result of this the Fijian church has no serious problem with its Christology. The Fijian seldom thinks to doubt either the deity or humanity of Christ. The purpose of the Incarnation is to defeat the devil on his own ground, overcome sin, and open the way of salvation to man. This is sufficient reason to justify the Incarnation.

Now it is interesting to note that the word for a complete change of face (i.e., a quiet person who suddenly flares up in anger) is built up from the same root, and so also is the word for "transfigure," or as its Greek form is, *metamorphose*. Though the connection is remote, the two great Christian words—"incarnation" and "transfiguration"—have come from this root *liā*.

Having settled the terminology for the establishment of the uniqueness of the Person of Christ, Fijian Christian thought then comes back to another concept of a divine spirit entering or possessing a human body. When the god entered the priest, he was said to be *curumi* (possessed). To be *vakacuru* (spirit-possessed) was to be possessed willingly for the purpose of becoming the instrument of the god for a specific task or utterance, and was the very opposite of *vakatevoro*, which was a hostile possession, injurious, and unwillingly possessed. From this distinction grew the doctrine that the Christian could be possessed by the Spirit of God and become His instrument for good works or preaching. The Holy Spirit was distinguished from evil spirits, and in church buildings the pulpit was set higher than the seat of the chiefs, for the word from the pulpit is the word of God.

Here again in the concept of spirit possession—willing and unwilling, divine and demon—we discover the theological potential of Fijian ethnolinguistics. Christianity was able to select from these ideas. Did she make any dramatic changes?

The dramatic difference was cultural rather than semantic at first. Possession by the Spirit of God was not confined to the priest class, but was open to all. This was literally proved by the experience of members in the class meetings and prayer meetings. During the 1840s, 1850s, and 1860s the Fijian people discovered through experience the doctrine we call the universal priesthood of all believers; and growing from this many fine souls have come to appreciate the high spiritual concept of the Spirit-filled life. As the experiences have developed, so the semantics have slowly come more and more near to our own higher moments.

The meanings of such words in any society will vary, of course, with varieties of religious experience. To some extent also, experience varies with varieties of culture and environment.

Bula (life) does not mean the same thing to all Fijians. For one it means escape from fear; for another, escape from sickness; for another, escape from hunger; and for still another, from sin. You greet your friend in the morning with this word, and wish him thereby escape from whatever danger or fear besets his path. In the Fijian word *bula* we have that state of life which provides him with what is to him most desirable. With a growing Christian experience, this great desire changes, and the word passes from a negative to a positive significance.

To the "primitive" weighed down by the fear of black magic, life is escape from this power. He is open to the message of the name before which devils fear and fly. To him thus Christ becomes *Ai Vakabula* (the One through whom one finds life; i.e., Saviour). Subsequently having overcome his fear through Christ, he develops a positive desire, maybe to build a church in his village, or to win his son for Christ, or to bring to an end a serious and long-standing quarrel in his tribe. Whatever it is, it is his great desire at the moment, no longer negative but positive; and this to him is life, to win this prize, to achieve this victory, to effect this reconciliation. He remembers how it was before he himself found Christ, the Life-giver. He prays earnestly and his prayer is heard, and Christ again gives him life—life more abundantly. Both negatively and positively Christ is *Ai Vakabula*, the Life-giver, but the nature of the life given is conditioned by his own experience and desire.

So the basic terminology for both the Person and work of Christ lay within the Fijian language and thought forms, but it was a dormant potential, which awaited discovery and application and development.

Oral Tradition and Christian Belief

Several Fijian chants were discussed in an earlier part of this study relative to the pattern of rhythm and its effect on worship and instruction. The same chants could also be used to illustrate how, in the preliterate stages of the church in the Fiji Islands, oral tradition played its part in the transmission of religious knowledge. The missionaries themselves were very much awake to the possibilities of this method of instruction and used it for teaching history, geography, hygiene, and mathematics, as well as the Bible.[45]

---

45 John Watsford was one who picked up the Fijian idiom and rhythm pattern and used it for the purposes of secular instruction. The following is an example of his craft. It was composed for use as a work song, after the pattern of the old Fijian house-building and timber-hauling songs, and would compare perhaps with the "Song of the Volga Boatman." The rhythm of the song had to fit the action of the work. Watsford began his service in Lau, hence there are a few Lakeban words.

Samu, Samu, Samu, Samu,	Beat, Beat, Beat, Beat,
Samu, Samu tikoga.	Beat and go on beating.
Kevaka da tawa samu	If we do no beating
Eda luva wale ga.	We'll have no clothes to wear.
Samu, Samu, etc.	Beat, Beat, etc.
Ke sa sega na tainamu	If we make no mosquito nets
Eda kaji kecega.	We will all be bitten.
Samu, Samu, etc.	Beat, Beat, etc.
Ni sa oti tu na samu	When we've finished beating
Eda qito lako ga.	We'll then go out to play.

Although it would seem certain that many of the early Christian songs and chants were actually written compositions, it is also quite certain that they were not all handed down in writing, but were deliberately prepared for oral transmission. The same may be said of a type of paraphrase used by pioneer missionary William Cross from the beginning. He made no known attempts at poetry and was not successful at word-for-word translations of the Scriptures, but his particular bent was to take simple Scripture narratives and write the story as one would narrate it to a child. This product he would recast many times, polishing the vocabulary and testing the rhythm of his composition, with the result that he wrote first-class narrative prose. Unfortunately no samples of his prose have come down to us, but we base our opinion on records and comments left by John Hunt, who was alive to this sort of contact and himself had a good grasp of native idiom. Cross would make out a number of copies for the men who had learned to read and send them out into the villages to read them. Everywhere these paraphrases were listened to with eagerness, and the gospel spread from there orally. Long before preaching reached the interior, and therefore long before folk had learned to read or write, these paraphrases were being recited from memory.

Thus it happened that for years afterwards messengers kept arriving at Viwa from remote interior where no evangelist had been. Oral tradition played a tremendous part in preparing the way for the evangelist.

These paraphrases and chants were also composed by the early native teachers who had been under the instruction of the missionaries, and although we have no way of identifying many of the composers, I have often heard these ancient acts of worship in the mountain and outer island villages. Many of them, I feel certain, never did exist in written form. Sometimes when I have tried to get the words of a chant, which seemed to me to contain obsolete words, an old woman of obviously great age has described how she learned the chant years ago from the old women of her young days. Sometimes I have picked on certain words and have been told that this one or that are very old, and the old folk themselves are not quite certain of the exact meaning. In the rhythm and the construction also there is a ring of antiquity which most certainly would have been edited by the young grammar-book Fijians.

Many of these chants are about heaven. Others are biblical narrative, but not always the terminology of our present Bible. Although David Hazlewood completed his translation of the Old Testament in the early 1850s, the full Bible did not appear in print until 1864 in London. For thirty years the narrative passages of the Old Testament had been recited and chanted in the villages of Fiji prior to this date.

The narrative was transmitted like this:

> *Na sucu i Mosese ka macala,*   We know of the birth of Moses,
> *Erau vunia tiko ko tinana,*   How his mother hid him,

Erau vunia e vula rua-ya.	How she hid him for two months.
Na waqa gasau erau dregata	She sealed the boat of reeds
Erau laveta ki matasawa	And carried it to the shore
Ciri sobu na gone matavinaka	And the pretty child drifted down
E sobu mai ka dua na marama.	And a woman also came down.[46]

I remember with a great deal of pleasure an occasion on the island of Koro, when at a monster service fifteen chants of this type were rendered by the women of fifteen different villages. The friendly rivalry was keen, and not one of those chants had been composed or suggested by a white man. It was a thoroughly indigenous expression of scriptural faith, and I was so caught up with the general atmosphere that I was from then on completely convinced of the transmissibility of the gospel through the cultural elements of the Pacific. Here is a gospel which can be perfectly integrated within another culture pattern, and here I found a cultural element which refused to break down, but took the gospel unto itself as its own.

At the same time, however, we must observe that it was selective. It selected those parts—the poems and narratives and ideas—which most fitted the local needs and ethos. It did not take our Christian ethics in entirety, for example, as we tend to think it should have done. Most Westerners, in their ethnocentricity, think that Christian ethics as we know them are the only Christian ethics; and if they want to argue the point from the Scriptures, they can, like Shylock, cite Scripture to their purpose. The islanders whose needs and way of life are different will select from different portions of Scripture. The narratives of the faith of the people who lived close to the herd and soil ring with a clearer message to them and is valid, although this may not seem so to the modern city dweller of cosmopolitan and democratic society.

We seek, either consciously or unconsciously, to impose our Western concepts and ethics on the "primitive," but quite often he does not take just what we seek to give him. He knows his needs and makes his own selection. We criticise him for not taking the full gospel, yet if we examined ourselves equally critically, we would see that we also are selective. There are segments of Bible teaching we reject as Hebrew or Greek thought of a particular period because they do not seem to fit our own peculiar political or social setup. We quote the parts of Paul which suit our purposes but bypass his views on Graeco-Roman status levels as not fitting our democratic ideas and teachings on human liberty. Yet the "primitive" who lives within a status society is completely mystified that we bypass them. To him they represent social security as well as ethics.

What then is the truth of the matter? Surely it is that the gospel has its own message in any form of society. Here is a gospel which integrates in any culture pattern, and in doing

---

46 My translation is very free. The use of the dual pronouns suggests parents rather than mother, but mother (*tinana*) is specific. This is a fragment from *Na Gauna Makawa* (Ancient Times) preserved in the records of William Aitken Heighway, who composed a number of such items himself about sixty years ago.

so it reveals what the real core of the eternal gospel is. This essential core may be stated thus, for Christians in either status or democratic society:

> Man has sinned and deserves to pay the price, but God, in His love, has desired man's salvation. The way is open through the Incarnation, the Cross, and the empty tomb; and Christ's work becomes effective for us through faith. We are assured of salvation from both the guilt and power of sin and called to a life of righteousness here on earth and union with Him beyond the grave.

There has been no difficulty in getting this essential core of doctrine through the cultural barriers to the Pacific Islander. It is now thoroughly indigenous. As a preacher, a foreigner of a different culture, raised with a different speech, and standing alone with my white face before a sea of brown smiles, I am thoroughly at home when I preach on the core of the gospel, for this gospel integrates well. But should I be foolish enough to urge the congregation in a fishing village to stand up for their liberty against their chiefs, they would perhaps listen to me with forbearance and courtesy, but would say among themselves that one shouldn't expect much from a foreigner. One immediately runs the risk of this once one gets away from the core of the gospel, for what is culturally right in one society is cultural dynamite in another.[47]

It is on the periphery, not in the core, that we find the peculiar cultural impact on belief in a given society. It calls for generosity and tolerance. Unnatural environmental factors also may lead to a peculiar cultural response, with bearing on belief. Sometimes these periodic emphases become a permanent stress in the religious outlook of a people.

Can we now focus this apparent digression on the subject under discussion? In general we are discussing the impact on belief; in particular we are discussing oral tradition. The question therefore which arises is—does Fijian oral tradition throw any light on changes of doctrinal emphasis due to ethnoenvironmental factors during the century, and to what extent have these become permanent?

The most obvious is certainly the strong and passionate doctrine of heaven, and it is strongly supported by documentary evidence from reports and records left by native preachers. The first impression one has when reading these documents is that it was an unhealthy overemphasis, that Christianity had got into a sidetrack, and that the desire for heaven had robbed her of an awareness of her task here and now on earth. A cursory reading of the documents could lead one to that finding, but nothing would be more unfortunate or unfair. The first essential is to pinpoint the period when the doctrine became so strong and then to examine it in the historic sense. Such an examination reveals the truth that the period of greatest emphasis just exactly coincides with the period of grimmest

---

47 Even in the communication of the gospel of comfort through pastoral visitation, one must proceed with caution. Dr. Winburn T. Thomas of Indonesia points out how the pastor's relationships with his people are conditioned by mores, by showing how in Muslim lands, for instance, pastoral visitation when the husband is at the office or in the fields would be resented, and thus have the opposite of the desired effect (1957).

persecution, when to proclaim oneself a Christian one day might well consign one to the cannibal oven on the morrow. There were literally thousands of Fijians who died in a real, living faith during this period.

In the written accounts left by Joeli Bulu and Jemesa Havea and in the oral tradition of narrative and chants, heaven was real and near and highly desirable. It was offered as the extreme opposite of the cannibal Fijian concept of life after death. This accounts for the popularity of the book of Revelation in the oral chants and the most common theme of all—the new Jerusalem.

To some extent it explains the popularity of allegorical preaching still today. For my own information, I have investigated this matter at length, and I am satisfied that it was neither an overemphasis nor a sidetrack, but a valid truth worthy of special emphasis at a particular point of history. It did no harm to the gospel core, but displayed it better within a suitable frame. Heaven preaching is not so strong today, because men are not daily called to face death for their faith; but I am certain that had the last war seen the foreigner victorious in Fiji, whose aim was to stamp out Christianity by persecution, that Fijian heaven preaching would have been found still strong in their thought.

Beyond the Bible itself, no translated work has so entered into the soul of Fiji as *Pilgrim's Progress*. Its allegorical form exactly fitted the Fijian cultural concepts. The young generation of today, which is ever turning to the West and its money economy, is not so familiar with Christian's adventures. When the writer came down to Fiji, they were used to illustrate half the Fijian sermons one heard, and preachers who had no copy of the book were still familiar with many of its episodes. The narrative of *Pilgrim's Progress* has long since passed into Fijian oral tradition, and I have known Fijians to argue that it is not allegory but fact. The wall between allegory and fact is thin in some cultures.

Although Fijian has no word for "personification," the people are thoroughly familiar with the figure of speech. One must not be surprised to hear a chant, which mentions faithful characters from the Bible, from the record of the church, and perhaps Christian and Faithful also from Bunyan's classic. They have become real. Without any real time concept, Abraham and Jesus, though separated by two thousand years, may be thought of together, and Luther and Wesley, and Christian and Faithful. There are no barriers of time or place to those who belong to the faith. Here is the church eternal. What time ideas the Fijian has had imposed on him by the foreigner, he has learned with difficulty; but in his belief, Bible time, and church history, and religious allegory are all the living present.

Examination of the contents of the following ancient chant reveals that thin also is the veil between earth and heaven:

Ha noda vanua ko Lomalagi,	Heaven is our land,
Na noda vanua vakarautaki,	Our land that is prepared,
Ratu Jisu ka sa hole cake.	Chief Jesus has taken up the challenge.

Dou sa tiko na veiwekani,	You remain here, my friends,
Au sa cibicibi tu ki Lagi.	I dance for joy to heaven.
Sa qai rawai ko vuravura-ri	The world is overcome
Sa qai tu me qali ki Lagi.	And is a subject state to heaven.
Sa leqa tani tu ko Setani.	Satan is truly in difficulties.

Now, to think of "overcoming the world" as leaving the world as a subject state of Jesus the conquering Chief from heaven, and as thus depriving Satan of his kingdom, is truly a culturally conditioned piece of exegesis. So too is the "dance of joy" (*cibicibi*), for this is the old-time term for the dance of joy that followed victory in war. Such phrases almost certainly date this chant to the pioneering period[48] when Christians found war about them on every side.

But surely a gospel which was transmitted by such cultural conditioning as this could never be considered a foreign imposition. It was part and parcel of their daily life.

God and the Land

With people who live close to the soil, the land plays an important part in their thinking about God. The doctrines of the will and purpose of God, divine providence, election, and covenant relationship were aspects of the Hebrew religion that received some colour and form from their beliefs about the land of Canaan. Nor is it uncommon to find that a "primitive" but landowning people, converted from paganism to Christianity, is quick to grasp the possibilities of these doctrines and to tie them up with their beliefs about their own land.

Laws of land tenure and "disposal" vary considerably, but the very existence of these laws and customs reveals how close a watch "primitives" keep on their land and how they have bound over the land with religious ritual control. The world has any number of examples of their resentment against white intruders. One of the major causes of such resentment is irregular land acquisition contrary to cultural taboos and sanctions.

It is amazing how many such races insist that lands cannot be lost or acquired by simple military conquest. The Kikuyu, of whom we have heard so much in recent years, believed the spirits of the true owners "would make it impossible for the new occupiers to carry out their agricultural activities with any hope of success" (Leakey 1953, 2–3).

Wanderobo [Dorobo] lands were divided into hunting territories on a family basis, and although these boundaries were natural formations of the landscape, the family land zones were known and respected by neighbours, and each family insisted that they were private property.

Dr. Leakey has shown how Europeans often disputed that hunting rights meant possession. However, whatever could be argued by the law of the white man, their own law

---

48   I have this chant from a typescript collection of items from the olden times, left by William Aitken Heighway. If Heighwey himself classified this as belonging to "olden times," it must go back to the pioneering days, as Heighway was himself at work in Fiji as early as 1887.

and custom insisted that hunting lands were inviolate property, and each family recognised the rights of its neighbour (ibid.).

Furthermore it is highly debatable, if in the most "primitive" landowning societies there was any real concept at all of land disposal. Did any white settlers ever really acquire the land of which they took possession? It is said they bought their land for coloured beads and iron axes, and the native people of today bewail the folly of their forebears. But this present generation knows the meaning of buying and selling. It seems certain that their grandfathers did not.

In the Fijian culture, for instance, there was no such thing as a land sale, even though the consuls did have printed forms for them. The foreigner's refusal to realise this basic cultural difference has led to much suffering and misunderstanding and bloodshed. There was a strong impression that the country was ruled under a kind of feudalism, in which the chief was the lord and owner of the land and the people the serfs. In reality the land was owned by the tribe, of which the chief was but a single member. He certainly had no rights of disposal. Since the time of Dr. Lorimer Fison, this has been recognised in Fiji, but the most fertile part (23 percent) had been alienated before any protection was afforded the native people.[49]

This problem of land ownership was one of the first questions presented to the new Council of Chiefs for decision after the Cession of the islands to Britain, and a firm decision for all Fiji was made—*A qele sa nodra na veitarataravi* (The soil belongs to the successive generations). It is not a chattel to be bought or sold.[50]

What is even more significant is the fact that every approved means of land "disposal" in old Fiji had its proper name, and in not a single case can we trace any permanent disposal. These occasions were tied up with birth, marriage, and death, and also other life crises; but in all cases the land eventually reverted to the original owner or his descendant.[51]

We referred above to the Kikuyu and Wanderobo. These two had interesting tribal interrelationships in land "disposal," but here again we are confronted with a strong mental resistance of anything approaching disposal as the white man understands it. How could a Kikuyu (an agriculturalist) acquire land from a Wanderobo (a hunter)? It was possible only by means of a ceremony of "mutual adoption," which solemn rites safeguarded both parties against treachery and made a transfer possible and produced friendly relationships between the spirits of the two tribes. This adoption gave them equal status and equal

---

49   Lorimer Fison presented the case for Fijian tribal land ownership in an address at Levuka soon after Cession—a linguistic and anthropological classic. Subsequently the government published the script (Fison 1903).
50   This subject has been dealt with at length in an MA thesis at the American University, Washington, DC (Tippett 1956b, 221–26).
51   The names of such transfers of land are: *ai kovu ni vanua* (bundle of land), *ai mudu ni liga* (shortening of the hand), *ai sere ni wa-ni-kuna* (untying of the strangling cord), *ai covicovi ni draudrau* (the branch of leaves), *ai vakatoka ni yaca* (the giving of the name), *a vanua ni cola buka* (land for hauling firewood), and *ai curucuru ni gone* (the child's entrance). For further detail see Bulicokocoko (n.d.).

obligations, and on the official occasion the Wanderobo tribe involved would invite other Wanderobo tribes to be present as witnesses. The solemn ceremonies performed were accompanied by sacrifices and prayers to the ancestral spirits of both tribes (ibid., 5–6).

In these widely separated cases, one in Africa and one in the Pacific, we observe in both cases a link between the land and religion. Any change of land occupancy had to be safeguarded by some religious rites and prayers.

This being so, then, what happens when the "primitive" landowners become Christian, and religious rites and prayers to their ancestor spirits are no longer effective?

In the case of the Fiji Islanders there has been a definite attempt to link up Fiji with Israel and to superinduce a new cultural interpretation on the Hebraic concept of the Promised Land. Some new twist of this reappears from time to time in the small nativistic movements, which are not rare, but quite apart from these the would-be indigenous historians of Fiji have usually tried to find some genealogical connections with the biblical figures of Genesis.

Thus, for instance, Dreketirua follows the biblical chronologies down to the family of Solomon, then through one Yala, later to Babylon, then back to Jerusalem, and subsequently under his son to Africa (4:17–18). Under later figures the line comes to Fiji. The sense of time, space, and sequence is shockingly bad,[52] and great world events are forced to fit into minor elements of Fijian tradition.

"The blood of Israel," Dreketirua says, "flows in the veins of our first leaders, Yala, Jerupi and Vasili, and thence to all their descendants. Among these are the native landowners of Fiji, chosen people, appointed to own the land and to eat the food provided there by Him who created it" (10:42).

This doctrine is the firm conviction of hundreds of Fijians today, especially among those of riper years. Dreketirua himself is a sane fellow, elderly, respected in his village, in close contact with commerce and industry, a schoolmaster and accredited local preacher.

His regular term for Fiji is *na noda Parataisi* (our Paradise), and he bemoans the fact that his people are "despised in their own land by those who are entering Paradise today" (Rokowaqa n.d., 2). He insists that Fiji was the Creator's special gift to the Fijian people; that this is the foundation on which they build, for so it was ordained by God. His regular terminology for God is *o Koya sa buli keda* (our Creator, He who made us), or *o Koya sa bulla na Paradaisi oqo* (Creator of this Paradise). Thus the work of creation would seem to find its greatest expression in two acts—the creation of the land of Fiji and the creation of the Fijian race to possess it. This is the widespread doctrine of election in Fiji. It does not claim

---

52   The same criticism applies to Rokowaqa's migration table. He has the ancestors of the Fijian people leaving Thebes (Egypt) in 178 BC for Tanganyika, departing thence in AD 122 for Fiji via Ceylon and Papua. By AD 1450 they were at Nakauvadra, after which followed three hundred years of wandering in Fiji, a period of native wars beginning with the establishment of the small kingdoms throughout Fiji about AD 1750. It is fantastic to try fitting his genealogies into his chronology (Rokowaqa n.d., 71) and other places.

that Fiji is the only divinely given land or that the Fijian people are the only elected people, but it does claim that the land of Fiji and the Fijian race were created for each other, just as were Israel and the Promised Land.

The present-day seriousness of such a doctrine in Fiji may be judged from the fact that the Fijian is no longer the majority in his own land, and he has lost possession of the most fertile portion. The immediate Christian problem is that with half the population Asiatic and landless, has the Fijian the right to go on holding the 77 percent of the land that remains (half of which he does not use)? Whether the church likes it or not, the question of the communication of the gospel is now tied up with these practical issues.

The supporters of Dreketirua's views have a plausible case, and their mode of presenting it is thoroughly scriptural. It is presented as the *will* and *purpose* of God that Fiji should be their *votavota tawa mudu* (eternal inheritance), and they are to *possess* and have *authority* over it—*me da mai taukena ka lewa noda Parataisi oqo* (Dreketirua 2: 3). It was God who brought them from Africa. In His strength only was that possible, because it was His *purpose* that they should *possess* and have *authority* over the land *forever* (ibid., 4:71). That is all strong doctrine and it does not end there, for it was *by the will of God* that the land selections were made (*na vanua sa digi oti tu e na lewa Vakalou*) and that the Fijian tribes *divided* and *possessed* their *different portions* (*me tawari kina na dui nodrai votavota*) (ibid., 3:16).

There was a brief period under British administration when the protective laws were relaxed and some Fijian lands were sold to become freehold property. Private planters, commercial sugar interests, and the church acquired lands at the time. Dreketirua is outspoken about this, and it is apparent that he has no solution for the future but that all lands should be Fijian and all others should be classed as foreigners and not permanent residents. Undoubtedly this has been the most common Fijian viewpoint, and clearly the church has done little until recent years to correct the matter.

A change of attitude has been coming slowly from the time of the new constitution of the church in the mid-1940s, when the church dispensed with the European Synod and formed a United Synod where leaders of all races could discuss matters of common policy such as education and evangelism.

The most significant change of all has come within the last two years among the Fijian ministers and theological students, so much so that surely the door is now open for the communication of the gospel to the resident Hindu in a way that we have not hitherto seen. As evidence of this change of attitude, I now set out the results of an attitude test done on fifteen theological students in October 1957.[53] They reveal a dramatic change in

---

53 The testing was done on a secret ballot principle, but the group itself was actively interested in tabulating the result. The disturbing element of the experimenter was thus eliminated by making the class the experimenter. These tests do not indicate the causes of the change in attitude, but merely the fact of it.

attitude among the young trainees for the ministry in Fiji. The test indicates the mind of this group and, of course, should be seen as a special group, not the rank and file.

Question investigated: Who should own the land in Fiji?

Response:

Great Britain	2
The Fiji government	3
The Fijian people	3
Each householder	7

Evaluation: 33 percent place their hopes for some solution of the Fiji land problem in the British administration either at home or locally. This strongly suggests the men are bewildered by the present situation. Those looking to Britain (2/5) feel that security and hope is in Empire. The others (3/5) favouring local government ownership perhaps feel the races within the colony will have to find their own solution. At any rate it will have to be done on an administrative level.

20 percent only still cling to full Fijian ownership, such as has been indicated above (Dreketirua). This is surprising and significant, a dramatic swing of opinion.

47 percent find the solution only in complete private possession of lands. This also is an important swing of opinion and shows a strong decay of custom over the last decade or so. It also indicates a feeling against the tribal ownership which is I feel a postwar development.

Question investigated: Does the ownership of the land imply any responsibility to use it?

Response:

Yes	13
No	2

Evaluation: This is a complete shift of opinion from the traditional position, which has pressed the claim that it is right and just to hold lands, even if unused, for the probable needs of generations to come. Even among theological students I think these figures would have been reversed as late as three years ago. Even among the senior Fijian ministers, mostly conservative, there was a similar shift of opinion in the 1957 Synod speeches. It was the general feeling of Synod that land ownership involves a moral responsibility for utilisation when there are so many landless people in the colony. This test reflects the Synod feeling.

Question investigated: Should the Fijian people dispose of some of their 77 percent of lands for the sake of the landless Indians in the colony? (dispose of = fully surrender)

Response:

Yes	11 (one qualified)
No	4

Evaluation: This shows that most of the students were prepared to be practical about their idealism in the question above. I confess I never expected to see the day when eleven out of fifteen Fijians, from any group, would cast a vote like this. It can only mean these men are wide awake to the grim situation which they will have to face during their ministries.

Reasons given against disposal; 4 voting so.

The Indian flays the land.	1
It is the Fijians' land by birthright.	2
It is needed for future generations.	1
Start this and there will be no end to it.	
It will mean large-scale racial strife.	

Reasons given in favour of disposal; 11 voting so.

Christian charity—Indians "being Fiji-born."	2
Christian charity—Indians being landless.	5
There will be war some day if we do not.	
Let it be sold and a native reserve fund established.	
They will aid in developing the country.	
We do not use it, so have no right to it.	
The earth is the Lord's and for the use of all.	

Qualification: Terms of disposal should be clearly stated so no subsequent misunderstandings can arise.

That list of reasons for and against the disposal of native lands is an interesting study in motives, and shows the state of theological and ethical ferment in the country at the present moment after a century and a quarter of Christianity.

Perhaps this changing attitude will open the door for a better communication of the gospel within the colony itself, for hitherto the strong doctrine of election has certainly hindered the Fijian Christian from the evangelisation of the Indian in his country. It must not be overlooked, of course, that the ministers and theological students represent a special group, and they are a very small minority, and it is unlikely they will convince their congregations overnight. They are, however, an influential group and not likely to remain silent.

Meantime the Fijian doctrine of election remains strongly entrenched in the greater part of Fiji. From the point of view of historical ethnolinguistics, we are interested in the fact that it did not exist in the early days of Christianity in Fiji. There is no trace whatever of the doctrine in the pre-Cession period. It is clearly a *cultural protective device that has evolved from the native concern at the rapid demographical changes brought about by the labour policy of the administration from the 1880s down to the Great War.*

The Fijian people had been reading their Bibles for years before the commencement of the indenture system, but they never found this doctrine nor put it in their preaching, their chants, or hymns. The inverse variations of indigenous and foreign population in the last two decades of the century drove the Fijian back to his Bible, and this time he found the doctrine of the election of Israel.

The struggles of Israel for the possession of what they believed to be theirs by covenant with God was something that now came to the Fijian with new light. From his new understanding of Israel he passed to the consideration of his own predicament, and so there sprang up the doctrine of the election of the Fijian people, but it should be noted that this was a cultural impact on religious belief, not *vice versa*.

Fijian theories of origin have never been in agreement. Epeli Rokowaqa, who was an ordained minister, prepared a list of seven different Fijian theories of origin based on the old Fijian myths. He had a habit of making slight variations in words, such as the changing of a vowel, and thereby twisting the meaning to suit his exposition. Sometimes I have deliberately twisted words thus for amusement and have been surprised to find that with many a Fijian it counts for logic, although I had meant to be funny.

Although Epeli denied the myths as they stand, he did not hesitate to recast one in this way to fit his Christian beliefs. Thus, for instance, he argues that *Ratu mai Bulu* (Lord of the Underworld) should be *Ratu mai Bula* (Lord of Life), and thus many of the claims of his ancestors could be tied up with his new faith with very little difficulty,[54] and so also he was able to identify the Fijian race with the Semites, and Tura of Fijian myth became Terah, the father of Abraham. The cause of all the confusion, Epeli insisted, may be put down to the time when their migrations took them to Egypt and some copied the customs of that land and deified their chief when he died. When *Ratu* was buried (*Ni sa bulu kina ko Ratu*), he became *Ratu mai Bulu*, and thus the true light was lost and the title *Ratu mai Bula* with it (Rokowaqa n.d., 16).

Epeli Rokowaqa's migration tables do not fit those of Dreketirua. The former introduced the Papuans into his account, probably because he was active at the time when the Fijian Mission to Papua was being pressed by the church. They came from Turkestan, via Egypt and Africa, because of famine in the land (ibid., 8), and en route to Fiji stayed a long time in Ceylon. His migrating groups met again, and eventually three large canoes left to seek the Promised Land (*me taura nodrai votavota*) to receive their inheritance. Similar

---

54 The anthropological status of *Ratu mai Bulu*, however, is absolutely unassailable.

circumstances occurred at Papua whence they were "guided to Fiji by the hand of the Lord of Life, the God of Tura (Terah), their ancestor, that the blessed land might be their inheritance" (ibid., 11).

The internal land divisions, according to Rokowaqa, were caused by the excessive hard-heartedness of Degei, who wanted "to be served and not to serve," which was a "dark attitude" and strong influence of the sojourn in Africa. Dreketirua and Rokowaqa disagree in these things, but they agree entirely in the claim that Fiji was God's gift, the inheritance of the Fijian people (ibid., 43).

The differences in the routes of migration and the chronology do not much concern us here, especially as neither is entirely consistent within his own writing. It is the unity of their theological emphasis that matters. It is a drift from the truth caused by the political and cultural predicament in which they found themselves. God guided them to Fiji. It was His firm intention that Fiji should be "their land and that of their descendants forever" (ibid., 243). "Each race of people has its promised land," argues Rokowaqa, "from the time when the world was divided among men and each race went out to seek its inheritance" (ibid., 8).

One would not suggest that European missionaries had done anything actively to develop such an outlook, but consciously or unconsciously some of the things they said and wrote did help to precipitate it, or at least provided an atmosphere which was not hostile to it. This is borne out by some of the national hymns in the current hymnbook.

Let us take a few examples.

Me tou sa mai doka	Let us come and praise
Na yaca i Viti ga,	The name of Fiji,
Me yaca dei.	To be an established name.
Sa loma ni Kalou	It was the mind of God
Me sa qui nodatou	That it should be our
Vanua ga ka no,	Land which lies (here),
Sa ka talei	And a precious thing.

That is a mighty long way from Billiam Edward Hiokson's "God bless our native land," which it purports to translate. The same hymn speaks of Fiji as:

| *Vanua sa qarai,* | Land that was searched for, |
| *Vanua sa kilai.* | Land that is known. |

If these words mean anything at all, it must be that the place was sought for and found at the end of a migration.

Another hymn which is quite popular has a verse that runs:

| *Vanua ka a dau nodra tu* | The land which has belonged |
| *Nai tubutubu ga e liu,* | To our forefathers of old, |

> *Na uma qele, me tu dei*
> *E na ligadra nai taukei.*

> May its soil be firmly established
> In the hands of the native people.

Still another has this verse:

> *Noda qase era bale era bulu no eke*
> *Na luveda era tubu, era tiko kina ne?*
>
> *Sa qai dredre me da beca na vanua ga oqo*
> *Sa solia raai vei keda ko Jiova, na Kalou.*

> Our fathers lie buried here
> Our children who grow, do they not live here?
>
> Hard it is for us to despise this land
> Which Jehovah our God has given us.

All these hymns date to the period during which this doctrine developed, and all were composed by white men, and (although I have extracted them from their respective contexts, which may not be fair) undoubtedly they did provide a suitable atmosphere for the development of the Fijian doctrine of election. The committee which approved the present hymnbook accepted them all in the above form.

The Theology of Original Hymns

In the first century of its history, the Fijian church produced about a dozen native hymn writers whose work is preserved and used. Their literary compositions provide us with some valuable data about their thinking. Some are attempted translations, but that the Fijian translators were sufficiently impressed with an English hymn to attempt a translation of it is itself of interest. Others were entirely original.

Viewed as a whole they represent a fairly compact body of orthodox theology, although those written for children seem to be confined to the joy of following Christ and living the good life. Some of these original hymns were composed for special occasions—a welcome service, opening a new church building, and so on, and in these the ringing bells of Sankey become the beating drums of Fiji.

The rhythm of the old Fijian war drum was taken over as the beat to call the congregation to worship. The drum was of yore the instrument of call, invitation, or communication of the will of the gods. It has come over to Christianity. Even in the heart of the city of Suva, with a new and thoroughly Western church built in the cruciform style, the native drum beats out, reverberating from the tower for each service. Tonga and Samoa have turned to church bells, but not Suva. The bells of the Fijian hymnbook are "drums of joy," and those who respond are the "citizens of heaven."

> *Qiri lali! Kailai Marau tikoga,*
> *Lewe i Lomalagi kecega.*

> Beat the drums! Shout! Rejoice,
> Citizens of heaven all.

Even in those few places where a metal bell has been imposed, the phrase is "beat the drum," not "ring the bell." This demonstrates that the true Fijian idea of the drum beating of call, invitation, and communication has been taken over for the call to worship; and where a metal bell is used, the drum concept is transferred to it. It is spoken of as *tataqiriqiri* (beating wood), even though it would be correct Fijian to say *tataqaqa* (ringing metal).[55]

Another Fijian hymn writer has put it thus:

Tou qiri lali ga,	Beat the drums,
Ka toro vei Jisu,	And draw near to Jesus,
Tou qiri lali tikoga,	Go on beating,
Ka marau tu.	And continue rejoicing.

We have already seen that heaven preaching was a feature of Fijian religious thought a century ago. This also has been reflected in their hymns. One Fijian attempted to translate the hymn:

Sweeping through the gates of the New Jerusalem
Washed in the blood of the Lamb.

Both in song and sermon the "drums of heaven" are continually in action, and are associated with rejoicing as well as invitation.

The drum-beating hymn cited first in this section of our subject ends with these lines:

Ni da curu yani ki na koro vou,	When we enter into the new village,
Qai marau ka tawa mudu tu.	Then will our joy be eternal.

The new Jerusalem, interpreted as heaven, is often spoken of as the new village.

Another hymn of Fijian origin places the writer in the position of a wanderer, prone to get lost in the bewildering changes of this life. He contemplates his life journey in the dark. Christ is the Light to lighten his path. Christ is indeed the way. Christ is the guiding Shepherd. With these three figures for Christ's guidance the result, no doubt, of his meditation on the Scriptures, he communicates the gospel in the medium of hymn singing. He gives one verse to each idea and brings the congregation in the last verse to the heavenly fold.

Au sa oai marau	I then find happiness
Nifu sa curuma tu	When I enter
Na bai ni sipi ni Kalou,	The fold [of the flock] of God,
Koi au ka sese tu.	I, who am so prone to wander.

One cannot help but feel that this hymn writer found it far from easy to be a Christian in this life and looked on heaven as a place of rest from his continual striving to keep on the right path in life. It is a hymn which seems to me to have grown out of a real experience of the grip of, and struggle against, sin.

The hymn we commonly sing in Fiji to the tune of "When upon Life's Billows" seems to me to have a much deeper quality than its English counterpart. Its opening stanza has the true concept of Christian grace for the sinner, and it goes on to give thanks for the work of

---

55   For further development of these words of double duplication, see Tippett (1954b, 229ff.).

this free grace among us—joy in the heart, preservation day by day, Christian fellowship, and the responsibility of service.

The same writer has given us a hymn on the theme of his own personal surrender to Christ. Unfortunately in our present hymnbook some other party has interfered with the words, so much so that the whole character of the hymn has been changed from one of humble petition to one of personal resolve. It is my recollection that about the 1930s the emphasis in the Church in Australia was more on personal action than humble petition.

In Tatawaga's hymn the actor was the Holy Spirit, and only by being so filled with grace could he find strength. In its modified form the singer offers himself to fight for the name of Jesus.

>   *Yalo Tabu me veivuke*   Holy Spirit be my help
>   *Qisi au me'u flomuni*   Make me thine own

has been modified to read:

>   *Vagolea na yaloqu*   (I) direct my soul (to Thee)
>   *Soli au me'u Nomuni*   And give myself to be Thine.[56]

Qisi au (Make me) is a strong and choice phrase which implies the whole action is God's. God is taking the sinner and making something new out of him. It implies a taking beyond the extremity of human achievement. The prodigal used the word when his own resolve had taken him back to the father but could take him no further—"Father, make me . . ." It is a passionate word and highly meaningful to the Fijian Christian.

>   *Me'u sinai e na loloma*   That I may be filled with grace
>   *Vakaukauwataki tu*   And thereby strengthened

has been changed into:

>   *Me'u sa la'ki valataka*   That I may go forth to fight for
>   *Na yacamuni, Jisu*   Your name, O Jesus

We are not so much concerned with the revised form, because we are seeking the theology of the Fijian hymn writers, not that of the European revisers. We note then that the anthropocentric hymns of the present hymnbook were originally theocentric and reflected a deep personal experience.

Most of the alterations would seem to have been made for the sake of rhyme and music (i.e., to fit the hymns to English music). Many will justify it on this score, but rhyme is unrequired in Fijian verse, and pious phrases are a poor compensation for personal religious experience. What is often lost is the atmosphere, and we are left with precepts rather than experience. It seems to me that this is an unjustified interference with an experiential heritage.

---

56   *Vagolea na yaloqu* is one of those pious phrases which actually means nothing, as it has no subject and the verb is causative, but *soli* implies the subject is *Au* (I); furthermore the whole hymn is anthropocentric in its modified form.

Au sa bula sara tu	Truly I live
Ni'u lomani mai Vua	Because I am loved by Him
E na siga ga oqo	And on this very day
Noqu bula au kila.	I know my salvation.

has been completely recast as follows:

Ni da masu vat a tu	When we join together in prayer
Tusanaka nomu ca	Confess your sins
Toro mai kivei Jisu	Draw near to Jesus
Ravi sara kivua.	Depend on him entirely.

Now even though the remaining verses are unchanged, this is a tragic facelift for the opening verse. Observe how the character has been lost. Here was a Fijian whose message grew from his own personal experience. Here is the doctrine of assurance. He *truly* lives: he *knows* his salvation, and he knows it *this very day*. In its place we have a pious platitude, a piece of advice which may or may not be followed. Again I say we are here concerned with the experience as in the earlier hymnbook, not the precepts of the current one.

It is amazing how in four short lines as set out above a Fiji Islander could so perfectly express a Christian experience and faith so identical with that of John Wesley, whose education and environment were so different. We might even say that the sins from which the two men had been saved were culturally poles apart, yet both rejoiced in the certainty of the gospel message of life.

One of the most impressive things about Inoke Buadromo's hymns is *the reality of the present*, or, as I often call the construction, the *timeless present*, when I'm thinking of it from a point of view of grammar. Theologically, it implies that the gospel is not a record from the past, but a glorious and victorious present. Buadromo speaks of the gospel record, when he reads it, as "sweet-sounding." The revisers, however, have made the "sweet-sounding" gospel one which is "widely-known and respected," and his immediately present gospel (*oqo, this* here) has been made distant, remote, and impersonal (*koyā*, the word for "that," not over there but afar off). This is an attempt to press religious experience into a few rules of grammar, and perhaps in the point of historic time the work of Christ demands the use of past tense and distant points of position. Technically and grammatically correct, however, something has gone; and because that something was a fundamental element of Fijian religious experience, we must try to recapture it.

The "sweet-sounding" gospel of which Buadromo sings is a word of joyful life which *is* Christ's word and work here and now. Neither the word nor Christ Himself are set in Palestine two millennia ago, but are real, here and now in the living present.

Under the modern influence of education, a certain stress has been placed on time and space and is being felt in Fijian grammar. The youngbloods are very particular about it, but if one listens to the older preacher, whose faith goes back half a century, one observes that he makes little if any differentiation between past and present. He is quite oblivious to tenses. He speaks throughout in the timeless present. I wish the world could hear his gospel before the changing grammar of the language robs the Fijian of his power to express this great experience. As the grammar becomes more formal, it loses its atmosphere.

The present-day hymnbook gives us the following verse:

Sa bulu tu na noqu ca	My sin is buried
Ni mate ko Jisu	For Jesus died
Au reki sara tiko ga	I go on greatly rejoicing
Ka vakacegu tu.	And am at peace.

It is correct in grammar and rhyme, and sounds like a normal English verse, and is easy to sing, but it lacks the colour of the original form in which Inoke Buadromo composed it:

Sa bulu tu na noqu ca	My sin is buried (atoned for)
E dra i Jisu	Through the blood of Jesus
Reki yaloqu, reki ga	Rejoice my soul, rejoice
Ka sa mamarau tu.	With a deep happiness.

The original expressed better that the joy is because of the burial of the sin. The depth of the happiness is obtained by the intensive form of *marau* (which form is not mentioned in the current dictionary). The mention of the blood is natural after the word *bulu* (bury) and colours its meaning, so that *bulu* is seen now to mean "atoned for." This would be immediately meaningful to any Fijian, for the word combination is culturally significant. The revised form would be meaningful only if he was familiar with the theology implied.

"Rejoice my soul" has an emotional and tonal quality quite absent from the colourless "I go on greatly rejoicing," and leads on not to peace or rest so much as to an intensive state of joy (*mamarau*).

This state of joy mounts even higher with the opening phrases of the chorus—"*Ue, ue, ue, oqo.*" No European wrote that. You cannot put it into English. You have to think it in Fijian. It is a passionate exclamation of surprise, excitement, and great pleasure. When a Fijian village congregation comes out with its full-throated "*Ue, ue, ue, oqo,*" one realises with a thrill that here is a deep communal experience that is thoroughly indigenous. Let us note also this repeating *oqo*, which means "now" as well as "this" and is expressive of proximity—the timeless present again:

Ue, ue, ue, oqo,	Ue, ue, ue, right now,
Sai koya dina ga	This is the truth indeed
Rarama levu ni Kalou	The great Light from God
Oqori ko Jisu.	Is Jesus.

The whole hymn is a song of personal salvation through Christ. He is the Light from God. He is the means of our approach to God. He is the atonement for my sin. I know this on the authority of Scripture, the sweet-sounding gospel. I know it right now—*Ue! Ue!*

It is only recently that the truth has come home to me that the Wesley hymns have made a similar use of the word "now." To name but a few examples: "Come down and meet us now." "Tell me Thy name, and tell me now." "Yield to me now; for I am weak." "All things in Christ are ready now." "Satan hear and tremble now." What then have we here? Either the early missionaries made a remarkable break through the barriers of culture with the thought and song of the Wesleys, or the Fijian preachers themselves had the identical experiences in spite of their tremendous cultural differences. I feel that both these were true, but whether this be so or not, I know that the basic experience of sin forgiven in the living present was and is a real thing which can be communicated and experienced by others within any culture pattern. The work of the Spirit of God is not prevented by cultural limitations.

In this section we have confined our discussion to theological points taken from the original Fijian hymns (i.e., hymns wholly the work of Fijian Christians). We have investigated the question of whether or not they have a definite theology, and if so what is it? We have found it basically orthodox but thoroughly indigenous.

As to whether or not culture and environment have influenced belief, we have found that the original hymns suggest cultural impact in several concepts—the call to worship and the drums of heaven, heaven preaching, the divine action in human life, the state of joy, and most of all the concept of the timeless present. Although none of these are really unique, they do represent, in several cases, an emphasis that has not been strong in the West, and particularly so in the religious liberalism of this current century.

The Christian Concept of *Mana*

We have already seen how some old pagan words were taken over for Christian theological purposes. No such choice has been bolder than the selection of the word *mana*, the supernatural power associated with sacred objects, places, and persons. Westerners have often expressed surprise that the church took over this word, which is so deeply involved with all forms of magic. Many white missionaries have refused to use the word at all, but the early missionaries, and especially those who were engaged in Scripture translation, found they could not do without it; and the evidence of this truth is found in the Fijian Bible itself to this day. I personally have no doubts whatsoever about their being absolutely right, for quite apart from the value of the idea for expressing belief, it was so essentially part and parcel of their life and thought that, without the capture of this concept for Christ, and a Christian interpretation of mana, I doubt if the church could ever have become really indigenous.

The concept permeated the whole fabric of culture and thought and was a positive factor of life. Although a great deal of evil was attributed to it, so too was everything worthwhile. To have shattered the concept of mana would have destroyed their capacity to accept basic distinctions—physical and spiritual, good and evil, etc.—and without this the communication of the gospel would have been made very much more difficult. It was through this concept of mana that they were able to fix their rudimentary ideas of theology, of ethics, of human obedience to a suprahuman will, of the existence of divine beings or a Divine Being, of prayer and sacrifice, of judgement and atonement. Mana ramified through them all.

The "primitive" islander had travelled a long way along his own philosophical highway before the coming of Christianity, and some of his ideas were well developed, and many of them were fundamentally right. Within the limitations of his natural environment, he had come to a point where he was capable of receiving the gospel. This is not to condone any of his ghastly practices of cannibalism, patricide, widow strangling, and black magic, all of which were admittedly tied up with the mana concept; but he had won much which needed direction and interpretation rather than extermination.

The quickest way I know of a missionary closing a door against himself is to say to the victim of black magic that it isn't real, it's just imagination, that such a power for evil really doesn't exist. The communicator of the gospel cannot start effectively from his own philosophic position. He must take up the position where the receiver stands. If he seeks to communicate to a victim of black magic, he must start from that position—the man is the victim of evil power. Behind that evil power is an evil person who is setting it in operation. This person too is real—he is no phantasmagoria—he is real and active, and using some ritual process to exert the evil force. The communicator is dealing with three factors—a sorcerer, a victim, and an unknown power. To the victim there is only one way of healing—another party who is stronger than the sorcerer and can break his mana. In the early days the priest of the tribe would be called, and he would use ritual means to counter the sorcerer's mana. The village would wait to see whether the priest's or sorcerer's mana was the stronger.

The communicator of the gospel must deal with this psychology and fit into this cultural pattern. He has scriptural support for the battle royal between Christ and the prince of devils, but he can only bring the spiritual power of Christ to save into the situation by admitting first the spiritual power of evil from which the victim is to be saved. It is a case of admitting the mana of black magic and offering the mana of Christ to counter it. This is the only effective antidote I know to the bane of black magic. I have far more sympathy today than I did before coming to the islands for Wesley's verse:

> Jesus the name high over all,
> In hell or earth or sky;
> Angels and men before him fall,
> And devils fear and fly.

Now before we can state the Christian concept of mana, perhaps we had better ascertain just exactly what it was in pre-Christian days. Space does not allow a long discussion of this. It is the subject for a whole book. We require rather a clear statement of what it was and how it operated in order to compare and contrast with the Christian concept. I therefore tabulate what I believe to be the essential elements after nearly two decades of observation and investigation in the part of the world from which English derived the word.

1. Mana is a *supernatural* power
   a. beyond the ordinary activities of man
   b. outside the common processes of nature
2. Mana is *impersonal*
   a. resembles a contagion or infection
   b. may have a material object as its vehicle
   c. may require a personal being to operate it
   d. may be accidentally transmitted
3. Mana is *amoral*
   a. good or evil according to intention of operator
   b. good or evil according to the rite used
4. Mana is usually the *product of a ritual act*
   a. operated by the correctly approved person
   b. performed in the correct ceremonial manner
   c. performed on the correct occasion or emergency
   d. dangerous if incorrectly done
5. Mana is *quantitative* efficacy may depend on the degree or quantity or strength of mana procured
6. Mana correctly used is *social* (i.e., tribal)
   a. Good:
      i. for prosperity, preservation, and growth of the tribe in peace and war
      ii. for maintenance of law, order, and custom
      iii. for control of weather and harvests
      iv. for the success of cultural functions
   b. Bad:
      i. against the enemy or foreigner
      ii. disciplinary—against idiosyncratic individuals in the tribe (View is tribal and social not individualistic.)
7. Mana, used individually, represents a corruption
   a. black magic—causing disease, killing by magic, wasting-away magic, stealing the soul, etc.
   b. enemy magic
8. The concept of mana *coexists with* the concept of *taboo*
   a. Mana is to *taboo* as electricity is to insulation
   b. *Taboo* safeguards:
      i. the unwary and uninitiated

    ii. the holy place from desecration
    iii. the weakening of the mana

That table of the nature and operation of mana should, at least, show the reader how there is no aspect of the life of the tribe or the individual in the tribe that is untouched by this power. It ramifies through the whole of the culture pattern, and is dangerous only when carelessly or improperly used. There can be no success or prosperity without it. Is there for the Christian such a power? Or, is the question as simple as that? Should it not be—is there for the Christian, just converted from a mana-saturated society, such a power? The Fijian church decided that there was. It is now our task to discover just what we mean by the Christian concept of mana.

The Fijian language has two words for power, *kaukauwa* (physical power) and *mana*. Most Fijians understand *kaukauwa* physically, though some who have been under Western influence may allow for it also spiritually, but it is rarely so used without a qualifying word, *kaukauwa vakayalo* (spiritual power). There is another word, *qaca*, but this implies conquest or victory and does not concern us here. The general use of these two words then would be that *kaukauwa* is physical power and *mana* is spiritual power. The latter is a power with which one cannot come to grips physically. It imposes a force from without. It rejuvenates or destroys the heart—depending on whose mana it is. A man in the grip of an evil power can only be saved by a greater power, also from without. His physical power is of no avail. Whatever wrestling with "principalities" and "powers" and "spiritual wickedness in high places" meant to Paul in the Graeco-Roman world (Eph 6:12), it has a literal enough meaning in the islands. And somewhere the missionaries really had to come to grips with heathenism on this level of thought, so they accepted the concept of mana and drove so hard into the heart of heathenism that devils did "fear and fly."

In the ancient sacrificial rites there was a point where the cry "*A! Mana!*" was heard. It was a response of the group in unison, very much like the "Amen!" of a Christian congregation after prayer, and of very much the same significance. It was a call to the deity to grant the request through the gift of his spiritual resources. This expression is still in use in the cultural ceremonial of the Fijian people, and used at significant points, such as immediately after the use of the name of a civil or social leader, that God's power may be with them. It is the mana of God they seek. When a civil ceremony of this kind is presented at a church festival or in honour of a ministerial visit, the proper words for the closing of a ceremonial speech are "*Me tubu ga na Lotu!*" (May the church grow!) and the response from the group is "*Mana! E dina!*"—their cry for spiritual power and their testimony of their sincerity in the request.

A study of the Fijian Bible shows, however, a much more frequent use of *kaukauwa* than of *mana*, and perhaps this may be interpreted as a hope on the part of translators to reduce the use of the word *mana* because of its heathen associations, or it may have been a conscious attempt to confine the word's use within a specific limited field. Whatever the reason for it, this policy involved the translators in the use of many qualifying adjectives, and it is highly probable that they were not entirely in agreement about the use of the word *mana* at all.

On the other hand, they showed no hesitation whatever to use the compound from this root, *cakacaka-mana* (works done as the result of mana) for the miracles of Jesus. *Ka-mana* (singular) and *veika-mana* (plural, things caused by mana) were used by the translators to render "signs," and in the case of "mighty signs" (Rom 15:19), *kaukauwa* and *mana* are used together. The English is—"through mighty signs." The Fijian is literally, "through the things caused by mana being mighty or powerful," which would be interpreted to mean physical manifestation of spiritual power.

I doubt if the average foreigner grasps these distinctions, but the Fijians themselves do. I have often heard it both in prayer and preaching, and on such occasions the theological potential has been brought home to me. It is important to note that there has been no attempt to confine *cakacaka-mana* to the miracles of Jesus. The worker of miracles (*dau-caka-mana*) had his place in the apostolic church (1 Cor 12:28), although it is more common to find passages so translated as to bring out the idea that the source of the power is God, or the Holy Spirit.[57]

An unusual form is *manamana*, in which the duplication provides us with the idea of mana in a multiplied form. Dreketirua uses the phrase, *na manamana ni veivakadonui ni Kalou*, the multiple mana of God's approval (Dreketirua 10:37). He is describing the pre-Christian assembly, and reading his monotheistic faith of today back into it. The point of importance to us here is the multiple idea. I take it from the context that the mana falls on all persons assembled to take part in the ritual.

The concept then might have been used to cover Christian episodes like, "They were all *filled with* the Holy Ghost" (Acts 2:4, emphasis added), and again, "They being afraid wondered, saying one to another, What manner of man is this! for he commandeth even the winds and water, and they obey him" (Luke 8:25), when each individual member of the group alike felt the power of the experience.

The word could be used for the power of the presence of God in a congregation deeply impressed by a sermon or an act of worship, *manamana* (multiple power).

Then what does the Christian concept of mana retain from the past, and in what way is it new?

I believe that the main points listed on the previous table would almost all still stand for mana to the Fijian Christian today with the qualification that Christianity has changed

---

57 Of God, through the Spirit—*dau caka-mana* (verbal form, Gal 3:5); work miracles (*cakava n aka-mana*), but the work of the Spirit (1 Cor 12:9–10); *cakacaka-mana*, as above, but the work of God (Heb 2:4).

the nature of many of the items mentioned. That does not concern us here for we are dealing with the concept itself.

The main difference is the availability of the mana of God to the individual Christian, who has direct access to God without the need of the priest. This is quite new.

The doctrine has a rich potential for deeply religious people and falls in line with the idea of the dispensing of divine blessing to man. On the other hand, it has its dangers, where religious experience is on a lower level and leads to sub-Christian faith, such as the school girl who places her Bible under her pillow so the mana of God's word can protect her from the thunderstorm or evil spirits; or the woman who desires her child to be baptised by the senior minister because a greater quantity of the mana of God is likely to be with him. Well, that is the nature of power—physical or spiritual—it may be a wonderful help or a grave hindrance.

Christ in Fijian Christian Thought

What does Christ mean to the Fiji Islander? Theoretically he is fairly orthodox, knows his catechism, and believes it. One does not find the wide variations of doctrine regarding the Person of Christ that one finds in the Western world. The Fijian has no time or place for a purely human Christ, although the preaching of the example of Christ for daily living is a strong tenet of Fijian exposition.

We have already had a good deal to say about Christ in this study. It is inevitable that He appear in almost every section, for He is central to them all. Under the head of "The Concept of Mediation" we discussed His work of priestly mediation. We also discussed him as the Life-giver. In discussing the root *liā* we dealt with the doctrine of the Incarnation, and in the study on oral tradition we met with an indigenous interpretation of *Christus Victor*. Personal salvation through Christ and the doctrinal significance of the timeless present were brought out in the section on "The Theology of Original Hymns."

All these were quite valid in their respective contexts, but they need now to be brought into perspective with each other so that we can see just what Fijian Christology has in it.

Two of the points mentioned reflect some communal or tribal influence. Christ is the High Priest, representing man to God and God to man. His uniqueness in this office springs from his being both truly God and truly man. He is the Priest of the fellowship (congregation) and renders a communal service. The priestly ministration of Christ is to the congregation, and this aspect of Christ's work for man is more deeply appreciated in the islands than in the West.

Likewise the struggle between Christ and Satan is not merely their personal conflict, but one between rival forces. The *soldiers of Christ* represent an army. Here again we have Christ's leadership of the community of Christians in the holy warfare, and hymns that speak of the Christian army and the forces of the enemy are among the most popular. The present hymnbook has a whole section on the *Holy War* and includes translations of hymns like "Onward, Christian Soldiers," "Stand Up, Stand Up for Jesus," "Soldiers of Christ Arise," "There's a Royal Banner," "Ho My Comrades," "Who Is on the Lord's Side?" "The Son of God Goes Forth to War," and so on. Many other hymns have the war theme as a base. "Yield Not to Temptation" begins, "*Vorata na meca*" (Resist the enemy).

The early missionaries came to Fiji at the end of a three-hundred-year period of wars. Weapon making was the most highly refined craftwork of the country, and the war vocabulary was most developed of all. As the wars continued until after Cession, the missionaries made good use of the terminology for developing a strong doctrine of the "army of the Lord"—a common phrase in prayers, sermons, and hymns. Actually this aspect of the church militant served well to sublimate the war instinct in early Christian converts. It aroused a strong sense of loyalty to both the leader and the group, and developed a sense of responsibility to resist evil and a willingness to accept hard discipline. Yet it must be seen as a communal concept—a soldier is never an individual.

In the end the victory must be with Christ. The forces of Satan are doomed to destruction, but meantime the Christian must be faithful and fight for his King. When Satan is finally overthrown, the kingdom of Christ will be realised. This conception of the kingdom is obviously conditioned by the view of wars, conquests, and kingdoms as they existed in old Fiji. The unification of all Fiji and the termination of the wars soon after Cession, when the British governor's forces subdued the last who held out against the new law and order, served as an illustration for the development of such a doctrine.

On the other hand, although these were strong communal concepts, it must not be imagined that there was no place for Christ and the individual.

We have already seen in the use of the continuous or timeless present, by means of the verbal sign *sa* and the *oqo* (this present, or now), that the Fiji time sense is continuous. He projects the Bible personalities into his present thought and activity. Many of the older missionaries were caught up with this construction. They used to call it the narrative tense when I came down to Fiji. Many of these ideas find a focal point in C. O. Lelean's translation of "And Didst Thou Love the Race that Loved Not Thee?"

Ko ni sai koyakoya tiko ga,	Thou art, yesterday, today, forever,
Koi Kemuni, Karisito Jisu,	Jesus, the Christ,
Kalou, tamata dina talega,	God, and truly man also,
Wekaqu dina tu.	And my true friend.

Here is the personal mediatorial work of Christ, bringing God to me and carrying my case to God, He having established a bond with me on my own level. The idiomatic structure of the opening line is best expressed as "yesterday, today, forever." It represents a continuous state.

We have also seen the bold step that was taken in the use of the phrase *liā tamata mai* and thereby captured the true significance of *in carnis* and firmly established the doctrine of the true incarnation of Christ.

The doctrine of the humanity of Jesus has been preserved in the Christmas hymns, most of which stress the idea of His birth. Some also mention him as Son of God, but all these hymns have been written by white men, and they all date in the last sixty years. Not one of them uses the phrase *liā tamata mai*.[58] There is no other phrase to so express the continuity of the life of the incarnate Son of God—his preexistence; the Word becoming flesh and dwelling among us; the Word existing from the beginning; the One who was with God but was found in form or fashion of a man and took upon Himself the form of a servant; the self-emptying. All these are expressed in *liā tamata mai*. The present Christmas hymns have lost the continuity with time back before Bethlehem, which shows that our hymn writers have stressed the narrative of the Nativity rather than its eternal significance. Yet the self-emptying is a strong doctrine in Fijian Christology.

Perhaps the hymn writers have implied more by the names they have used for Christ—*Tui ni Sautu* (King of Peace), *na Mesaia Vakalou* (the Divine Messiah), *Karisito Turaga* (Christ the Lord), *Matanisiga ni Yalododonu* (Sun of Righteousness), *na Luve ni Kalou* (the Son of God). Yet all these terms require interpretation, and it is highly doubtful if any except the last are really meaningful to the average Fijian.

There is, however, one name which is meaningful throughout Fiji and for which most children in a Fijian village who have reached an age of understanding could cite a text: Jesus, the name of Him who saves the people from their sins (Matt 1:21).

The sacrificial death of Christ on the Cross, or should I put it in terms of the shedding of the blood (as they usually do), is the strongest of all doctrinal emphases in Fijian Christology. The Fijian view is orthodox, but having sprung from a sacrificial society the sacrificial terminology is more meaningful than it is to the Christian in the West. That point has to be made. One often hears a criticism that the church imposed an overemphasis of soteriological and sacrificial concepts on the island people. But let there be no mistake about it, they were a sacrificial society and without it they would have found little satisfying about Christianity.

The current hymnbook is divided into sections about Jesus Christ—His teaching, His death, His resurrection, and so on, arranged in historical sequence. The book of 1877 used the plain sectional heading *Nai Soro* (The Sacrifice), and one-seventh of all the hymns in the book were in this section. In the present book these have been reduced to about half their number, although the new book is two and a half times as large. The dropping of

---

58 The phrase was used in William Aitken Heighway's translation of "Christians Awake!," which has unfortunately been dropped from the last edition of the hymnbook. He used *liātamata dina mai*, the *dina* intensifying the phrase with "truly" (hymn 17 in the 1913 edition).

many sacrificial hymns occurred in the thirties of this century, and although the present hymnbook still reflects this character of its predecessor, the reduction of sacrificial terminology throughout, appears to have had no noticeable effect on Fijian preaching, which still emphatically stresses the atoning death of Christ and the power of the blood, a doctrine which has been highly acceptable culturally from the beginning. Theories of the atonement do not particularly worry the Fijian, and even the theological student finds it a burden to have to think them out. What does mean a great deal to him is that his own sin alienates him from God. This he knows from experience. His long sacrificial traditions tell him that an atonement of some considerable cost is demanded to set things right again and restore the broken fellowship. The idea that Christ's death on the Cross provides this atonement entirely satisfies him. His concept of atonement is functional, not theoretical.

Even the theological student has to grasp certain common points before theories of atonement mean anything to him. The basic fact of experience is twofold—estrangement from God through sin, and reconciliation made effective through the death of Christ. If he can be led to see that a ransom theory implies first man's separation and then man's restoration, then it attains some meaning. He can grasp the idea of the great gulf fixed between man and God which must be bridged from the divine side, but it all has to come in pictures, not in philosophy.

The average thinking Fijian can see the Cross as the action of God, the divine initiative, the inability of man to save himself, and God coming to his aid in Christ. It ties up with his belief concerning God that he always has been, still is, and always will be in control. It also ties up with his own experience of salvation—at least I have found it so in scores of cases that have come under my personal contact.

An interesting sermon was preached at the Methodist Youth Camp at Davuilevu in 1957 by Rev. Maika Tora, who chose the "Self-emptying" as his theme. The word *kenosis* he explained in his own way in the light of the fact that Paul used it in connection with the injunction, "Let this mind be in you, which was also in Christ Jesus" (Phil 2:5).

He stressed the point that this was God's *only* Son, quoting Scripture and adding that there is no record of any substitute having been appointed to attend to His heavenly duties during His absence. So He "put his glory by" and assumed human flesh, leaving the place in heaven vacant. Here is the doctrine of the continuity of the life of the Son of God—pre-existent, incarnate, and then glorified—even though he ran perilously close to injuring the unity of the Godhead.

His application was, to say the least, novel. Turning from his theological point to the delegates to the camp, many of whom had high rank, and all of whom had left their responsibilities behind them at home, he exhorted them to come to the camp in the same mind as Christ came to earth. They were to forget their rank and status. They were to completely identify themselves with the delegates from all parts of Fiji, and by this identification they would both understand them and make their own contribution to the camp. This illustration shows the speaker's mind on the completeness of the self-emptying and the completeness of the identification.

Yet I am not sure that all Fijians would go as far as Maika Tora in the matter of the self-emptying.

We cannot claim to have answered the question with which we began this section, without some reference to Christ in personal experience on a less theological level, using "theological" in a theoretical sense. Earlier we discussed the term *Ai Vakabula* (the Life-giver). It was shown that, both negatively and positively, Christ is Life-giver. Christ saves the Christian from fear, from black magic, from hunger, from anger, or any other thing which threatens his life, his security, or his peace of mind. We saw also how having set his life right with God through the help of the Life-giver, he invariably acquired some great desire, some social service, some proof of his personal salvation for the benefit of the group or fellowship. Again in Christ he finds this possible. To him it is life and Christ the Life-giver. In saving him from his personal fears and sins, the Life-giver removes the problem and negatively gives him life. By showing him fruit worthy of repentance and inspiring him in applied Christianity, the Life-giver revealed new life in service—that is, positively. Negatively He saves by driving away his fear; positively by reinstating the sinner within the fellowship with a new life for positive service. The new life now is a life of joy.

Both these aspects of life-giving are going on all the time in the island church.

The Saviour is a personal friend, the Companion of life's road, who appears as He did on the road to Emmaus and causes the hearts of those who walk with Him to burn within them. This is a real experience and another example of the timeless present.

In fairness to the facts, however, let us recognise that the islands are very much like other places. There is variety of religious experience. All men have not the same degree of faith. Where there is pride and arrogance and indifference, there is a poor conception of salvation. Where men and women realise their shortcomings and crave the forgiveness of a true Saviour, Christ Himself is there, and those who trust Him find His promises true. This applies everywhere, regardless of cultural and linguistic limitations. Truly He is Saviour of the world.

PART THREE

Communicating the Gospel beyond Cultural Barriers

INTRODUCTORY STATEMENT: BREAKING *DOWN* OR BREAKING *THROUGH* CULTURAL BARRIERS

The process of communicating the gospel has two aspects—transmitting and receiving. This is the normal sequence, but we must reverse the order in this study, for unless we understand first the capacity for reception we can scarcely evaluate our methods of transmission.

A person who desires to appreciate the peculiarities of reception within a culture pattern not his own must first realise that the people with whom he is dealing have a time record as long as his own. They have already passed through phases of cultural and religious development, of ferment, of stagnation, of revolution, and consolidation. Their cultural histories have counterparts of our own Middle Ages, Reformation, and Age of Reason.

In modern times Christianity has been given to the world (for two thousand years is a short time really), and has been received as one of many revolutions in the history of thought, but this revolution differs from others particularly in the exclusive claims it makes. In the form in which it is usually transmitted it leaves little room for religious syncretism as other revolutions often did, and as a result conversion to Christianity, alas, often means a direct imposition of Western Christianity.

In the two earlier studies in this book we have seen how Christianity is quite capable of integrating itself within the pattern of non-Western cultures. It is the confirmed viewpoint of this book that the communicator of the gospel should set out to break *through* into the pattern of life of the people with whom he works. His task is to communicate the soul of the gospel so that it becomes thoroughly indigenous and meaningful to the receivers who yet continue living in their own culture pattern.

This is not to say that life is to remain exactly the same as before. Change is inevitable, and especially where Christianity is received, but if the gospel is culturally communicated, it will become part of the culture itself and will be retained throughout the social changes that must come.

On the other hand, if the gospel is given in a form that is a cultural imposition, we can hardly be surprised if it breaks down under the strain of rapid economic and social change we are facing in these postwar days.

Missionaries seem to do shorter terms of service these days than did their predecessors, and this makes a full understanding of this truth imperative. Modern methods of communication can be used and integrated within the culture if the transmitter is willing to pay attention to the cultural outlook of the receivers and if his own faith in the universality of the gospel is big enough.

Unfortunately, however, many capable transmitters of the gospel have their eyes so fixed on the ultimate and culturally divorced goal that they seem quite incapable of appreciating that the receivers stand at some specific transition point, and it should be at this point where personal contact and identification is made. Much very good and devoted work is lost and may even cause irritation by the refusal of the communicator to make contact on the receiver's level. Such transmitters often become disillusioned, give up the task as hopeless, and retire from the field early, blaming the receivers or their own predecessors, whereas in reality the trouble is that they have been breaking *down* cultural barriers instead of breaking *through*.

Before we can come to grips with the subject of breaking through another culture, we must first of all recognise that there are basic cultural differences and be open-minded on this matter. We must also recognise that we ourselves are selective, and grant others the right we claim for ourselves, even though their choice or judgement may differ from ours.

The wise communicator will be alert to any such differences of selection and, rather than imagining he is always right himself, will probe these matters to discover why receivers within the other culture make selections in the way they do.

In this study we now turn to three questions—the matter of reception or capacity to receive, the matter of transmission of the gospel, and finally to ascertain whether or not we ourselves can discover anything about Christianity from a young church just feeling its own theological emphasis.

8

RECEPTION

Thinking Mythically and Thinking Scientifically

Is it not Bultmann who gives us the idea that much Christian dogma is not suitable for people with our rational and scientific conception of the universe, and therefore we should disentangle ourselves from these "myths" and get to the core of truth in them so that it can be restated rationally? Now we do not intend taking up this discussion with Bultmann, but simply to observe that he represents a body of people who want to be *selective* with the Scriptures.

What has been spoken of as the "mythical approach"[59] has a far greater appeal to millions of people on the mission fields of today, and one of the great dangers of sending students from the young churches overseas to the West for study is that many of them return to their people and try to express scientifically the truths which would be better received "mythically."

To put this in a practical example valid for a missionary—a perfectly reasoned piece of Pauline logic may have no effect whatever on an island congregation, and the transmitter of Paul's gospel who delights personally in the apostle's logical argument is hard-pressed to get his message a hearing, unless he does so by means of a series of pictures. It would not be fair to say the congregation is unable to receive the message of Paul. The problem lies in the mode of communication.

My own experience has been that it is fatal to preach Paul's gospel without Paul. If I can present in pictures a man of faith, facing a human situation, especially if I can present it, as an old Fijian would, in the timeless present, and particularly if the local scene has a parallel, then there is no difficulty whatever with the reception of the most advanced ideas of Paul. But if I present only a train of thought, detached and abstract, then certainly I will achieve nothing.

Students of the Bible School in Fiji presented biblical dramas. The purpose of these dramas, during my years in charge of that institution, was to show the public how the

---

59 This does not mean legend (i.e., distorted history). We are speaking of myth as a mode of expression. Myth, used thus, does not imply any distortion. True history can be expressed either mythically (pictorially) or scientifically (rationally)—both are legitimate.

books of the Bible came to be written, that they all came out of real-life situations, and to project these facts into the timeless present. The characters were real and the audiences literally lived the scenes themselves. One of the most successful was based on Paul's letter to Philemon. It was successful, not because of the quality of the acting (although that was good) but because of its clear reception by the audience. Again I remember with great satisfaction the way in which the audience received the market scene in the drama of Amos the prophet. The students presented the dishonest trading and trickery of the Bethel market with great reality. No sermon could ever have presented more effectively the motives behind the message of Amos.

The power of the mythical approach lies in the fact that it is free from the bondage of time and space. In the above episode the audience was present in the marketplace of Bethel, both geographically and historically, nor could they refrain from making comments among themselves on what they saw and heard. It was not a play about a place they had never seen or a time long before they were born. They were not in a class having a biblical matter explained to them. It was real life. Bethel was really before them.

One of the most remarkable experiences that a missionary can have in the pulpit is on that day when the muse truly comes to him and he is really caught up with the atmosphere of a dramatic narrative and unconsciously the congregation, forgetting they are in church, begin to make comments on the narrative. They are away in some other land in another period of history. They face real truth in good, descriptive narrative—it is quite apart from time and space. I well remember once describing an event of over a century ago in China, a country where I had never been. In the very front of the congregation sat an old Fijian, who was so taken up with the description that he cried, "Alas! Alas!" throughout the dramatic part, and leaned forward in his seat shaking his head seriously from side to side, his face intent, his body tense. Finally the story took a pleasant turn, and then he sank back with a sigh and a smile and said, "Thank you! Thank you!" I chatted with the old fellow afterwards. He had been to China that day, although he put the clock back a century to do so. He was free from the bondage of time and space.

We foreigners do not often strike these purple passages because they are limited by our linguistic attainments, and even then one may speak a language fluently and grammatically, and be able to explain all kinds of involved problems in technically sound sentences, and still not achieve this state of sympathy and attention. Perhaps it depends more on rhythm and idiom than on grammar, but more still it depends on the transmitter finding the hidden potential in the theme he is to transmit. Every now and again one gets a sudden inspiration—"Ah! This will just exactly suit my people." It is never translated. It has to come to you "mythically."

One of the problems faced by all missionaries who have to teach the Bible is to get a time sense into biblical history. A people that thinks mythically rather than scientifically finds it difficult to understand that two thousand years lie between Abraham and Christ. We therefore have to be patient with their preachers who read Christ into the Old Testament in passages which have no direct reference to him at all.

The last sermon I heard by an untrained native preacher was on the text, "the iron did swim" (2 Kgs 6:6). The point of the sermon was that it was the cutting of the tree to be put into the water which caused the lost axe head to rise to the surface, and that tree was compared with Christ and His work of raising the lost from the depths to which they had sunk. Now, over a long period of time, I have heard this remarkable exegesis from three different preachers, and have good reason to believe the sermon outline can be traced back to a white missionary about the turn of the century or a little before. It has been in circulation for sixty years and meets with a good reception in the villages—why? Obviously, to the audience the errors of time do not matter, nor is any fault found with the very forced allegory. What really matters to the congregation is that the story does represent a truth expressed in the allegory—the truth that Christ restores the lost and raises the fallen. For this reason they receive the message.

Social change in city and industrial areas and the rise in the educational standard of the congregation which is learning time and sequence, are raising a new problem. The villages still live in the timeless present, but city dwellers are coming under slavery of clock and calendar.

Culture Change and the Capacity for Reception

Let us now take a brief excursion through the variations of religious experience in the Fiji Islands, remembering how it was stated at the outset that each race of people has behind it a long sequence of change. Fiji offers us some considerable documentation for such a study in the sequences of religious development over the last 150 years. More particularly will we consider the aspect of attitude or mental set, in order to appreciate capacity for reception. As there seems to be some benefit in dealing with the matter historically, we divide our time sequence into four—Pre-Christian, Early Christian, Nativistic Christian, and Transition Christian.

Pre-Christianity

Prior to the coming of Christianity the Fijian had the concept of the communicability of the will or mind of his deities (i.e., the intellectual basis for a doctrine of divine revelation was already existent). The instrument of revelation was usually (but not always) the priest, and revelation was not confined to one place. It could be a priest's house, or in a forest, by a stream, under a tree, or by a rock on the seashore. Even so the properly specified place where people sought the mind of the deity was the grove or high place associated with the town concerned.[60]

---

60 Variously known as *sava, sau tabu*, etc., according to locality.

How does a Christian Fijian view the pre-Christian rites that sought the revelation of the mind of the deity at the tribal sacred grove? Some there be who speak of it all as dark, or at least they will so speak of it to a missionary. But others, like Opetaia Dreketirua, himself a preacher, consider the old tradition as true, according to its light and in the line of revelation that led up to the revelation of God in Christ in Fiji. It is partly through the medium of his appeal to tribal heritage and loyalty that Dreketirua presses the claims of Christ, saying He is the natural fulfillment of their tribal inheritance.

Dreketirua attempts to tie the fortunes of his race with those of Israel, and this would lead us to expect some such interpretation of Christ's own words to the effect that He came not to destroy the law and the prophets but to fulfill (Matt 5:17). Therefore the *qaravi kalou mai na sava* (ritual approach to the deity at the sacred grove), if followed to its logical conclusion, demands in the end that men will come to Christ in faith and hate sin. Dreketirua says that he rejoices that he has been born in the time of the gospel, but stresses that in all time growth and prosperity have depended on serving God according to one's light. He makes his evangelistic appeal on this basis (Dreketirua 10:39).

Elsewhere, Dreketirua claims that the cultural pattern of Fijian society and the system of chiefly administration maintained an integrated whole, and through this historic unity God has blessed them all. While it is true their chiefs in pre-Christian days did not know the One True God, yet in their ritual and law-making they had His guidance all the same.[61]

This concept, strange as it may seem to us at first, is quite consistent with the Hebrew prophet's concept of the pagan Cyrus as the Lord's "anointed"—"I girded thee, though thou hast not known me" (Isa 45:1,5).

Dreketirua reminds us of the Athenian altar "To The Unknown God" (Acts 17:23). It prepared the way for Paul's statement of truth to them. Its counterpart in Fijian ritual, he argues, is the first cup of *yaqona* (the ceremonial beverage) at the pre-Christian ceremony at the sacred grove. This cup was poured out as an oblation with the ceremonial words:

A livi nai sevu:	The pouring out of the first offering:
Nai sevu ki na Sava Levu.	The first offering to the Great Sacred Grove.

This ceremonial formula is followed by a homily to stir up the people and to bring upon both them and the land the *mana* or power of God's approval.

The ceremony had to be accompanied by the right presentation of food, fruit, and fish. *Ai sevu* is equivalent to the firstfruits, but in this ceremony it is also the name of the first cup of *yaqona* which accompanied it. The important element to observe, however, is that it was not merely a piece of ritual—it was *an act of faith*. The blessings which followed would be success in war, perhaps, but it was done at the sacred grove to ensure the security

---

61 "Perhaps it is true that our fathers did not know the True God, but it was the breath of the Holy One, the Son of God, who led them in their administration and tribal law-making" (Dreketirua 17:92).

of their society. The formula and ritual had to be correctly performed, and a blunder by priest or worshipper could bring disaster on them all.

I find it interesting that Dreketirua should associate this offering of the cup with the Athenian worship of the Unknown God—something of a safeguard and perhaps as an anticipation. Unknown power undoubtedly existed and was viewed both negatively and positively.

To what extent this sense of anticipation really existed in the pre-Christian days would be hard to determine, but it is quite certain that hundreds of Fijians, looking back from the present, read it there. Therefore we take cognisance of the belief.

Early Christianity

The following record is extracted from the archives, from the minutes of a meeting chaired by Thomas Baker, who was martyred in the interior. It reads: "Conilio Ramasi is dead. His heart was right and his knowledge of God, as his portion to the end, was clear."[62]

His heart was right and his knowledge of God was clear—to what extent could we expect that in Bua in 1865, when Fiji was still more than half cannibal? It is the opinion of a white man, but the opinions of white men tend to vary.

Nearly two decades later Bromilow wrote from Lakeba:

> The doctrine of *assurance by faith* has a strong hold on the hearts of our people; and of those who are joined to our Church we have met few who cannot clearly say that Heaven is theirs.
>
> The testimony of the dying constantly shows that Heaven is not a mere metaphor to their minds, but a reality. (Annual Report [hereafter AR] Lakeba Circuit 1883)

Yet his contemporary, Jory, at Bua, wrote at the same time of the "blunted moral sense of the native through generations of base living" so that "it cannot be wondered at that the type of Christianity seen in the average Fijian is not the highest" (AR Bua Circuit 1883).

However, 1883 is within the period of British administration, and just far enough into it to be influenced by the disillusionment and economic depression that followed soon after Cession. The wars and persecutions were over, and problems of violent culture clash were upon them.

The 1840s and 1850s are well documented. Let us consider a few references prior to the conversion of Cakobau, say.

> Nasavu: "Some have found peace with God through faith in our Lord Jesus Christ, and the members in general are growing in knowledge and holiness." (Hazlewood, AR Nadi Circuit 1851)
>
> Muanaicake: "Many who had only the form of Christianity have sought and found the power. They are very consistent and evidence their faith by their works." (Ibid.)

---

62 Bua Circuit teachers' meetings minutes, entry at Dama, 15 March 1865.

> Viwa: Members are clear "in their views of Christian experience and practice. Some who have given up their professed heathenism have not given up their sins and are therefore resting short of the great design of Christianity, which is to make men holy in heart and in life." Revival experiences of 1846 had "all the outward marks of genuineness." (Hunt, AR Viwa Circuit 1846)

There are scores of such references, and in general they create two definite impressions. The early missionaries felt their converts fell into two clearly differentiated groups. John Hunt, one of the greatest evangelists of the church in the Pacific, used to speak of a "two-fold conversion":

> In most instances those who have renounced their former superstition have felt but little of the power of Divine grace until they have been a length of time under religious instruction. In these cases a two-fold conversion has been necessary; the first from heathenism as a system, the second from the mere form of godliness to its power. (Hunt, AR Viwa Circuit 1845)

Sometimes the second was long delayed. Hunt spoke of cases that had been delayed for as long as five years. There were some remarkable cases, however, in which the converts came at once from intense darkness into brilliant light. One such was Varani of Viwa, who from the start showed "a determination to declare himself a Christian and leave the consequences with God." Eventually he died a martyr in the cause of peace and love.

Yet although Hunt looked for and longed for this real experience among them, he did not expect too much immediately. He felt that

> a people just delivered from the power of a most sensual and diabolical heathenism may be expected for a length of time to present many things inconsistent with the pure and elevated piety of the New Testament. Many who are sincere are inconsistent in some things; though in most respects the direct opposite of their former selves.

He then qualifies this by adding that many are "above suspicion," and he contrasts Varani, who is "zealous and consistent," with Namosimalua who is "much better for his Christianity" but has a "restless and ambitious spirit" (Hunt, AR Viwa Circuit 1847).

David Hazlewood felt the mission was making real progress by 1850, and spoke of a "more enlightened belief" and a more spiritual experience.

> In the public services we have had many blessed visitations of the Spirit. Sinners have been awakened and souls saved. Our members generally appear to be growing in grace and more and more grounded and settled in the saving truths of the gospel which has delivered them. Their belief is a more enlightened belief, their experience more spiritual and their outward conduct in general highly satisfactory... Our cause is also extending among the heathen. (AR Nadi Circuit 1850)

The terminology of these reports has to be seen in the light of their position in history, but it is quite apparent from these quotations from the archives that the young church was making an impact on paganism and winning converts. It is also clear that after a short term of instruction the formal conversions usually became spiritual. There is no room for doubt that this was a characteristic pattern. The first converts came to Christianity as a system for a multiplicity of reasons—some valid, others not so. Yet the great significance of the first conversion was that it represented a real change of mind, a new mental set, a breaking through a barrier of mental resistance, and the convert's willingness to place himself under instruction.

Hunt admitted that many in this group had quite a sound and constant belief in God, and some of them died in the faith although still ignorant of the true nature of religion. For many it ended there, but thousands passed on into the full experience of new life. Hunt, Hazlewood, and Watsford in particular, somehow managed to "break through" and transmit a real spiritual experience, even while yet surrounded by cannibals. They trained many of their converts; and there are names like Joeli Bulu, Paula Vea, and Josua Mateinaniu who should be classed among the great evangelists of the Pacific, as their work often reached out beyond the frontiers where the white men were working. Because they were successful evangelists, we may well ask what sort of a gospel these men preached.

They communicated the gospel in a day of intense and bitter persecution, and not only were they communicating new beliefs to the heathen, but they were communicating the gospel of power to those who had taken up their personal crosses in this era of persecution. This undoubtedly explains the reality of the book of Revelation to them. They were not, as we have often been told, hellfire preachers—that belongs to a later day—but heaven preachers they were on a grand scale. It was so real that it broke the barriers and came as the timeless present. A score of deathbed scenes have survived in the written records, and the reality of heaven is outstanding in them all. It was no negative doctrine of escapism but one of high aspiration and positive certainty, and it rings through their testimonies and hymns. The later hell preaching was an inferior instrument of evangelism and used only with a subsequent generation which grew up after the end of cannibalism, and which understood not the real greatness of the salvation of its forefathers.

It is, of course, in the second generation and third that the missionary strikes his problems, as Jory's reference above suggests. A gospel that is valid for a day of bitter persecution, or for the church undercover, tends to reveal a quality which may disappear when life is easy.

The worship of Yahweh in early Israel had to face this identical problem. While Israel was wandering in the wilderness, security demanded unity, and the personality of Moses held them together to some extent, but after the conquest it was a different matter. Could the Mosaic reform be taken over and retained by the following generations who were now scattering throughout the land and developing their own sectional interests?

The message sounded by the Judges was that Israel must preserve its allegiance to its own God. When the people turn to *Baalim* and *Ashtaroth*, the Lord will deliver them into the hands of their enemies; but if they repent and cry to the Lord, He will send a deliverer.

It is always with the later generations that the real testing time comes.[63] The characteristics of the early church in Fiji revealed a strong militant form of Christianity, dynamic faith accompanied by not a few miracles, Pentecostal experiences, a strong doctrine of the Spirit, a real awareness of heaven. This was a form of Christianity which grew out of its environment—a life of adventurous faith and the facing of death daily.

Later generations did not have the same dangers to face, but lived through depressing days of foreign imposition, land alienation, the bitter disillusionment that came after Cession, rapid depopulation, and economic depression. More and more has tightened the grip of commercialism, and Asiatic indenture went on for four decades.

This was a new world for which the Fijian was not prepared. The bitter experience played havoc with the Fijian's moral standards and, apart from the enthusiasm that accompanied the Jubilee in 1885, the last quarter of the century saw the church adopting a rather negative form of religion, of which a strong trace remains with us still.

The same factors caused movements of other kinds on the outer fringe of the church, and to some of these the next section is devoted.

Nativistic Christianity

Nativistic movements like cargo cults (as some of the more recent forms in the Pacific have been called since the war) are by no means peculiar to the postwar period. The history of such movements in Fiji goes back to the beginning of British rule in the 1870s, but over the last thirty years there have been numerous serious disturbances over much of the south west Pacific. Each decade has added to the list. In 1913 it was in Saibai, in 1923 in the New Hebrides, and in Papua the "Valhalla Madness" lasted for six years, in 1941 there was the John Frum movement in Tanna, and in the Solomons "Marching Rule," the Raluana trouble and the naked cult in Santo, the Assisi cult, and the Times in Fiji.

These are the cries of frustrated islanders who want to live their own life in their own way. Sometimes they want the foreigners' goods, but they all seek to rid themselves of his rule. The movements are essentially religious and appeal to the religious instincts; all of them have a developed religious ritual and have a centrifugal force radiating from a strong personality, usually a mad prophet. All have a hodgepodge of Christian eschatology and biblical genealogies interwoven with their own ancestor mythology (Tippett 1956, 253–58).

Epeli Rokowaqa listed three such movements in Fiji within his experience; one was terminated by military force under Governor Thurston in Macuata, and the second from Colonel North ended with the parties concerned being sent as prisoners to Kadavu. The third he called the Number Eight Movement (Rokowaqa n.d., 42).

---

63 Welch discussed this problem in Israel (1953, 58ff.).

It is significant that one can trace no records of such movements prior to Cession, and though the Cession was a voluntary act on the part of the chiefs, yet there were many of the rank and file who were strongly opposed to it. Immediately on top of the Cession came the measles epidemic in which forty thousand Fijians perished, wars in the interior, depression, and disillusionment. The growth of sugar brought major social and commercial changes. Nativistic movements were almost inevitable.

Just two years after Cession, the Methodist district meeting was faced with a movement in Matuku which took the place by storm. The Fijian minister of the island became the victim of two self-appointed "angels" and every preacher with the exception of one (who belonged to another island). The district meeting removed the minister from office, although he had been a useful man and had some standing. Among the things taken over from Christianity by this cult was the rite of baptism, which was done in the name of the Great God (Minutes of District Meetings 1876).

This was the first, and the church was at a loss as to how to interpret it. Some thought it compared with a peculiar outbreak reported in Savoy a decade or so earlier. The emperor had sent an eminent French physician to investigate the case, and he had described it as a disease of hysteric demonopathy. However, examination of the minister revealed him to be in perfect health.

A decade later Fiji was faced with the *Tuka*, which spread through the mountainous interior and required military force to terminate it. This was also a revealed religion built on a combination of ancient and original legends and a good deal of Scripture extracted from its context. The name of Christ was replaced by two Lords—the Spring of Life and the Humble Lord—and the recipient of their revelation became the Chief Justice with the title, *Navosavakadua* (Speak once and for all). The days of the week were renamed after Fijian heroes and heroines, temples were established with women attendants, a set liturgy and hymnology were used, and miracles were worked.

The devotees began their worship service with the following prayer:

> I pray to the Life,
> To Your Lordships, the Two Lords—O the Springs of Life!
> Please think of us and take care of us
> At the present time that we may escape trouble,
> O Springs of Life!
> We pray to thee that our sins be wiped out, O Springs of Life!
> To Your Lordships, the Two Lords, at Burotukula, O Lord! O Lord!

Then the worshippers sang together this hymn:

> Hallelujah! All are well.
> Hallelujah! Hear us please our Two Lords.
> Hallelujah! Hear us please *Waicalanavanua*.
> Hallelujah! Hear us please *Adi Sovanatabua*.

> Hallelujah! Hear us please *Lekanikurotukula*.
> Hallelujah! The Holy Day of our Life.
> Hallelujah! Long live our Lords.

A careful examination of the story of their beliefs will reveal that it was an attempt to select many elements of the biblical narrative, which appealed to the Fijians, such as Noah's ark and the miracles of Jesus, and to modify them sufficiently to force them into the legendary history of Fiji. The cult added the attraction of offering immortality to its devotees.

The psychological motivation was to dispense with the white man's administration, and his religion with it, retaining only what could be Fijianised and claimed as their own revealed religion. The *Tuka* spread throughout the inferior and caused the government much embarrassment, so that it had to be dealt with by military force.[64]

The third on Rokowaqa's blacklist was himself a disciple of the *Tuka*, and had been the publisher of the *Tuka Gazette*—a handwritten record. He was eventually sent to the asylum.

These movements have the habit of flaring up again from time to time. You never really know that one is quite extinct. In my own time I have seen several, one of which in particular gave the government much concern.

This was a widespread organisation known as *Na Gauna* (The Times), which spread through the Wainimala area and had little pockets of followers all over the place. Its leader was eventually exiled to Rotuma. One place up the Sigatoka Valley had been completely won over to this cult, and the people all lost the money they had invested for their places in heaven. In 1941 I conducted the first Christian service in the place after the movement had died down. As an effort at worship it was a rank failure. The place seemed to have been left in a state of nervous and spiritual exhaustion, a complete contrast to other villages on the bank of the same river.

Three years later I ran across two movements on a smaller scale on the south coast of Kadavu. One was of short duration, but the other, though confined in area, has had a long life. The prophet built himself a temple and ran his own worship services and worked miracles. Both these movements had good followings within the confined area and, it seemed to me, had grown up as a result of pastoral neglect by the minister. This fellow confined his ministrations to the village where he lived, and no Christian ritual had been performed in the offending villages for a tragically long time. Time after time I have found that where a Fijian minister neglects the celebration of the sacraments, some magical rite will spring up, for although these movements are basically cultural ferment through the conflict of

---

64 This movement is well documented. The best sources are Sutherland (1910) and Brewster (1922, 236–48) and other references in the same work. See also Thompson (1903, 140–45). Thompson and Brewster have also more to say about the cases cited by Rokowaqa.

indigenous thought and foreign ideas and domination, they are also a clear sign that the existing communication of the gospel is ineffective.

Transition Christianity

The genius of Ratu Cakobau of Bau was his appreciation from the start that the Fijian social fabric could not retain its stability while members of the society were divided in their religious affiliations. Thus he planted the church squarely in the heart of the village system. However, from the date of the Cession, two decades later, when the government was no longer the *Vanua* (native kingdom), the social system has slowly but definitely been disintegrating—too slowly for some, too fast for others. Yet Cakobau saw the change was inevitable and remained a loyal supporter of Britain until his death. In his last years he retired more and more from public affairs and lived truly for his faith and the centrality of the church in the chiefly island. He died in days of unrest, but to the end he remained a solid pillar of the young church.

Dr. Langham wrote of him and the times:

> We cannot but feel concerned at the apparent disinclination on the part of many to submit to the new state of things, and who, in some instances do not hesitate openly to express their disappointment therewith... We sorely miss the grand old chief, Cakobau, whose loyalty to the British Government was always conspicuous; whose sympathies were invariably with his people; and whose wide-spread influence was invariably exerted in the interests of Christianity. His last words showed where his trust was, and that he knew Whom he had believed. (AR Bau Circuit 1883)

It was not for Cakobau to anticipate the terrific influx of Asian population, but he did foresee the commercialisation of his land. Unfortunately the fine example he left was not always followed by other chiefs, and the irresponsibility of some and their ways with wine and women have turned many of the rank and file to favour the democratic way of life.

For several decades the Fijians were a dying race, but the crisis has passed and the race is increasing steadily again. Through those decades of depopulation the social system fell into decay, and the Indian-Fijian population figures varied inversely. Right into this century political and economical writers felt the Indian must take over from the Fijian. Commercialism was adamant about having its labour supply.

It was not until after this last war that the Fijian really seemed to possess himself of a new lease of life. New opportunities have opened up such as he never had before. The church reconstituted herself and dispensed with European authority to a large extent—even our stations are now determined by the Fijian brethren. New church buildings have introduced new aspects of design and ornament. The power centre of Synod has shifted from the voice of the representatives of the two great kingdoms of Sau and Itewa to whichever representative can best state his case. The transition moves apace. Stipends have increased out of all recognition. The youth movement in the church is active and progressive.

The question will naturally arise now—what about the mythical and rational approaches in this transition period of today? What is the mind of the young men selected for theological training on this question? They will be ministers for the next thirty or forty years, and so we want to know what their approach is. Will they present truth mythically or rationally?

For all interested in the communication of the gospel on the mission field, this is a valid question. In the first place, let us admit frankly that their lot will not be easy. Their congregations will be divided between those who cling to tradition and those who have discarded it. I decided to attack this question by means of an attitude test with class participation, working on the exegetical problems we have to face when studying the opening chapters of the book of Genesis. These at least should disclose whether these young men of two worlds are thinking mythically or scientifically.

We have seen how the Fijian people rejoice in the Old Testament narratives because of their atmosphere. Where we stumble over these early narrative laws, they tend to discover the basic truths involved, partly because they are removed from time and space just as were the Hebrews who used those episodes centuries ago. The young people of Fiji are going to ask more questions than their fathers did about the critical problems of Genesis 1–11. Their fathers were concerned with their timeless truth, and these problems did not often arise.

The writer therefore took a group of sixteen theological students at Davuilevu, Fiji, and presented them with three of the long-standing posers on Genesis. This group, with one exception, comprised the same students as were tested on the matter of land ownership, and who in that case revealed a group attitude which was distinctly modern. Let me tabulate the results of the test.

> Question: Why was the sacrifice of Abel acceptable and that of Cain not so? What is your personal opinion?
>
> Responses:
>
> | | |
> |---|---|
> | The sacrifice of Cain was surely offered in the wrong spirit. | 12 out of 16 |
> | The sacrifice was the wrong kind. It should have been a blood offering. | 6 out of 16 |
> | The offering was incorrectly presented because the best portion was withheld. | 5 out of 16 |
>
> One stated all three as possible reasons but was himself noncommittal.

Evaluation: The second and third answers suggest that, however modern these young men may be, socially they are conservative here. To offer an imperfect sacrifice was a crime, and likewise to present it incorrectly.

A Fijian would have supplied these answers a century ago. On the other hand, that twelve men out of sixteen should mention the spirit of the worshipper shows they have left their fathers far behind. This is the high morality of the eighth-century prophets. One student actually cited Hebrews 11:4 to indicate the quality difference in the offerings. One developed the idea of the fat as the best piece and therefore the key to the spirit of the offering and the desire to draw near to God on the part of Abel.

Question: How do you account for the biblical statements about the ages of the patriarchs?

Responses:

They probably calculated years differently from us.	3
Possibly names of tribes, not individuals.	1
Years exaggerated as in old Fijian stories.	3
Either first or second above.	1
Either first or third above.	2
Stated all three possibilities but noncommittal.	5
The years do not matter, but the events do.	1

Of the five who stated the three possible answers, three said it was an open question. Two said these were the only explanations they could offer, but they were not personally satisfied with any. Four expressed surprise that the years should be held of any great matter. The teaching was the important thing.

Evaluation: That four should stress teaching and one events as of importance and years of no importance surely reveals a strong sense of the timeless present. In no case, however, was there a refusal to consider the problem. Almost every student had doubts about the figures being in our years; one reasoned the complete incompatibility of the ages and dates of childbirth, etc. There was a strong tendency to view them in the same category as their own hero stories, especially hero stories which housed customary law and taught tribal morality. These men think solidly, but it is still within their own cultural concepts.

Question: How do you reconcile the flood story of Noah, the righteous man, with the account which follows of his drunkenness and exposure?

Responses:

It shows wine as opposed to the will of God.	2
Anti-Canaanite propaganda for Israel's benefit.	1
Shows the attitude of the J source to wine.	1

Warning that wine leads to sin and should be avoided.	1
Even a good man can fall. Moral vigilance.	6
First and last reasons above.	1

Four men gave invalid answers, merely giving the narrative and making no attempt to interpret it.

Evaluation: The twelve men all directed their attention on the second story, not that of the flood (i.e., all recognised the problem of such a story being in the Bible). They arrived at different solutions but all used the same method of attacking the problem—looking for the motive of the story. The class was all pro-Noah. With the exception of two who were facing the problem historically, the whole class was prepared to take the story as a timeless and unlocated piece of narrative law on the dangers of wine.

On the whole then, we may feel that these young men are falling into step with Western Christianity, but a good deal of their thought is still within their own cultural modes. Perhaps this should make them well fitted for the communication of the gospel in their new day, this age of transition.

Meantime the foreign communicator should note the effect of culture change on the capacity for reception and make his contact on appropriate levels.

Warning: Ethics Is Culturally Conditioned

We glibly speak of *Christian ethics*, or of things being *ethical*, as if these terms stand for something solid, undeviating, and universally meaningful within Christianity. Yet when the point is pressed we invariably find them solid or undeviating only within the culture pattern of the speaker.

Many a Westerner has been a failure as a communicator for trying to force Western Christian ethics into a chiefly communal society. He will probably retort that *Christian* ethics are part of the gospel, and that acceptance of the gospel means acceptance of the ethics of the gospel. But, alas, it isn't nearly as simple as that.

The gospel is a stimulus. Ethics is a response. Nor is the process even a simple stimulus-response one, for the action takes place within a confined field in which there is an integration and interaction of other stimuli. The gospel itself may be the master stimulus, but the various configurations of a culture pattern are also potent forces which influence the resultant ethics in any society.

To "grow in favour with God and man" implies two aspects of activity on the part of the subject. Growing in favour with God implies some cultus or provision for worship by means of which that relationship may be developed. Growing in favour with man implies the acceptance of a set of standards by means of which your living is acceptable to brother man—ethics, if you like. Each of these has to be both individual and social. Each has to integrate within the pattern of life in that particular society. If the gospel is to be valid in that society, it must integrate in this way. This makes it inevitable that both form of worship and ethics of life will be culturally conditioned.

Although it is true that the gospel challenge may divide brother from brother, as Christ himself indicated, it is quite another matter to impose on a convert a foreign element that will cut him off culturally from his own society, and the basic position of this study is that such an imposition is wrong and unnecessary because the gospel integrates in any society.

Our Lord Himself was born within the Hebrew culture; in its devotional pattern He found His daily strength; in its sacred literature He found the seeds of the gospel of His Person and work, His doctrine of sin, and the divine purpose to forgive and save. Many who followed Him in the early days of Christianity did so within the Hebrew culture pattern. Many great ideas of the Christian gospel—like repentance, forgiveness, and salvation—are by no means confined to the New Testament. The difference in the New Testament is that these great ideas were personalised in Jesus Himself. The ideas belong to the Bible.

The great characters of the Old Testament like Abraham, Moses, David, and the prophets were discovering aspects of the gospel without the advantages we have of the historic revelations through Christ and the Holy Spirit. Is there any reason to doubt the faith which led Abraham forward into the unknown? Christianity retains in its sacred literature the records of Jewish faith and experience, which were the Scriptures to Paul and Timothy (2 Tim 3:15–17), and to Jesus himself.

H. A. Hodges has given us a concept which he calls "The Abrahamic Presupposition," insisting that Abraham is the model for Jew and Christian alike; that the true Christian is the spiritual child of Abraham, or has a similar attitude to God as Abraham had. Here was a man who committed himself unconditionally to God and thereby received the promises and won the title of *friend of God*.

Such an attitude of mind, Hodges argues, presupposes not merely the existence of God, but also something specific about the character of God—that He controls the world in a purposeful way, fitting human beings into their respective places in His designs; that He communicates with them in ways they can fully understand, by commands, promises, and guidance. Hodges calls this the Abrahamic Presupposition—the presupposition of both Jewish and Christian thinking (1949, 28–29).

This then would be true for David and also for Paul. There is a similarity in the spiritual aspirations of these three figures—but their ethics were vastly different, because they were different in their cultural conditioning, spaced out as they are on the timeline at thousand-year intervals.

Religion and morality have been compared with the two wings of an airplane, without which the craft would be incapable of flight (Scott 1942, 134). The validity of such a figure is agreed only within certain limits. Religion and morals are not parallels. One is an internal stimulus and the other is an external response. I would not risk my life in that airplane. Abraham and I may have similar religion, but we have different ethics or morality.

The tendency of Christian preachers when speaking of the Old Testament heroes is to ask the congregation to consider the narrative historically and not to judge them by Christian standards. This explanation may satisfy a Christian in a Western city, because he belongs to a time-ridden culture; but it offers no comfort to a Pacific Islander, who reasons that the accounts of Abraham, David, and Paul are preserved in the one body of literature and therefore belong to the same time group. The God of Abraham, David, and Paul is the same God. He cannot understand the explaining away of their ethical differences on a temporal basis.

But there is another matter he perceives more clearly than we do. Temporal differences do not matter when he sees the three men belonging to three different culture patterns.

A century and a half of violent culture clash has introduced the islanders to foreigners of every type and race, and they have found Christians in many of the groups. They fully realise that though they serve the same Christ their worship and Christian practice is bound to differ. They love nothing better in conversation than to question foreigners about how they worship and practise their religion at home.

Now let us return to our Old Testament heroes, remembering that Christian preachers, especially island preachers, love preaching about Abraham and Moses and David—and they are Christian sermons. In spiritual experience they had some remarkable affinities, as did Paul. They were alike pioneers of experimental faith. Each lived in a period of social ferment and maintained a core of faith through cultural transition, and the Old Testament characters all helped to prepare the way for Christ. Yet culturally they were vastly different.

Abraham lived under the pattern of Semitic nomadic patriarchal society; Moses after forty years training in law and ritual in Egypt, and forty years influence of Semite transhumance society in Midian, had the task of leading a herd of freed, or rather escaped, slaves through that wilderness to the Promised Land which was to be their inheritance. Between Moses and David lies the settlement of Canaan, a few centuries of local wars, and the evolution of a fairly well-organised monarchical society. Paul, the nearest of them to us, came from the cosmopolitan world from which Western civilisation itself sprang, with Greek language and philosophy and Roman law and efficiency that led to a *worldview*, not unsimilar in its own way to our own day, in spite of the Middle Ages which lie between us. These four men were all Hebrews, yet their cultural environments differed vastly.

We Westerners tend to see these characters as marking points of religious evolution in a long time sequence, which we call *progressive revelation*. But many a non-Westerner sees them as chosen men of God with a common basic faith, but the applications of which vary because they operate under quite different culture patterns which call for the different emphases, and as a result of this there are variations in the ethics and the form of the cultus.

From the Bible itself we can argue out these two viewpoints, and if we are open-minded, we shall have to admit the strength of the non-Westerner's case. Progressive revelation satisfies us because, consciously or unconsciously, we have an evolutionary complex in the West. It is true only within very broad limits. It doesn't account for some very high thoughts in very early sources, and it depends on attributing late authorship to anything religiously well developed, like the fifty-first psalm, for example. Every highly developed thought found in newly discovered inscriptions in the Middle East serves to remind us that progressive revelation applies only in the broadest sense. Obviously the whole truth is not with the West.

Paul was a tentmaker. Supposing he had been a nomadic tent dweller instead of a Roman citizen (quite apart from the time element, you may imagine him the patriarch of a present-day patriarchal tribe, if you like), would he have pressed an ethic of persons "behaving like worthy citizens"? In the first place the terminology is foreign to the nomad and the concept itself. It implies an individual freedom within a city society that does not exist in patriarchal society. In patriarchal society such individualism, which the city dweller considers his right, would be considered as disloyalty, and indeed would have threatened the whole structure and security of the tribe.

On the other hand, in patriarchal society the ethics of being *one's brother's keeper* is higher in actual realisation than is ever likely to be achieved in city life, because patriarchal society is itself an extended family. It has been part of our ethical idiom to urge ourselves to be our brothers' keepers, but it is largely an ideal, and never will be more than this if we insist on the ethics of the independent rights of the individual. We have a strong ethical conflict here that is determined by cultural outlook. The Westerner will fight tooth and nail for his personal rights and consider it ethical. The patriarchal society people sink themselves in the family. The oldest narratives that have come down to us through the biblical patriarchs, probably in oral tradition at first, include the story of Cain and Abel. This is patriarchal ethics in the form of *narrative law*. Narrative law is a pictorial method of teaching tribal ethics and is still found today among communal societies. That this is the most ancient of laws must create difficulties to anyone who desires to press in detail the doctrine of *progressive revelation*. The best one can do about it is to press for progressive revelation within each culture pattern.

This does not mean that either the patriarchal concept of brotherhood or the Pauline concept of worthy citizenship was wrong, but that each was culturally conditioned because each had to operate within its own peculiar ethos. Worthy citizenship was vital in one culture pattern but fatal in the other. In a society in which security depends on a high degree of interpersonal loyalty, individualism has to be sacrificed. Progress in such a society depends on the wisdom, foresight, and capacity for leadership found with the patriarch of the tribe. However, in the Greek and Roman cities of Paul's day, particularly at the trade centres and intersections of the highways where the Christian groups began, often in private homes or in secret, and where people from various races and different social status gathered in the faith, and where no one was born to leadership and all who came did so on their own personal decisions, it was natural that individualism should figure more prominently. In patriarchal society there was a completely unified body, whereas in Paul's day the church was a Christian minority within an unchristian world.

I have not chosen a lone example in developing the cultural differences in patriarchal and individualistic society. We could, for instance, deal with economics. Paul's ethics of money would have been quite meaningless in the exchange economy of patriarchal society. Again his ethics of the family life, of the relationship between man and woman, or father and son, were thoroughly conditioned by culture—they had to be so to be valid.

Paul had the advantage of standing at the crossroads of culture. His Greek, Roman, and Jewish patterning come out in his imagery—military, commercial, political, architectural, athletic, and so on. Often his doctrine and ethics were actually formed from these cultural elements (and, be it noted, that he seldom mixed his cultural figures but confined his imagery to that of the culture of his audience). Because of our affinities with the Graeco-Roman world, we have taken over many of his cultural metaphors—ransom, adoption, stewardship, for example. In some societies these doctrines are meaningless as they stand. The imagery of Jesus, on the other hand, is strongly coloured by the environment of rural Palestine and seems to me to contain many ideas missing from Paul.

The great ethical issues of Abraham's day were being fought out around matters like human sacrifice, for instance, which was a cultural tendency among his related nations, and continued long after his day (1 Kgs 3:27). The well-known story of Abraham and Isaac is another case of *narrative law*, for on this point Hebrew patriarchal ethics stood out as different from that of her neighbours.

Many of the problems we stumble over in studying the Bible are caused by our failure to appreciate cultural conditioning. Let me put a few examples before you.

In the days of my unregenerate youth I was a burden to my poor Sunday school teachers, for I was wont to ask the most embarrassing questions. I confess I devised many a sly trap for my unsuspecting mid-Victorian teachers, whose patience was more commendable than their learning. This is the sort of proposition I would set before them:

> Why is there commendation of Rahab the harlot in the New Testament? Why did God spare the harlot when all the rest of her fellow citizens perished in the judgement? How could a harlot be justified by good works?

My long-suffering teachers had not realised that the great variety of ethics in the Bible are all culturally conditioned, and so they could not answer these questions. I know now that Hebrews and James are two books in the New Testament with somewhat heavy Hebrew cultural conditioning, and that one strong strand of Jewish ethics is that God will use even a person who does not know Him to fulfill His purposes—witness Cyrus of Persia (Isa 45:5). His willingness to use Rahab the harlot to protect the spies sent forth in the name of the Lord was interpreted as an *act of faith* (i.e., faith manifest in works; Jas 2:25,26).

The Jew saw no difficulty in the use of Cyrus and Rahab for the the fulfillment of God's will, because this was the highest end, and as persons who were used to bring about that end they were specially blessed. The Western Christian is not so confident about this, but the Jewish Christian found it no problem. It did not condone the daily arts of Rahab, but admitted that even the sinful person might be an object of divine grace.

Hebrew ethics has also a strong concept of *common responsibility*. Because of the sin of Achan (Josh 7), punishment fell on the whole nation. This has been used repeatedly by Christian preachers and teachers in modern times to demonstrate the error of theft or deceit, because we ourselves have developed a strong ethical resentment against theft and deceit. That is reading our own minds into the Bible story and is not its true teaching. In its context the sin was the breaking of a taboo, the sin of disobedience of a specific command of God. Jericho was to be the first city to fall to Israel in their conquest of the Promised Land, and as with all the gifts of God received by Israel, the firstfruits were to be dedicated to Jehovah and presented as a burnt offering (James 1940, 122–24). By breaking the divine taboo of the firstfruits Achan had sinned against society and against Jehovah. Such a sin threatened the security of the whole, and to some extent the whole society did suffer on its account, and the offence could be removed only by the family to which Achan belonged paying the price. In passing, I imagine that the majority of Pacific Islanders would agree with the Jews on this point—to them the sin would be disobeying God rather than thieving.

All these narratives, especially narratives of tragedy, in the Old Testament have to be seen culturally. For us to use these stories as the basis for teaching on twentieth-century Christian ethics is to ask for trouble from enquiring teenagers who will demand the setting of Achan beside Jacob, say. Many a Christian has a strong resentment in his heart against Jacob, or more particularly against the narrative. It seems wrong that Jacob and Rebekah should stoop to a mean trick to defraud Esau of his tribal birthright and to achieve their purpose. Even if the Bible hero suffered privations as a result of the fraud, the fact still remains that he did receive the blessing and his children inherited the promises. Christian ethics resents this, and I never remember a Sunday school teacher or preacher who answered the difficulty for me in the days of my youth.

Again the ethics are cultural. The big issue at stake is the attitude of the two twins to the family birthright. Birthright is a tremendously important matter in any society based on the family. To despise one's birthright was to refuse one's responsibility to the extended family, and a major form of tribal disloyalty. To place one's momentary hunger before one's tribal responsibility was an indication of the unworthy spirit of Esau, and reveals Rebekah as an astute and observant woman who had the interests of the tribe at heart.

The written narrative is a significant cartoon of the characters, although it is doubtful if this changeover could have been effected had they not been twins. However, apart from this, the narrative is an important statement on tribal ethics—the responsibility that goes with birthright. Birthright is not being born to privilege, but being born to responsibility.

The Fijian people have a saying they use of a firstborn who fails to mature properly or live worthily of his birthright—*Ulumatua vakasabote*. It literally means "the firstborn who falls like the early breadfruit" and alludes to the manner in which three or four breadfruit form on a branch, the younger fruit outstripping the first in growth and causing the first to fall unripened to the ground. To be unworthy of one's birthright is a social and ethical tragedy in any communal society.

We must be satisfied with these examples and return to the point which called for them. The Western missionary working within a communal or extended family society often has trouble with his Christian ethics. He must first reorient himself to the *confined society* in which he works, and realise that it is an *organic whole* and that here *personal interests are subordinated* to those of the family or tribe—the direct opposite of life in a modern Western city, where the rights of the individual are sacrosanct.

Unless such orientation is effective, the missionary is likely to return home after a short service, claiming that the religion of the young church is shallow and insincere, that the natives are liars and thieves, indifferent about sexual morality, and so on—a Western view. Investigation usually reveals that a good many of the faults found fall within cultural elements where the islands differ from the West. Eliminate these elements and their ethical standards stand up to our own very favourably.

This is not to say that island standards are free from criticism. By their own requirements they themselves admit they are far from perfect, and I would not try to defend them for any of their shortcomings. At the same time even their shortcomings are usually culturally patterned and must be evaluated in this light.

Take the boy-girl relationships outside of marriage, for example. In true Fijian village society (excluding towns and industrial areas), offences will be found more often than not to be between young people known as *veidavalini*, and must therefore be seen in the light of the cross-cousin kinship pattern, which was common in a large part of the group. Even in those places where the cross-cousin system does not apply, the majority of illicit boy-girl relationships were, until very recently, said to tie up with the kinship pattern. Any foreigner who criticises the sex standards of the Fijian people should first set out to get the facts straight, and that will lead him deeply into the whole matter of Fijian kinship. This is only fair. The West has practically no kinship pattern, except for a few anomalous taboos that are survivals from the past, so a Westerner is obviously hard-pressed to reorient his thinking to the ethics of a strict kinship pattern.

Thus also in the Old Testament the birth of Ishmael is justified by Semite law and custom, though it would be quite unethical in our own society.[65]

Our Bible in the Christian church being the whole Bible, we must have an attitude to these Old Testament narratives which we have been examining from the point of view of ethics. We have tried to remove the problem by differentiating between Hebrew and Christian ethics. To the thinking person, however, this is just as unsatisfactory as trying to differentiate them as Old Testament and New Testament ethics. Rahab the harlot receives her honour in the New Testament in two different books. Some other explanation must be found.

Nor should we overlook the fact that the ethics of the patriarchal period are very different from those of the days of settled life under the monarchy, and yet these are both Hebrew and both Old Testament. The same thing applies in the New Testament—to a lesser degree, but it still applies. We must also account for the fact that, throughout the history of the church, it has been necessary to emphasise different elements of ethics at different points of history. Clearly both Hebrew and Christian ethics are culturally conditioned and periodic.

The church historian has made it impossible for us to define properly what Christian ethics really is. He has taught us to speak of Roman, Greek, Palestinian, Syriac, and English forms of Christianity, and in later times of nonconformist, episcopal, reformed, evangelical, and many other forms of Christianity; and nowadays we think of our Christian theology as Continental, American, or British; or as liberal or fundamental; or as theocentric or anthropocentric. All these are said to be Christian, and all have their different ethical responses. Christianity has been tied to national movements, and loyalty to national peculiarities has been declared an ethical issue. Christianity may be national or ecumenical, but the ethics of nationalism and ecumenicity are usually diametric opposites. A high church communion considers certain ritual a moral responsibility, but in certain extreme Puritan bodies all possible symbolism is dispensed with.

This being so, we should be wise in our administration of religion outside our own environment and culture pattern. To press high church ethics in a communion with the opposite point of view, or vice versa, can lead to schism and do untold harm. In exactly the same way a violent individualist or democrat in a communal society may undo years of faithful work, even though he does so with the best of intentions, and the result is calamitous.

Any man can serve God best in his own natural environment; as in Kipling's great poem, Mulholland was sent back to the lower deck of the cattle boats, the place where he

---

65 Sarai had been barren for ten years. It was legal for her to give her *own* female slave to Abram to raise a son for her. The initiative had to be hers (Gen 16:1–16).

was culturally most at home.[66] The danger of all foreign missionary enterprise is that the missionary may try to take his own culture pattern with him. To be aware of the danger is to be forewarned. There is no aspect of the communication of the gospel that is easier to stumble over than this matter of ethics. We tend to confuse ethics for the gospel, the response for the stimulus, and thereby we expose our foreignness and render much of our work ineffective and reduce our capacity for identification.

We are discussing capacity for reception of the gospel, and we have learned that Christian ethics from the West must be seen as culturally foreign, and therefore tread carefully. The receivers of our communicating are much more ready to receive our gospel (for this is universal and integrates in any culture) than our ethics (which are merely the response of the West to the gospel). Can we not give them the gospel and leave them to "work out [their] own salvation" (Phil 2:12)? Their capacity to receive the gospel is high; their capacity to receive our Western ethics is much less certain.

---

66   The story is told in Rudyard Kipling's poem, "Mulholland's Contract" (1896).

9

TRANSMISSION

Identification of the Communicator with the Receivers within the Culture Pattern

In one of his books Kluckhohn, the anthropologist, describes a Southwestern archaeologist scanning a new site and looking at a few broken fragments of pottery. From these fragments he can predict other styles of pottery, forms of weaving, architectural elements, stone and bone craftwork. He can do this because he knows the pattern. Without a pattern it could never be done, but because there is a pattern, and because he has studied it thoroughly until he knows it, he can, from small fragments, predict the general whole. He can recognise the culture from one of its configurations. This configuration is the key to the whole (Kluckhohn 1949, 48).

The whole pattern of any culture is an integrated and operating organisation of many configurations. We do not say that all cultures have all these configurations. Sometimes environmental factors have prevented the development of one. Some Pacific islands, for instance, have no pottery manufacture because no suitable clay is to be found there, but some configurations are found everywhere. One of these universal configurations is religion. There is no race or culture of which it can be truly said that they have no religious sense. Even though some culture may have forced itself into a purely negative position about religion, this in itself is an attitude to religion, and therefore an admission of its existence. Anti-religion is not a-religion.

Thousands of years ago, when the people of the Old Stone Age lived in caves that are now two miles beneath the surface of the earth, a great change was taking place in their way of life. They lived by hunting bison, mammoth, rhinoceros, and a type of reindeer, all of them species which are now extinct. They appear to have had a kind of religious ceremony to aid their hunting, and this ceremony involved the development of the art of mural painting. Into the bodies of the animals they painted on the walls of the caves, they threw their spears, and, so we are told, they believed they had already wounded the animal in spirit. Subsequently they went out to kill and capture the body. As time went on, this ritual demanded better and better artists; and the primitives set aside a group of their number, freed them from their duties as hunters, and were themselves willing to support these ritual artists so they could perfect their specialisation. Some of their painting is really remarkable; their unexpected degree of perfection puzzled the experts—an animal half-turning its body to vigilantly drink at a stream, for instance. In the same caves where some of the best murals are, research workers have found scores of flat pieces of bone and stone—rough sketches we would call them, small-scale trials of the same murals. Many of them show lines as if a master hand had been correcting an inexpert student (Childe 1954, 40–41). What have we in this scene? Here is a segment of a pattern. Configurations of the painting art, of its instruction, of religion, of the art of hunting, and the economics of food supply for a group of cave dwellers of the Palaeolithic Age; and these configurations are perfectly integrated. There is interrelationship and interaction throughout the whole scene. Each aids and depends on the other. Each is the other's inspiration.

We see then that this integration is also an interdependence, so the configurations must be in harmony and on a common level; they must have real affinities, they must be completely meaningful to each other, and a strong overdevelopment in one configuration must still be significant to the others. Let one configuration so outstrip the others that it dominates them or upsets the equilibrium, and the general integration of the whole is lost. Then we have a culture clash, which is often the sign of disintegration or decay.

We see this in many parts of the world where "primitive" people living under a communal system on an exchange economy are reaching out for money and wealth, obtaining it and spending it without a corresponding development of their living pattern. Life suddenly seems to get all out of joint, behaviour becomes irrational, moral standards and quality of workmanship suffer, youth becomes disrespectful and age disgruntled—all because one configuration has gotten out of relationship with the rest.

The social function of religion in any society is to maintain that society's integration and equilibrium. This does not mean that religion should not seek improvement unto perfection. We are not thinking here of drives, but rather of the mode or machinery of religion by means of which the people of a particular society may best and most effectively worship God, and receive comfort and guidance commensurate with their needs and aspirations at any given point of time. The methods and modes of their religion must be culturally harmonious with their lives.

When we speak of Christianity as a *universal* religion, we do not mean that we hope to find a basis for some unity in a world church through one particular form or mode of worship or even a common philosophy, and certainly not through a common language. We find it difficult to speak of Christ breaking down culture like that. Rather we think of Him breaking *through*. There is quite a significant difference. A thing is broken *down* when it ceases to be of value, or when it needs replacement by something better. It implies a state of rottenness or badness. To carry this on to its conclusion, in modern missions it implies that Christ Himself is to be seen through Western eyes, and disapproves non-Western culture patterns. Yet Christ Himself lived and died within the Hebrew pattern of His day. From his twelfth year He was a son of the law, a position He never rejected. Furthermore He deliberately stated that He did not come to break down (destroy) the law.

Yet He did break through the law for these first disciples, for Mary of Magdala and the woman of Samaria. He broke through the barred door of the room of fear and said to his fearful followers, "Peace be unto you" (John 20:19). Surely this means that for all men everywhere who believe, behind any barrier, within any walls or "curtain" or culture, whether these barriers mean imprisonment or not, whether they are good or bad, Christ can break *through*, answer the problem, comfort the sufferer, guide the lost, strengthen the weary, and bring joy to His faithful servant. Even when physical conditions do not change, Christ can still break through with a valid word for the situation, and can give the Christian an opening for Christian expression in spite of the walls or barriers. Such a Christ is surely universal.

Let me safeguard one point. This does not mean that Christ teaches us to be so content with our lot that we are led into no work of social reform, nor does it mean that we may blithely tolerate social injustices because they seem to be cultural. This is not the point under discussion. What we are stressing here is that when we think of the indigenous cultures of the mission fields we must not assume: (a) that they are inferior to our own, and arising from this, (b) that they must inevitably disappear. The white missionary must always be on his guard against his natural or inherent egocentricity, his tendency to think of Christianity as Western, and of his own pattern as the only road to progress. To do this will make us break down culture rather than break through it.

If the reader feels disposed to argue with me on this point, I suggest he take a sheet of paper and jot down everything he can call to mind from ecclesiastical vestments and ritual, to properties, church investments, social aids, money-raising devices, and so on which have been introduced through the centuries by the church, but were not features of the original apostolic Christianity. Let him consider this truth when he looks over the formidable list, that we could drop *every one* of those things from our religion and still lose nothing of apostolic Christianity. It should impress on us that the mode or form of our religion is cultural and environmental—then why force this cultural conditioning of two thousand years of European history on the young churches?

If a cultural element from the West fits the pattern of a young church, then all is well, but for the most part the missionary will have to find a way of breaking through. This means learning the culture of his area, speaking the language, eating the food of the people, and as often as possible with the people, trying always to see things through their eyes.

Surely this has bearing on evangelism everywhere. Even in hometown evangelism the truth is often overlooked that localities have their own peculiarities, with their own vernacular jargon and mental outlook. The evangelist would hardly speak in the same way to a gathering of rural farmers as he would to a university assembly or at a midday gathering of factory workers. The first commonsense principle for the communicator of the gospel is that he must get as quickly as possible into contact with his audience on a level that is perfectly meaningful.

If that applies within the local cultures in the homeland, how much more in the foreign land?

To achieve effective transmission of the gospel means first and foremost that one must accept the basic culture pattern of the people.

Communicating the gospel means more than leading men from sin unto life (although this is a primary element of it). The gospel involves more than salvation as an initial experience and act of faith; it means ministering daily help, care, prayer, comfort, guidance; it means making the whole gospel available at any time and every opportunity. This is a full-time task and involves close identification with the receivers.

The visiting evangelist who brings to a community an experience of revival may have been used by God for a great work, but he does not stay to follow up his cases. He misses out on the identification which is so necessary to confirm and strengthen the decision that has been made. He only communicates one aspect of the gospel at one time. The full gospel requires a full-time communicator, living with or closely identified with his flock. Maybe he will have to confine much of his own personal life within the little limits of their life pattern. One thing I know—the closer the identification, the more effective his communication.

The heavenly Father Himself recognises this principle. He Himself was unable to break through into the living experiences of humanity until His own Son assumed the physical limitations of human flesh, took up His abode with man, spoke his language, suffered as man suffers, was tempted in all points as we are. Then, and only then, was God Himself able to communicate effectively His gospel to mankind. When "the Word became flesh" and "dwelt among" men, then men were able to say they "beheld his glory" (John 1:14 ASV). Real identification is an essential of effective communication.

When meditating on the matter of identification I often find myself thinking of Father Mapple, who ministered to whalemen at the Whalemen's Chapel at New Bedford, in Melville's great story of a century ago. The pulpit was built high and constructed as the bow of a ship, and was approached, not by means of steps, but a rope ladder. Father Mapple, dressed as a whaleman, would come in, grasp the rope ladder which dangled over the side of his ship, look up in the fashion of a true sailor, ascend, swing himself on board, and haul up the ladder after him. Then he would gaze out over his congregation. The wall of the chapel behind him was painted as a storm at sea, black rocks, snowy breakers, flying scud, and dark rolling clouds. A small ray of light struggled through the clouds and threw a spot of light on the deck. His ship was on its passage out (Melville 1892). Father Mapple's sermons were salted with the sea itself, for he had been a harpooner in his day. He truly ministered to whalemen and "dwelt among" them. To some of us that may seem a bit theatrical, but one reads his sermon on Jonah, as it is in *Moby Dick*, and Ishmail's meditations on it, and one feels Mapple's identification with Ishmail was certainly real, and one wonders whether it was fiction at all.

To give another example of good identification from a completely different period and scene, I call to mind Richard Baxter, who pressed this very point with English pastors and preachers in a most decadent period of English history. He pressed that their ineffectiveness was the result of no identification through pastoral visitation.

The object of our pastoral care is all the flock . . . to which end it is presupposed necessary that we should know every person that belongeth to our charge . . . Doth not the careful shepherd look after every individual sheep? And a good schoolmaster look after every individual scholar, both for instruction and correction? And a good physician look after every particular patient? (Baxter 1950, 75)

Occasional sermons, radio voices, nicely printed literature may all catch the eye and ear, and open hearts; but it takes personal identification with both the individual and the group to really communicate the gospel, for the gospel is not a thing of a fleeting moment—it is a continuous and growing experience to those who know it.

Let it be noted that identification must be with both individual and the group. The virtue of Baxter's argument was that it provided for the individual within the group. A converted individual without any genuine group affiliation is liable to become a serious problem. Therefore there must be a group pattern to which the convert belongs and with which the communicator of the gospel can identify himself.

Faulty identification means faulty contact, and faulty contact means distorted transmission and reception. A vigorous transmission without proper contact or identification leads to religious position, and this creates mental resistance or resentment. Imposed religion is formal only. If the posing force is relaxed or weakens, the formal religion will quickly disintegrate—unless the imposition has been so vigorous that the original pattern has been obliterated. In this case it lapses into materialism.

If, on the other hand, the communicators break through a cultural barrier without injuring it and transmit a gospel which integrates, this gospel will share the adventures of the culture and always be valid to any changing situation.

Mental resistance may not be always apparent on the surface. The oppression of an imposed religion may have driven it underground. The only visible evidence may be an increasing drift from religion to materialism. It seems right then that we should turn aside for a moment to investigate this tragic alternative.

The Cultural Significance of Mental Resistance

David Hill, the great missionary of China, described an incident on one of his journeys when he heard the sound of praying in a tiny *T'u Ti Miao*. A man was inside, reciting prayers in the dark and beating a wooden drum alternatively with the ringing of a bell. So intent he was on his purpose that apparently he did not notice Hill, though his temple was but six square feet. Impressed by his earnest praying for enlightenment, Hill lay a Christian tract on the shrine and went on (Rattenbury and Hill 1949, 63–64).

Hill had respected the man's private devotions to the extent that he did not interrupt as some evangelists may have done, but he left a tract to do its own work. We do not know the result of this act, but it raises a basic issue. What would be the reaction of a devout but unenlightened man when, at the conclusion of his devotions, he discovered this Christian tract? What would be his psychological response? Would he read the tract or not? Would he be able to find in the tract that for which he was earnestly but blindly seeking, or would it stir up a cultural or religious resentment against the unknown person who had placed the tract on his shrine?

I make no attempt to answer this question, for I know too little of the Chinese people, but I know well what would be the effect on a hotelkeeper if I so impersonally left an anti-liquor track under his door.[67]

A method which is effective in opening up one mind for the gospel may do untold harm in closing another. It is therefore imperative that the communicator understand what he is doing. There are some evangelists who do win converts, but for every one they win, they close the hearts of ten. This problem is real enough within one's own culture pattern, so it follows that the man working outside his own pattern should be particularly careful. Perhaps we may appreciate the problem better by returning to Sapir's theory of phonetic law and linguistic drift mentioned earlier in the book. We saw that in linguistics changes could be rapid and acceptable as long as they did not disturb the basic pattern.[68] But disturb the linguistic equilibrium and there is immediate resistance. I have pointed out that this also applies to a culture pattern.

Then, what is the significance of this to the communicator of the gospel? It has both a positive and negative significance. It opens up a way for the communicator to break through the cultural barrier without dislocating it, but it also issues a warning of the danger of disturbing equilibrium and creating thereby a strong mental resistance. Sapir makes

---

[67] The Christian tract is a useful instrument for leaving behind after one has made a personal contact and is better not used impersonally. If the man was merely searching for truth, he might read the tract, but if his prayers were a matter of deep faith, he would be resentful perhaps, and this would raise a barrier against the gospel.

[68] To give an example from Sapir (1949, 187), here is a series of consonant changes that have a constant pattern in English:

p t k		b d g
b d g	which corresponds, point for point, with the Sanskrit series:	bh dh gh
f th h		p t k

the point that one language actually encourages a phonetic drift which another language resists. The communicator is always faced with this problem culturally, and he must view it rationally. He must achieve culture contacts and avoid culture clashes. He may achieve the former by accident, but he can only avoid the latter by thoroughly saturating himself in cultural understanding of the people among whom he labours, both in its historical and contemporary culture. This takes time, and it means that a man is not really effective until he has been a few years on the field. I fully realise that this will be distressing to mission boards which approve short-term appointments, but it is absolutely true nevertheless.

Kluckhohn, the anthropologist, has described culture as like a map. He points out that this is not the real territory, but an abstraction of it. However, he says, if you know the map you can find your way about the territory (Kluckhohn 1949, 29).

Like the maps said to be used by Columbus, certain parts of which were endorsed "Here be demons," so our map of culture warns us of going carefully in certain matters. We take a locality map and see written here "quicksands" and there "No road this way" and we know that certain things are to be avoided. It is negative advice perhaps, but we do not ignore it.

In this way the cultural map of the people I serve reads that it is dangerous to press individualism too hard, to stifle rivalry in church collections, to force native music into Western rhyme and rhythm, to refuse Old Testament concepts, and so on. Even though I can give a good reason for doing any of these things, my cultural map warns me on the point. Westerners take the ethnocentric view that this is progress, but I honestly must write it "progress." We start by thinking that everything "progressive" to us is progressive to people in other cultures, which may not be so at all. If they clash with the basic pattern, they cause mental resistance, which, if serious, leads on to complexes and pyschological abnormities, which can hardly be called progress.

What we do is often to press for independent individualism, which means death to communal society and leaves people suspended between two conflicting cultures and at home in neither, whereas a little more careful thought may have made it possible to provide an opening for some individualism within the status or communal society instead of being in conflict with it. A good example of this was the creation of the native ministry, which represents a degree of individualism but does not irritate the basic pattern. In other words the individualist has to be given a status in the communal society.

The very opposite is seen in the drift of individuals to the industrial centres, in search for money and facilities for spending, isolated from their culture, misfits from every angle. To be normal and effective progress, the changes should resemble phonetic drift and remain within the basic pattern. I use these merely as examples of the same factor (individualism) of change *within* or *without* a culture pattern—one acceptable, the other producing resistance from the communal society which is injured thereby.

As fire is a good servant but a bad master, so with cultural forces. We must be aware of this and cautious. It is even possible for the strengths of one culture to bring death to another, as we have seen time and time again.

Consider Paul's journey to Arabia after his conversion. Supposing that he had stayed there and done his missionary labour among the Arabs, and the gospel had been given to the world by Arabs instead of Europeans, so that today we were on the receiving instead of the transmitting end, and the Christian missionaries to us from Arabia pressed that in the name of progress we must sacrifice some of our individualism and personal freedom for the preservation of human society, and changed our musical forms of rhythm and rhyme and perhaps our musical scale. Some of us would feel perhaps that Christianity was a bit of an imposition, and I'm quite sure we would have many nativistic movements to resist it.

This is not a bit fantastic. It might well have been so. I trust it will help us see what I mean by saying that an imposition of Western theology, ethics, and ritual on a non-Western people may well create mental resistance.

Yet I firmly believe these people can receive the gospel, and will receive it gladly—if it is not an imposition which breaks down their culture but an integrated configuration within it. It is then of primary importance that I know my people culturally and prepare my food in the form which appeals to their palate.

Transmission through a foreign language is at best a second best, and it seems essential also that the communicator should acquire some knowledge of indigenous idiom and poetic forms. Forcing hymns into English rhythm should be done with care, yet music is essential in communicating the gospel. The current American tendency to set religious themes to song hits no doubt has its appeal in certain quarters, but it is a powerful irritant in others. Sapir points out that there are basic differences in the culture patterns of verse. Greek and Latin verse depends on the principle of contrasting weights; English on contrasting stresses; French on number and echo; Chinese on number, echo, and contrasting pitches (Sapir 1949, 230). These differences arise from the unconscious habits of the people concerned. The communicator, to be effective, must captivate the indigenous system, which is more likely to be achieved by trying to think in the language than by translating from his mother tongue. Sapir says the prose of Milton is not English but is semi-Latin in magnificent English words (ibid., 227). Perhaps that is why Milton makes so little impression on so many of the English rank and file.

I remember two missionaries. One had remarkable fluency and correctness of grammar. I have sat amazed to hear him explain some highly involved procedure with perfect ease. The other made many mistakes and his vocabulary was not nearly so extensive, but it went deeper into the culture of the people. The former was everywhere admired for his skill at exposition and translation, but the Fijians themselves never thought of it as anything but excellent translation. The other man, despite his imperfections, was always communicating within their own world of cultural and religious experience.

Only by throwing oneself into the cultural concepts of one's people, sympathising with their point of view, and always starting to deal with them from the point or level of their present position, and sharing with them those things which go beyond religion (i.e., by real identification) can one become a real communicator of spiritual experiences to them. One must always start with them, not from one's own Western philosophical position. The former will avoid mental resistance; the latter may well cause it.

Transmitting the Essential Core

The essential core of the faith must be preserved, at all costs. So much has been said about the need for the communicator adapting himself to his new environment that the central truth could have been endangered. This criticism is often aimed at the missionary who presses the case for real identification. It is, however, a challenging experience to the missionary to find himself forced to evaluate his own faith and separate its cultural paraphernalia from its essential core.

I remember as a youth being presented with a supply of small decision cards by an older evangelist who stressed the claim that every Christian should be an evangelist. These cards bore the drawing of a hand with one word on each finger. They were the five great words of Christian experience, according to my friend: Sin, Love, Sacrifice, Faith, Salvation. The truth was driven home to me there and then that this was the five-finger exercise which provided the basic theme of the message of the Christian evangelist.

Since then I have read hundreds of devotional and theological works, many from publishers other than my own denomination. A very large percentage of these works have concentrated on one or more of these themes. The ministry of comfort, the work of the Holy Spirit, and life everlasting are doctrines often introduced under these heads. The configurations integrate. It is not so easy to separate them. The obvious absence is the doctrine of the church. This is the weak spot of freelance evangelism. To these five I think we shall have to add this sixth—the fellowship. There must be a group or church into which the convert is absorbed. There can be no solitary Christians as the Wesleyan tradition has it.

Other doctrines will vary in importance and emphasis according to cultural needs and environmental peculiarities; for instance, people under persecution develop a strong eschatology as we have already seen; but if you tamper with any of the six points I have mentioned, you will so weaken the fabric of the whole that the configurations will not integrate. Your religious experience is out of balance—be you an individual Christian or a church congregation.

The five-finger exercise presents the plan of salvation viewed in relation to eternity. It needs the doctrine of the fellowship (the church) to bring it back to earth and fix it in the human scene for practical functioning and application.

This finger-pointing of the essentials made a great impression on me as a young man. I prepared an object lesson talk for young teenagers using a larger hand with each finger in a different colour. I had a device by means of which the colour was not apparent until I was ready to talk about it. I avoided theological words by naming the fingers—"I have sinned" (black), "He loved me" (blue), "He died for me" (red), "I believe" (gold), and "I have eternal life" (white). The colour system played its part also in the communication of the message. I was just starting out as a preacher at the time and used the object lesson with good effect.

Years later, when ministering to a dark-skinned people under completely different cultural conditions, I remembered the old object lesson I had used in my youth, and I made use of it again, with exactly the same results. The same device, the same message, was communicable equally effectively within two completely different culture patterns. This is the integrating gospel, the essential core of the faith, the universal Christianity, which can fit every culture.

In the years of my theological training the essential core was threatened. In those days an attitude spoken of as the social gospel was being pressed as a way of salvation, and many dispensed with the red finger of sacrifice and explained salvation without atonement. There have also been attempts to whitewash the black finger of sin (i.e., dispense with judgement), saying it is incompatible with the God of love, and some thereby have literally "made shipwreck of their lives."

Often, when I have knelt on a *pandanus* mat of a native house and tried in my halting Fijian to help young men and maidens, old men and women, and older children across that gulf which means to pass from death unto life, this truth comes home to me—they are taking the same step I took on a certain day long ago in Melbourne. They know nothing of the atmosphere of a city of over a million people. Their background and mine are poles apart. Their home life, their education, their habits of life, their pleasures and occupations could hardly be further removed from me. Yet we have knelt there together at the focal point of personal history, and felt the same way about our sins, and the greatness of God's love, and the way Christ bore our sin that day, and the step of faith we took, and the sudden certainty of life eternal. This experience was—not mine or theirs—but *ours*.

Yet again, the application of this experience within the fellowship would be different for each of us. The common point for us was simply that there had to be a fellowship. The experience had to have a valid and integrated place in life.

When I say that the concept of sin is common to us, I do not mean that we think in an identical way about what is sin. That, like ethics, is culturally conditioned to some extent. The common point is that to both of us there is something which tends to separate us from

God and dim "the spiritual glow." Sins have been crystallised by the codification of laws, and therefore vary in different communities and cultures, but sin refers to our relationship with God, and this is an experience within all cultures.

The concept of atonement must be very close to a universal one. Wherever sins are recognised there is also an approved mode whereby the offender may seek to free himself from the penalty: maybe a large-scale restitution, a sacrifice presented, or an act of humiliation or atonement. This is very much more widespread than the average Westerner realises. A religion without a plan of salvation is of very little use, even to a savage. That "the wages of sin is death" (Rom 6:23) is a universally understood statement; yet, strangely enough, all cultures seek ways and means of resisting the verdict.

To millions still today this is merely a blind groping in the semidarkness, but it is because mankind has been conscious of his shortcomings and hoped in some salvation that religious rituals have developed the wide world over. The strength of Christianity lies in the perfection of its doctrine of salvation, and its personal concentration in a Saviour who is both God and man; who, without sin, is yet perfectly identified with man. This is real and historic, not mere abstraction. This truth (it is not merely a doctrine, it is an experienced truth) seems to satisfy people of otherwise widely different cultural tastes, and seems to answer the seeking hearts of men everywhere.

The wide world is dotted over with altars to the Unknown God, and the Christian communicator of the gospel must realise that the essential core of the message he communicates is the perfect answer to the searching hearts of his listeners.

Yet whether he be presenting the truth to his own folk at home within his own culture pattern, or in some foreign land where the pattern is strange to him and he himself is a stranger, he still has to persuade his listeners to take that step of faith which alone will make Christ *their own.*

Intellectually the cross of Christ was a stumbling block to the Jew and foolishness to the Greek, yet to both Jews and Greeks, who took that step of faith, it was the power of God unto salvation (1 Cor 1:23,24).

Here then is the essential core of experiential Christianity in all cultures, that "God so loved the world, that he gave his only begotten Son, that whosoever believeth in him should not perish, but have everlasting life" (John 3:16).

The Continuity of Apostolic Experience

The Acts of the Apostles is certainly an unfinished book. It ends leaving Paul for two whole years in his own hired house, receiving all who came, preaching Christ and the kingdom of God freely and with confidence (Acts 28:30,31).

It has neither literary conclusion nor closing blessing. If ever a literary composition ended in unfinished action, it is the Acts of the Apostles. This literary characteristic is symbolic of a real fact. The acts of the apostles and the communication of the gospel are going on and on. The apostolic concept of time is not determined by clock or calendar; it is eschatological, and we are still in the same period of time as the Christians of the early church.

In the communication of the gospel in our day, therefore, the communicator must establish this feeling of continuity with the apostolic church. This is much easier to achieve on the mission field than in the home church, because Western cities are enslaved by mechanical clocks and daily time programs. We have already seen that "primitive" societies have trouble with Western time and space ideas, but they have thought forms of a timeless present which simplifies the preservation of this continuity of apostolic experience by projecting the Scripture narrative and experience into their own as if it were contemporaneous.

The Westerner tends to think this is a mere figment of the imagination, but this is not so—it is a completely different time sense, and as far as it relates to our thinking about Christ, we have a great body of Scripture evidence to support the continuous life of Christ. It projects both backwards and forwards—"Before Abraham was, I am" (John 8:57,58), and "I am alive for evermore" (Rev 1:1-18). Do we not in our own liturgical exercises bind ourselves with Christians of all ages; and irrespective of time or place or race, do we not look forward together to the consumation of our eternal hope in glory? We sing the *Te Deum* in the present tense and put praise into the mouths of the apostles and prophets and martyrs of the church, and thus we see the church as whole and timeless because it is above time.

There are few hymns of history which catch better the supratemporal and supraspacial nature of the Christian church than the *Te Deum*. This is one reason why it is so acceptable on the mission field.

Wherever Western culture imposes itself on others, its time and space concepts are also imposed. This gradual but constant loss of concepts like the timeless present, throws an increased responsibility on the communicator of the gospel to establish the continuity with apostolic experience.

By apostolic experience is meant the converting of men and women of all types; the knowledge of salvation in the Person of Christ; the discovery of Christian fellowship through such things as the breaking of bread, prayers, baptism, meeting from house to house with gladness and singleness of heart, continuing steadfastly in the teaching of the apostles (Acts 2:41,42,46,47).

When the Lord adds "to the church daily such as should be saved," (Acts 2:47) when the church is active and growing, when she is realising the great potential of her fellowship and rejoicing in it, we may feel we are not merely in touch with the apostolic community but actually part of it. We ourselves are experiencing one of the unwritten chapters of the Acts of the Apostles.

A few weeks ago I enjoyed the unusual pleasure of sitting in the pew at one of our Fiji Indian churches. It was a baptismal service in which five converts from Hinduism were received into the faith. Three of these represented a family, and I thought of the baptism of the Philippian jailor and his household (Acts 16:33), of Lydia and her household (Acts 16:15), and of the household of Stephanus (1 Cor 1:16), and felt at once the continuity of apostolic experience.

To feel this continuity is a great source of strength to the young convert. The apostolic church lived in the power of the Holy Spirit, and the full resources of that same Holy Spirit are available to him, as Christ Himself promised it would be so. This is indeed "good news" to the new Christian, who, after his decision, may have to face a very hostile world and be subject to much testing.

The trouble with a good deal of Christian evangelism is that it becomes an end in itself, and thereby it ceases to be apostolic. I have found it necessary in my own evangelistic work in Fiji to have by me a small booklet, which I specially prepared for this purpose, of making conversion the beginning of a new life, not an end in itself. The booklet's title, being translated, is *The Way* and it provides, in some fifty-odd pages, a study of what I feel it means in life to be Christ's men, and how the help of God may be obtained day by day through the Holy Spirit as we "work out" our salvation in life. The booklet, I am led to believe, has proved useful also to those being received into church membership. It has no special merits in itself, and no real originality, but only seeks to answer the problem left in the hearts of many converts after the departure of the evangelist—after conversion, what next? The communicator of the gospel is honour-bound not to neglect this aspect of his transmission of faith.

The apostolic answer to this question of what follows conversion was found in the fellowship—the meeting together, breaking of bread, hearing instruction, praying, and building up the fellowship with gladness and singleness of heart, and in witnessing beyond the fellowship. Whenever we find a congregation which feels the entity and strength of its fellowship in this way, we have evidence of the continuity of apostolic experience, and it is not as rare as the cynics would have us think.

Naturally enough in any area the fellowship will be culturally conditioned to some extent, for if it is to be fully realised and vital it must integrate in the pattern of life there; when we meet at these deep religious levels there must be nothing imposed—it must be perfectly natural. The responsibility is with the communicator to reach the level of the fellowship, not theirs to adjust themselves to him.

The obvious reason for this is that all foreign communicators are at best birds of passage. The fellowship must live on after his departure. An imposed form of fellowship of a foreign pattern is of little immediate value and no permanent value.

There are communicators who build up huge projects around their own personal dynamic. They make a brave show for a time and maybe leave some momentum, but in time nothing remains and people say it was a great venture but it needed an X to carry it out. Had X seen to the establishment of a truly indigenous fellowship and set it to explore its own potential, he himself may have been less impressive to the general public, but his fellowship would have remained as a more permanent contribution weaving itself into the fabric of society.

The genius of the apostolic church was that it provided a relevant message and an integrated fellowship within its own world living in and acting upon society, not foreign and isolated from it.

Every country and society has its own peculiar mental and social problems. If they are to be effectively and permanently faced, they must be faced indigenously. The church must be an indigenous force within its own culture pattern, and to be such a force it must have a valid message, and requires the daily strengthening of a real living and integrated fellowship. This is to discover the continuity of apostolic experience.

10

DISCOVERY

The Dormant Potential

Whenever a culture suddenly comes face to face with the fact of Christ, and an integrated fellowship is established within that culture, so that Christianity is substituted for the old religion, we are faced with the possibility of a dormant potential being there, which may someday be the unique contribution of that young church to world Christianity.

History reveals how God has raised many movements and communities to serve as correctives to the church or to facilitate the rediscovery of lost truths. Western civilisation is prone to think it has all the answers, and its Christianity evidences the same shortcoming. No branch of the church as we know it may entirely claim it has the whole gospel.

Over these recent days I have been looking back over my own faith and experience and asking myself to evaluate it in the light of the changes it has undergone since I left Australia nearly two decades ago to live and work among an island people. What has living in the Fijian fellowship done to my concept of religion? Do the changes that have come to me suggest the dormant potential which the church at large should discover?

In the first place my outlook on the Old Testament has been revolutionised, and I have found treasures I never knew to have existed; it has deepened my appreciation of the unity and wholeness of the Bible, and compelled me to face up to the question that the Scriptures to Jesus himself were the Old Testament—a useful exercise to anyone who feels the gospel is confined to the New Testament. I found myself more able to appreciate the nature of the real struggle between Hebrew and Canaanite religion, and some of the Old Testament heroes have become real characters to me as they were not before. Intellectually it has been a revolutionary and invigorating experience; and I have found that, apart from the fact that the Old Testament is anticipatory of Christ but the New Testament reveals him as an actuality, the main differences are cultural and periodic only. Because of this I have been forced to read and think more and more of the whole Bible.

Psychologically it has forced me out of the rut of stereotyped Western religious experience in which I and my comrades had been buried. The difficulty of a man getting in a rut is that he is confined to solid walls on both sides and can only advance along a hard-baked track, one misses the scenes and colours of the roadside, and the only consolation is that the track has been followed before and must lead somewhere. My religion was vital and active in its own way, and I knew the joy of sin forgiven and the keeping power of Christ, and the stand I took was orthodox and dogmatic—yet it was still a rut in which I was travelling. When I came to the islands I found the road less hard and sunbaked and found it possible to leave the rut and travel the open road with Christ.

Travelling the open road with Christ means getting one's religious ideas into correct perspective. At some time or other we have all packed our bags for a journey. How we consider each item before putting it in! We evaluate everything. Something has to be discarded. Is this essential or can we do without it? A man cannot carry too much baggage as he travels the open road. Not that one is discarding his beliefs without thought, but one has to be asking what is really essential, and gradually one gains a much deeper appreciation of the essential core of the gospel.

In reality I have discarded little. My confession of faith has remained firm, but I know now what I did not know then—if some cataclysmic change came into my life and confronted me with the dreadful decision of throwing overboard everything I could possibly cast away without jeopardising my hopes for eternity, I think I could now make that decision calmly and safely. Once, the thought of jettisoning one single traditional doctrine would have precipitated extreme mental agony within me. But now I can say I know which parts of my religious bag and baggage are merely aids to worship and which parts are essential unto salvation.

The third thing I can say about the impact of the island sojourn on my faith is that those essential doctrines, and especially that of the work of Christ Himself, have been richly deepened, because I have explored these things in the hearts of people outside my own culture pattern. The concept of the mediatorial work of Christ means more to me now than it did, and I have learned more the art of seeking the will of God for me and submitting to it. I have become less anxious for the morrow, and when I have revisited "civilisation" I have been shocked at the high tensions and mental disturbances of people whose main problem is really an unwillingness to wait patiently on the Lord.

Living for a long period outside one's own culture pattern has a broadening effect. It throws the spotlight on our own arrogant ethnocentricity. We discover that all the best things do not belong to one race or language or culture, and we see too that our development of the doctrine of human freedom has been done at the expense of our Christian duty to the group and the love of our neighbour. A little solid thinking on points like these helps us to see ourselves as others see us.

The sum of this is that in many ways the communicator has been the receiver—I have found the gospel where I never thought to seek it before; I have been lifted from my theological rut to travel the open road with Christ; I have found my devotional and spiritual life deepened, my faith refreshed, my social outlook more tolerant of others, yet I am more critical of myself. Certainly the communicator has been the receiver.

The question now arises—*what* has been received? Something has been drawn from the dormant potential of the young church in the islands—something that has been lost at home, something needed at home to correct our own perspective. Is this the purpose of God that we should communicate the gospel to them, eventually to receive it back by retransmission with emphasis on elements we have bypassed or missed? It could well be so.

For a practical example, let us admit that we have a rather feeble concept of the will of God for man, and man's recognition of the right God has of making demands on him, and the virtue of complete submission to that will. It is seldom preached and has poor reception when it is. It is becoming more fashionable to go to the mission field "for the sake of experience," for instance, than because the will of God has possessed the person concerned and he has learned to yield to God. We have ceased to stress this doctrine, and the loss is surely ours.

Will it be from one of the young churches that this truth comes home again, and when it comes, will it be in the form we knew or a varied form—say, as a holy sacrifice we lay at Jesus' feet, signifying that submission to the divine will is itself a high sacrificial form of worship? Can we not hear, even now, the words of the Christian poet of India, Narayan Vaman Tilak?

> Whate'er within the future lies
> Bring thou to Christ a sacrifice,
> Establishing a faith complete,
> O soul of mine, at Jesus' feet.
>
> Thy will upon His altar lay,
> And go thou forth with Him today. (Winslow 1923, 115)

Can we perhaps recapture the primary meaning of sacrifice, and then see our wills presented as a sacrifice to Him, and having so worshipped let us go forth on the open road with Him?

Or again, are we to be led back to the noble concept of work as serving God, instead of as a necessary evil to provide us with food and clothing and entertainment? Is this guidance to come from the young church, whose Christian hymns were based on "The Song of the Hoe" and "The Boatman's Song"?

Or are the communal societies of the Pacific to remind the West that its continual emphasis on individual freedom and "progress" is at the expense of one of the earliest known laws of human history—that I am my brother's keeper (Gen 4:9–12).

The more deeply the communicator digs in the culture of his adopted field of service, the more he will discover dormant potential that lies there awaiting discovery by the world church. The more he digs the more these truths impress themselves on his heart, and he feels that someday he will be compelled to go home and communicate there the gospel as he found it in the foreign land. With the present-day development in the young churches, the retransmission of the faith is a real possibility of the near future.

Nor should we imagine that such retransmission can only be a rediscovery. It may well be an original development of something that has never hereto germinated.

Writing to illustrate a different point altogether, Ruth Benedict has described the growth of Gothic architecture from a mere "preference for altitude and light" to a "unique and homogeneous art" (1946, 43). Without conscious choice and with no set purpose, but from a local bias, the technique was slowly integrated into a perfect form. Benedict uses this to illustrate what goes on within cultures. We use it to illustrate the kind of thing which may be anticipated in the religion of the young churches.

What possibilities, for example, lie in Tilak's concept of the Christian laying his will as a sacrifice on the altar? It is not merely calling the West back to the lost meaning of sacrifice, but also to a concept of the will of God and man's submission. They are two germinal ideas that are integrated here—and possibly these two ideas may not have been integrated before, so that it could well produce a hitherto unexplored field of religious experience.

We are in the realm of discovery. The idea of discovering something new in the integration of two known factors was appreciated by the late W. H. Davies, the nature poet. Standing in the wet grass one day he became entranced by the combination of a rainbow and a cuckoo's song, and feeling that the sheep and cows required some explanation of his strange behaviour he explains that "a rainbow and a cuckoo's song may never come together again, may never come, this side of the tomb."[69] Davies had the soul to appreciate the inspiration of the integration of two beautiful things, and he stopped to enjoy them when others would have passed them by.

But the beauty was there for any who had the soul to see. In the same way I feel certain there is a dormant potential in the young churches, and sooner or later their indigenous theologians will give us their poems and paintings.

> Not for a handful of jewels is earth called the mother of riches,
> But for the mines of gems that lie hid down in her bosom.[70]

The Integrating Gospel

Ratu Seru Cakobau, whose name in native idiom means "Bau is at war," was known in the concert hall songs of the West later on as "The King of the Cannibal Isles." His enemies knew him as "The Centipede," but he called himself *Tui Viti*—King of Fiji. These names are an index to his character.

---

69 This experience is described in a poem entitled "A Great Time," which I believe was originally published in a book, *The Bird of Paradise*. I know the poem myself from Benn's Augustan Book of Poetry on *W. H. Davies* (Davies 1925).
70 Narayam Vaman Tilak. His own translation.

This ferocious figure, who is reported to have devoured a thousand human bodies before he came face to face with Christ, had a good many reasons for accepting Christianity. History has assembled a score or more—political, social, and religious[71]; but here we are not concerned with the reasons for his conversion, but rather the factors which hindered his decision for so long. It seems to have been a genuine conversion.

Cakobau, in spite of his power as paramount chief and warrior, was not a free agent. He knew his conversion would have hundreds of ramifications throughout every aspect of political and social life. Before Cakobau actually bowed the knee to Jehovah, three decisions had to be made. The first was his personal decision to accept Christ as his Saviour, which was made in private with his wife and a missionary present. The following day he called together the chiefs and leaders of his kingdom and informed them of his change of heart. None dared to stop him, but several pressed that the time was hardly opportune. Long discussions eventually terminated with general approval—the kingdom agreed to accept the conversion of its War Lord. The next day the heads of the royal house were called for a similar discussion with the same result. The social group had approved. The following day being Sunday, Cakobau, followed by his household, became Christian by a public act of worship.

What was the precise significance of this series of discussions, and why was the great War Lord, who killed and ate enemy or friend as he desired without anyone's approval, so without freedom in this matter of deciding for Christ?

He felt he could not preserve the unity and strength of his kingdom or the security of his household without this approval. He felt that only thus could he abandon the gods of his fathers. He was chief, and tribe and kingdom were involved in his actions. He took all their traditional religious practices with their whole paraphernalia, including the thirty temples of Bau and the sacred grove on the mainland opposite, and of his own volition he destroyed them all completely. In the great gap they left, he set Christianity fair and square in the centre of the Bauan social system. It happened that way in Bau.

The only culture pattern he understood depended on sound and efficient integration. He would therefore have no conflicting religion. The function of religion was to maintain the social integration and security of the whole tribe and kingdom. There must be no division, and he elected to stand or fall by pressing this principle. No other high chief took quite so bold a step. Some of his lieutenants deserted him and fought against him in the Battle of Kaba a year later, but Cakobau proved the reality of his new religion by setting the disloyal captives free and thereby astonishing all Fiji.

We are concerned more with the phenomena than the historical events at this point, for the really remarkable thing about this narrative is that the Bauan social system,

---

71 These factors are tabulated and evaluated in this volume, see *The Christian: Fiji 1835-67*.

cannibalistic and polytheistic and military as it was, *took over Christianity in a day*. It made the necessary adjustments and set the full organisation at work immediately; its preaching, its educational system, its status pattern, its taboos and relations, its forms of worship and classes and prayer meetings. Of course this did mean scores of modifications in social life, but the documents, which are numerous, show not a single trace of cultural shocks.[72] The completeness and thoroughness of it all surely reveal the capacity of Christianity for integrating in culture patterns different from that in which it was born, without the dislocation of basic social elements.[73] Cakobau removed all traces of paganism from his island. From the scattered stones of the heathen temples he built a great church, which still stands. He set it centrally in his island to symbolise the centrality of the new faith in their society, and the cannibal killing stone was uprooted from its position and set up in the church as a baptismal font, for which purpose it is used still. The furniture of the church was arranged to fit the culture pattern and so it remains.

I have talked with Fijians of this kingdom, a few of whom still remember the Christian period of Cakobau's amazing life. They state plainly that Christ came to them "in the fullness of time" and that the integration of the church in their social system was perfect.

One old Fijian insists that the True Light came to Fiji at the very point of time when his forefathers had evolved a sacrificial system that needed such an advent to bring the different parts into integrating relationship. Fijian life needed a new perspective, he says. He uses an interesting word, *veidutaitaki*, from *dutai* (to fit together). The word can mean "put into perspective," or is used in a court of law when the judge sums up the great variety of evidence throwing it into correct relationship. So my old friend argues that Fiji had reached this point where she required the gospel only to provide the key which would lock the whole mosaic together.

This is Fijian reasoning and not mine, so I take it he found nothing alien in the gospel, but rather found in it all of the requirement for perfect integration.

On the other hand, there have been nativistic movements and there has been mental resistance of one form or another, although most of these may be traced to the influences of commercialism, alienation of land, administrative policy, and other secular factors. I do not think the church is free from inclusion in the list.

Knowing that we have a gospel to transmit and that the gospel will integrate, the communicator is very unwise if he employs any methods which tend to disintegrate.

The late Ruth Benedict described the chief of a tribe of Californian Indians. He was the leader of his people and a Christian. His present life was lived in the agricultural pursuits

---

72   Documentation is set out in detail in this volume, *The Christian: Fiji 1835–67*.
73   For a more detailed evaluation of Cakobau's conversion and the place of his form of Christianity in the Bauan culture pattern, see "Christianity and the Bauan Social System" in Tippett, *Cakobau Papers* (1954a), a multigraphed collection of newspaper and magazine articles and radio talks relative to the occasion of the Centenary of Ratu Cakobau's Conversion in 1954.

of an irrigation area, but his dreams were in the past. One day, without any apparent cause, he broke in on his narrative with these words: "In the beginning God gave to every people a cup of clay, and from their cups they drank their life. The cup of every people was different, but each people dipped into the water. Our cup is broken now" (Benedict 1949, 19).

The chief and his people found themselves between two cultures, trying to make the best of the dominant one, but dreaming wistfully of the cup that was broken.

Hundreds of chiefs and tribal leaders the wide world over are in that position today, with no alternative but to choose the way of the money-economied West and thereby drink from another's cup. The situation calls for the deepest of sympathy, for often their choice of the cup of the West is a choice of desperation. Their wistful dreams are for the cup that is broken.

The economist and the child welfare worker and the health service officer and the schoolmaster may look at these things impersonally and call them progress. The communicator of the gospel must take cognisance of things that are intrapersonal. He has to focus his attention on that wistful longing. Somehow or other, even in a rapidly changing cultural environment, and particularly if the transition is imposed rather than voluntary or the result of a tension choice, the communicator of the gospel has to present his message in a form and manner that will satisfy the desires which cause the wistful longing for the broken cup.

The function of the communicator of the gospel is to do what was the work of the priest of the tribe in pre-Christian days—to aid the maintenance of the mental stability of society, and to see that the changes which are sure to come, do so in a way that will cause no violent cultural shocks. In this intrapersonal field, which, because it involves worship, must be on both the individual and group levels, there must be an overlap. The yearnings of the past must be satisfied, and yet activities must be directed to something vital in the changing present.

World missions today are faced with a situation which bristles with difficulties. I feel certain that no religion but Christianity has the capacity for this task, but it must be a Christianity separated from colonialism, commercialism, Westernism, and democracy. The task is to pilot the leaders of the young churches so they can lead and inspire their own people in the new world and the atomic age, with faith and practice adequate for the new but still satisfying the yearnings for the broken cup. The communicator of the gospel has to provide the ways and means for maintaining mental equilibrium in spite of social change. The gospel is the integrating configuration which alone can bind the whole together.

When mass migrations have interfered with a country's demography, and the indigenous people find themselves a minority in their own land, and powerful commercial interests have captured the country's economic policy, and foreign ideas are imposed on every walk of daily life, and cultural features of three continents strive for mastery in a Pacific Island group, the Christian mission has a problem of the first magnitude on its hands.[74]

One thing is clear, however; that in most cultures it is religion which has performed the function of integrating. Religion is clearly the integrating configuration of culture. Every Christian communicator must realise that—it is axiomatic.

Change is inevitable, but the communicator of the gospel has to see that shocks are reduced, that cultural inheritance is utilised, that wistful longings are satisfied, and that no cultural voids are left to generate discontent.

Human societies are like organisms. They have natural ways of warning of the existence of these dangers. In one society it is nativistic movements, in another revolution, and in another an excessive number of neurotics. They all point to the same thing—the religious configuration within the pattern is inadequate for its task.

The universal cry among people mentally disturbed today is for a faith or a gospel that will integrate the forces of life and bring peace of mind and ease the wounds that torn personalities reveal.

I know only one gospel that has the capacity to reintegrate either individual or group personalities—the gospel of Jesus Christ. There are many evidences of this truth, and by no means the least is the manner in which the great non-Christian religions of the world have all been forced to modify their doctrine and particularly their social application in the light of Christianity. In Hinduism, for example, Christianity precipitated a whole series of reform movements which have endeavoured to captivate Christian ideals of service.[75]

Shushil Kumar Rudra wrote in a paper on "Christ and Modern India," "to distracted India with its whole head and heart sick there has come a message of hope, a message of no rigid hide-bound system such as caste, of no regulations of a book, such as the Quran, but of a living Person" (Andrews 1912, 248). Principal Rudra felt that the hope of India lay not in a philosophy or doctrine but in a living Person—not even in writings, however sacred, but in the living, risen Christ, who reveals the heart of God and the sonship of men.

Tilak's great poem, "Insatiate," reveals this same desire for the Person of Christ.

> The more I win Thee, Lord, the more I for Thee pine:
> Ah, such a heart is mine.
> My eyes behold Thee and are filled, and straightway then,
> Their hunger wakes again!
> My arms has clasped Thee and should not get Thee free, but me,
> I cannot let Thee go!
> Thou dwell'st within my heart. Forthwith anew the fire
> Burns up my soul's desire

---

74 This description fits many other fields besides that where the writer works.
75 For further reading on the point I recommend C. F. Andrews (1912).

> Lord Jesus Christ, Beloved, tell, O tell me true,
> What shall Thy servant do? (Winslow 1923, 98)

It was a brilliant inspiration which gave Walter Marshall Horton the title for his book on Jesus—*Our Eternal Contemporary* (1942). He, whoever liveth and maketh intercession for us, is not likely to pass out of man's knowledge with a changing culture, nor is He likely to find any cultural barrier strong enough to keep Him from the hearts of believers. He is, indeed, the Eternal Contemporary, and He is this in every culture pattern. The gospel that reintegrates the personalities of individuals and societies is the gospel of a Person.

This has been brought home to me in my preaching in the islands. More and more I am driven away from texts that are theological abstractions, and more and more I am forced to deal with persons or the One Person. If I want to speak of a Pauline idea, I must speak of Paul himself. He has to be set as a living character in a real-life situation first—and let me confess it has deepened my appreciation of Paul. I can see better now how a church which stresses theological abstractions runs the risk of missing the Person Himself.

A gospel revealed in a Person by its very nature implies personal relationships. The narrative of the life of Jesus Christ gives us a core of belief—the Word with God, the self-emptying, the Incarnation, the humanity, the ministry of love, the preaching in parables, the clash with the forces of evil, the trial, the self-giving on the Cross, the Resurrection, the continued ministry, the Ascension, the indwelling Christ. Of course these are theological concepts, but coming through a personal and historic life they are not hard to understand. The believer comes to know Him, and knowing Him these all fall into place. If the communicator of the gospel follows the cycle of the Christian year, there is preaching on each phase in turn. In a way this is a creed, but more it is an introduction to a Person, and that creates a personal relationship.

This same gospel of the Person has also its social aspect, for though Christ worked with individuals, He also worked with a group. He selected a band of followers and subjected them to instruction and discipline. You cannot read the life story of Jesus without being aware of the tremendous importance He attached to that group. Much of His preaching was directed to them. To them He gave figures like the little flock, the shepherd and the flock, the vine and the branches—all group studies, or pictures of the integration of their fellowship in Him. If Christ is our Eternal Contemporary, then the fellowship is coexistent with Him.

Professor John W. Bowman set out to investigate what was the intention of Jesus, as a study of the Synoptics. His conclusion was that He intended to found a fellowship of those who share the kingdom experience—something to continue after the fall of Jerusalem and the breakdown of old Israel, but gathered "from among all peoples and nations, a piece of Messianic activity," as he puts it (Bowman 1945, 11).

Communicators of the gospel, then, are engaged in introducing people to Christ Himself and this fellowship in which He is eternally present.

In a way Christ Himself is the gospel, and we are "introducing" Him rather than communicating. He *is* the gospel. This needs no translation, for the truth is transmitted through a personal relationship. This goes on in every cultural setting. He draws together the severed elements of both individual personalities and the group. He is the gospel that integrates—the Word of life.

To introduce others to Christ we must be able to say with John that that "which we have heard, which we have seen with our eyes, which we have looked upon, and our hands have handled" is the Word of life. We *declare*, we *bear witness*, we *show* it. Why? "That ye also may have fellowship with us: and truly our fellowship is with the Father, and with his Son Jesus Christ" (1 John 1:1–5). This same Jesus alone is our own Eternal Contemporary; the fellowship is eternally coexistent with Him; we can speak as do the Pacific Islanders in the timeless present, saying, I am His and He is mine—now.

REFERENCES CONSULTED OR DISCUSSED

Manuscripts, Journals, and Correspondence

Fison, Lorimer. n.d. Tonga Note Book. Unpublished manuscript.
———. 1871. Vosa Vakaviti [The Fijian Judged by His Own Words]. Unpublished manuscript.
Hunt, John. 1846. Correspondence to London Committee. Wesleyan Magazine.
———. n.d. Journals of John Hunt. Methodist Overseas Mission.
Lyth, Richard Bursdall. n.d. Journals and note books of Richard Bursdall Lyth. Mitchell Library, Sydney.
Tippett, Alan R. n.d. Press cuttings and magazine articles on nativistic movements, etc. Writer's own scrapbook.
Williams, Thomas. n.d. Journals of Thomas Williams. Mitchell Library, Sydney.

Material from Archives of the Methodist Church in Fiji

Annual Reports:
    Bau Circuit. 1854, 1855, 1883.
    Bua Circuit. 1883.
    Lau Circuit. 1883.
    Nadi Circuit. 1850, 1851.
    Viwa Circuit. 1845, 1846, 1847.
Bua Circuit teachers' meetings minutes. n.d.
Fiji District Miscellaneous Resolutions Book. 1854–67.
Minutes of District Meetings. 1876.

Editions of Fijian Hymnbooks and Catechisms Used

Ai Vola ni Meke e na Vosa Vaka Viti. 1877. Sydney: Cook.
Ai Vola ni Sere ni Lotu Wesele e Viti. 1913. London.
Ai Vola ni Sere ni Lotu Wesele e Viti. 1936. London: M. M. Press.
Nai Vola ni Sere ni Lotu Wesele e Viti, vata kei na Taro kei nai Vakarau e so. 1938. Sydney: Epworth.

Editions of Fijian Bible Used

London, 1864. Hazlewood. Revised by Calvert (Genesis–Esther) and Lyth (Job–Malachi).
London, 1902. Langham and Heighway's revision.

Editions of Fijian New Testament Used

Viwa, 1847. Hunt.
London, 1867. Calvert's revision.
London, 1879. Calvert's revision.
London, 1899. Langham and Heighway's revision.
London, 1901. Edition with references.
London, 1947. Lelean's revision.

Vernacular Works Cited or Used

Bulicokocoko, S. T. U. n.d. *Fijian Idioms, Colloquialisms, Customs.* Colony of Fiji: Education Department.
Dreketirua, Opetaia. n.d. *Ai Vola Tetegei.* 2 vols. Unpublished manuscript.
Heighway, W. A. n.d. Manuscripts of Hymns, *Mekes*, etc. Unpublished manuscript.
Hunt, John, and James Calvert. 1908. *A Vakatusa ni Lotu.* London.
Moore, William, trans. 1867. *Ai Tukutuku kei Vulagi Lako.* Originally published as John Bunyan, *Pilgrim's Progress.*
Raiwalui, Anare K. 1954. *Nai Vosavosa Vakaviti e So.* Melbourne: Oxford University Press.
Rokowaqa, Epeli. n.d. *A Tukutuku kei Viti.* Suva, Fiji.
Seru, Paula. n.d. *Cabe ni Lotu ki Kadavu.* Unpublished manuscript.

General Works Consulted

Andrews, C. F. 1912. *The Renaissance in India.* London: Student Volunteer Missionary Union.
Apocrypha, The.
Barclay, William. 1955. *A New Testament Word Book.* London: S.C.M.
Baxter, Richard. 1950. *The Reformed Pastor.* London: Epworth.
Benedict, Ruth. 1946. *Patterns of Culture.* New York: New American Library.
———. 1949. Anthropology and the abnormal. In *Personal Character and Cultural Milieu,* ed. D. G. Haring. Syracuse: Syracuse University Press.
Bowman, J. W. 1945. *The Intention of Jesus.* London: S.C.M.
Brewster, Adolph B. 1922. *The Hill Tribes of Fiji.* London: Seeley, Service & Co.
Bromilow, W. 1904. *Vocabulary of English Words with their Equivalents in Dobuan, Fijian and Samoan, with a short Dobuan Grammar.* Geelong, Australia: H. Thacker.
Bullinger, Ethelbert W. 1924. *Critical Lexicon and Concordance of the English and Greek New Testament.* London: Longmans Green.
Calvert, James. 1860. *Fiji and the Fijians.* Vol. 2, *Mission History.* London: Alexander Heylin

Capell, A. 1941. *A New Fijian Dictionary*. Government of Fiji.
Childe, Gordon. 1954. *What Happened in History*. London: Pelican Books.
Childs, S. H. 1943. *A Life of Holiness*. London: Sheldon Press.
Churchward, C. Maxwell. 1941. *A New Fijian Grammar*. Government of Fiji.
Davies, W. H. 1925. *W. H. Davies*. London: Benn.
Dewar, Lindsay. 1949. *An Outline of New Testament Ethics*. London: Hodder & Stoughton.
Durell, J. C. V. 1910. *The Self Revelation of Our Lord*. Edinburgh: T. & T. Clark.
Edwards, Maldwin Lloyd. 1951. *The Methodist Ecumenical Conference, Oxford, 1951*. London: Epworth.
Erskine, John E. 1853. *Journal of a Cruise Among the Islands of The Western Pacific*. London: John Murray.
Fison, Lorimer. 1903. *Land Tenure in Fiji*. Suva, Fiji: Government of Fiji.
Hayden, Howard. 1954. *Moturiki: A Pilot Project in Community Development*. Sydney: Oxford University Press.
Hazlewood, David. 1850. *A Feejeean and English Dictionary*. Vewa, Fiji.
———. 1872a. *A Fijian and English and an English and Fijian Dictionary*. London: Sampson Low.
———. 1872b. *Grammar of the Fijian Language*. London: Sampson Low.
Heighway family, eds. 1932. *Not as Men Build*. Sydney: Methodist W.A.O.M.
Hodges, H. A. 1949. *Christianity and the Modern World View*. London: S. C. M.
Horton, Walter M. 1942. *Our Eternal Contemporary*. London: Harper & Brothers.
James, E. O. 1940. *The Social Function of Religion*. London: Hodder & Stoughton.
Kahn, Robert I. 1956. Kodesh, Mishpat and Chesed: A Philological Approach to Some Attributes of God. In *Religion and Life*. Abingdon.
Kendall, Henry. 1869. *Leaves from Australian Forests*. Melbourne: George Robertson.
Kipling, Rudyard. 1896. *The Seven Seas*. New York: D. Appleton.
Kluckhohn, Clyde. 1949. *Mirror for Man*. New York: McGraw.
Leakey, L. S. B. 1953. *Mau Mau and the Kikuyu*. London: Methuen.
Lightfoot, J. B. 1913. *St. Paul's Epistle to the Philippians*. London: Macmillan.
Mariner, William, and John Martin. 1820. *An Account of the Natives of the Tonga Islands*. Boston: C. Ewer.
Martin, John, ed. 1817. *An Account of the Natives of the Tonga Islands*. 2 vols. London: J. Murray.
Melville, Herman. 1892. *Moby Dick*. Boston: Page.
Moore, Arthur J. 1951. The Methodist Tradition in the United States. In *Proceedings of the 8th Ecumenical Methodist Conference*. Oxford.
Nettleton, Joseph. 1906. *John Hunt: Pioneer, Missionary and Saint*. London: C. H. Kelly.
Parrinder, G. 1946. Worship in Protestant Missions. *International Review of Missions* 35: 187–93.
Rattenbury, Harold B., and David Hill. 1949. *Friend of China*. London: Epworth.

Roth, George K. 1953. *Fijian Way of Life.* Melbourne: Oxford University Press.

Sapir, Edward. *Language.* 1949. New York: Harcourt Brace.

Scott, Anderson. 1942. *New Testament Ethics.* Cambridge: Cambridge University Press.

Smith, C. Ryder. 1946. *The Bible Doctrine of Salvation.* London: Epworth.

Snaith, Norman H. 1944. *The Distinctive Ideas of the Old Testament.* London: Epworth.

Sutherland, W. 1910. The *Tuka* Religion. *Transactions of the Fijian Society, 1908-10*: 51-57.

Thomas, Winburn T. 1957. Theological Training in Indonesia. *British Weekly*, 31 October.

Thompson, B. 1903. *The Fijians: A Study in the Decay of Custom.* London: W. H. Heinemann.

Tippett, Alan R. 1944. The Snake in Early Fijian Belief. *Transactions and Proceedings of the Fiji Society of Science and Industry* 2: 279-96.

———. 1954a. *Cakobau Papers.* Suva, Fiji: Methodist Mission. Multigraphed.

———. 1954b. An Interesting Aspect of Sound, Movement and Decay in the Fijian Language. *Oceania* 24: 229-33.

———. 1956a. Methodism in the South West Pacific. In *Proceedings of the 9th World Methodist Conference, Lake Junaluska.* Methodist Publishing House.

———. 1956b. *The Nineteenth-century Labour Trade in the South West Pacific.* MA thesis, American University.

———. 1967. *Solomon Islands Christianity.* London: Lutterworth.

———. 1968. *Fijian Material Culture.* Honolulu: Bishop Museum Press.

———. 1970. *Church Growth and the Word of God.* Grand Rapids: William B. Eerdmans.

———. 1971. *People Movements in Southern Polynesia.* Chicago: Moody Press.

———. 1973. *Verdict Theology in Missionary Theory.* Pasadena: William Carey Library.

Trench, R. C. 1865. *Synonyms of the New Testament.* London: Macmillan.

Waterhouse, Joseph. 1866. *The King and People of Fiji.* London: Wesleyan Conference Office.

Webster, W. M., and W. Wilkinson. 1855. *The Greek Testament*, 2 vols. London: J. Parker & Sons.

Welch, Adam C. 1953. *Prophet and Priest in Old Israel.* Oxford: Basil Blackwell.

Wiant, Bliss. 1946. Oecumenical Hymnology in China. *International Review of Missions* 35: 428-34.

Williams, Thomas. 1860. *Fiji and the Fijians.* Vol. 1, *The Islands and Their Inhabitants.* London: Alexander Heylen.

———, and James Calvert. 1884. *Fiji and the Fijians.* 2 vols. London: C. H. Kelly.

Winslow, J. C. 1923. *Narayan Vaman Tilak: The Christian Poet of Maharashtra.* Calcutta: Association Press.

the CHRISTIAN: FIJI 1835-67

THE MISSIOLOGY OF ALAN R. TIPPETT SERIES
DOUG PRIEST, SERIES EDITOR
DOUG PRIEST, EDITOR

CONTENTS

The Christian: Fiji 1835-67

Foreword 161
Preface 165

PART ONE

CHAPTER 1 Christians—Nominal and Otherwise 173
CHAPTER 2 Ratu Cakobau's Conversion 177
CHAPTER 3 The God of Battles 187
CHAPTER 4 The Clash of Cultures 197
CHAPTER 5 Cakobau Himself, His Kingdom, and His House 209

PART TWO

CHAPTER 6 The Fijian Evangelical 219
CHAPTER 7 His Simple Faith 223
CHAPTER 8 Revivals—Viwa, Ono, Kadavu 239
CHAPTER 9 The Christian under Persecution 253
CHAPTER 10 Comparative Merits of Factors Examined 257
Key to Abbreviations 265
References Cited 267
Index 277

FOREWORD

In 1954 the Methodist Church in Fiji was preparing to celebrate a significant moment. One hundred years earlier Ratu Cakobau, a Fijian chief of considerable influence and power and notorious for the violence and cannibalism of his community, had converted to Christianity. It was being said that the conversion of this man and other chiefs had been the reason why Fijians had chosen to become Christian—loyalty to their chiefs and political convenience. Alan Tippett challenged this understanding. In his view, this question had been "somewhat superficially evaluated by historians and anthropologists." For some years he had been studying this question. Why had Fijians chosen to become Christians? What did Christianity mean to them?

By the time Alan Tippett had completed this manuscript, he had lived and worked in Fiji for thirteen years, having arrived there in 1941. He was immersed in the life of the Methodist Church in Fiji as missionary, circuit minister, and teacher. He had learned to speak and read the Fijian language and taken great interest in Fijian history and culture. All these factors contributed to his thinking as he asked himself: Why is there a Christian church in Fiji in the twentieth century? Was it simply the result of political expediency, or a response to a military victory, as some writers suggested?

He began his work by thinking as a historian, gathering evidence from as many primary sources as possible, both from his own growing collection of documents and from relevant archives and libraries. Some of this material was from private sources and not available to many other historians. The writings of those contemporary with the earliest years of mission contact in Fiji suggested that there were many conversions prior to the conversion of Ratu Cakobau, conversions that were not following his example but risking his wrath. The written evidence also suggested that the Christianisation of Fiji had been very uneven, with the result that some regions remained heathen long after the conversions of chiefs or the outcomes of major battles for local power. As he read material from private journals and letters as well as secular and religious publications, he concluded that the answers to his questions were far more complex than secular writers suggested.

As well as thinking as a historian, Tippett also thought as a linguist. His capacity to read and translate from the Fijian language gave him access to documents that were closed to most historians, and he used this well. It also made possible some significant interviews to collect oral history from elderly Fijians with long memories.

Added to this, he thought as a statistician. Irritated by sweeping statements based on hearsay and preconceptions, Tippett took the time and trouble to study in detail the church reports over the years that recorded numbers of church attenders as well as church members. Church attenders may well have been following the lead of the local chief with little interest or commitment to Christian faith. Those who became church members had been through a demanding and extended period of preparation before being admitted to the privileges and responsibilities of membership. Tippett studied this evidence and made his analysis of the timing, location, and numbers of Christian converts. He concluded that the largest influx of new Fijian converts did not coincide with either the conversion of a chief or a decisive battle for political and social power. Others had not explored this source of information.

Alan Tippett also thought as an anthropologist. He had lived long enough in Fiji to be familiar with the local culture and worldview. The independence and agency of the Fijian people was clear to him, and he rejected the notion that missionaries could force their beliefs on others. Traditionally, Fijians from time to time had chosen to abandon a god who was deemed to have become impotent in favour of another. Understanding their social framework and the ways they incorporated or rejected aspects of their traditional world into a Christian life was part of Tippett's approach to his task.

The political implications of any movement toward Christianity by the Fijian people were also part of Tippett's thinking and analysis. It was clear to him that, in common with many other societies, there were political and social reasons why people might choose to attend Christian worship. Having been the Methodist minister in both the island of Bau, dominated by the chief, and in the growing town of Suva, he observed the differences between the "chiefly church of Bau" and the "democratic church of Suva." Two very different contexts, he noted, but while both could be accommodated within Methodism, each context presented very different political challenges.

Tippett offered a prophetic voice as he considered the importance of Ratu Cakobau. It seemed to him, writing in 1954, that the key significance of the conversion of Cakobau to Christianity was not so much that he had influenced large numbers of Fijians to follow his example. More importantly, he had "welded together the church and the chiefly system." As Tippett foresaw, this was to shape the nature of the Methodist Church into the future. Some of the contemporary challenges to the contemporary Methodist Church in Fiji in the twenty-first century can be traced to this welding together.

By the time Tippett was writing this work, he had been educating Fijians in the Bible School at Davuilevu for a number of years. It was natural for him to think as a teacher, posing questions, providing evidence and possible conclusions, and offering summaries at the end of each section.

Most importantly, Alan Tippett brought to this work his thinking as a Christian believer and a Methodist churchman. In his own experience he had observed the stages through which many passed. First there was a change from a belief in another way of thinking to conversion to Christianity as a system, which would include attendance at worship. Later, after further instruction, some people moved to a deeper spiritual experience which led on to formal membership of the church, with the associated rights and responsibilities. Tippett observed that while, for some, their Christianity was superficial, influenced by the political and social forces of their day, for others it was a profound and life-changing experience.

In the second part of this book, Tippett moves away from his discussion of the political, military, and secular influences on Fijian Methodism where he challenges the conclusions of other historians and anthropologists. Bringing out new material, gathered from primary sources and often translated from the original Fijian language, he writes from the heart of the spiritual experience of the earliest converts and preachers, their faith, and religious revivals. From this he concludes that the revivals in Fiji had much in common with similar religious experiences in Great Britain and North America a century earlier. This evidence persuaded him that the reason why there was still a Methodist Church in Fiji in the twentieth century was not because of the power of the chiefs, or because of the evident potency of the mighty "God of Battles," but because a spiritual force and faith had transformed a society. The witness of former cannibal chiefs, who now showed mercy to those in their power instead of consigning them to cannibal ovens, spoke more strongly than any political argument. This was, Tippett believed, from God.

The approach which Alan Tippett took in preparing this early manuscript set a pattern for his later work. It was thorough, well researched, carefully thought through, and meticulously documented, using all his skills to gather the evidence as a historian, theologian, anthropologist, and Christian thinker to present a scholarly monograph. While acknowledging the reality of the points made by secular historians—the influence of political and military power to direct followers toward Christianity as a system—he concluded, on the evidence, that "the Methodist struggle for Fiji was fought and won on a spiritual plane." In later years Tippett would become known internationally as a Christian scholar and educator who would influence the thinking of many. Many other books would be written by him on issues of mission. His private collection of books, journals, and manuscripts would continue to grow until it became an exceptional collection to be shared with others. For the rest of his life he would continue to study, be curious, think deeply about evidence, challenge ideas, and develop his skills in the fields of church history, anthropology, theology, and missiology. He would always struggle to control his fascination with interesting sidetracks, as so many varied ideas and disciplines caught his attention. From time to time he would speak a prophetic word that was wisdom to those who heard. He would be a trusted mentor for many. The seeds of all this can be found in *The Christian: Fiji 1835–67*.

After the death of Alan Tippett on 16 September 1988 a memorial minute was recorded at the meeting of the World Mission Committee of Uniting Church in Australia on 4 November 1988. This national body was the successor of the Methodist Church in Australia that had first sent Alan Tippett to Fiji as a missionary. The minute outlined his long life and ministry, his awards, publications, and academic achievements with his "great accomplished and faithful service of the gospel."

Fittingly, the memorial minute included an extended quotation from Tippett's final writing shortly before his death. In an "Afterthought and Declaration" added to an article on the new shape of syncretism in postcolonial mission and ministry, he reflected on what he had learned over many years and what he wanted to say to those who followed. The primary word that he wanted to share was of the centrality of the gospel. Listing a series of accounts of experiences and writings from the Old and New Testament, he wrote, "I find that biblical history and revelations have always spoken to those human situations and show up to us of other eras and cultures just what is continually at stake." Studying the evidence, as he had always done, he concluded, "The spiritual cohesion between these portions of scripture is so strong that I must say with Paul 'Woe is me if I preach not the gospel.' I must stand by the Book as I stand by the Lord himself."

Margaret Reeson
Church Historian
Canberra, Australian Capital Territory
August 2014

PREFACE

This study purports to investigate the nature of religious experience among the early Fijian Christians (i.e., in the foundation period of the history of the church in Fiji). It does not deal with the experience of the white missionaries except insofar as they influenced or were influenced by the native Christians. For the purpose of this study the term "Fijian" has been extended to include also those Tongans who had become more or less permanent residents of Fiji, and in particular the early Tongan teachers—like Bulu, Vea, and Havea—from whose writings I have drawn considerably in my evidence.

The need for such a study as this becomes apparent when one realises that most of the historians who have written on the subject have indicated two main causes only for the spread of Christianity in Fiji in so short a space of time.

1. The inevitable result of the conversion of a powerful chief was the conversion of his tribe.
2. Victory in war compelled the defeated party to acknowledge that Jehovah was indeed the God of Battles.

Now any thoughtful person dwelling for a moment on those will see that, were there no other or no deeper causes, there could only have been a political and militaristic church as a result, nor would it explain the sudden displays of mercy by the newly converted.

In reality, the acceptance of these two reasons creates far more problems both for the missionary-minded thinker and for the historian than it solves. Hence this investigation. One must admit, of course, however unpleasant, that these were two reasons for the rapid increase of attention given to Christianity at the time. The term *Ai Valu ni Lotu* (Wars of Religion) is still met in some parts, but as to what this sort of conversion meant, the reader is referred to a most important statement by missionary Horsley, quoted in the text. As one studies the documents he comes, time after time, to the activities of men like Butuki, Mateinaniu, Varani, Raitono, and dozens of other Fijians like them, and feels at once that he is in possession of pieces of a jigsaw that just do not fit the scene given us by historians up to this date.

Therefore the whole matter comes in for review, and we set out to discover, if we can, the relative importance of these causes of "following the chief," of "victory in war," and whether or not there was a "genuine religious experience" that played a part in the building of the native church. If so, then just what kind of an experience was it—a sort of "rational conviction" or a "religious enthusiasm"? What was the extent of each of these factors as causes for the rapid spread of Christianity in Fiji? Such a discovery should give us a clue to the nature of the early Fijian church.

The publication of this study is in connection with the celebration of the centenary of the conversion of Ratu Cakobau, one of the events commonly stated as the cause of Fiji's acceptance of Christianity. That was 30 April 1854. This event certainly set a seal upon the Methodist Church in Fiji, but just exactly what that seal was, we shall shortly investigate.

I have called the study—*The Christian: Fiji 1835-67.* Why 1835? Why 1867?

1835 is really the official year for the beginning of Christianity in Fiji. I mean by that the year the full organisation of the home church was brought to bear on the group, its finances, its resources for printing and administering the means of grace. I mean the presentation of the case for Christianity in the chiefly way and by means of correct introduction by the king of Tonga to the king of Lau, in the traditional way (Williams and Calvert 1884, 230; Hunt 1846, 75). 1835 is the official beginning.

But that statement needs qualification, for there were Christian evangelists in Fiji before this. Gill's survey of Pacific missions, a century ago, stated the Wesleyans came to Fiji in 1829 (Gill 1856, 305). It is quite possible that Wesleyan missionaries did call at Fiji in that year, but they did not establish a mission, although within a very short time from that date they were making preparations, and men sent to Tonga were designated for Fiji but were first to get the "feel" of things in Tonga.[1] The Tahiti teachers who went to Oneata were brought to Fiji by Takai (Williams and Calvert 1884, 231), the first Fijian I know to have become a Christian. He had to fight to get them from the London Missionary Society, who had agreed with the Wesleyans to zone these seas, and Williams agreed on the understanding that the Wesleyans should take over the work.[2] But though they gave a good demonstration of practical Christianity, they made no attempt to use the language for preaching and praying, and Takai was disappointed (Hunt 1846, 82-83). Takai had to take them from Lakeba to his own island to protect them (Williams and Calvert 1884, 230), and it was Takai who pressed for a Fijian teacher as soon as Cross and Cargill arrived.[3] Takai was the driver—for more than five years before the mission began. He himself was a bit of a globetrotter and had been converted in Tonga (Hunt 1846, 84), like Mateinaniu

---

1   British Conference designated two for Fiji, sent to Tonga 1832. See also *Missionary Register*, March 1834, 121.
2   Williams, *Missionary Experiences*, 75.
3   Journal of Cross, 12 February 1836 (Hunt 1846, 82).

(Cargill 1841, 110–12; Williams and Calvert 1884, 232) and Butuki,[4] also Fijians. Having made that qualification of preliminary work done, the official start of the mission is 1835.

The year 1867 is a suitable date for the termination of this study. There is so much evidence that there has to be a date fixed, and 1867 is, I think, about the best. It allows us to arrive at a fairly advanced stage of the nominal conversion of the coastal peoples of Fiji. It also introduces us to the mission to the interior, which was creating a great deal of interest in the sixties and began with a flourish under Thomas Baker and, for him at least, came to a sudden and tragic end in that year, 1867. This thoroughly awakened the home church, which had become complacent in thinking Fiji was converted, to the fact that Baker, Fison, Langham, and Carey had been crying out for some years of the needs of the interior.[5] In those days also we find ourselves in the midst of the earliest attempts at local constitutional government, forced upon them by Britain's adamant foreign policy and refusal to accept the offer of Cession. The year 1867 also gives us a good clear field of more than a decade from the Battle of Kaba in which to observe the statistics and obtain therefore some idea of the numerical effects of the battle. Thus we test the claims of the earlier historians. Beyond all this, 1867 is as late as we can safely go prior to that heavy infiltration of white men—planters, traders, fugitives from justice (a mixed assembly of very good and very bad)—who so complicated life that the issues I wish to evaluate are far too difficult to untangle. In many ways, then, 1867 marks the end of a period.

Sources

As much as possible I have endeavoured to keep myself out of the picture. We are studying the native Christian. What I think about the form of their faith, or their theology, or their religious enthusiasm, does not really matter, as long as I can give a true picture of what they believed and thought and did. I have no doubt that the reader may not always react to these things as I have. I leave the reader to form one's own opinions. My work then has been mainly the assembling of selected material, the arrangement of it, and here and there a simple confirmation that such and such a thing continues to be so to this day as I have found myself.

The study is almost entirely prepared from primary sources, either published at the time, or original manuscripts, of which I have been through some thousands. Where secondary sources are used these are mostly volumes from which extensive primary material is available in the quotations. On furlough recently I examined material in public and private libraries in New South Wales, Victoria, South Australia, and Tasmania, but time was against me. But I have drawn from the Mitchell Library (Sydney), Melbourne Public Library, and that of the Patterson Street Methodist Church in Launceston, for some important

---

4 Journal of Lyth (2:112).
5 *Wesleyan Missionary Notices.* (Aust.) correspondence 1865.

statements made in this monograph—original manuscripts in the former and original publications in the other two. To these institutions I am deeply indebted. I also thank the families of several retired missionaries who have helped me. Apart from these all my other source material is in the colony of Fiji.

The most valuable source of all in this particular study is that terrific assemblage of material in the archives of the Methodist Mission in Fiji. I have been wading through this off and on for years. It includes annual reports from the circuits, school reports, baptismal registers, statistics, reports of committees, minutes of meetings, letter books, and endless bundles of correspondence inwards, and other documents. Most of the official reports handled at Bishopsgate by Henderson are here also, but these go on and are not terminated in the mid-1950s. There is, of course, a great deal of repetition in them, but studying these over the years has given me a sort of background that has become more and more clear as I have proceeded. This picture I have tried to give in this monograph, and though I state many references to specific items in my text, the overall picture is that of the archives as a whole.

Therefore, whenever I have read statements like this—"For more than ten years there were few converts. When, however, a few high chiefs were won over, progress was more rapid"[6]—I know that sooner or later this monograph will have to be given to the public.

Now the mission archival material has some gaps—flood, fire, and hurricane, no doubt, account for them. Fortunately I have been able to find in my own library a good deal of published primary material to fill most of those gaps. The missionaries of the period wrote long letters and reports and kept journals, and most of their material was published in the *Wesleyan Magazine* and the *Wesleyan Juvenile Offering*, and in the later period when this field came under the Church in Australia the *Wesleyan Missionary Notices* did the same thing. I have these fairly complete, and the few that are missing I have examined in Launceston. In addition to these my library contains a great many missionary letters, documents, journals, and newspaper cuttings spread out over the last century, and other similar material has been loaned to me from time to time for purposes of study. Any student using this script and studying the references will observe that quite a number are from unpublished sources in my private collection.

Whenever possible I have made use of nonmissionary sources like Seemann, Erskine, Wilkes, and others—mostly seamen and travellers—but the reader will see at once that the nature of the theme demands a heavy use of mission material.

Some of the original publications used freely are fundamental to the study. Of these I should refer to the following, in particular Calvert's *Fiji and the Fijians*. Calvert came in 1838 and left finally in 1865. He was a great collector of other men's notes. He quoted fully

---

6 Colonial Report of Fiji, 1951, 68.

and freely. In 1865 no white man knew more about Fiji than James Calvert. I use both his first and last editions. Waterhouse's *King and People of Fiji* (together with the Bau annual reports) cannot be done without for the study of the conversion of Cakobau and the events before and after. Rowe's *Life of John Hunt* is indispensable for the study of the Viwa revivals. It was compiled from Hunt's original documents, journals, and letters, and with access to Hunt's widow for any needed confirmations. It quotes freely. With it one should use the Hunt reports in the mission archives, and his published correspondence in the *Wesleyan Magazine* and his own publications. Nettleton's *John Hunt* also adds revival material not found elsewhere.[7]

Lawry, Young, Calvert, and others provide native testimonies given at love feasts. In any study of Fijian religious experience these are important.

The Baker, Langham, Carey, and Fison letters and reports in *Wesleyan Missionary Notices* (Australia) during the 1860s are extremely valuable historical material—both for the religious and secular historian—that as far as I know have been practically untapped. My use of them in this monograph has been mainly to establish the narrow confines of the Christian era a decade after Kaba.

In order to evaluate the peculiar revival experiences of Viwa, Lakeba, Ono, and Kadavu, it becomes necessary to relate them to similar phenomena in the outside world. I have therefore made heavy use of two entirely different types of sources—Tyerman's *Life and Times of Rev. John Wesley* in three volumes, and Knox's recent work, *Enthusiasm*. Both of these are rich in quotations and references to primary sources, and both writers were thorough in their examination of Wesley's own material. Other Wesley sources I have used sparingly. Their validity in this study is but for a single point—to establish whether or not there is a connection between the Wesleyan revival at home and those of Viwa and other places in Fiji.

In connection with the nature of the faith of the native Christians under persecution, it is difficult to say that one source is more important than another. Possibly in my references I have drawn more from Thomas Williams' Journal, a Mitchell Library manuscript, which we have in published form through the labour of Henderson. But I do refer to Margaret Cargill's *Memoirs* and to Fison's *Autobiography of Joeli Bulu*,[8] and one might well have used many other sources. One does not have to go far to find evidence of the persecution of the early Christians.

In connection with the actual experiences of the native agents and ordinary Christians, the testing of their faith in times of crisis, and for those most important (for this

---

7   One year after Tippett wrote the present volume, he completed his own biography of missionary John Hunt (2013a).—Ed.

8   Fison encouraged Joeli Bulu to write his autobiography (Fison 1873). It has been translated and annotated by Tippett and Kanailagi (2013b).—Ed.

study) deathbed statements of faith, my source, wherever possible, has been a native document. These comprise two types: (1) stories told and letters written by natives and translated into English by missionaries for publication (from the idiom they are manifestly translations, and usually it is so stated) as books, like *Old Sefanaia* and *Autobiography of Joeli Bulu* (Fison translations), or as short stories and letters in *Juvenile Missionary Offering* and other missionary publications; and (2) I have also a small assortment of original native manuscripts, and two of these are of considerable length. These are in Fijian and I have had to translate whatever I have quoted. For a study of native faith and experience these have, to me, become fundamental.

Such is the scope and nature of this monograph. I regret the impossibility of maintaining a single style of writing throughout, but that one part should be statistical and another psychological is the nature of the case.

The writing has involved me in a good deal of self-restraint, for it has not always been easy to go on without engaging in asides. Politics, for instance, persistently kept cropping up, for some of the missionaries and some of the Tongan teachers later did get tied up in local politics. But though they differed greatly among themselves in their political views (as in the church today), I feel their religious experiences were fundamentally characteristic. I hope that this little work will help the reader to clarify in his mind some of the issues that have been much misunderstood, especially regarding the nature of conversion among the early Fijians, and just what the effect of the conversion of a chief or a victory in war meant, and how far afield such influence would be felt, and whether or not there was a real spiritual factor in the conversion of Fiji.

No one will challenge the statement that the evangelistic attack on Fiji was an extremely dangerous venture from the start—it was dangerous for the missionary and dangerous for the Fijian who became involved before his chief, or the petty chief before his superior. Yet this happened—that is a fact which history cannot dodge. The venture called for brave spirits, men and women of faith from among the people. If we can discover the nature of that faith, we shall also discover the key to the conversion of Fiji.

These words of John Wesley to Alexander Mather in 1777 serve well to end this introduction: "Give me one hundred preachers who fear nothing but sin and desire nothing but God, and I care not a straw whether they be clergymen or laymen, such alone will shake the gates of hell and set up the Kingdom of God upon earth."[9]

Alan R. Tippett
Bau, Fiji
1954

---

9   Journal of Charles Wesley II (Carter 1851, 215).

PART ONE

1
CHRISTIANS—NOMINAL AND OTHERWISE

"The King of the Cannibal Isles," as they used to call Ratu Cakobau, of Bau, the chiefly kingdom of the Fijian Group, made history when, on 30 April 1854, he "bent the knee to Jehovah" (AR Bau Circuit 1854). "Bending the knee" was the traditional phrase for a public act by means of which the person witnessed to all that he was rejecting his heathenism and placing himself under Christian instruction. This particular event is being remembered this year—its centenary. Meantime it raises the whole question of the nature of conversion in those days in Fiji, a matter which has been somewhat superficially evaluated by historians and anthropologists and, for the sake of future study, ought to be corrected.

The remarkable rapidity of the conversion of Fiji may be judged by a simple statement of statistics, comparing Fiji, for example, with Tahiti, where a larger team of missionaries had been placed and concentrated on a single station where their lot was comparatively easy, when compared with conditions at Rewa, Nadi, and Somosomo in Fiji. A decade and a half passed and there had not been a single convert (Ellis 1830, 1:183, 185). In less than the same period of time in Fiji, and in the face of much more hostile opposition and greater linguistic difficulties, there were some remarkable results achieved—five mission stations; 37 churches and 23 other preaching places where regular worship was conducted; almost 4,000 under systematic religious instruction (and over 1,700 of them full members); about 50 day schools and roughly 2,000 attending, 38 paid catechists, and 117 unpaid assistant teachers; and 68 local preachers, tested and approved.[10] This represents a more or less well-organised Christian community in action—and we must admit, a rapid piece of Christian conquest.

Now I deliberately chose to quote the statistics of that particular year so that I could add this fact—no really big chief had yet "bent the knee." Tui Nayau was the first big chief to do this, and that was in 1849,[11] still half a decade before the decision of Cakobau to follow. It is important that we should note the existence of this organised Christian community before the conversion of a big chief, because it is evidence against the claim that Fijians would not become Christian before their chiefs. Against persecution of their chiefs,

---
10   1848 figures from Lawry and Hoole (1850, 109).
11   19 October (Williams and Calvert 1884, 331).

indeed, had this happened.[12] True, there were Tongans in these statistics I have quoted, but they were not enough to affect the truth of my contention.

The Rev. Robert Young, special commissioner from the British Conference, sent to the Pacific to examine the state of affairs in the colonies and the islands, to ascertain whether or not they could safely be constituted a separate conference, visited Bau before the conversion of Cakobau. He described it as "the deepest hell on earth" to a British audience upon his return to England.[13] Later, before terminating the same address, he stated that there was another side to the picture: "We have 3000 of the people in church fellowship, 4000 in the schools, and 6000 regular attendants on the ministry."[14] Again, I have a reason for quoting those particular figures, which as I have said were pre-Cakobau conversion. Yet there are many who would have us believe that the Fijian church began with and exists only because of the conversion of Ratu Cakobau. Let it be noted rather that this six thousand worshipped in spite of Ratu Cakobau, and the figure returns to my mind whenever I hear the phrase *Na Lotu nei Ratu Cakobau* (The Church of Ratu Cakobau). There are, of course, many parts of Fiji where that phrase is never heard. Even within Bau itself there were many attending worship prior to the conversion of Cakobau (AR Bau Circuit 1854; AR Viwa Circuit 1853), just as there were twenty-five hundred in Tui Nayau's domains prior to his conversion,[15] and one thousand in Vanua Levu before Tui Bua joined them.[16] So the point should not be missed that whatever happened after the conversion of a really big chief, there were many Fijians who had the courage of their convictions, despite the price to be paid, and quite irrespective of the religion of the chief. Some people have stated that this was disloyalty. Well, Cakobau did not find this to be so, neither with individuals nor with villages. He threw many tests on the loyalty of Varani, and proved his loyalty time after time,[17] and the Christians at Koro, having special responsibilities to Cakobau, were sorely tried, but Cakobau was forced to admit he could better trust them than his heathen subjects there. Loyalty could be proved either in war or labour (Williams and Calvert 1884, 316). Against the opposition of Chief Wetasau, the people of Yadrana persisted with their Christianity, saying their new religion would not affect their loyalty or the amount of their tribute. This cause in Koro, by the way, had been under a Christian teacher four years before the conversion of Cakobau (AR Viwa Circuit 1850, 1851), and Christian teachers were also established at other Lomaiviti islands in Bau's domain—Gau and Batiki (AR Viwa Circuit 1853). As a matter of fact a list of the small Christian causes within Cakobau's own

---

12 One priest and few friends only remained heathen (Williams and Calvert 1884, 331).
13 In address at 1854 annual meeting of Wesleyan Missionary Society, WM, 1854, 2:755.
14 Ibid., 756.
15 Lawry and Hoole (1850, 109) show 2,500 by 1848.
16 Ra Masima *lotu*-ed August 1855. Over one thousand at worship—stated by Malvern, letter quoted (Williams and Calvert 1884, 534)—an increase of four hundred for year.
17 Varani's peace efforts in Vanua Levu, death in Ovalau, etc. Viwa loyalty specially mentioned in AR Viwa Circuit 1851.

realm but prior to his conversion is interesting—Namata, Kaba, Gau, Batiki, Kiuva, Nairai, and Koro (ibid.; AR Bau Circuit 1854). Kaba and the last three were long-standing causes (AR Viwa Circuit 1850–53).

The same test might be applied in the domains of Tui Nayau, where, for instance, nine years before his conversion the island of Oneata was half Christian and where Christianity had made such an impact in Lakeba itself that cannibalism there was already extinct (Wilkies 1944, 233). That was in 1840.

Nine months prior to the conversion of Cakobau, the Tongan preacher Joeli Bulu wrote to the London Committee urging them to send more missionaries and describing events that had taken place some time before. "The chiefs were not wishful to *lotu*," he wrote, "but some of the people did, and lived as Christians."[18] The letter also shows something of the wide distribution of Christian enterprise before Ratu Cakobau's conversion.

---

18   Bulu to LC, 9 June 1853, from Lakeba, WM, 1855, 2:1149.

2

RATU CAKOBAU'S CONVERSION

Having begun by establishing the existence of a live Christian cause beforehand, let us now examine this great event, the conversion of a great heathen chief, and its effect. Cakobau was as great in his Christianity later as he had been in his heathenism—a moulder of events. His conversion certainly did make an impact on the church and on Bau.

Cakobau's conversion did mean that many followed him into the church—that was inevitable, and it is undeniable. It is true that after the conversion of any paramount chief this happened—many, no doubt, because he was their chief, and they would be as diligent as he was, no more and no less, and there would be little appreciation on their part of the spiritual significance of their action. Its meaning would not go beyond a knowledge that for them at least, cannibalism, widow strangling, and such customs which robbed human life of value had come to an end. There is not a shadow of doubt that thousands got thus far and no farther. Time after time in their letters and reports the missionaries bemoan this fact.[19]

Yet in one very real sense it was a conversion. They left their gods and became attenders at worship, sang hymns, bowed in prayer, heard the reading of the Scriptures, and listened to a sermon. They had, in fact, got where many of our own have got.

Whatever motive lay behind that decision (and the motives recorded are legion), it was for each one of them an intelligent act. Yet it was far from what we usually think of as conversion. In the general thought of Bau that day, it was a political not a personal act. It was a sober, uniform performance and quite devoid of the customary tension and excitement associated with individuals making so great a decision, and knowing full well that the club may be awaiting them at the door on account of it. This difference is a fact based on the documents. Calvert described it thus (and he was there):

> We assembled in the large Stranger's House. The chief was preceded by his grey-headed priest, with a long beard. His children stood, with many others, in the front; his wives, sisters and chief women, not a few, and other females on the right hand: he and the male attendants were on the left. All were dressed, many

---

[19] See Annual Reports and letters in *WM*.

of them in Tonga cloth. They were orderly, serious and attentive, not like new converts. About three hundred assembled.[20]

Now that paragraph introduces a number of interesting points, which throw some light on the nature of this conversion. Firstly, there is the presence of the priest—still, be it noted, in his own prominent position. Secondly, the very law and order of everything indicates a state occasion rather than a personal event—"not like new converts," adds Calvert. Then we note Cakobau still had his "wives" (plural). Waterhouse described it: "The priest of his household gods, and all his wives (about fifty)."[21]

A week later some three hundred more embraced Christianity,[22] and the process went on week after week until, about the end of June (AR Bau Circuit 1854), roughly a thousand had come over, and after thirteen weeks some 1,300 had become Christian.[23] These we may feel were directly or indirectly converts because of the conversion of the chief. Some were the timid people who hesitated to do it before; others saw it as a political event; his family would naturally follow the father, and quite a big family it appears to have been. I say "indirectly" because they did not all come over at once; it went on for three months, right under the eye of the chief, and that some took three months to take the step indicates a strong unwillingness to do so. Furthermore there were other events in the interim, may I say, like the plagues of Egypt.

On 8 May and thereafter there had been some iconoclasm. Temples were despoiled of their ornaments, sacred objects removed or destroyed, and the sacred grove was felled. That this was inspired by Waterhouse, as has been suggested, I am not prepared to admit, but there is no doubt about his approval of it. His own correspondence shows that.[24] It must be remembered that the destruction of the sacred ironwood groves had been a precedent set by Viwa, and the cause at Viwa had prospered tremendously after that event, which had been entirely the inspiration of Namosimalua the chief, whose sacred grove it was. He had deliberately done it to prove his loss of faith in his old gods—a rational conversion was Namosimalua's, if anyone's was (Rowe 1860, 73).

If there was evidence that Tongan teachers were in Bau at the time, one might have suspected them, but the teachers are mentioned impersonally, and Viwa teachers would have been equally capable of it. Anyway the new converts were not at all confident in their iconoclasm, and one of the teachers sought Jehovah's protection for them as they cut down the trees. This does strongly suggest that the teachers or missionaries had placed some such test of faith upon them. There were ancient myths about those famous trees, of how once before they had been felled in an act of sacrilege, to be found growing again in their

---

20 Calvert to LC, 20 May 1854, from Viwa, WM, 1855, 1:89.
21 Waterhouse to LC, 1 June 1854, from Bau, WM, 1855, 1:464.
22 Ibid., 465.
23 Report, Waterhouse to LC, 18 August 1854, ibid.
24 Waterhouse to LC, 1 June 1854, WM, 1855, 1:465.

places in the morning. I myself have seen groves of sacred *vesi* trees, of which the identical tales are told. I quote the Waterhouse passage for the reader to form one's own judgement:

> 9th.—An attack was made upon a sacred forest in our vicinity. The carpenters were conveyed by water to the spot. Solemnly bowing before the Great Creator, one of the teachers prayed aloud, and besought him to prevent any evil from coming to them while they attacked "Satan's forest." They felled some of the monster ironwood trees, which have been considered sacred for ages. Some of the poor carpenters trembled very much, lest an evil spirit should kill them. (Not very certain of their new faith, that is apparent.)[25]

The story, however, savours more of the spread of the gospel in Polynesia than in Fiji, for apparently iconoclasm was there the accepted thing, and one reads of great public burnings of idols (Ellis 1830, 1:210–14), and missionary books still exist with plates of these events—idol burning with missionaries as spectators.[26] But in Fiji this was not the rule. With the exception of Waterhouse, all the missionaries were agreed that there were no idols in Fiji (Waterhouse 1866, 390), and I believe they were right, but Waterhouse says otherwise. To the Fijian a deity would appear in or speak through some "shrine," which might be animate or inanimate. The destruction of a shrine did not destroy the god, whose punishment could still fall upon the person who desecrated his sacred object. Williams says,

> Idolatry, in the strict sense of the term, he seems never to have known; for he makes no attempt to fashion material representations of his gods, or to pay actual worship to heavenly bodies, the elements or natural objects. It is extremely doubtful whether the reverence with which some things such as certain clubs and stones, have been regarded, had in it anything of religious homage.
> (Williams and Calvert 1884, 183)

My own research would show these objects to be charged with *mana* through having been shrines of the deity, or places of revelation, or some such thing at some time. Seemann specifically states he saw no idols, and he travelled about a good deal and visited many temples (1862, 154). Erskine also noted, "The Fijians are said not to worship idols" (1853, 252). Waterhouse disagreed.

However, whether the destruction of an idol or the desecration of a sacred object—property of a deity—its prospects were terrifying enough, and when such objects were destroyed with no apparent harm falling upon the perpetrators of the iconoclasm, they could well be led to think either that their gods had deserted them or that Jehovah was indeed a mighty God to protect his own thus. Undoubtedly there would be many conversions on this account. And those conversions must also fall, on this occasion, in that 1,300 listed above. Two elements are clearly involved—the definite act of Cakobau's conversion, and the progressive events of desecration of objects held to be sacred without serious

---

25 Waterhouse to LC, 1 June 1854, WM, 1855, 1:465.
26 See title page in Williams, *Missionary Experiences*, with scripture passage, Isaiah 2:18.

consequences. So we cannot say with certainty that there were more than about six hundred who just "followed the chief." So much for Bau itself.

Similar results were achieved after a longer space of time in the islands in the Bauan realm. Within twelve months Batiki and Nairai had virtually become Christian, and Gau had a strong Christian cause (AR Bau Circuit 1854). Some of the groups along the mainland coast came in and followed Bau, but many of them flatly refused (AR Bau Circuit 1855).

The Bau Annual Report of 1854, written in June, within two months of Cakobau's conversion, says:

> At the plague spot of Fiji—cannibal Gau—there has been a shaking among the dry bones and many have lotued [accepted the *lotu*, or become Christian—A.R.T.]. Several scores have become Christian at the island of Batiki and teachers are now fully occupied with their legitimate work—preaching and schools. A general change has taken place at Nairai, where we have sent a qualified teacher, with those who lotued at Bau, numbering upwards of a hundred. (AR Bau Circuit 1854)

The report was written just after the chief's conversion; the movement had begun before. The conversion of Cakobau speeded it up. Twelve months later we read:

> At Gau, with a population of more than 3000, two-thirds of whom are professing Christians, we have placed two teachers. We have sent another teacher to Batiki, where the entire population, nearly 700, sit under the preaching of the Gospel. Nairai is perhaps most advanced. Among the population of nearly 1000, the whole of whom are now Christians, there are several who seem to be taught of the Lord. (AR Bau Circuit 1855)

These extracts show that there was a strong mass movement[27] into Christianity in early 1854 and 1855—before Kaba. Indeed we may say that in the islands of Lomaiviti there was a dominant Christianity prior to Kaba. Most of them stood to stand or fall with their chief. In Koro the acceptance of Christianity was delayed because of internal wars (AR Bau Circuit 1854). There is, therefore, a strong case for the claim that these islands, in the main, "followed the chief." But I qualify that by stating again that there had been a growing cause there before, and in spite of his opinion. I qualify it further by saying that there was iconoclasm here also. For instance there was a case of a ritual act of worship being performed before a sacred tree at Gau, "decked out in the finest Fijian draperies." At this very moment a Tongan teacher Abraham (there were several of that name) arrived, escorted by a Bauan chief, who would have some authority there as a messenger from Bau. The Bauan "sacrilegiously tore down the gaudy ornaments, whilst Abraham preached unto them that

---

27 Tippett's use of the term "mass movement" follows the usage of J. Waskom Pickett in his 1933 book *Christian Mass Movements in India*. Donald McGavran's book *The Bridges of God* was published in 1955, whereas this Tippett volume was published in 1954. Though McGavran worked with Pickett in India and was well aware of the term "mass movements," he later chose the term "people movements" instead. Tippett's later writings use the term "people movements" rather than "mass movements."—Ed.

they ought not to "think that the Godhead is like unto a tree." The terminology is Waterhouse's, and he is writing for home readers. I cannot imagine Abraham would begin by speaking of the "Godhead." The outcome of the act and the sermon was that about a hundred "bent the knee" (AR Bau Circuit 1855). Nor was Abraham the only person who seems to have had some such roving commission in these islands at the time. Another, Benjamin, was winning converts in Nairai and about the time of Kaba was moving on to Gau. Wakaya and Moturiki had also been visited.

The same reports indicate quite clearly, however, that there were many who remained heathen in spite of Cakobau, and in Nairai a village was burnt in protest. Even after the Battle of Kaba there were many Bauan towns which refused to turn to Christianity. Many of the Lasakau people on Bau Island itself, though they fought as loyalists with Cakobau, remained heathen (ibid.). (Let it not be thought that Kaba was a purely Christian vs. heathen affair.) Indeed, three months after Kaba, fifteen months after Cakobau's conversion, only four mainland villages had become Christian—Rewa, Nakelo, Naitasiri, and Suva (ibid.).

Two important facts emerge from all this. Firstly, there was a definite limitation of the area influenced by the conversion of Cakobau. Although after a year or so there were nearly nine thousand Christians in the Bau area, these were mostly in the islands and very near at hand, and they represent nothing like the whole population (AR Bau Circuit 1854). Not even within Bau itself was this so. There were about one thousand Christians here (AR Bau Circuit 1855) out of a population of about 1,500 at the time (AR Bau Circuit 1854). Of the three thousand in Gau, two thousand were Christian (ibid.). On the mainland some who did turn Christian, like them at Namata, apostatised after a short time (AR Bau Circuit 1855). The conversion had no influence at all along the long Ra coastline, or outside the Bauan area. Lau, of course, was already Christian.

The second fact made apparent by the statistics and reports is that this influx of people into Christianity was no more than an increase of people to worship, and as such they were received and welcomed and brought under instruction, but they were not received as members. The increase in membership went on at much the same rate as before, and it can be dogmatically stated that everywhere the statistics indicate increased congregations after the conversion of an important chief—but nothing more.

Now as to the spiritual experience of these new converts, manifestly they had very little, but they were quite willing to be instructed. A good deal of this instruction they accepted readily enough, but much went only skin-deep, and—let it be noted well—at no time was there any compulsion of any kind placed upon converts, and no man was advanced a stage in his status within the church except at his own request. He heard sermons as to why he should. But the initiative had to be his. Not until he expressed his desire to go further in the church were specific moral standards demanded of him. Thus, looking ahead, say to 1860 when the Bau Circuit figures show 15,461 people attending church, there were only 2,744 of them who had been admitted to membership—about 17 percent (AR Bau Circuit 1860). The difference between the religious experience of that 17 percent and the other 83 percent was beyond recognition. It was on this large percentage of mere nominal Christians, who had come in for a great multitude of different reasons, that the preachers poured their messages and prayers. They were a mixed lot. Many of them retained the heathen outlook on life, even to the making of simple offerings at wayside shrines (Seemann 1862, 195), which many still do without thinking what it means. Naturally the early missionaries were disappointed that so many of these would-be Christians did not advance greatly, but it should not be overlooked that when the revivals came it was among this 83 percent that they came—but we have not yet reached that part of the study. It should not be imagined that that 17/83 ratio was average for other places. The ratio varied greatly. In Bua and Cakaudrove the ratio was worse for a long time, in Viwa and at Lakeba it was very much better, but the differentiation between them was always there—and still is.

In the case of Bau there was one good explanation of this ratio. Even after Bau accepted Christianity she clung to polygamy. In June 1855 we read, "None of the chiefs have yet formally renounced polygamy, etc., and the common people are afraid to take the lead" (AR Bau Circuit 1855).

And twelve months later we hear of "the beginning of the public renunciation of polygamy in Bau. Without the example of the king, but by the simple force of religious instruction, by the creation of conscience and the fear of God, the sanctities and benefits of marriage were introduced" (AR Bau Circuit 1856).

It was not until 1859 that the missionaries found it necessary to write the laws of marriage into their books in Bau, though they had been codified in 1853 in Viwa.[28]

The question of marriage was but one of the factors that held up reception into membership—though I am of the opinion that it was the major one. It is important to point out the popular error that the missionaries forced marriage on the natives—that is, Christian marriage. They did nothing of the sort. They preached its virtues to those who had of their own volition placed themselves under their instruction. A man could have fifty wives and worship in church every Sunday in those days—as Cakobau did for three years. That man could enjoy all the privileges of worship, instruction, and pastoral guidance, but he could not be admitted into the inner circle until he accepted the standards of that circle. In other words, the missionaries asked no more than certain heathen secret societies demanded of their devotees—different in kind but no harder. As I read the evidence, the preaching emphasis was for a deeper religious experience among those who were mere nominal Christians. It had to be an experience sufficiently real to demand fruit of itself. That is, if the Christian discovered this experience, he should of himself see at once the

---

28   See Bau Records between 1859 and 1860, time of Fordham, in handwriting of Collis.

true standards he should adopt in life. But without the experience he is not likely to desire a much higher standard.

The report mentioned that began—"the beginning of the public renunciation of polygamy in Bau"—significantly enough also contains this statement:

> Penitential scenes have been witnessed almost every Sabbath since the reopening of the Chapel. Whilst there has been much mere animal excitement there are several genuine cases of conviction and some clear instances of sound conversion. (Ibid.)

A little simple calculation from further information in the same report reveals that the temporary chapel was rebuilt, and these scenes followed, and then shortly after is the beginning of public renunciation of polygamy in Bau. The sequence is quite clear—it is the fruit of a religious experience. It seems therefore wrong to judge these missionaries on the basis of establishing a clash of culture. Let us remember—it was voluntary: the enjoyment of religion was not denied to any by not accepting Christian marriage—when undertaken it was usually the response to an intellectual and emotional experience, and a desire for it. In the fifties when it became so relevant, I feel the majority of the missionaries would have taken this view.

The celebrated heathen chief Wetasau continued a polygamist for two and a half years after his conversion, before taking the further step. There is evidence here also that he experienced a deeper change of heart before taking the step, and all his wives found greater happiness afterwards (Williams and Calvert 1884, 325).

We find, as we would expect in the light of this fact, that baptism, marriage, and membership on trial tend to go together. Bau Circuit statistics show that three years after Cakobau's conversion there were 1,373 "members" in the circuit, but 1,114 of these were in the islands of Lomaiviti. There had been revivals in these islands. Membership in Bau itself was small (130), but a hundred of these were new members that year the penitential scenes were witnessed. In all the remainder of the Bau mainland towns, though there were 23 preaching places, there were only 19 members. Figures like that demand recognition.

The missionaries, however, were not quite free to be radical on the question of marriage. They had the directions of the Wesleyan Missionary Society before them:

> No man living in a state of polygamy is to be admitted a member, or even on trial, who will not consent to live with one woman, his wife, to whom you shall join him in matrimony, or ascertain that this rite has been performed by some other minister; and the same rule is to be applied, in the same manner, to a woman proposing to become a member of the Society.

But regulations or not, the missionaries to a person showed their mind to defend this position, and Calvert sets out his arguments together with this statement for whoever wishes to read (ibid., 270).

Let it not be imagined, however, that the matter was simple. Some of the difficulties involved by the policy (and the missionaries were not unaware of them) have been mentioned by an independent observer in 1860. Methodism may have had numerical gains by a change of marriage policy, but she maintained her position (Seemann 1862, 33).

For the time being Cakobau was quite satisfied just to worship. Nearly three years after his conversion, he publicly renounced polygamy on 11 January 1857 and abandoned eighty wives (having already stated his wives at about fifty, the balance would no doubt be those classified by Calvert as "other females") and was baptised with the name Ebenezer. His experience had grown considerably, and that growth was represented by this step (AR Bau Circuit 1857).

Before we pass on to the second question, there is one matter which must be evaluated if possible. It concerns the messages sent by Cakobau to the islands and his armies after his conversion. In one source, Waterhouse tells us the messages sent were "directing the inhabitants to renounce idolatry."[29] Were this so, it is remarkable that a third of Gau, and many others who remained perfectly loyal to Cakobau even when everything was against him, should flatly refuse to obey—even still after his authority had been confirmed in the Battle of Kaba. However, there is another record about those messages, and the source is the same man. Some years later when Waterhouse was writing this up in a book, he used again much of that original letter, word for word, but further away from the heat of the moment he wrote not "directing" but "authorising" (1866, 262). I feel Waterhouse was right in making that alteration. Unfortunately it does make a great difference—and it is a tremendously important point when we come to evaluate the nature of these conversions. Were they authorised or directed to become Christian? Strangely enough, Calvert, the other figure in the drama, seems to have omitted this detail entirely. It was in Koro, one of these islands, where I first met the phrase *Na Lotu nei Ratu Cakobau*. In my three years in Nadroga and three in Kadavu, before this I had never heard the phrase once, but during that week in Koro I believe I heard it fifty times. I deeply regret I cannot settle this point. The nearest I can get is that Waterhouse deliberately changed the word, so the chances are it was authorised, not directed.

Recapitulation: We began this study by considering the effect of the conversion of a paramount chief on the church statistics, and from this study we have discovered that:

1. Many became Christian irrespective of the chief's opinion, and did so prior to his conversion.
2. Many did follow the chief into the church, but their conversion was purely nominal and not based on any spiritual experience. It was, however, an intelligent act and brought them under Christian instruction.

---

29 Waterhouse to LC, 1 June 1854, from Bau, WM, 1855, 1:465.

3. Under instruction some were led into an experience later.
4. There is no evidence at all that church membership derived any benefit or increase by the conversion of Cakobau or any other big chief. But the size of the ordinary congregations increased considerably.
5. The conversion of a big chief by no means brought all his followers into the church or even led them to attend occasionally. In the case of Cakobau, many of his loyal followers remained heathen and cannibal for years.
6. The conversions which followed the conversion of a powerful chief were secular and political in character and not emotional; they were mass movements and impersonal and stood out in contrast with the usual personal decisions the missionaries had been familiar with up to 1854.

I shall return later to the religious significance of Cakobau's conversion, and the Bauan conversions will be seen later in contrast with other mass movements of a deeply spiritual and emotional character at Viwa, Ono, Kadavu, and other places, but meantime this matter of the effect of Kaba must be investigated first.

3

THE GOD OF BATTLES

Some historians have laid much stress on the number of conversions achieved because of the result of war. I am sorry to say that there is some degree of truth in the assertion. Many did become Christian because of the results of war. However, it was one of several causes, and it has been grossly overstated—of that there is no shadow of doubt. The means was not consciously used for the propagation of the gospel. Kaba was fundamentally a political issue—it was the authority of Cakobau that was at stake, first of all, and there were heathen fighting beside his troops and the Tongans (AR Bau Circuit 1856). At the same time there was a Christian cause in Kaba, and a Christian teacher was resident there throughout the whole time (ibid.). After the battle ended in favour of Cakobau, now a Christian, it was natural for many villages, which had been in doubt about religion, to ask for teachers. It was a way of thanking Cakobau for sparing their lives, as it were. In the case of the wars of Ma'afu in Vanua Levu, there was a more positive and aggressive plan of campaign. Once again it was dominantly a political issue, but religion did figure. To the nature of these I shall return in a moment, but meantime let me state the question for investigation.

To what extent may the conversion of Fiji be attributed to these wars? To what extent were they causes, and to what extent were they just factors which speeded up already existing processes? Did the church benefit numerically from these wars—either in (a) members or (b) attenders at worship?

There were nearly nine thousand at worship in the Bau Circuit (excluding Viwa Section) about the time of Kaba (ibid.). The increases after the battle were confined to Rewa (and its allies) and the towns of the Bau area, which had been among the rebels.[30] Even these, the statistics show, did not come into the church immediately, as we should expect were the result of the battle, the determining factor. This did happen in other parts of the Pacific, as for instance at Bunauia in Tahiti (Ellis 1830, 1:247–57). It came more later on in the second year following, and even then it was not by any means a clean sweep, but came step-by-step. There were still rebellions against Bau throughout 1858–59, and even after the termination of wars in 1859 (August), in the following months when "most

---
30   But still only twenty-three preaching places on Bau mainland even two years later (AR Bau Circuit 1857).

of the rebel towns presented their peace offerings, some of these towns," we read in the handwriting of Collis over the signature of John Smith Fordham, "continue professedly heathen" (AR Bau Circuit 1860). This sort of statement does some harm to statements like "The Battle of Kaba set a seal upon the triumph of the white man's religion. Almost immediately afterwards the people embraced Christianity in hundreds and thousands; islands went over to Methodism en bloc, etc." (Henderson 1931, 49). There are three wrong words in that statement—"immediately," "thousands," and "en bloc," which waters the statement down to something like this—In the years following Kaba, hundreds embraced Christianity, especially in the islands of Lomaiviti and the kingdom of Rewa. Even then it requires qualification.

What the Battle of Kaba really did for Christianity was that it opened up a huge area for evangelism, for the going and coming of Christians. It created an interest in their message and guaranteed them a hearing, as it were, along the Rewa and Tailevu coasts. But it did not by any means win them.

It certainly did not win Fiji for Christianity, as some believe. In five years the Christians in the Bau domain increased from nine thousand to fifteen thousand (AR Bau Circuit 1855, 1860), and there were big advances in Rewa, where the Christian cause had been driven underground through the Bau/Rewa war, and where hundreds were awaiting such an event as Kaba. It may have speeded up events in Kadavu, though this place was really evangelised from Viwa, with Lauan agents, who were there before Kaba.[31] The main holdup to Christianity in Kadavu had for a long time been the vigorous persecutor Qaraniqio—and he was dead. His death, more than the victory of Kaba, speeded up the work there. The result of Kaba had no effect on the hill tribes (Cooper 1888, 35–36), or upon the long coastline of Western Viti Levu, which was evangelised from Viwa[32]; the Yasawas were evangelised from Bua (AR Bua Circuit 1856–60), Vanua Levu, or Taveuni; and, of course, Lau was already Christian.[33] Let us not overestimate the event.

Now let us go over that paragraph a little more carefully. In five years the area under the immediate power of Bau only produced six thousand converts—which is less than the year before it. Let it not be thought the heathen were not there to be converted. In that same five years the mission had increased its staff in that area by one white missionary and one schoolmaster, three native ministers, a further 95 catechists, and 354 extra native teachers. An increased staff like that must have been responsible for a good number of those six thousand conversions. It all shoots the proverbial peas through Professor Henderson's "immediate," "thousands," "en bloc." Furthermore, where did those 95 catechists

---

31   Sent by Varani, who died before conversion of Cakobau. Fijian manuscripts.
32   Lived their own life irrespective of Bau. Witness Lyth, Journal (5:20–23).
33   See Lau statistics (Lawry and Hoole 1850, 209).

and 354 teachers come from? A few came from Tonga, but mainly they were the fruit of the Viwa and Ono revivals, and came from the church in Fiji before the conversion of Cakobau.

As far as Kadavu was concerned, several missions had started here, and all had promising beginnings, but all came to tragic ends at the hands of Qaraniqio or his satellites. The ultimately successful mission was commenced by Varani of Viwa,[34] using Paula Vea, and establishing him at Yale under the care of the chief. This Christian cell had commenced to grow before Kaba; and eighteen months after Kaba when Vea began a proper circuit register, he had a staff of two graded catechists, two on probation, and five local preachers caring for stations, sixteen local preachers on trial from Matuku, Lau, and eight more who were Kadavans, and eight local exhorters. There was an advanced organisation at work.[35] There were 153 full members, and another 114 on trial. Unfortunately there is no record of the number attending worship, but the number of Kadavans who had got to full membership, and the status of exhorter and preacher, indicates that the work was successful from the very start. The very nature of these statistics shows we are dealing with a completely different kind of movement from that which we have seen at Bau. In two years Kadavu had produced twice as many people who were judged to have experienced a spiritual conversion, and were willing to accept full Methodist standards, as the whole Bau coastline of Viti Levu. And its roots were pre-Kaba. It is my own belief that as Rewa became more and more occupied with holding out against Bau, she became less and less able to restrain the church in Kadavu. Moore realised this and saw the growing interest in religion, and soon he had a team of Lauan teachers, under Vea, establishing themselves at many points along the Kadavan coastline (Williams and Calvert 1884, 385). The white missionaries were not established in Kadavu until 1862 (AR Kadavu Circuit 1862), but by this time there were 10,460 adherents with sixty-seven chapels and seventeen other preaching places.[36] Its consolidation had been excellent, and its isolation kept it free from the disturbances of the mainland, although it still had not finished fighting out its own internal wars.[37] The more I study Kadavu, the more I am convinced that if Kaba had any influence at all on the place, it was indirect.

As for the interior, much of it was not subdued until after Cession—and then not by Bau (Cooper 1888, ch. 5). Thirteen years after Kaba, Cakobau's men had marched inland to deal with the murderers of Thomas Baker and party and met with ignominious rebuff (Brewster 1937, 117).

The coastline of Western Viti Levu was evangelised from Viwa. Hunt had visited them in 1843, and Lua had carried the small cause in Nadroga, but though a chief, his following

---

34 Vernacular manuscripts from Kadavu.
35 Circuit Meeting at Tavuki, 21 February 1857, in Kadavu Circuit Register.
36 Kadavu Circuit Register, 1862.
37 White to AC, 4 October 1864, *WMN*, January 1865, 472–73.

was small. Lyth had visited them in 1848, immediately after the death of Hunt, and teachers were left there.[38] The Yasawas were evangelised from Bua—an entirely independent movement which had no relation to Kaba (AR Bua Circuit 1856-60).

If Kaba had bearing on the conversion of Vanua Levu, why were the couple of years that followed years of severe persecution for the Christian party? Vanua Levu was at war for the whole of the fifties—Bua and Macuata, as Bau and Rewa had been in Viti Levu.[39] It all shows what a frightfully local thing Kaba had been. Five years after Kaba, Buretu, a few miles from Bau, on the Rewa delta, was a strong, fortified, and unconquered heathen town. Its few Christians had become apostates, and one of the finest heathen temples in the Group was found there in that year (1860) by Seemann (1862, 135).

Nor did Kaba open up the whole of Rewa; it was only the coastline. Nearly a decade later Langham wrote, "The Lotu is spreading inland from Rewa, but there is fighting inland at Nadroga."[40] That was written in October 1864—almost ten years after Kaba—and it was just moving in from the coast. Jesse Carey, stationed at Rewa in 1865, and responsible for 150 miles of coastline, wrote:

> Religion is acknowledged by three important kingdoms and a number of lesser ones. But within the limits, and under the jurisdiction of these, there are not a few tribes still clinging to heathenism. While adjoining each and stretching inland from every part of the coast, are tribes as dark and savage, as revengeful and cannibal in their dispositions and habits, as any of whom the pioneers of this mission wrote.[41]

Later on in the same letter Carey adds, "Nearly every inland tribe, settled, say within a line eight or ten miles from the coast, is still heathen and cannibal." He worked Viti Levu, Rewa coastline; the year is 1865, ten years after Kaba. That same man Carey received a letter one day from one of his teachers. It read like this: "Sir, I write to inform you that the chiefs in whose dominions we are stationed have just assassinated a great number of people, 55 of whom have been distributed to the adjacent villages where they have been devoured."[42]

That also is Rewa coastline, ten years after Kaba.

Then what of the Viti Levu coast on the Bau side, stretching out to Ra and Ba. I read in one place of a massacre at Koroveitoga,[43] and within a few days another at Nabeka,[44] both in Langham's area; and the mail previous to this both he and Fison speak of the death

---

38 Journal of Lyth (5:20-23).
39 Many references in Journal of Williams, also AR Bua Circuit and AR Nadi Circuit throughout the 1850s.
40 Langham to Moore, 11 October 1864, and forwarded to AC, *WMN*, 1865, 472.
41 Carey to AC, 18 January 1865, from Rewa, *WMN*, 1865, 490.
42 Translated by Carey in same letter.
43 Fison to AC, 16 March 1865, *WMN*, July 1865, 509; also Journal of Fison, November 1864.
44 Journal of Fison, January 1865 and same letter 16 March 1865.

drum near Natutuniba—a hundred bodies for the ovens.[45] Then there is an account of the murder of some Bauan Christians[46]; and nearby tribes, like Vugalei, for instance, still fighting with Bau[47]; and persecution of Christians and strangling was going on at places ten and twenty miles only from Bau[48]—and all this a decade after Kaba.

By this time it had become quite apparent that the conversion of the interior would require new tactics, and the Annual District Meeting of 1864 pressed the Conference in Australia to establish a new post, appointing one of their number as missionary to the interior.[49] In anticipation of approval, land was procured and a mission house built "just within the border," as Carey described it,[50] at Davuilevu. Calvert inspected and bought the land.[51] That Davuilevu (present Dilkusha) should have been considered just within the borders of the interior, just shows us what a very short distance inland the *lotu* had spread to this date.

By October 1865, Thomas Baker was in residence there,[52] although Fison had been nominated by the district for the position.[53] Baker, in his first letter to Australia afterwards, makes a most interesting comment—that below him is Christian, and above (except for two small towns) is heathen. From his door he sees the first heathen town.[54]

I do not recall ever having seen a reference to the mission to the interior so stated by any of the historians, who have been so quick to attribute the growth of the church to Kaba, nor have I seen any attempt by them to evaluate the Heathen League, which agreed that no single town should *lotu* alone, but only if they all agreed to do it together.[55] But knowledge of this policy on the part of Baker is the key to his own policy, which was from the start, on his own word, to try to break the connecting link. Thus his first drive led him through Viria and Lomaivuna to Soloira.[56] In 1865 he travelled along the Waidina and left his boat at Navakadua and climbed high mountains into Soloira. The fruit of this journey was the conversion of the chief of Soloira—he had achieved his purpose. We note here the first of a type of reference we shall investigate in a few moments. Baker is careful to state the nature of this conversion—"He now abandons heathenism as a system, and formally professes to be a Christian."[57]

---

45 Langham to Moore, 11 October 1864.
46 Langham to AC, 20 June 1865, WMN, July 1866, 574.
47 Moore to AC, undated but 1864, WMN, January 1865, 472.
48 Langham to AC, 20 June 1865, WMN, July 1866, 577–78.
49 Carey to AC, 18 January 1865, from Rewa, WMN, April 1865, 490.
50 Ibid.
51 Calvert to AC, 16 January 1865, from Ovalau, WMN, April 1865, 488.
52 Baker to AC, 16 October 1865, WMN, July 1866, 574.
53 Carey to AC, 18 January 1865, from Rewa, WMN, 1865, 490.
54 Baker to AC, 16 October 1865, WMN, July 1866, 576.
55 Ibid., 575.
56 Ibid., 574–76.
57 Ibid., 576.

Almost every letter of Langham's over 1865–66 speaks of attacks on Christian parties, burning of houses, and plundering of teachers along the Ra coast.[58] Bua and Yasawa letters over the same period show tragic similarities—much persecution, but a spreading church.[59] Baker, now in the interior, had done good work in the Yasawas and was a good pioneer evangelist after he had learned the language, which gave him trouble at first.[60] He revisited Soloira and found a good increase of Christians in Soloira itself. He arranged for the stationing of fourteen teachers there.[61] Then a few months later he made that fatal journey into the very heart of Fiji, where he and his party were murdered on 21 July 1867.[62] Kaba lay twelve years behind—and this is the Fiji that became Christian as a result of that battle! A study of the Baker records leaves no room for such an assumption, not even for Viti Levu, let alone Fiji.

And much the same thing has been claimed for Ma'afu's victories in Vanua Levu. Well, let it be observed first of all that there were seventeen thousand Christians in Vanua Levu when Ma'afu put in his appearance,[63] and that cause had grown against bitter persecution, and thousands more had died for the faith. I shall return to that later when dealing with the nature of faith under persecution. What it lacked in theological depth, their simple faith more than made up for in strength (AR Bua Circuit; AR Nadi Circuit 1847–59). After Ma'afu had done his work and things settled down a little, there were still only twenty-two thousand Christians in Vanua Levu (AR Cakaudrove Circuit 1860). The Bua report of 1860 shows that there may have been some increase on account of the wars. We read, "In the Dreketi and Macuata districts about 5000 are willing to be instructed." That is suggestive, but I cannot say more than that (AR Bua Circuit 1860).

For the whole of his time in Fiji, Ma'afu was a source of trouble to the missionaries. He sought to become a member one month and was expelled the next. Then he would show up again quite repentant on the surface. He was too important to ignore, too crafty to trust, too dangerous to let beyond one's sight, and his Christianity was but a political device. But so important a place did he hold in Lau, which was the Christian stronghold, that he could not be ignored by the missionaries. He came to Vanua Levu by the invitation of Tui Bua. The best account of it all is Seemann's (1862, 254–55). The paramount chiefs of Bua and Macuata had been at war for years. Old Ra Gagavoka died and bequeathed the war against Ritova to Batinamu, who was assassinated in an expedition to this end. His successor, Tamai Vunisa, was a diplomat, whose biggest problem was to prevent the Christian/heathen struggle

---

58 Langham correspondence 1864–66 in *WMN* of the period.
59 Correspondence from Rooney and Brooks over same period in *WMN*.
60 Island of Viwa, Yasawa, had become Christian under Baker about 1864. Rooney to AC, 26 November 1866, *WMN*, July 1867, 19.
61 Baker to AC, 7 January 1867, *WMN*, July 1867, 20–22.
62 Full report and correspondence in *WMN*, October 1867.
63 Calculated from AR Bua Circuit 1860, AR Nadi Circuit 1860, and AR Cakaudrove Circuit 1860.

from dividing his forces. He was followed by Ra Masima, who, under Tongan persuasion, and with Tongan blood in his veins, became Christian. He invited Ma'afu into the war. But as his daughter reminded me when we were talking of the matter, Ritova had the help of Mara, and that was a formidable enough combination for any poor chief to have to face.

Ra Masima's portrait is in the Bua church today, and it seems to me he was a character of the days of the judges, and God to him was the God of Battles. Adi Mere, his daughter, told me slowly (for she was very old) but quite proudly of her father's wars. They started from Savusavu, she said, and followed down the coast to Dama. Men were sent ahead to ask in each area whether or not they wanted to *lotu*. An affirmative reply gained them a supply of *sulus* (clothes); a negative meant war. The Tongans were with him. So the hosts of the Lord marched on.

But it was not as simple as all that, and Ra Masima had taken a page from Ma'afu's book. He had come to the conclusion that the only hope for unity along his coastline was as Christians, and above all things, as long as Ritova lived, and Mara and Tui Levuka, he must have unity. This was gained under the name of *Nai Valu ni Lotu*.

I have no hesitation whatever in pointing out that, though political ends were gained in this way, and some people—perhaps a few thousand—were brought a step nearer to the *lotu*, it did no real good. They were brought near with a mental barrier that made true conversion really difficult, and for years to come the area concerned produced few outstanding Christians, and it had to be carried by Lau and Kadavu almost to the end of the century.[64] The church had been made a political tool by Ma'afu first and then by his copyist. In the first case the missionaries were extremely annoyed, and a severe letter of rebuke to Ma'afu is still in existence,[65] but it was too late. The Tongans were not Christians but were the uncontrollable youths who had fled from the rigour of King George's Christian laws (Pritchard 1866, 290). Seemann's judgement is that Ma'afu made dupes of the Vanua Levu missionaries (1862, 254–55). Anyway, for the immediate purpose of this study, let us note that the absolute maximum number of adherents that could possibly have been gained, supposing there were no other agencies at work (which is not so, of course) by both the exploits of Ma'afu and later in the Savusavu wars, is less than 5 percent of the population. I make that statement so that at least we may keep our thinking in perspective.

Now it seems only fair to Tui Bua, that having placed him in this position, I should make an important qualification. When a rebellious tribe or an enemy at the back door is defeated and, instead of being made food for the ovens, is frankly forgiven on the one condition that the people *lotu*—was that compulsion? What did this mean?

It has been explained by a missionary on the spot at the time in these terms:

---

64 Many references in minutes of church meetings in Vanua Levu in later part of century.
65 Full text of letter in Seemann (1862, 254).

> It is just the same as though he had said, You shall not kill and eat men, women and children anymore; you shall not bury your old and infirm parents alive, you shall not strangle your widows, you shall not dash children's brains out against a stone or tree, or tie them to dangle to death from the masthead of your canoes; you shall not murder and eat all shipwrecked individuals; you shall no longer destroy yourselves wholesale as you have done . . . You shall lotu . . . The chiefs and the people who are heathen only take it in that light.[66]

It is a long letter, but enough is quoted to show what the phrase meant, and how it was used. The victor said, "You have been defeated in war. You are my prisoners. But I shall set you free, if you *lotu*." There was no compulsion to join the church, either one denomination or another. It simply meant there had to be a change of human values, especially the value of life itself. And coming from a missionary in Fiji at the time and in defense of Tui Bua, that is a very important statement. So do not let us be too hasty about judgement in this matter.

Even with this qualification the percentage of converts as a result of all the wars is a very small one indeed. Lest the reader should still not feel convinced about Kaba, let me add on the authority of William Moore that ten years after Kaba there was still only about a third of the population of Fiji that had come under Christian instruction and worship.[67] In fact a careful examination of the statistics gleaned from many sources indicate that the period of greatest expansion was in the middle and late sixties, a period which could hardly have been influenced by Kaba or Ma'afu's Macuata wars. The three years immediately prior to the death of Baker saw an increase of approximately forty-four thousand adherents, and over seven thousand additional members. Moore gave the 1864 figures as sixty-four thousand.[68] Calvert gave the figure of 107,771 prior to the death of Baker.[69] The twenty thousand converts of Rewa and its dependent states had taken seven years to win.[70] The six years following Kaba showed an increase of only six thousand members; the three before the death of Baker, seven thousand.[71] The forty-four thousand converts of that same three years is placed beside the thirty thousand over the period of twice as long after Kaba.[72] And Fiji was still far from won for Christianity. In fact I shall jump ahead to twenty years after Kaba, or shall we say to after Cession. I compare the statistics of 1876 and 1877, and discover that there are more than ten thousand converts from heathenism that year—3,537 of them in the Rewa Circuit and 5,170 of them in Cakaudrove, and even, be it noted, 554 in the Bau area itself—after Cession and the twenty-second year after Kaba.[73]

---

66 Horsley to Houlding, 14 November 1865, CB.
67 Moore to *Christian Advocate*, 15 March 1866, CB.
68 Speech reported in press in Australia, CB.
69 Calvert to *Watchman*, 30 November 1867, CB.
70 1855 statistics as in Henderson (1931, 222), with 1861 given by Royce in *The Herald* letter, 11 September 1861, CB.
71 Moore's 1864 figures and Calvert's.
72 1855 figures and Royce's.
73 District statistical returns of 1876 and 1877.

But there was something at Kaba that counted for much more than the victory. It will be remembered that this was a war between loyalists and rebels, and many villages had swung away from their rightful chief and were arrayed against him, who should have been able to depend upon their loyalty. Nor can it be disputed that some had become rebels purely because they thought that the results would go that way. Yet they were defeated—routed, we might say. The loyalists had taken some two hundred prisoners; and what should have happened to those prisoners before Cakobau's conversion, when it was said the Bauan ovens never cooled (Seemann 1862, 77), we know perfectly well. They knew also, and they also knew what would have been done to their villages. But that they were frankly forgiven, and even Koroi Ravulo among them (Waterhouse 1866, 292–93), was something the heathen just could not understand. Could this be Cakobau? From this point Cakobau "shocked" the heathen by his complete change over from the heathen way to the Christian way. There had been other instances of this new spirit. An astonished spy, taken plotting against Cakobau, had been sent home unharmed and advised to *lotu* (AR Bau Circuit 1855). Another case is recorded of captives who were liberated and told to go home and tell the rest of the people what a fine thing Christianity is (Lawry and Hoole 1850, 48–49). Previous to this Cakobau had spared some Koro captives, whom he would most certainly have killed before his conversion (AR Bau Circuit 1855). Much earlier, the same thing happened at Ono—"To the astonishment of the heathen, who had been so abusive and cruel, and contrary to all Fijian precedent, the lives of the conquered were spared, and their ill conduct freely forgiven. Hereby a greater victory was won" (Williams and Calvert 1884, 279). But that this same sort of thing could really happen to Cakobau was "shocking" to every Fijian who knew him. What had happened to Namosimalua (Hunt 1846, 110) and to Varani (Wallis 1851, 65ff.) had now happened to Cakobau, and he had stood the test.

It stood out all the more in contrast because the Lasakau people, who were loyalist but not Christian, had also taken prisoners in that battle, and these they treated in the usual way (AR Bau Circuit 1855). This contrast made a great impression on all who were spared, and certainly many there were who became Christian because of this mercy that it had brought to Cakobau.

Recapitulation: To what extent was war the cause of the spread of Christianity in Fiji?

1. The plain evidence of statistics is that war, and especially Kaba, did not really cause a great landslide into Christianity as has been claimed.
2. That to some Jehovah was a God of Battles cannot be denied, but when Fiji is viewed as a whole they represent a very small percentage of the people.
3. The astonishing display of mercy towards captives, after the victory, by Christian warriors, made as great an impact as the victories themselves.
4. The wars concerned are seen to be political primarily. At Kaba it was the authority of Bau that was at stake. Loyalists were opposed to rebels. Heathen

loyalists fought with Bau. Bua/Macuata wars were long-standing. The primary issue in Tui Bua's later fighting was the unity of Bua.

5. The few areas where the *Valu ni Lotu* had operated did not produce any real spiritual leadership until a new generation had been born, but had to be carried by other areas.
6. The nature of such conversion was merely the abandonment of cannibalism and other practices which conflicted with Christian humanitarianism. Such converts were free to attend church—some did, some did not. There is no evidence that church membership increased at all by these means. Congregations were enlarged a little, and areas were opened up for instruction.
7. The main benefit of war (if there can be such a thing) was that long-standing fighting came to an end; political issues, which had long hindered the progress of Christianity, were settled one way or the other; and the field was open for the going and coming of preachers. This was a great benefit to the Christian cause—but, be it noted, an indirect one.
8. At the same time it all led to a new problem—the rise of Tongan power in Fiji. This became a problem to the church, and led to the termination of the use of Tongan teachers.
9. Wars generally militated against the spread of the church—first heathen wars and then political wars. In areas at war, statistics invariably show that progress was slower than elsewhere. They certainly interfered with the experience of Christians (AR Viwa Circuit 1851, etc.).
10. The very necessity for the establishment of the mission to the interior, a decade after Kaba, and the fact revealed by the statistics that there were still thousands of converts in Rewa and Vanua Levu after Cession, clearly reveals Kaba and the wars of Ma'afu and Tui Bua as mere local skirmishes, with little direct or indirect effect upon the spread of the church elsewhere in Fiji.

4

THE CLASH OF CULTURES

We have heard a great deal in recent years about the clash of cultures. It reminds us that there is a wide range between the Christianity of the New Testament and the heathenism of old Fiji. To what extent was this idea of the God of Battles a natural stepping-stone from the ancient order, via the Old Testament, into the New? To what extent did Christianity clash with the old culture, and to what extent did it build upon it? Was it a Fijian or a white man's Christianity that was given to Fiji? Did the church provide something the Fijian could really appreciate and worship in, or was it a remote and meaningless theology to him?

The Fijian war gods figured a major place in the life and thought of the old Fijians. Success in war meant security; defeat meant, at the best, slavery, but more likely death. Fijian beliefs about life after death, especially for those who were feeble in war, were pretty grim (Williams and Calvert 1884, 203–05.). At one time in the mission period, there were seven wars being waged in Fiji.[74] It was therefore inevitable that many would never get beyond the outlook of the Old Testament prophets of the earlier period and the dramatic struggles between Baal and Jehovah, which were reenacted dozens of times in Fiji. Thus for many Kaba was such a struggle, because the rebels had made full heathen sacrifices before the battle and the Christians had turned to prayer. (Though what the poor heathen loyalists had done, I cannot say.)

> All the heathen oracles predicted the destruction of the Christian "powers that be" and the heathen waited with impatience for the day in which Christianity was to be "upset." The enemy sought by costly sacrifices to propitiate their numerous deities, whilst our people endeavoured to humble themselves under the mighty hand of God. (AR Bau Circuit 1855)

So writes Waterhouse, for whom it was a Jehovah/Baal struggle, and true (in anticipation of something the reader has yet to meet) Bau itself had become officially Christian; but as I have already stated for Cakobau, the statesman, the issue was Bauan authority, and most of his subordinate chiefs knew this—and so did his enemies.

---

74 Journal of Williams, 16 September 1843.

Even so it must be admitted that there were many who did see this as a Jehovah/Baal struggle, and the victor was a truly great and powerful God. That was not a new teaching given by Christianity, but a survival of their old ideas of war and religion. Even though this was seldom the reason given for individual conversions, most converts would think that way at first, and many never got beyond it.

How did a Fijian view his god, once strong, but now vanquished? We still hear the term *kalou lasu*, to which Henderson, with his Western mind, took great exception. Today the term means "lying god," but that conception of lying is one derived from Christian ethics, which has, even yet, not been fully appreciated by the Fijian people. A "lying god" in those days was one that was false, or impotent, in the sense that he could not do what his devotees begged of him. It had no bearing on truth. It meant that the deity was receiving sacrifices but impotent to hear prayers—he was a false god, at least for the time being. The term was Fijian, not the white man's, for the Fijian had often found his gods were "false." He would usually make an offering of "farewell" and worship another deity. This was often done by Fijians when "farewelling" their gods and turning to Christianity.[75] The "farewell" offering was to leave the way open for return. This was normal Fijian procedure and represented no culture clash whatever.

Sometimes, especially when a priest was involved, it would be done in a different way. When the prayers of the people had been offered for some time in vain, and clearly the deity was impotent, priests had been known to make a public announcement to the effect that the god had departed from them. It was then open for them to worship another deity, and also it excused the priest's failures. (By "prayers of the people," I mean on their behalf by the priest.) There was a case of a god who left an island because Jehovah had beaten him sore (Rowe 1860, 71), and another of a Rewa god who left his abode because of the arrival of Mr. Hunt (ibid., 74). This also was characteristic and the people were polytheistic, and places like Bau had dozens of temples—in fact Bau was sometimes called "God-land" (Carey 1891, 20; AR Bau Circuit 1854), having over thirty heathen temples (Waterhouse 1866, 43). And no doubt there were many who accepted Christianity who never grasped the meaning of its monotheism, and who entered it rather as a trial more than a matter of faith. To this day the term used for "Almighty God" really means "Mightiest of Gods" as well.

When a Fijian left his old gods, made his sacrifices, joined the *lotu*, and accepted the humanitarian way of life, it did not really involve him in any serious culture clash, except that he was subjecting himself to a different set of taboos. This sort of adjustment was being made all the time in that period when the religious system was breaking up under forces which predate Christianity.[76] One might even find places where cannibalism itself

---

75 Many references, like Williams and Calvert (1884, 306).
76 Sorcery, for example. See Cargill (1841, 116–17).

was under a taboo: I mean heathen places.[77] I am speaking now of the changes met by folk who simply acknowledged Jehovah and went no further, the thousands of converts who never got into the inner fellowship. The only serious adjustment they had to make was to accept a greater value for human life.

But that last indicates that converts were not all of the same type. Indeed, early missionaries and native preachers spoke of two kinds of conversion, and it is essential for all research students to understand the differentiation if they are to work over missionary material. The first was a mere formal change over from heathenism as a system to Christianity, and the second—usually after some instruction in the church—a spiritual experience. Thus wrote Waterhouse of Bau, "Bau is converted from heathenist to Christianity; we now labour for Bau's conversion from sin unto holiness."[78]

We have already met a similar statement from Thomas Baker, of the chief of Soloira: "He now abandons heathenism as a system, and formally professes to be a Christian."[79]

However, we can go back much earlier than either of those statements. From Viwa we find Hunt writing, for instance:

> In most instances those who have renounced their former superstition have felt but little of the power of Divine grace, until they have been a length of time under religious instruction. In these cases a twofold conversion has been necessary—the first from heathenism to Christianity as a system, and the second from the mere form of goodness to its power. (AR Viwa Circuit 1845, 192)[80]

Such variety in religious experience is apparent from most of the early reports. Cross, for instance, in 1842, said of his 356 Christians at Viwa that some had a "satisfactory sense of acceptance with God, and others, though firm in their adherence to Christianity were still earnestly seeking the Gospel salvation" (Hunt 1846, 145).

Let it not be imagined for a moment that only the white man was aware of this obvious difference in the experiences of Christians. Here is an interesting quotation from one of the native ministers who had been in a difficult spot for some time:

> Of the spiritual state of those who have but lately entered class, it is of a few only that we are really sanguine. They speak clearly about repentance and justification through faith in Christ; yet though many "old things" have passed away, we do not see the fruits of the "new creation." They have more religious talk than religious spirit. I write this of the trial classes. They attend regularly on public worship, and their conduct in God's house is becoming. They are at home in the day and Sabbath schools, showing a teachable spirit, and that is our hope.[81]

---

77 At Nakelo (Seemann 1862, 179).
78 Waterhouse to LC, 1 June 1854, WM, 1855, 1:465.
79 Baker to AC, 16 October 1865, WMN, July 1866, 576.
80 Writing is John Hunt's. See letter to Lincolnshire friends (Rowe 1860, 240).
81 Eroni Fotofili to Nettleton, 27 April 1871, WJO, 1872, 10.

One would not pick that as a mature minister's report, of over eighty years ago, but it is. This expectation of two different conversions is the key to an understanding, not only of the church system introduced, but also to this variety in religious experience in the Fijian Christians. And to determine the extent to which it clashed with their culture we shall have to understand first what the system was. What sort of a religious experience was desired by the Christian leaders?

The Wesleyan system was built on the expectation that people would "grow in grace." The outer court, as it were, was open to all. Any could worship. When people attended regularly but did no more, they were termed "adherents." "Membership" involved a status in the church, and a right to speak on its policy. It required certain standards, and members were first received on trial. Beyond this there were other positions—exhorter, local preacher, catechist, native minister, class leader, and so on. So the church was geared for service and responsibility. To speak in the name of the church, naturally one would be expected to obey its rules—is there any society that would not ask this? Discussing polygamy, I have already pointed out that no restrictions were placed on adherents, but a person could not become a member until Christian standards were accepted. This did not deny him the right of public worship, fellowship, sharing in praise, and prayer. Much criticism has fallen on missions by the careless statement that too much was demanded of their converts. The obvious rejoinder is—what converts? Of men who came over from heathenism in the wider group, little was expected—it was, to use Eroni's phrase above—"our hope." But to those who professed a religious experience a new standard was expected as the fruit of that experience. Shortly we shall examine the nature of those experiences and the fruit, but for the present let it be clearly understood that two types of conversion were sought, and both were voluntary, and the church system was geared to fit this "growing in grace." If the system is geared to fit the emotional growth of the people, and Christian exercise is provided at each stage, there does not seem to me to be any clash there, for no adherent was demanded to maintain the standards of, say, the preacher. So if there was a serious clash, it was not in the church system, and we must look elsewhere for it.

In the early period most of the converts came in small groups of two or three. Reading Williams' Journal for the year 1847, say, will impress this on one's mind,[82] but as time went on there was more mass movement. The groups were larger and the motive less pure. The early cases being more personal and stronger, advancement was a little more rapid. This is understandable. But when the mass movements began, the church had to be particularly careful about the experience of all who got beyond the outer circle. That is still the Methodist position—a religious experience is expected before reception into membership.

---

82 November/December. Journal of Williams, 28 November 1847; 5, 6, 19, and 30 December 1847. See also Fison (1873, 33).

We have already observed how political or secular events might give rise here and there to mass movements into the outer circle of the church. We also have to admit that, despite the vigilance of the church leaders, many did get through into "status," to fall later or to be discovered as not in possession of a real saving experience. Nor is it at all surprising to find that six or seven years after Kaba there is quite an increase in expulsions from membership (from membership, not from the church), and in particular John Smith Fordham found it necessary to tighten up standards. He remembered Milvan Bridge and the influx of pagan ideas afterwards. Many of the reasons given for these expulsions make us smile today, and we must admit also that the leaders themselves varied in severity.[83] We have to view the matter historically. There is no doubt about the mind of the missionaries. They felt they were standing at the crossroads—what they determined would possibly determine for years to come the strength or weakness of the Fijian church. Severity, they felt, a lesser evil than leniency, if the latter was to weaken the Christian witness for a century to come. They were wide-awake men, and what they did they had given careful thought to before they acted, and their policy was their considered judgement, not something done in the heat of the moment. It is all very well for men of today to look back and say that this or that was too hard—it should never have been demanded of people just out of the heathen state. The question in their minds was "What kind of Christianity will this be?" Was it too interwoven with Fijian mythology and heathen ethic? Their answer was an emphatic negative, and it led to a strong discipline for any who accepted responsibility or status, and this had led to criticisms from some of the anthropologists of today. The obvious rejoinder is that the discipline did not apply to any but those who sought status. They did this of their own volition. They knew well beforehand and had testified they had a personal experience that would stand by them. If they fell from grace, they were expelled only from that status—they were never denied the right of access to God in prayer and worship. That, I feel, is how the men of that day would have answered the critics of today. If in some ways the discipline of the church had weaknesses, it was also the reason for its strength in many ways.

I suppose as we look back some eighty to ninety years or more and think about it, it may seem that this rigid discipline must have been a jerk to their metaphoric backbones. But I do not think it was so real to them, because the step was never undertaken lightly or without due warning or without a period of trial, and many there were, and still are, who were quite happy to remain adherents.

Furthermore, such a system suited the situation in Fiji, and it was not as far removed from their native culture as we might imagine. The classification of people into groups according to office and responsibility; and the statement of factors which might lead to promotion or demotion, to honour or disgrace; the service required and the taboos imposed;

---

83   For example, "for cursing his aged mother," "for selling water as coconut oil," "for swearing at a papist teacher and wishing him dead." Mostly they were war, revenge, sex.

reception into membership after a course of instruction, and reception by means of a rite, after which the rules and standards must be strictly observed or discipline will be administered; what is this description—the ancient Fijian social system or the Fijian church? It fits either perfectly.

There were conceptions and beliefs against which the missionary, by his very presence there, was bound to strive; but to take these and change them for the Christian teaching, and thereby uplift their living, is not necessarily a change of culture. For instance it may be, as it was in Fiji, a change within a culture. For though the myth and morals of the ancient culture have given way to the Bible and Christian ethics, yet the cultural system of the race has been fundamentally retained.

To give a few simple examples, let us begin with the Scriptures themselves. Realising the place of hero worship among the Fijians, the missionaries made good use of the hero stories of the Bible, always with the moral included, and these were narrated by the teachers whenever folk could be gathered together in the normal Fijian way. And among the mission agents were men like Josua Mateinaniu who had been famed beforehand as dancing masters (Cargill, 1841, 111). These men composed poems for chanting and dancing, again after the Fijian manner. The Fijians astonished the missionaries in their capacity for memory work and provided them with catechisms that were suitable for chanting in their own way, and there are records of such material that was intended to serve for a year's instruction, being so appreciated that it was absorbed by memory within a matter of a few days (AR Viwa Circuit 1846–47).[84] Learning by rote may horrify some modern educationalists, but it was the ancient native system. Realising the traditional and linguistic pitfalls of a foreign language, the missionaries concentrated on giving their agents greater responsibility—giving them the details and leaving them free to deal with its application. Even so, among the white men, some, like Hunt, developed an ability to Fijianise his biblical narrative and illustration to a remarkable degree, and there is something about Hunt's translation and rhymes that had a true Fijian ring about it (Nettleton 1906, 83–84).

Let an independent observer speak—Captain Erskine—who, after witnessing several episodes in which Calvert had taken part, wrote of:

> the judgment shown by the missionaries here in retaining the usual habits of the people, when not militating against the great reform they hope to effect. Even in performing the church service, part of it is chanted in the same manner as their old songs used to be, a custom which not only makes the repetition of prayers easy and agreeable to Christians, but attracts occasional heathen visitors, who are always prepared to listen. (1853, 200)

And again at Nadi in Vanua Levu after attending one of Hazlewood's services he comments:

---

84 Also Hunt to Hanna, 1 December 1847 (Rowe 1860, 234–36).

> Some parts of the service, such as the Te Deum, were chanted in the most judicious arrangement, not only as assimilating the worship to their old customs, but as attracting many heathen listeners standing outside the door, who seemed, with respect and attention, to enjoy the music going on within. (Ibid., 223–34)

It must also be remembered that the Fijian of that day, despite his fierce exterior, and his human sacrifice in so many forms, was not entirely dark—he knew the rudiments of prayer and worship; understood sacrifice, priesthood, and temple; all of which had their Christian counterparts. The manner in which these facts have been recorded by the missionaries shows they were well familiar with them. Cross, Cargill, Williams, Hunt, Fison, Waterhouse, and many others, have left a terrific assemblage of research into the primitive religion of Fiji, not always equally evaluated, but still collected. These men borrowed freely from the pagan terminology, and they preached in heathen temples.[85] A theology developed from the old Hebrew sacrificial system was far easier to explain in Fijian than in English, a fact which came home to me within my first year in Fiji when I tried to describe one of the Hebrew feasts.

It must therefore be quite apparent that being converted did not mean the isolation of a Fijian from his natural culture, and what is more, were this thing called Christianity so much of a culture clash to them, how do we account for the way in which the heathen loitered about the church windows to hear the music and sermons? Time after time one reads—"A number of heathen were present." A good example is the opening of the new chapel at Tiliva.[86] Lawry wrote, "Some Lotu, others behold and enquire" (Lawry and Hoole 1850, 85). Cargill gives many such references, but sometimes to about thirty or more heathen listening respectfully.[87] There must have been contact to bring them and keep them like that.

The deeper experience was demanded for the people who sought office, because of the differences in ethical and moral requirements. This could be, and often was, a highly emotional experience. Joeli Bulu, writing to the London Committee asking for more white missionaries, gave an account of events gone by as he had seen them, and said:

> The Lord poured out His Holy Spirit in the manner of olden times: thus it was that many were converted to God. Sinners repented of their sins, hard hearts became soft, and dark minds were enlightened, and the foolish were made wise, and those who were dead spiritually were quickened, and the cursed were blessed.[88]

---

85 At Bau in 1851; Journal of Cargill, 10 January 1837, at Nukunuku; *WM*, November 1838; AR Viwa Circuit 1851. See also Williams and Calvert (1884, 316, 445); Hunt at Ba (Rowe 1860, 221); *WJO*, 1848, 123 for some of many.
86 Journal of Williams, 24 April 1850.
87 Cargill to LC, Journal extracts, 3 January 1836, 19 and 22 May 1836, etc.
88 Bulu to LC, 9 June 1853, from Lakeba, about Nadi, *WM*, 1854, 2:1150.

I give that quotation for the sake of its terminology, not from a European, and yet who, having read his life story, would say that those terms had no meaning for Joeli Bulu? And he had been a mere hearer for some time before the emotional experience, of which he speaks, came to him.

The conception of a group of more intense devotees within a larger group offered no serious cultural barrier to the Fijian of that time, who was familiar with all sorts of societies and cults. Not that these cults were like the Christian church, or its membership within, but I simply make the observation that an inner circle professing a deeper experience was not an altogether foreign idea.

I do not intend at this point to investigate those mass movement demonstrations of emotionalism that led to fainting and wailing, for I shall come to them later. But let them be noted here (Rowe 1860, 165ff., 172ff.; Williams and Calvert 1884, 283; Nettleton 1906, ch. 6, etc.). They came to people under Christian instruction, and whatever their explanation, they had their counterparts in British Wesleyanism and were akin to some apostolic experiences.[89] But even these presented no violent culture clash, for Fiji was familiar with trances and spiritual tension, such as was associated with a priest's inspiration. Descriptions are legion. Lockerby gives a good premissionary example,[90] Williams also describes priest inspiration in detail (Williams and Calvert 1884, 190), Waterhouse's term is "paroxysm of inspiration" (1866, 405), and Joeli Bulu describes another (Fison 1873, 34), and Fison described how a new priest was chosen from the priest clan by means of an inspiration test (n.d., 32–33). So that however different the meaning or use, the Fijian people were not unfamiliar with the characteristics of inspiration, and the description of pagan and Christian inspiration is achieved by means of the same vocabulary. The word *curumi* (inspired) is an example. One could make a long list of words from the heathen ritual, taken over for use in Scripture translation—*soro, vale hi soro, Kalou, vakalougatataka, vakarokoroko, masu, ai madrali, ai bulubulu,* and so on—they are all heathen words, but we never think of them that way today. Christianity has itself over the years charged them with new meaning.

Many of the cultural elements taken over from heathenism but charged with new content in Christianity still persist unto this day. Sometimes the white workers find them unpleasant and express their disapproval. But they still continue. One, for example, is the manner of receiving the annual offerings, which has been criticised as noisy and ostentatious, too obviously competitive and designed to shame the poor giver. But let it not be forgotten that it is the traditional method of the Fijian to bring forward his gift, the people coming one behind the other, and then for a presentation and dedication. Others there are who dislike the Fijian chanting of psalms or catechism. Yet it is not by any means without appeal when one develops a taste for it and an understanding of it. It offers a special field of

---

89 Scores of references in Wesley's journal. See later sections of this monograph.
90 Journal of Lockerby.

leadership to the women and is essentially part of their ancient culture. The preservation of this was the work and genius of Hunt, who prepared the basic catechism. Hazlewood tells of the children assembling every Sunday morning at Ono to chant the catechism (Williams and Calvert 1884, 288).

Hunt's Testament has been described by an old missionary as "a paraphrasic version in the idiom and rhythm of the classic Fijian as spoken at Bau" (Nettleton 1906, 40), which later versions sacrificed for the sake of more literal translation.

> Some of the parables were translated and printed on sheets, to be sung to native lyrics in the schools. Long before the New Testament could be printed as a whole, the young people had the gospel set to music, and were charmed with the story of the Good Samaritan, which they chanted in the schools and also in the home. (Ibid., 41)

Messrs. Hunt and Lyth spent some of their time in isolation at Somosomo in preparing a collection of hymns, based on Wesley's selection, and intended to take its place with the Fijian people. These hymns were prepared for congregational use. "Their native lyrics could be adapted to the Te Deum, the Magnificat or any of the psalms" (ibid., 83–84).

In one way all this shows how the ancient culture was preserved as much as possible, but on the other hand it also shows how eminently suited for the evangelisation of Fiji was the Wesleyan system of worship. Shortly we are to examine the similarities between the Wesleyan revival and that of Fiji, but here, while commenting on music, let it be noted that in the Methodist revival responsiveness to rhythm was intensified "by recurring periods of compelling emotional excitement, followed by the discipline of organised routine and good works in the newly-formed societies" (Dimond 1932, 90). This alternating of experience and service, of worship on the mountaintop and application in valley service inspired a responsiveness to rhythm and fire and the music of words. "Only a long experience of the emotional waves that are set up by the atmosphere of Methodist song can enable the investigator to discern the genius of creative imagination which is manifest in the hymns and music of the revival" (ibid., 98). If Dimond is right in that, it offers a clue also to the remarkable revivals of Viwa and Ono—and these came right out of their real Fijianness.

These things I am describing came from "heathen worship," its form and method, purged and sanctified. It is essential here and now that the critic realise that there was such a thing as worship in pre-Christian Fiji. As Tui Nayau said to his daughter before his conversion, but after hers, "I shall wait a little longer and then decide. I build no temples. I do not attend heathen worship" (Williams and Calvert 1884, 323). We note he had become indifferent about his old religion. Some heathen priests had learned much of the art of prayer, and several examples of their prayers have been preserved.[91] For all the horror and ugliness, the hate, the murder and revenge of the ancient Fijian religion, there was in it just

---

91   For example, Fison (1873, 48); Baker letter, 16 October 1865, *WMN*. Best example I know is in Hazlewood (1850, 63–64).

the same a basic structure on which the missionaries could start to work—its belief in Divinity, in life after death, its use of sacred persons (priests) and places (like temples), with its use of prayer and worship, its idea of community worship. The elements of religion were there, and the vocabulary. And the early missionaries rejected nothing they felt could be sanctified in the worship of the true God.

Recapitulation: Did the form of Christianity given to the Fijians by the missionaries and native preachers represent a serious culture clash? Was it a white man's or a Fijian church?

1. What clash there was, was a clash with the culture, not the clash of culture.
2. The general form and method of worship of Christianity, hymns, chants, offerings, and so on were essentially Fijian, understood and appreciated by them, and attractive to the heathen also.
3. To some extent the theology of the God of Battles, and the prophetic Jehovah/Baal struggles of the Old Testament, was a natural stepping-stone from heathenism and has been slowly discarded by following generations en route to the New Testament. (Qualifying this, however, Christology had a very important place with those in membership.)
4. Two types of conversion are noted, one formal and the other spiritual; one leading to attendance at worship, the other to membership and responsibility. A classificatory system is found to be truly Fijian.
5. No serious discipline is demanded of the new nominal convert (adherent), but a rigid discipline is imposed on any seeking status or responsibility. This is voluntary. It is subject to a period of trial, to instruction, and a rite of admission. As a system it offers no cultural clash. The Fijians were familiar with taboo, which is compared with discipline. It was never expected without a prior spiritual experience.
6. The phenomena and terminology of "inspiration" was known and accepted. Christianity took over the terminology of heathen worship. As time went on it acquired new meaning. New theological terms acquired meaning by means of the use of suitable narratives—the prodigal and his father, the Good Samaritan, etc.
7. The genius of the Fijian church was that it provided a place for converts at all stages of religious development, and this considerably reduced the "clash" and aided growth in experience.
8. Allowing for the fact that Christian missionaries did come to Fiji to destroy inhumanity and cannibalism, etc., and to introduce the people to Christ, the Saviour of all people, and that this inevitably involved a clash in itself, there was no more. It certainly cannot be said that the Christians were like the

proverbial "ducks out of water"! It certainly cannot be said they were deprived of their culture and lived in a white man's culture, theological and unfamiliar. Shortly we shall investigate the nature of their religious faith.

5

CAKOBAU HIMSELF, HIS KINGDOM, AND HIS HOUSE

The publication of this study on the nature of religious experience among the Fijian people is made relevant by the present "Centenary of the Conversion of Ratu Cakobau," and having made some attempt to clarify a number of issues on which there has been some confusion, it now becomes necessary for us to examine the exact significance of this important event—and this is no easy matter, so tied up it is with tribal and political issues.

If what I have claimed is true—viz., that his conversion as such did not bring a really great number into the church, except perhaps in the islands of Lomaiviti, where there was already a growing Christian cause—what, we may say, is the value of going further? The conversion of Cakobau had another effect of great importance on the church which demands stating, as we shall do in a moment.

One often hears people stating in a single sentence that Cakobau was converted because of this or that—but the matter is nothing like so simple. For a long time Cakobau had been interested in Christianity and at times most generously disposed,[92] and sometimes he was a hostile persecutor.[93] For a long time his daughter had been a leader of the Christian women in Bau.[94] Carefully observing the missionaries, he had long been convinced that their purpose was not self-interest, but rather to help Fiji and the Fijians (Williams and Calvert 1884, 444, 462, 478). On one occasion after Calvert had tried to save a case of widow strangling and departed unsuccessful, Cakobau said to the people who remained: "How the missionaries labour to save life! They take any trouble and go anywhere for our salvation. And we are always trying to kill one another" (ibid., 463). Among those missionaries was John Hunt, whose life and work, and especially his triumphant death, had made a profound impression upon the chief (Rowe 1860, 272). Later he confessed that he was "favourably impressed towards the Christian religion, when I saw it made dying not only easy but triumphant" (Nettleton 1906, 116). Besides the lives of these men were those of Fijians, great heathen warriors, who one by one had become Christian, and been equally

---

92 Especially 1847–49. See AR Viwa Circuit 1847–49; Williams and Calvert (1884, 488).
93 Prior to and after this period. Heavy persecution 1845 after Varani's conversion; began again 1850. Viwa 1845, 1850.
94 For ten years before Cakobau's conversion (AR Viwa Circuit 1844).

great in another way. None was more respected by Cakobau than Varani, and when he died Cakobau cried in anguish, "Varani is dead and I have lost my right hand."[95] These were early and continuous factors which, no doubt, allowed him to keep his stake in religion through his family.

Not to be overlooked also was the Christian witness of the schools, dispensaries, and such institutions, particularly at Viwa, which he inspected with much admiration,[96] and upon his visit to Lakeba he was astonished at its complete transformation under Christianity (AR Viwa Circuit 1852). The dying Hunt had sent him a message. "Tell Cakobau," he said in his last struggling breath, "Tell Cakobau to remember the exhortation, that it is in his interest to embrace Christianity—and to remember his promise to become a Christian"[97]

To these we must add a great accumulation of purely political factors, which Cakobau might well have felt was a concentrated effort of Jehovah against him, for many, he knew, were praying to God about him. I summarise them thus:

1. The revolt of Ovalau (Williams and Calvert 1884, 485ff.; Waterhouse 1866, 207ff.).
2. The opposition of the Levuka whites, who controlled shipping, arms, and ammunition (Williams and Calvert 1884, 488; Waterhouse 1866, 216).
3. The blockade of Bau (Williams and Calvert 1884, 488; Waterhouse 1866, 216).
4. The seizing of the ammunition and revolt of Kaba (Waterhouse 1866, 204–5).
5. The second burning of Bau (ibid., 204, 231).[98]
6. The defense of Rewa (ibid., 202, etc.).
7. Series of small defeats—Verata, Kaba, Sawakasa (ibid., 178, 243, 256, etc.).
8. Passive resistance against his levies and taxes, and his unpopularity on their account (Williams and Calvert 1884, 481ff.; Waterhouse 1866, 197).
9. Death of Varani on a peace mission in his interests.[99]
10. Assassination of Tuikilakila.[100]

Such a sequence of calamities must have caused Cakobau some very serious thinking. Calvert and Waterhouse called on Cakobau, and so writes the former:

> We found him very thoughtful. He referred to the murder of his relative, the old King of Somosomo, who had been killed in his bed while asleep, by his son and nephew, and was evidently affected. I told him that the deceased had been well instructed by several missionaries, etc., etc.

We can well imagine what Calvert and Waterhouse made of this opportunity.[101]

---

95 Contemporary series on *Christianity in Fiji*, no. 111, on Varani, CB.
96 Calvert to LC, 28 October 1852. Also Wallis (1851, 30).
97 Journal of Lyth (5:10).
98 First, 1852; second, 4 March 1854.
99 See Young, "Varani of Fiji," *WM*, 1855, 1:407ff. Also AR Viwa Circuit 1854; Williams and Calvert (1884, 485ff.); Waterhouse (1866, 211–15, 252).
100 Calvert to LC, 20 May 1854, *WM*, 1855, 1:88–89.
101 Ibid.

In addition to the above, there were certain repeating factors that disturbed Cakobau. There was, for instance, the complete agreement on the part of commanders of visiting ships, traders, naval men, and missionaries, on the wrong of cannibalism, widow strangling, and other customs of his people, so that many of them had urged him to accept Christianity. To name a few of them—Erskine of the *Havannah* (Williams and Calvert 1884, 456); Fanshawe of the *Daphne* (Waterhouse 1866, 174ff.); Pollard of the *Bramble* (ibid., 177-78); Home of the *Calliope* (ibid., 197ff.); Owen, trader of Adelaide (ibid., 206); Wallis of the *Zatoff* (Wallis 1851); McGruder of the *St. Mary's* (AR Viwa Circuit 1852-53). These all came in this same period of the missionaries' continuous attack on Cakobau, and it is by no means a full list. The full home correspondence with Cakobau is preserved[102]; also the detail of the speeches by Erskine (1853, 187), Pollard (ibid., 292), and others.

In addition to these there were some purely religious factors—the prayers of the people and the persistence of the missionaries—who never missed a chance of putting the challenge to him. The conversation referred to above with Calvert went from Tuikilakila to himself. He was sick at the time. Calvert told him "he had been well instructed by several, and that the Lord had also afflicted him for his profit, so that he also would be without excuse at God's dread tribunal." His affairs were in confusion and beyond the power of human unraveling (Williams and Calvert 1884, 489).[103] From my reading of the records, I imagine this to be a normal Calvert attack. The men differed greatly in this respect. There does not seem to be much evidence of success with this type of reasoning in the early period. The Fijian Bulu had just as much to fear as hell. However, Cakobau was attentive and asked "if the Lord did undertake cases when human wisdom failed, and where it was customary for affliction to be rendered useful in bringing people to God." He was more interested in a possible solution of his problems than the events of the judgement. There was a religious element in it all the same. Within his own household the prayers of Adi Samununu were being continually offered on his account (Waterhouse 1866, 256). For long he had been convinced of the uselessness of his own household gods (ibid.; Williams and Calvert 1884, 443).

Then there were those two events which actually are supposed to have brought things to a head—the disclosure of Consul Williams' newspaper correspondence (Waterhouse 1866, 244-47)[104]; and the personal appeal of George of Tonga, his letter from Australia, and his visit (ibid., 243-44).[105]

It has been suggested that he turned Christian to gain Tongan aid. It could have been so, but I have found no direct evidence to this effect. There were good reasons for keeping

---

102 WM, 1853, 1:481-86.
103 Also Calvert to LC, 20 May 1854, WM, 1855, 1:88-89.
104 Text given.
105 Text of letter given.

Tonga out of it, and Cakobau was not unaware of them. The simplest explanation is that it was a real conversion, and he felt he was doing the right thing. There is evidence that it was quite a religious decision. For instance his last questions were very significant—"Will not God cast me off, if I call upon His name, whom I have so ill-treated?" (ibid., 257). It was something new for Cakobau. It was an emotional moment. He wept. He had a new and foreign spirit of meekness. So he reached his personal decision to become a Christian (ibid.).

For most people it should have ended there, but not for Cakobau. He knew he was a political figure, and the hope of his people's paramountcy in Fiji largely rested with him, either as a heathen or a Christian. He had no intention of seeing any breakup of Bau through his decision. Next day he took it to council and again the next. He never lost sight of his responsibility to the clan and the grim reality of the political situation with which they were faced (ibid., 257–58). Ultimately the council followed him. Some tried to delay his decision a little, but his mind was set, and the religion of Christ was officially accepted both by the family of Cakobau and by the kingdom of Bau. In this form it came, not by the decision of Cakobau, but by the council of the chiefs under his leadership, and it came at a time when they were faced with dire peril.

Now this peculiar twist which Cakobau gave to the whole affair, making his personal act accompany a political change, is so important that I shall quote in detail the records:

> The day following (his personal decision) the king held a full meeting of the chiefs and governors from the adjacent towns on the mainland. Smothering his new-born feelings, he appeared in their midst as an acute man of the world. Having referred to the contrast between his own country and that of Tonga, and having expressed the wish to make some beneficial changes, he requested the missionary to state the purport of King George['s] despatch and to translate the consul's letter. This was done. The missionary added a few remarks on the importance of the human soul. A long conversation ensued. Some endeavoured to cause the king to procrastinate, but he remained firm. (Ibid., 257)

That was what happened on Friday, 28 April, as described by Waterhouse, the missionary present. He had moved into Bau in late 1853 (ibid., 223–25).

> On Saturday Cakobau assembled his male relatives and the principal chiefs of the city. The political aspect of the question was fully discussed. A near relative of the king ventured to remind Cakobau that he himself was the only man troubling Fiji; and that if he resolved to become a Christian, the whole country would rejoice. It was eventually resolved that the king and Ratu Mua should wait on the missionary, as a deputation, to make inquiries. The result of this interview was deemed satisfactory, and the deputation returned to the meeting and made its report. It was then resolved that the religion of Christ should be substituted for the vain traditions received from their fathers. (Ibid., 257–58)

The religious service in which Cakobau actually "bent the knee" took place on the following day, Sunday, and has been already described. For our purposes at the moment we should try to remove from these quotations those phrases which are obviously the missionary himself, and get away from opinions to basic facts. (I am not questioning his opinions, but looking for facts.)

It is clear that the drama comprised four distinct acts on four days, brought to a head by King George's letter warning Cakobau of Consul Williams' attack on him in the overseas press.

1. There was a session Cakobau had with his wife, Adi Litia Samununu, and Waterhouse, in which he made a personal decision, somewhat emotional and probably with some religious conviction. Thursday, 27 April 1854.

2. On Friday it was put to the chiefs of the kingdom of Bau, extending beyond the confines of the island itself. The social and religious aspects were discussed frankly, its probable effect, their relationship with George of Tonga and with Consul Williams. The king explained his decision. Some would have hindered. He remained firm. No one actively opposed him. So the kingdom of Bau accepted Christianity. Later some did leave Cakobau and join the rebels, but they did not do so at this time (AR Bau Circuit 1855).

3. Saturday, 29th. The matter was now discussed by his clan. It was an independent act and no missionary was present. Questions arose, were referred to him through a deputation, answered; and the discussion went on. The house of Cakobau in this meeting officially accepted Christianity as their religion.

4. Sunday, 30th. The personal, national, and family decision was ratified by the ritual act of public witness, and they placed themselves under religious instruction. The family priest preceded the king into the building, for his offices were more than religious. He did not become a Christian, however, but continued a heathen and died one (Williams and Calvert 1884, 491; AR Bau Circuit 1856).

It is not difficult to see that such a sequence of events would have important bearing on the nature of the Christian church in Bau, which is (as I, the present resident missionary in Bau can declare) entirely different from the church in most parts of Fiji. To compare the democratic church of Suva with the chiefly church of Bau (and I have ministered to both congregations) is to find oneself in two completely different worlds.

Cakobau's religious experience, as with most of us, progressed in stages. Though his initial decision had signs of having been a sincere religious one, it was not until 1857 that he had advanced sufficiently to present himself for baptism. But from this point he developed rapidly in the faith. But this was not so with all his friends and relations. Many never got beyond that initial step. This indeed has constituted a serious problem in every chiefly place, or in every place where the church is "chiefly" rather than "democratic"—a problem still met today.

The need of that first conversion from heathenism to Christianity has gone, and the chiefs who are now born in the Christian society often fail to see the need of that spiritual conversion, which would bring them into line with the fellowship of members. Yet they claim their right as chiefs to determine the affairs of their people, a right which is theirs by native tradition. So the young church faces a serious dilemma—is its policy to be determined by those who have a deep religious experience, or by those who are born as chiefs? There are some villages, known well to me, where the leading chief has experienced a sound conversion, and here, without any doubt, we find Fijian Christianity at its very best; but there are others where the chiefs think little more than of food, liquor, and women—here the church is compelled to be democratic or perish.

The present constitution of the church, which was evolved within our own committees, endeavours to honour the native traditions and social structure. Each area sends its lay representative to Synod, and he is the intermediary between the church courts and the chiefs. It works fairly well, but problems do arise, and more often than not these are a clash between a democratic but spiritual fellowship and a chiefly but unspiritual authority. Fortunately these cases are not common, but they do arise.

In fairness to those who have gone before, let it be pointed out that there was no other alternative. If the church was to be received by the people, it had to be in a form that would fit the Fijian way of life. Control had to be maintained, and the moral dislocation of life was sufficient without inflicting a foreign system upon the people.

Sometimes in recent days Fijian chiefs have stated that the church has become too democratic. Undoubtedly there has been a democratic trend, but the greatest cause of this has been the shortcomings of the chiefs themselves. A chief who looks upon the people as "my people," and cares for their place of worship, and sees that the Fijian minister is well set up with the needs of life and is paid when the pay is due, will never find that his church is anything but chiefly. But if he neglects worship, and lets the building fall into disrepair, and makes his minister wait months for his pay, while he himself is more concerned with liquor, he is equally certain to find the congregation, having got on without his support, grows democratic. My strong feeling is that village Christianity still prefers to be chiefly. In the towns, however, we are in a different environment.

In ancient times even a chief had to obey the rules of his tribal religion and observe its taboos, and this religion maintained the chiefs' authority. So if the chiefly system is to continue, it will partly resolve on whether or not the chiefs maintain the religion of their people. To neglect it is to speed democracy on its way, and this is slowly breaking down the system on which their chieftainship stands.

Now Ratu Cakobau was a penetrating thinker, and as long as he lived, he thought of "my people." He saw the value of Christianity; he saw that it had many forms; he saw that sooner or later Fiji must accept it. Long before his conversion he stated this (Williams and Calvert 1884, 478; Lawry and Hoole 1850, 54), and so had Tui Dreketi (Rowe 1860, 71–72), and so had Tui Nayau (Williams and Calvert 1884, 315), and Tanoa (Wallis 1851), but all had wars to finish first. The struggles of the early church, the persecutions it suffered, and its faithful spirit were not unobserved by Cakobau. He realised that this could be a frightfully disrupting force in a land, or a unifying force, and for Bau's sake he strove to bind this new religion to the chiefly system as the people of Fiji knew it.

The importance of Cakobau's conversion and the decisions of the April meetings of 1854 was not so much that many others followed and became Christian, but that Cakobau thereby welded together the church and the chiefly system, and in doing so he virtually determined the course of events for the following century. He assured Christianity of a hearing, and he preserved the only system of effective control that was workable at that time. I feel myself that Cakobau, not the missionaries, was the "actor" of the drama.

Kaba was inevitable after that, and Cakobau had no illusions about that. The rebels were increasing, the net was closing in. Sooner or later he would have to fight—not for Christianity, but for his own authority, which Kaba reestablished. His display of mercy to the captives was a public confirmation of his new faith. A hundred years have passed since Cakobau "bent the knee." For that century the impress of Cakobau has been upon it. The chiefs own the property, care for it, finance their circuit sections, carry their ministers and catechists, and assist the general central funds. But it is the peculiar genius of this church that it provides avenues of service and fields for Christian self-expression for all its people, and at the same time it may be geared for the chiefly system in the villages or for a democratic body in a town or industrial area, without any serious dislocation.

What the next century holds in store, who can tell? As long as the chiefly families raise men with interest and faith and zeal, the predominant position in village Christianity is theirs by right of birth and tradition. But should they, on the other hand, show their inclination is towards things less noble, then I have no doubt it will be an automatic gear change to the democratic. For the time being the decision still lies with the chiefs.

Recapitulation: What was the nature of Cakobau's conversion and what bearing had it on the Fijian church?

1. The conversion of Cakobau was the result of a combination of a great many factors—social, political, and religious.
2. His personal decision was not without emotion and would seem to have been quite a spiritual one in a way.
3. The kingdom of Bau was acquainted of his mind before any public act took place, and no objection was raised.
4. The house of Cakobau discussed the decision from the social and religious angles and resolved to accept Christianity as their official religion.
5. The personal, national, and family acts were ratified by public rite of "bending the knee."

6. The most important consequence was the welding of the church to the chiefly system. It is thus part of the Fijian culture. This has been so for a hundred years.
7. The church, however, is so constituted that it may be geared to the democratic system in towns or industrial areas.
8. As to whether or not the church clings to the chiefly system for the next century will largely depend on the character of the chiefs in the local areas and their interest or otherwise in it.

PART TWO

6

THE FIJIAN EVANGELICAL

By its very nature this section of the monograph is quite different from the first. The former section was mainly a study of cause and effect, of secular, political, and military factors that made some impact on the church, and to what extent. The conversions with which we dealt were mainly nominal, and we endeavoured to relate them to a church system. To the nature and effect of Cakobau's conversion we devoted a good deal of space. All that we now leave behind—we are in a different world. This world is one, which, unlike the last, has not been studied to any degree at all by the historians, and which does not involve us in the critical problems of the last.

Had the factors stated in the last part represented the whole story, there would have been no Methodist Church in Fiji today. The real cause of its existence is, without any doubt at all, the work of the Fijian and Tongan evangelical, and his work is best studied in the early period, before any big chief was converted, and before there was any thought of a God of Battles. The church in Lakeba before the conversion of Tui Nayau and in Viwa before the conversion of Ratu Cakobau are the best for study. And please note now that we are passing beyond that outer circle of adherents, mere nominal Christians, to the members, the leaders—the evangelicals. What was the nature of their spiritual experience? What did they believe? What kind of a faith did they have? How did they die? How did they stand up to persecution? What was the nature of their revivals? The questions, surely, indicate the change of tone.

We have seen that the leaders of the church awaited a second conversion, a spiritual experience, before admitting a person into the real flock. Spiritual growth and increased responsibility were expected to go together. Both white missionaries and native Christians looked for "outpourings of the Spirit" (the common phrase used),[106] or "fresh manifestations" of God's love, as Hunt used to put it,[107] which were expected to lead on to new service. Thus, for instance, James Havea could divide his life into a series of stages, each

---

106 See most Annual Reports (e.g., Viwa Circuit 1845).
107 See account of Hunt's death (Rowe 1860, 267, etc.).

itself the response to a new spiritual experience (Havea n.d.), and the same phenomena exactly can be found in, for example, the life of William Cross (Hunt 1846, ch. 1).

Indeed, the more one penetrates into the old records, the more he realises that the religious experiences themselves, which the Tongan and Fijian Christians enjoyed, were remarkably similar to those of the evangelicals of Britain and America; or, to use their own terminology, the manifestations of the Holy Ghost in Viwa or Ono or Kadavu might well have been accounts from Cornwall or New England. By merely changing the names of the places and people, the love-feast testimonies from one place might well be taken as from the other. There are pages and pages from the missionary journals telling of these, which might as well come from Wesley himself, or Robe of Kilsyth, or Edwards of New England.

Before evaluating any of these experiences, I wish to make three observations.

Firstly, may I ask, if this is so, how can the secular historians say that there was no response to the preaching of the missionaries in the early days? I think I should have little difficulty in producing up to about fifty specific references to religious experiences that have come from the result of their preaching, and I think I could still do that and confine myself to the first decade of the mission. It is something I have never ceased to admire as I have gone through the records—that these early missionaries seem to have got their messages across in a truly remarkable manner. They taught solid Christology. They gave the doctrine, but with it a narrative. The narrative stuck, the teaching was obvious, the name of the doctrine was appended (Nettleton 1906, 40). But what is more than this, they did get converts. Let the reader not imagine that their preaching was fruitless.

My second observation is that a great many of the initial conversions were accompanied by emotional displays, and, as much as could be expected from a heathen, some were spiritual experiences. But it was more with Christians who had been for some time under instruction and guidance that the real spiritual revivals came—in class, prayer meetings, and divine service. This again was so also in the Wesleyan revival.

As a third observation may I point out some remarkable similarities about the nature of the preaching and acts of devotion from which these revivals sprang. Tyerman has pointed out that great revivals mostly sprang from one type of preaching (1870–71, 1:223). Christian David of Moravia was preaching salvation by simple faith in Christ (ibid.); Jonathan Edwards in New England, justification by faith alone (ibid., 1:218); James Robe in Kilsyth, regeneration (ibid., 1:223). Wesley wrote to Whitefield of how such a movement began when he was arguing on the cause and fruit of justification.[108] On such occasions as these the outbursts of intense enthusiasm were experienced. Such an outburst was experienced at Viwa in Fiji in 1844 at Pentecost, and others followed. In a prayer meeting Hunt stated the purpose as "confession of sin, and pleading for God's mercy through Christ"

---

108   Wesley to Whitefield, 16 March 1739 (Tyerman 1870–71, 1:224).

(Rowe 1860, 180). It usually began so, and shortly I shall devote a whole section of this monograph to these revivals, but meantime be it noted that whether they started in a sermon, a prayer, or a hymn, it was usually some aspect of soteriology.

In those three respects I find the evangelical experience of Fiji similar to that of England. The value of preaching; that the deeper conversions came after a period of instruction; and that some aspect of soteriology was the theme of sermon, prayer, or hymn when it began.

Was there, you may want to ask, any striking difference between revival experience in England and in Fiji? The only difference that is immediately apparent as one goes over the records is that in Fiji they were often associated with baptismal services. One does not greatly wonder at this. In a heathen country where converts were being won, there were many baptisms; and because of the personal sacrifices involved in a heathen environment (for converts were not all attached to mission stations but had to live among their own people), probably baptisms were times of crisis when feelings long suppressed came near the surface. In addition to this the statement of fundamental experience and saving grace would have to be stated in the service. That these experiences could be so real to Englishmen and also to Fijians just coming out of cannibalism shows the essential uniformity of the nature of man, his openness to conviction of sin, and grace through Christ by faith, and certainty of life everlasting.

7

HIS SIMPLE FAITH

Simple it was, but how strong! As one reads the accounts of these native Christians, their experiences at sea and in war and under persecution, there is one thing that stands out—*faith*. A good deal of their logic differs from ours—but it is a form of logic for all that. And there is a confidence and quality about this faith that is not found among the heathen in their religion. Then whence did it spring in their hearts?

By bringing a score or more somewhat similar episodes together for purposes of comparison, I have discovered some facts, which, to me at least, are very suggestive. I am struck by the number of these converts who went off into the forest alone to pray—before their conversion. Bilivucu had done it (Fison n.d., 14), and he also found a boy doing it (ibid., 26). James Havea did it (Havea n.d.). Joeli Bulu did it (Fison 1873, 12). So did Varani.[109] Well, having established that this was so, you may still ask what was strange about that? The strange thing about it was that it was not Fijian—it was Christian. Heathen prayed, that is true, but they always used a priest. But these men were out in the forest, alone, on their knees, praying to an unknown God. They had no priest. They were neither begging nor enquiring. On their own evidence, they were fighting against a conviction. They were wrestling with God. Without guidance and without instruction they were in agony, feeling in the dark for God. That is not my figure, it is Joeli Bulu's. He was like a man in a dark house feeling for an exit—and the door was suddenly opened before him (Fison 1873, 15). Their going out alone and hiding in the forest shows there was also an element of resistance there. Such men were bound to find a mighty faith once they got their feet on solid earth.

A large percentage of the few thousand who were converted before any great chief had "bent the knee," had wrestled their way into the Society, and they came in knowing very well they might lose their lives that day for doing so. Their missionaries had come to Fiji in that same spirit. A more timid person once said later on to Calvert, "But weren't you afraid to die out there in Fiji?" and Calvert replied quietly, "We died before we went" (Nettleton 1906, 27).

---

109   Hunt to LC, WM, 1846, 2:926.

Our Fijian pioneers would not have put it that way. Their logic was different, but their faith was as strong. It had come by a realisation that if they became God's men they might well be in glory on the morrow, and they needed then a sheer sense of dependence and resignation to serve or die as He might will. Time after time their love-feast testimonies bring out this element in their faith.

There were some attractive elements about Christianity that often drew the heathen quietly to go and hear a preacher,[110] and they were not obliged to commit themselves in any way. But often the message got through, and, as with Bilivucu, he would find himself saying, "My soul longs to know that God. What shall I do?" (Fison n.d., 14). Then those lone visits to the forest would begin. It was such a sermon that first challenged Joeli Bulu also (Fison 1873, 12-13), and James Havea (n.d.) and Necani Cataki also,[111] and old Silivanusi,[112] who had heard Cross preaching like that; and Joeli Keteca had been so challenged by another Fijian,[113] and so it went on. These men I have mentioned became preachers and were all fine evangelists in their day. They were convinced of sin by preaching, and by preaching also most of them found the gate of life. Quite by accident my examples were all men, possibly in my subconscious was the fact that they all became preachers. It might serve as a corrective to the idea that only women were among those early converts.

Missionary journals preserve records of love-feast testimonies like this from Cross:

> Some renounced their false gods in profession only, and continued to live in sin, until by the preaching of the Gospel they were brought to repentance. Some remembered the particular text and sermon, which had been of use to them in bringing them "out of darkness into marvelous light." "And this," says Cross, "was not confined to the Tonguese," and the date, 20th July, 1837, less than two years after their arrival, and 12 years before the conversion of their chief. (Hunt 1846, 93)

One of the great things the church provided was an organisation within which the people could express their faith and grow in grace. Let it not be forgotten that their experiences were progressive. Joeli Bulu used to tell that after that first sermon had sent him off into the forest to pray, another on the wheat and tares took him a stage further (Fison 1873, 12-13), and still another led him on to real repentance (ibid., 14); and then there was a testimony, during which he fainted—but found life (ibid., 15-16). It all shows his experience had to be battled step-by-step, and the battle usually began long before the "knee was bent." Coming thus into the Society, they grew.

Koroi Tukana, a Bauan warrior, stated that he had a "favourable opinion of Christianity long before he embraced it" and had been expelled from Bau on account of it. That was

---

110   Journal of Williams, 24 April 1850; Cargill to LC, Journal extracts, 3 January 1836, 19 and 22 May 1836, etc.
111   Journal of Hazlewood, 29 December 1848 (Williams and Calvert 1884, 289).
112   Ibid., 290.
113   Ibid., 289.

nine years before the conversion of Cakobau, during the persecution of 1845, which had arisen because of the Viwa conversions that year. Here are his words:

> I did not at first think of Christianity at Viwa. I began at Bau. I was in Viwa some time before I renounced heathenism. At length Litia persuaded me to become a Christian. I wish to follow Jesus on earth, and then to see Him above. I desire that my friends may lotu. I have now no God but one. We formerly thought sin right; but we have learnt to think differently. We now see sin in the light of the Lord, and we desire to follow His steps. We are now concerned about our friends who are eating one another. This is my mind. (Lawry and Hoole 1850, 60)

That man had then been attending worship for three years.

Ilaija Varani stated his experience had been one of growth, that when he first professed Christianity it had been very rudimentary. "I have nothing else to speak of but 'the love of God,'" he said. "I professed religion some time before I knew His love, but now I know it. Now I wish to do what He approves and to hate what He disapproves" (ibid.). Yet his initial experience had been a spiritual one.

Silas Faone, a Tongan teacher, put it like this—"When I was in Tonga I had the love of God, but it was not complete. In Rewa I had it also. Now in Ono my love is perfected" (Williams and Calvert 1884, 285). Joeli Moto had repented genuinely four months before "the Spirit of God bore witness with his spirit that (he) was his child,"[114] and Silivanusi, previously mentioned, used to quote Paul's pressing towards the mark of the high calling of God in Christ Jesus as expressing his own personal experience.[115]

So much were these young Christians compelled by circumstances to cast themselves on God, that from this there grew a feeling that God Himself was in the events of their everyday lives—any testings were sent for the good of their souls, or for the good of their witness, and any deliverance from calamity was evidence of His grace towards them. So in good or bad, in life or death, they praised God. Nor were they unlike the missionaries in this respect. The records these Fijians and Tongans have left of their remarkable deliverances, especially in storms at sea, bring out the nature of this faith.

As one typical example of many, I quote James Havea—and I am translating from his own handwriting:

> When the waves were big and terrifying, they asked me that night, when we were allowing ourselves to run before the wind, if I thought they might die. My reply was that nothing was difficult for God if it was His will that they live a little longer upon this earth for there were plenty of places where He could take us. [They were sailing in the Lau Group. A.R.T.] But if, on the other hand, it was His will that we should enter that place where there is neither wind nor wave, then we ought right now to consider our lives and our sailing, whether our prows be headed straight for life eternal, or whether we be drifting away to

---

114 Journal of Hazlewood, 29 December 1848 (Williams and Calvert 1884, 290).
115 Ibid.

> destruction. And they were silent and afraid. And many were the sharks which followed, waiting to devour us; but we were spared by the power of God, for after two nights like this and on the third day we entered the reef at Nairai and our canoe drove hard on the sand so that there was no need to anchor her, but we all ran to land and were soon warming ourselves before a fire and rejoicing in our having been spared through the continuing love of God. (Havea n.d.)

They were thirty degrees off their course and 120 miles from their desired haven. When I consider the whole of the tale from which I have extracted that portion, I am reminded of many similarities with Paul's voyage to Rome, nor was the faith of James Havea far from the kind of faith manifested by Paul on that occasion (Acts 27).

In very much the same way, Joeli Bulu lived through a storm and after prayer experienced a "stilling" of the storm as had happened of old on Galilee. Even the similarities in the telling are remarkable (Fison 1873, 67–71). In times of war,[116] in the mountains and along the river courses (ibid., 57–59), in many strange places,[117] in shipwrecks,[118] and hurricanes,[119] on land, and on sea these men experienced astonishing deliverances. That there could ever be so much need for deliverance shows only the peril of the days in which they lived, and if there is only one thing we could say about these men, it would have to be that they had found a faith adequate to their experience. The old gods of Fiji were no mere idols of wood and stone, they were gods of action, many of them deified ancestor heroes, who had proved their might on earth; but none of them were gods like unto the one true God, whom they had now come to serve. The deliverances of the psalmist they knew daily (Fison 1873, 29–41).[120]

They cherished the Scriptures and read daily the portions they had, and what is more, they applied them to daily life. This strikes one forcefully quite frequently, and it is a strong characteristic of their form of faith. Let me give a couple of examples from the story of Bilivucu, the *Mata ki Lakeba* from Vuaqava (the official representative and messenger of this island to Lakeba, the island of its paramount chief), who later on took Sefanaia as his Christian name. I select two of many examples to bring out this childlike faith in applied Scripture.

> Another man hit me on the head with an earthenware cooking pot, because I was zealous in beseeching him to lotu, and then he abused me when the pot was broken. I went away to my house sorrowful, for my head was very sore, and so was my heart because of the insult. [The pot was a kitchen thing. To be hit with a club was no insult, but with a pot was. A.R.T.] When I entered my house I sat down and thought what I should do, for the insult was very grievous, and a

---

116 Fison (1873, 39–41) for a good example.
117 Havea's experiences in Tonga as a prisoner supply abundant examples (n.d.).
118 En route to Beqa (ibid.).
119 For example, Nadi hurricane and flood, 1848 (Fison 1873, 67–71); also Havea (n.d.).
120 Also Psalm 46:9–11.

great anger sprang up in my soul, till I began to look at the place where my club was hanging on the wall. But a voice said within me, "That is not the way," and I answered, "Lord, what is the way? Tell me what I should do." And with that I looked up—for I had been sitting with my head bowed down—my eye fell upon the Book which lay near me, where I had put it down after my morning prayers. I stretched forth my hand and took it up, and when I opened it, this was the word I saw, "Blessed are they which are persecuted for righteousness['] sake, for theirs is the Kingdom of God." It is in the Sermon on the Mount. "My Lord! My Lord!" I cried. My anger fled away, and my soul, was filled with joy. I leaped to my feet, took my best cooking pot and ran with it to the house of the man who had struck me. "This is to replace the pot you have broken," I said. The man stared at me in amazement. "Here is a wonderful thing!" he cried, and went to his sleeping place, and brought a whale's tooth, and laying it down before me as his atonement, he asked my pardon for striking me. "Be of a good mind," he said, "Let this tooth of a fish be my atonement for the evil I have done." I took it up for if I had not taken it up he would have been ashamed. "I take your atonement," I said, "but none was needed, for you have given me the Kingdom of Heaven. Hear now what my Lord says about it," and then I read the word to him from my Book, which I had brought with me together with the pot. He asked for more, and I read him the whole of the Sermon on the Mount—to him and his friends, for the breaking of the pot had been noised abroad, and many of them came to hear the news. (Fison n.d., 22-25)

The second will have to be abbreviated, much as I regret it. It tells of a disease left on the island by a white man's ship. A number died. A kinsman of Sefanaia, still heathen, was seriously ill, and a grave had been dug for him within the house, and the wailing party had assembled.

One day I was reading my book and I came to the word that was written by James: "Is any sick among you? Let him call for the elders of the Church and let them pray over him, anointing him with oil in the name of the Lord; and the prayer of faith shall save the sick, and the Lord shall raise him up." I rose straightway and taking my Book and a bottle of coconut oil, ran to my kinsman's house. He was lying close to the fire and his face was as the face of the dead. "I am come to report a great thing to you." I said: "You have been offering that fat pig of yours, and other wealth besides, to the gods, that you may live, but you have grown worse and worse, and here is this God of mine, who will heal you for nothing, if I ask Him." And I read to him. "Shall I report you to Him?" I asked. And he answered, "That I may live." So I poured the oil on him and rubbed it all over his body, and then I knelt down and prayed to the Lord for him. Before I came to the end of my prayer, he threw off his covering and sat up. "I live!" he cried. His wife was sitting by him, and he said to her: "Bring hither a sulu, that I may put it on. Put one on yourself, and let our children have one apiece. This house is lotu today."

And Sefanaia prayed with the family, giving thanks and seeking guidance for them in the way. His kinsman, now hungry, asked for fish, and an amazed crowd gathered to see

Tuiwai eating food and two young men filling in an empty grave. With an epidemic on the island it requires no imagination to guess what happened after that. And Sefanaia had to point out that he could not heal them; he could only present their petitions to the Lord. But many times he prayed and all for whom he prayed, recovered, and the church grew (ibid., 46–50).

Those stories were selected to illustrate the faith these men had in the Scriptures as a sound means of guidance, as God's directions for human life, and their boldness to apply them, where most of us would have had faint hearts. Here is one of the tap roots of the early Fijian church. These people, and especially those of them who were called to positions of leadership, had an experience like that of the Hebrew patriarchs. They were called out into an *unknown*, and they had to go out in faith, with nothing to cling to but God. They were called to be "God's men." It was a challenge *of faith* and *to faith*, and many were the mighty deliverances, which only increased that faith.

It may be fairly safely said that there were few, if any, political or convenience conversions in the first stages of the mission—say, up to the conversion of Tui Nayau in 1849.[121] And as a general statement that would be fairly sound up to the conversion of Cakobau in 1854. Clearly the forties was a period of great spiritual advance, when, in the face of persecution and death, Christian characters were forged and faith discovered. They were great men, and they had great stories to tell—and they certainly knew how to tell them. For every theological doctrine they had a Bible story, and they had a lived experience and a faith that was infectious.

This faith must be viewed historically. Many of us may disagree about their logic—that is not my concern here. But we cannot doubt the reality of their faith. As Paula, an old man of Viwa, who had learned Christianity under the preaching of Cross, said:

> The lotu in my mind has been something like a tree, that grows up by degrees, and grows quite straight; it is not turned aside by anything . . . I was a bad man, but God loved me. The wind blows on me (That is, the evil words of men), but I am like the tree that moves not. I praise God only. (Lawry and Hoole 1850, 59)

The spearhead of Christian attack on the strongholds of heathenism was in the hands of men like this. Their faith was intrepid. Some of them, like Joeli Bulu, Paula Vea, Iliesa Takelo, and James Havea, were Tongans by birth (though when a man dies and is buried in a land after facing death there for forty years, it is hard to think of him as anything but a native); but among their own people also were raised up Fijians of the same stature and faith—Josua Mateinaniu, Joeli Keteca, Juliasa Naulivou, Taniela Kipa, Ilaija Varani, Malakai Butuki, Aisake Ravuata, Johi Toki, Josaia Raitono, Esekaia of Bua, Jioji of Dama, and dozens of others who are mentioned in the records only as Rupeni, Paula, Sefanaia, and so on. And they came from every division of society—some were carpenters; some were fishermen;

---

121 The last priest and a few friends "bent the knee" with him (Williams and Calvert 1884, 331).

some were warriors; some, like Raitono and Bilivucu, were royal messengers; some, like Varani, Jioji, and Esekaia, were chiefs in their own areas; and some, like Rai and Solomoni Raduva, were priests. Whether there was the conversion of a big chief or not, wars or not, in fact, in spite of these things, Hunt was able to write before these causes arose, "There is a Church in Fiji!"[122] Hunt knew he had gone well on the way to getting what Wesley had desired—a hundred preachers who feared nothing but sin and desired nothing but God.[123]

Later on in the fifties, sixties, and seventies, when the mere nominal conversions had increased so much, the church never passed out of the hands of these men, or men of this kind; and in the last quarter of the century, when evangelism of the heathen at home had more or less been achieved, this was the type of man that Fiji sent away to New Britain, New Ireland, and Papua, and later to the Solomons, many indeed to lay down their lives there. Of course they had their shortcomings, but who among us has not? But I am speaking here of the intense quality and intrepidity of their faith.

These men were *called*. The evidence would suggest that folk in each status—"class leaders," "prayer leaders," as well as "preachers"—generally had a sense of *call*. These offices were prepared to undertake such work, always dangerous in those days, because they had experienced a religious force, of which this was the fruit. I have in my possession details of several calls of this type. Both Joeli Bulu (Fison 1873, 17–20) and James Havea (n.d.) had definite calls to come to Fiji. In the love-feast testimonies it was no uncommon thing for someone to say that he had enjoyed a new experience and was ready to go or serve God where he was wanted (Ami Rara for example),[124] and this is the remarkable thing—in every case I have seen, almost without exception, it is stated that after a brief period of waiting the opportunity would be opened. This applied to Bulu (Fison 1873, 19) and also to Havea (n.d.), and to scores of others.

He who believes in a God of history has no trouble with this sort of evidence. The determinist historian has to evaluate it as best he can. The evidence is that there were many *calls*, and usually they are followed immediately by *opportunities*. It may be answered that in those days there were almost always opportunities, and this is true—but it is still remarkable. However, we are investigating their experiences and what they thought. Their belief was that God called them, and also opened up the way. He was to them a God living and acting in life about them.

In view of that, it is not surprising that dreams figured sometimes in such calls. Havea, for example, dreamed of his commission to take the gospel beyond Tonga. He did not just dream it as an adventure, it was a specific warning that he should prepare himself for this purpose. The experience was not unlike the call of Paul to Macedonia, except that the

---

122 Journal of Hunt, early 1844 (Rowe 1860, 165).
123 Wesley to Mather (Carter 1851, 215).
124 Hazlewood's account (Williams and Calvert 1884, 290).

foreign land was not specified. No such enterprise had been mooted—so it was not exactly in the air at the time. Yet like a bolt from the blue, things happened—the canoe materialised, the appeal from Fiji, the missionary's choice fell on him, and all so suddenly that without being able to farewell with his folk, he found himself in deep water on the way to Lau (ibid.).

No aspect of the faith of these men was realer than their certainty in life to come. Heaven was the dominant element of their preaching—it was continually ventilated in their sermons and their personal work. It may come as a surprise to many to know that these men were far more heaven than hellfire preachers. Mind you, I do not say there was not plenty of hellfire preaching, and the Methodists never did avoid the doctrine. But as a means of evangelism it was used only by Calvert and Waterhouse, and to a lesser degree by Lyth. Hunt used it but little, and then not alone. I have been through a large portion of Cargill's Journal, in which he recorded the subjects on which he preached and the texts. Although there is some repetition of preaching, I noted twenty-one different sermons used—and not one could be linked with hellfire preaching.[125] The native preachers were more absorbed with the glory of the new discovery and certainty of heaven than trying to frighten others of hell. (I am speaking of the early period. Later on when heathenism had gone, native preaching changed, but that is beyond the field of this survey.)

May I put it like this—sermons on "the wages of sin is death" were much less common than sermons on "the wages of sin is death, but the gift of God is eternal life." There is a good deal of evidence for that claim. References to hell in native testimonies do exist, but they are few and far between. On the other hand, references to heaven would require some pages just to list them. After having been through statements of early conversions numbering into three figures, I must admit that evidence of conversion by preaching the fear of hell is so scant that, if used, it was clearly a failure. There are occasional references to converts having feared hell, but they were not convicted of sin by this type of preaching. On the other hand, the preaching of heaven undoubtedly did impress the heathen. Heaven preaching turned many a person to seek Christian instruction and the way. It was a most useful device for gaining the heathen's attention and his sympathy.

Not one of these preachers would have said that a man was *saved* by just desiring heaven; but they rejoiced greatly, because to desire heaven was to open the mind and the heart—and people who did this were sure to find the way before long. A number of them had been through this experience themselves. Take, for instance, the case of Joeli Bulu, who served Fiji for forty years. It was a desire for heaven that led him to join the Christians (Fison 1873, 9), but under the unpleasant threats and pressure of his friends and relations he had to drop the *lotu*. Then he writes:

---

125 Cargill's last Journal.

> No sooner had I spoken than grief sprang up within my breast. "I have thrown away the good land," said my soul within me, and stealing away into the forest I knelt down and prayed to God ... though indeed I knew not what to ask Him for. All I knew of the lotu was the good land among the stars. (Ibid., 12)

I can only find one reason why heaven as a doctrine, or an element in preaching, should have been so important in Fiji as a stepping-stone to sound conversion. It was so real in the hearts of the preachers, and they were so certain of it, and their preaching of heaven was so pulsating with glory and the reality of it all, that many a heathen said within himself (on their own confessions later), "I should like to know that land!" The real sincerity of a preacher, and the feeling that he has an experience to share, is halfway in a listener's heart to a converting experience for him.

Now if heaven featured in preparing men for conversion, it was even more prominent in the testimony of dying saints. Fortunately for our study, the period we are investigating was one which saw many Christian biographies written, and it was the custom, if possible, to use triumphant deathbed scenes as the climax of a book or article. And, after all, is there a better place than facing death to see the real nature of a man s faith?

Both the white missionaries and the native preachers realised that there was good illustration for the Methodist doctrine of *assurance* in these deathbed testimonies, and they recorded them in full detail. A simple person who could not understand a theological statement of such a doctrine could still learn its meaning from the plain description of So-and-so's dying, his certainty of Christ, and life eternal.

One of the best examples of such a description is preserved for us and had been copied in half a dozen publications at the time. I refer to Hunt's triumphant death. Of this kind of statement it is a classic example. It comprises a chapter in his biography, the climax of the book (Rowe 1860, ch. 14). The Conference obituary is built on it.[126] Lawry (Lawry and Hoole 1850, 138–39), Calvert (Williams and Calvert 1884, 440–43), Waterhouse (1866, 155),[127] Wallis (1851, 322–24), and Young used it (1858, 317–19),[128] while yet in the news. From time to time it reappears, in whole or in part—Blacket (1914, 242–43), Colwell (1914), Burton (Burton and Deane 1936, 29), Miss Lapthorne (1935), and article writers in *Centenary Record*,[129] *Missionary Review*,[130] and ever so many other papers. These references I know without chasing. The array serves to show it was indeed a classic example of a deathbed testimony. Evidence within suggests they are all from a common source. In addition to this there is a less printed vernacular tradition, which provides other facts like the presence of Gavidi and Inoke Bakoso's dirge for the burial.[131] A primary and original source exists in the Mitchell

---

126   Minutes of Conference, 1849.
127   Last prayer of Cakobau.
128   When visiting grave.
129   *Fiji Methodist Centenary Record*, 28.
130   *Missionary Review*, January 1939; 6–8 September 1947, 3:16.
131   *Ai Tukutuku Vakalotu*.

Library, Sydney, in the Lyth Journals. This was the doctor who attended him, and he expresses his surprise at the clearness of Hunt's thought to the last.[132] This story was used throughout the whole Christian world to encourage believers. We now ask the question—have the native people left any Fijian counterparts of this type of literature?

The missionaries often translated such accounts from letters written by Christian native teachers. They all carry the same imprint. Said dying Ana: "My faith is strong and lively every day . . . My soul is prepared to enter heaven, there to be at peace."[133] Asefa Vakatekau, a Kadavan student whose studies were terminated by sickness, went home to die. His last words were: "Ratu Jovesa, you stay. Be very earnest in the Lotu. I today shall take my crown."[134] Marika Galu's dying words were: "I know that I shall enter heaven, not as a stranger, but as an *owner* of the land through faith alone"—a citizen of the colony of heaven.[135] The almost identical words were said also by Paula Mafi.[136] A child, Elijah, whose parents were not Christian, died telling his mother, "Near to me now is the heavenly land."[137] Nor were they limited to deathbed scenes. Their preaching, as I have shown, pulsated with heaven. Ifereimi Tukana wrote, "When I look down into my heart, I see the Lord is there; wherefore do I go about rejoicing in these days, because, plainly as the things which I perceive with my eyes, do I see that I have laid hold upon eternal life, on which I shall enter when I depart from this world."[138] Tomasi Navunisunu, a native minister, described a service he conducted at Cicia, in which, as he was about to give out a hymn, up jumped a young man, Setareki Seileka (later himself a native minister, and murdered with Thomas Baker in the interior) with some others "and sang a new hymn, which I had never heard before—'Will you go to the Eden above?' and truly my soul was hot within me as I listened, and my eyes filled with tears. It is indeed a fine hymn."[139] These references all come from papers and have been translated by missionaries using the vernacular letters. There is another source of such accounts—viz., the actual extant native manuscripts—and I now proceed to supply in detail two accounts of deathbed scenes from the writings of Joeli Bulu, which I translated for the purpose of this study.

> A man of Ono, named Rupeni, a true Christian, fell ill one night. He sent a person asking me to go to him. I went to his house and when I saw how seriously ill he was, I asked, "Rupeni, how are you?" and he replied, "I am very weak." "How is your soul?" I said, to which he replied, "My soul is at peace for I know the love of the Lord. But the sickness is heavy upon me and causes me pain."

---

132 Journal of Lyth (4:334–37; 5:1–12).
133 *WJO*, 1871, 20–21.
134 A. J. Webb, *WJO*, 1871, 110.
135 *WJO*, 1869, 85.
136 Rooney, *WJO*, 1872, 81.
137 *WJO*, 1869, 63.
138 Ifereimi Tukana to Fison, 31 May 1871, *WJO*, 1872, 21.
139 Letter from Fiji, *WJO*, 1869, 63.

"What are you thinking?" I asked again, and he replied, "I think only of my Lord and Saviour." "Then let us pray," I said, and as we prayed he was unable to rest because of his suffering and he said: "Lord Jesus, have mercy upon me." After prayer we sat watching him and talking about his soul. Clearly he was ready for death and so I went away again to my house. At daybreak I went again to see him, and when we saw each other I asked, "Rupeni, how is it with you?" and he answered me thus, "I am very weak. I know that I am about to go to the place where I am ready to go." "Where?" I asked, and he answered me, "To heaven." "Are you certain?" I added, and his reply came: "It is a long time now since I became sure of eternal life by faith in Jesus." Looking at his face I saw that it was like the face of a man who had found great treasure. Then he commended the care of his children to me, saying, "Joeli! If you love me, love my children. Teach them religion that they may know Jesus as their Saviour." "I will look after them," I agreed, "but you attend to yourself now." And he added, "Truly, the love of God is with me, though my pain is great. Even so, this pain is a trifle, when I consider the good things I shall receive from the Lord on His Throne." As we talked on thus, he added, "The time for my going is near," and seeing that death was near we prepared to take him to the great house, for he was of chiefly line and had many relations who were gathering to see him. So we took him away to the bigger house, and (it seemed to us) he died as his relatives gathered and embraced him and performed our usual customs. Great was the wailing because of the death of a friend so useful in the land. Presently we saw that he was still breathing slightly. Then he opened his eyes and raised his hand, beckoning and saying—"Let there be no weeping, no weeping." Now when we saw this and heard his voice we were all silent and afraid on account of what had happened, and the sick man spoke—"Why are you weeping?" "We weep," answered a relative "because of your death," to which the man replied "Weep not for me, but for yourselves. As for me, I live. Weep not like that, the Lord and His angels are hastening for us to go, but I have one word yet to say to you—be zealous in religion. If you love me, hold fast to the lotu." And he began to testify of his Lord, saying: "In health I have believed the scriptures, and therein I found salvation. From the Bible I learned of heaven, and believed, and this day I shall see in truth those things I have believed but not seen, things that Paul speaks about, and I have read of them in the *Vunau Lekaleka* (*Short Sermons*, written by Hunt for use of native agents and printed at Viwa), all of which tell of my Saviour and of the heaven which I am now going to possess." The sick man went on, "Don't you see the Lord? Behold the house is full of angels who say the Lord is hastening for our departure. Farewell! My love to you all." Thus ended his earthly life and the angels took the hand of his soul and led him away to heaven. But as for his father, wife, children and relations, indeed, all of us who had seen and heard, we were filled with joy so that it was not like a day of death, but rather resembled a festival, wherein we had found the love of God, both to the dead and to ourselves. So our faith was strengthened and we all said there is nothing on earth like unto true religion. (Bulu n.d.)

And the second account is this:

Taniela Kepa, a Christian preacher of Ono, had been appointed to Kabara, but suffering a great deal from sickness, was returned to his own island to recover, but grew steadily worse, and during this period Joeli Bulu came into contact with him. One day Kepa said to him: "Every day I have clear witness with my spirit that I have salvation through Jesus Christ, and I also know that should I die just here, eternal life in heaven is mine." Joeli goes on: Another day I asked if the love of God was still with him, and the sick man replied that he had had a peaceful night for his soul, and he found great help in the love of God and was receiving that in which he had hoped. I therefore read 21st chapter of Revelation to him and the sick man rejoiced as he heard the words of the Book (the chapter being an account of heaven), and said, "I am going to heaven. I know there is nothing to prevent me. I am ready for life above. I am not in two minds about anything. I know that if my life is terminated today, I shall but go to heaven." Then I suggested prayer and while I prayed the sick man wept, and went on weeping after I had finished, so that I asked him why he cried; and he said, "I weep in love for my Lord. He loves me and His love is greater than mine. The salvation of my soul is clear and therefore I do not fear death, for I know that if my soul and body are parted I shall go to live forever in heaven through Jesus my Lord." And many were the other good words he spoke about the love of God. His sickness grew worse and I went to see him again on the Sunday, and when I saw him I knew that death was near, and I asked: "How is it with you, Taniela?" Whereupon he said: "I am ready now and the time is near for me to leave this earth for the world above." He asked me what day it was and I told him Sunday. "This Sunday," he commented, "I shall spend in heaven with my Lord." I asked him how he knew and he told me it was the Lord's will, whereupon I enquired if he had seen the Lord this day. "Yes," he said, "but you do not see Him. Talk less for He is present now. He has come for me. Behold the Lord." And he stared forward and did not move, and his face was as the face of one who was far from being sick, and he said, "Joeli! Do you see that post there?" "Yes." "You are sure you see it?" "Yes." "As for me, as surely as you see that post, so surely do I see the Lord." And with those words he placed one hand on his breast and raised the other to heaven and died, and thus there went to heaven a man of God, and his very dying was to us a useful sermon, more useful even than his very useful sermons and his leading us in class. Herein we know the worth of true religion. This is the story of Taniela Kepa, a true Christian. (Ibid.)[140]

It might be fitting to follow up these two accounts with this reference to Joeli's own passing: "Soon after midnight Joeli passed away, and died nobly as he had lived. He was quite conscious to the very last, and the expression of the grand old face was simply beautiful—so radiant, as of one without a shadow of doubt concerning the home he was so near" (Cumming 1881, 312, 316).

---

140 My translations are literal. Fison translated *Autobiography of Joeli Bulu* (1873) and places post episode in the other story. *WJO* sets it with a third person. I follow the Bulu manuscripts.

These accounts are long—not as long as some of their English counterparts—but they have a peculiar value to us here as they are pure native accounts, absolutely original and primary source material, which I have translated. They show clearly the place of heaven in the minds of these early Pacific Island Christians. But there are other things also that may be observed, and let us remember that these are quite typical cases, and my only reason for selecting these particular cases is that I have them direct in the vernacular without a European intermediary. Let us note also the place of Jesus. Here is a good corrective to any who may think that the early Fijian did not get beyond the Old Testament, Jehovah, the God of Battles. These deathbed testimonies, and there are dozens of them, all show the same strong belief in a real personal relationship with Christ, the Saviour. The same thing is demonstrated in the love-feast testimonies.

These testimonies are by no means stereotyped, but are saturated with phrases showing the place of Christology in their minds, phrases like:

1. "I desire only to follow Jesus"—Luke, a Bauan six years before the conversion of Cakobau (Lawry and Hoole 1850, 60).
2. "I know no Saviour, only Christ"—Josua, one of the first converts (ibid., 61).
3. "I found no Saviour on earth, only Christ"—Necani Cataki.[141]
4. "We now see sin in the light of the Lord, and desire to follow His steps"—Koroi Tukana, expelled from Bau for Christian sympathies nearly a decade before Cakobau's conversion (Lawry and Hoole 1850, 60).
5. "We used to rejoice in worldly assemblies, but now we meet to speak of Jesus. I am happy on account of Jesus"—Taniela, a Viwa man (ibid.).
6. "I wish to spend the whole of my life doing something for Jesus"—Varani, the peacemaker (ibid.).
7. "I wish to trust in Jesus. I desire to give Him my heart, that I may not be separated from him"—Susana, at Viwa (ibid., 61).
8. "I asked: 'What shall I do to be saved?' The word was heard quickly. 'Believe in the Lord Jesus Christ'"—Matiasi (Young 1858, 274).
9. "I was a bad man, weak—full of bad, but the atonement of Christ has crushed the bad"—Leonitasa (ibid.).
10. "I was bad, dark, weak—but Jesus saved me"—Etileti of Lakeba (ibid.).

And so it goes on, one could produce hundreds of examples.

Let it not be imagined that this is largely meaningless Hebrew jargon to them. The complete terminology for the Hebrew sacrificial system is found in the Fijian dictionary, and they are not new words. Besides these we may place an equally large list linking their belief in Christ with certainty of heaven, like "I know my Saviour, and when I die I shall be

---

141 Journal of Hazlewood (Williams and Calvert 1884, 289).

in heaven"—Susana of Lakeba (ibid.). All the examples I have selected, and they have been selected at random, date well before the conversion of Cakobau, and many of them before that of Tui Nayau. I think that they should be sufficient to justify the conclusion that there was a strong personal religion in the infant church in Fiji within the first decade and a half from the arrival of Cross and Cargill.

To such statements as those just listed may be added reports of mass movements into the church at Lakeba and other Lauan islands, even as far as Ono, at Viwa in particular and later in Kadavu and other places. I am speaking of those mass movements, which some have called "enthusiasm" and others "revivals." We are about to investigate the nature of these religious movements, and when placed beside these native testimonies the reader may judge the historical value or otherwise of the official statement of the colony that "for more than ten years there were few converts. When, however, a few high chiefs were won over, progress was more rapid."[142] The mass movements we are about to examine mostly fall within those ten years.

Recapitulation: What, then, was the nature of the faith of the early Fijian Christian, whence did it spring, and in what was this trust placed?

1. The faith was simple but strong. It was a faith in a living and active God, who could be known as a Person.
2. This faith was usually the result of a sequence of events, through which the person had battled his way into a religious experience. Private prayer in the forest and the direct impression of preaching and testimony played a big part in their *wrestling*.
3. It was thus a *growing* faith. The circumstances under which the Christians lived forced them to throw themselves unreservedly on God Himself and resign themselves to His will.
4. Suffering is taken either as an opportunity to witness or a discipline of value to the soul.
5. Deliverance from trouble, sickness, death, danger at sea, etc., are occasions for warning and then praise and improved service afterwards. But in suffering or deliverance it is God who is the actor—man's lot to resign to His will.
6. This conception of God and man led to a fearlessness, which astonished outsiders. They saw themselves as God's men. To whatever office they aspired they believed they were *called*, and such advances in status were invariably preceded by some spiritual or emotional experience.

---

142 Colonial Report of Fiji, 1951, 68.

7. Hellfire evangelism, though used, was not as common as often thought (at this period), and it was never greatly successful. The doctrine was accepted but not overdone.
8. Assurance of heaven, on the contrary, was a regular feature of their belief, preaching, and testimony, and is shown to have played an important part in leading people to enquire about Christianity and in strengthening those about to "cross the last river."
9. These Christians of experience are found to have a faith in Christ, the Saviour, His work and sacrifice, and are poles apart from the political converts, who usually thought of Jehovah, God of Battles.

To this extent their faith was individualistic, but there was also a corporate experience they shared, that we now investigate.

8

REVIVALS—VIWA, ONO, KADAVU

No study of the religious experiences of the early Christians in Fiji would be complete without careful examination of the strongly emotional mass movements that features the midforties in Viwa and Ono, and again much later in Kadavu. And let us admit at the outset their remarkable similarity with movements in Britain and America a century earlier. I shall aim to collect and tabulate data and to make comparisons and contrasts, in the hope of ascertaining whether or not there be any connection between them all.

About a century earlier some astonishing scenes had been witnessed in widely separated places, three examples of which I set out now for the reader to consider before we investigate similar phenomena in Fiji.

The first comes from the narrative of Rev. James Robe, of Kilsyth, Scotland:

> Sixteen children began to hold prayer meetings in the town of Kirkintilloch, and the godly excitement became general. On every hand were heard cries, groans, and the voice of weeping ... Young converts held prayer meetings in fields, barns, schoolhouses, and the manses of their ministers. Cambuslang, Kilsyth, Campsie, Kirkintilloch, Auchinloch, St. Ninian's, Gargunloch, Calder, Badernoch, Irvine, Long Deghorn, Kilmarnock, Larbert, Dundee, Bothwell, Muthill, Edinburgh, Glasgow and other towns, villages and parishes were visited with a most gracious outpouring of God's Holy Spirit ... Not a few converts, about one-sixth of the whole, suffered such distress of mind, and were under such powerful religious influence, that they not only cried and shrieked aloud, but trembled, fainted and were convulsed in their bodies most mysteriously ... Some were seized with such trembling that their friends had to render them support. Many of the females went into hysterics. Numbers, on finding peace, broke forth into rapturous weeping and had their countenances so lit up with serenity and brightness that their neighbours declared they had obtained, not only new hearts, but new faces. (Tyerman 1870-71, 1:222-23)

So much for Scotland, as reported in 1742. Let us now turn to America, to New England, where the Rev. Jonathan Edwards reported:

> In many instances conviction of sin and conversion were attended with intense physical excitement. Numbers fell prostrate on the ground, and cried aloud for mercy. The bodies of others were convulsed and benumbed. As chaos preceded

creation, so in New England confusion went before conversion. The work was great and glorious, but was accompanied with noise and tumult. Men literally cried for mercy . . . From one end of the land to the other, multitudes of vain, thoughtless sinners were unmistakably converted, and were made new creatures in Christ Jesus. Frolicking, night-walking, singing lewd songs, tavern haunting, profane speaking, and extravagance in dress were generally abandoned. The talk of the people was about the favour of God, an interest in Christ, a sanctified heart, and spiritual blessedness here and hereafter. The country was full of meetings of persons of all sorts and ages, to read, pray and sing praises. Oftentimes people were wrought up into the highest transport of love, joy, and admiration, and had such views of Divine perfection and the excellencies of Christ, that for five or six hours together their souls responded to a kind of sacred elysium until the body seemed to sink beneath the weight of Divine discoveries and nature was deprived of all ability to stand or speak. Connected with this there were no enthusiastic impulses, or supposed revelations, but trembling reverence, and the mildest meekness and warmest charity . . . The New Jerusalem, in this respect, had begun to come down from heaven, and perhaps never were more the pre-libations of heaven's glory given upon earth.[143]

During Wesley's ministry in England similar events were not uncommon, and they were not limited to the services conducted by Wesley. Kingswood, Bristol, New-castle-on-Tyne, Everton, and Weardale were among the places that witnessed such events. In the early period "stricken cases were frequent and numerous" (ibid., 2:312). In Wesley's experience they were more common in fields, barns, and private meeting places, but there were cases in churches. The phenomena would disappear for a time and then reappear suddenly at some unexpected time and place. In 1758 under the ministry of Hicks and Berridge they broke out at Wrestlingworth and Everton—everything described above—fainting, convulsions, strong crying, and many falling prostrate on the ground (ibid., 2:312-13, 331ff.). Wesley himself saw the same thing when preaching in the church at Everton that year (ibid., 2:313). Preaching in Hicks' church at Wrestlingworth a year later, "two or three fell to the ground and were extremely convulsed; while one or two were filled with strong consolation" (ibid., 2:331). Just prior to this Berridge had written to Wesley,

> The word is everywhere like a hammer, breaking the rock in pieces. People fall down, cry out most bitterly and struggle so vehemently that five or six men can scarce hold them . . . At Orwell ten people were broken down in one night, only by hearing a few people sing hymns. At Grandchester, a mile from Cambridge, seventeen people were seized with strong convulsions last week, only by hearing hymns sung . . . There has been a wonderful outpouring of the spirit of love among believers; in so much that they have fainted under it, fallen down and lain upon the ground, as dead, some for hours.[144]

---

143 Edwards' account of New England revivals (Tyerman 1870-71, 1:218-19).
144 Berridge to Wesley, 16 July 1759 (Tyerman 1870-71, 2:332).

Again Wesley writes of another service at Everton:

> One sunk down, and another and another. Some cried aloud in agony of prayer. I would willingly have spent some time in prayer with them, but my voice failed, so that I was obliged to conclude the service, leaving many in the church, crying and praying, but unable either to walk or stand. (Tyerman 1870–71, 2:333)

Then as late as 1772 in Weardale (where Wesley had earlier prevented the Society turning Dissenters, on account of the curate, "whose life was no better than his doctrine,"[145] and where in a twenty-mile valley there were only five places of worship when the Methodist chapel was put there in 1760[146]) we find Wesley there for a week, with repetitions of this kind of thing daily, some "dropping to the ground as dead," "six lay on the ground together roaring," and another "struck to the ground so distressed that he was convulsed all over.[147]

That should be sufficient material from England, America, and Scotland to refresh the reader's mind on the nature of the phenomena we are about to examine in connection with Fiji. As to what the reader may think of these things is not my immediate concern. Much has been written about them, and they have been variously evaluated by Tyerman (1870–71, 1:223, 467–69) and others down to Knox in 1950.[148] Indeed, to a limited extent, Wesley himself tried to evaluate them[149] and these bring out interesting points. The reader is simply referred to them. Some assemblage of the main facts was necessary here for purposes of comparison, but not only for this reason. They provide part of the religious and emotional background from which the men who evangelised Fiji came, and I feel that there is little doubt that the revivals of Fiji were but a projection of the above-mentioned revivals.

I now turn to the Journal of John Hunt. The year is 1844 (ten years before the conversion of Cakobau, five before that of Tui Nayau, less than a decade after the arrival of Cross and Cargill), and the entry is dated 26th May and tells us of the events of the day before, which happened to be Sunday. Hunt had baptised ten adults and was exhorting them to remain true to their promises. So he writes:

> Some already began to sob and cry, and showed that it was with the greatest difficulty they could contain themselves. Almost as soon as I commenced baptising the candidates, the Queen of Viwa was completely overwhelmed. Her heart seemed literally to be broken; and though a very strong woman, she fainted twice under the weight of a wounded spirit. She revived, only to renew her strong cries and tears, so that it was all we could do to proceed with the service. The effect soon became more general. Several of the women and some of the men literally roared for the disquietude of their hearts. As soon as the baptism

---

145 Quoting Wesley, 16 July 1759 (Tyerman 1870–71, 2:406).
146 From manuscripts (Tyerman 1870–71, 2:503).
147 Journal of Wesley, 4 June 1772.
148 Knox (1950, ch. 21), on "Wesley and Religion of Experience."
149 See Wesley pamphlet of Edwards revival; also Tyerman (1870–71, 3:124–25); Knox (1950, 535).

was concluded, as many as could, chanted the Te Deum. It was very affecting to see upwards of 100 Fijians, many of whom were, a few years ago, some of the worst cannibals in the Group, and even in the world, chanting—"We praise Thee, O God; We acknowledge Thee to be the Lord!" while their voices were almost drowned by cries of brokenhearted penitents ... The Queen came to our house after the service, and with a countenance full of sadness, and eyes full of tears, said, "Mr Hunt, I am afraid." I directed her to the Lamb of God and prayed with her. She requested the use of my study, in which she could pour out her soul unto God without interruption. I, of course, let her have it; and there she prayed until God spoke peace to her soul.[150]

The year that followed this was one of spiritual growth in Viwa. Hunt described it as one of "great harmony and spiritual prosperity," true of both the Fijian and the English class meetings, "filled, unutterably filled, of glory and of God" (AR Viwa Circuit 1845). Good Friday had seen the event for which they had all prayed for years—the conversion of Varani, a sound New Testament conversion.[151] This slow but steady movement that continued throughout 1845 may be said to have reached a climax in October. Let us return to Hunt's Journal—19 October 1845:

After I had prayed, I gave a short exhortation, stating the design and meaning of such meetings as we were now holding. Paul then prayed and the feeling increased, which was the more remarkable, as he is a calm old man ... Another prayed ... without being called upon, and by the time he had finished most of the people were engaged in prayer. The feeling and the praying became general. Some cried aloud. Clear and decisive work commenced ... Many were pricked in the heart, and cried in agonies of prayer for mercy ... the flame spread. The meeting was not very long, but the praying continued after it was concluded; and indeed, the praying commenced that night continued till most of the people were saved. To describe what followed is impossible. Every meeting became a penitent meeting and almost every family altar a penitent form ... Some of the instances of conversion were very remarkable. A person would be seized all at once and thrown into the most extraordinary distress. Most of the women fainted two or three times before they found peace. On some occasions the men were so violent, both in their sorrow and joy, that it was almost dangerous to be near them. There was no way of managing them but by throwing them on the ground, and holding them there, which sometimes had to be done for hours together, and in some cases the strength of four or five men was required to manage them. Yet there was nothing wild or silly in what they said; indeed, in general we were astonished at the manner in which they expressed themselves, both in prayer and praise, and in their exhortations to others after they had found peace ... Our public services were most extraordinary times. Sometimes before we reached the chapel we heard the cries of penitents ... to hear the preacher's voice in prayer was out of the question ... people were praying

---

150 Journal of Hunt (Rowe 1860, 165–67).
151 Many accounts exist. All the missionaries wrote to London Committee of it. See also AR Viwa Circuit 1845.

all over the chapel with all their might, and several of them prostrate on the ground, fainting or overcome by the power of their emotions. (Nettleton 1906, 75–81)[152]

This went on for days, and about a hundred persons "professed to obtain the forgiveness of sins through faith in Jesus Christ" (Rowe 1860, 184).[153] The Viwa Circuit extended along the coast to Nakorotubu and over to Ovalau and to Vanua Levu, where there were causes at Tiliva, Nadi, and Solevu. The influence of the Viwa revival was soon radiated through the native agents to all these places (ibid.; AR Viwa Circuit 1844–46), and but for a few months, this was ten years before the converstion of Cakobau. Hunt, writing to London, described the scenes more briefly, but in much the same terms:

> Some of the worst cannibals in Fiji were suddenly seized with the most powerful conviction . . . They wept and wailed most piteously; and some were so agitated as to require several men to prevent them doing themselves and others bodily harm. Yet there was nothing foolish in what they said . . . What some of them had long heard without much apparent effect, was now of the greatest use. Conversion to God is the only proper means for making theological knowledge practically useful. I never saw this truth so clearly illustrated as in the case of some of the older members in our society in Viwa. We had long mourned over their apparent inability to understand the plan of salvation by simple faith in Jesus. Their class-meeting statements showed a defective experience: they were, in fact, servants, not sons of God. Now the difficulty was removed and the faith-inspiring Spirit . . . and testimony . . . was made clear and satisfactory.[154]

It is useful to have that opinion of an eyewitness, who was at the same time a great evangelist and a careful observer of spiritual experience. The same letter states also the spread of the experience throughout the circuit, so that eight months later when the annual report was written there was an increase of over two hundred in the society, but even this figure "gives but a poor idea of the extent of the good work."[155]

Nor is it to be imagined that the missionaries were themselves unaffected by these events. They frankly begin their annual report by admitting, "We ourselves have shared in the blessedness in no small degree" (AR Viwa Circuit 1845). "We have often prayed that God would show forth His mighty power as in the first ages of Christianity," Hunt wrote to the London Committee, "and convert men at once from heathenism to saving Christianity. The Lord has heard our prayers and we have some remarkable conversions of this kind during the last year" (ibid.). Missionary Watsford was also present at Viwa during these days. He acquired great proficiency in the language in a remarkably short time, and the translation of the fourth Gospel in the Fijian New Testament is a memorial to this, but at the time of his

---

152 Quoting Journal of Hunt, 19 October 1845.
153 Quoting Hunt.
154 Hunt to LC, 6 November 1846, WM, 1847, 2:930–31.
155 Ibid.

witnessing this revival, he had been but a short time in Fiji. He left us a three-and-a-half page account of it (1900, 51–54), though a half century had passed before it saw printer's ink. The value of his account is more in the particular interest he took in a couple of cases—for example, Noah, who was a Fijian he had engaged to teach him the language:

> The floor of the church was wet with the tears of the penitents. When the wave of power first broke upon us, Noah jumped upon a form, and, his black face shining, cried: "This is that which was spoken by the prophet Joel, 'And it shall come to pass in the last days that I will pour out my spirit upon all flesh.'" (Ibid., 52)

The reference shows something of the general disturbance that must have taken place to make it possible for him to jump up on forms and shout out Scripture.

[There is a slight historical problem here. Immediately upon his first retirement Calvert prepared a mission history. It was published within twelve years of the events. He states specifically the revival took place just when Rewa was destroyed, in October 1845 (Williams and Calvert 1858, 271-72). Hunt's Journal, quoted by Nettleton, gives the same date and is an entirely different source (Nettleton 1906, 75-81). Rowe, Hunt's biographer of the time, who had access to the Hunt papers and Mrs. Hunt to consult, also places it in 1845 (1860, ch. 11). This source places it as simultaneous with the Ono revival (ibid., 184, footnote), which Calvert states definitely began the Sunday after Whitsuntide, 1845 (Williams and Calvert 1858, 76),[156] but in October he was himself in Ono and observing its result. The 1844 outburst at Viwa was on Whitsunday (Lawry and Hoole 1850, 59). There might well have been more than one Whitsuntide experience, as these were often selected for baptismal services. Watsford gives just the year, 1846 (1900, 51), but was writing fifty years later. A Hunt letter in Wesleyan Magazine, 1847, dated the first week in November, states last "week."[157] The remainder of the letter, however, is an account of the year, and it strongly suggests a misprint—"week" for "year," and furthermore, even if no misprint, it would not bring the events into the correct week. The penitent prayer meetings definitely started in October 1845, and from this I feel we can safely take record as I have set it out in the text. A.R.T.]

The Sunday following Whitsunday witnessed a similar outburst on the small island of Doi, off Ono i Lau. There was no white missionary within one hundred miles at the time. Worship was being conducted by Necani Cataki—a local preacher, a powerful speaker, and a man of strong faith—who was ordained some time later. During his sermon,

> the people began to weep aloud. The preacher was much affected and sank down, unable to proceed. A note was sent across to Ono to the head teacher, Silas, who immediately came and again assembled the people for service; but the emotion and excitement were so great that he was not able to preach. They then prayed together, and, as in olden time, the Holy Ghost fell upon them in great power. Silas begged the people to go with him to Ono, and they crossed over, dividing themselves into parties for the different chapels where the prayer

---

156 Unchanged in Williams and Calvert (1884, 283).
157 Hunt to LC, 6 November 1846, WM, 1847, 2:930.

meetings were held. The holy influence now spread on all hands. Old and young became alarmed and earnest about their souls. In a few weeks about 200 persons showed good signs of having been truly saved. Great was the joy of these new converts, and whole nights, as well as days, were spent in praise and prayer. (Williams and Calvert 1884, 283)

That is Calvert's account. Several months later he visited the place and was astonished to discover that some eighty people had been permitted to engage in the work of preaching and exhorting. As to what he discovered upon their examination, we shall return in a moment.

Over three years later Hazlewood found the people of Ono greatly affected on the occasion of the Christmas prayer meeting and service. "Many of the people wept and shouted aloud for joy at the commemoration of the birth of the Lord of life and glory."[158] It was here also that Joeli Bulu had those deathbed experiences, which have already been narrated.

Nor were these experiences limited to Viwa and Ono. Mrs. Calvert, writing to her daughter, Mary, who had been taken to England, said: "There has been quite a revival among the native children at Lakeba; and Sikovi (Wetasau's daughter), Victoria and some others are thought to be truly converted to God. I met their class and was much pleased with them" (Rowe 1882, 33). This was written in September 1950. Mrs. Calvert did not then know her child had died. This, be it noted, was a revival among the children already inside the church. It took place somewhere about the same time as the conversion of Tui Nayau.

Sooner or later the question must arise and be answered—what became of these movements? Did they have any lasting effect, or were they just sheer emotionalism? Was there anything specific to show in the church after, say, a matter of months or years, that could be traced back to these events? We have already noted their similarity with revivals in England, Scotland, and America, and again, what Knox calls "the law of diminishing returns" (1950, 233) is found to apply to Fiji also. Wesley himself admitted that "these circumstances are common in the dawn of a work, but afterwards very uncommon."[159] Though there have been many revivals from time to time since, and I myself have seen hundreds of people pass through such converting experiences—some with considerable emotion, some with tears, and some with radiance—but I have never seen anything approaching these descriptions I have quoted.

At the same time it was not entirely limited to the early period. Langham reported a case at Nairai in 1864 of a man "roaring by reason of the disquietude of his soul." He had previously been a local preacher, but having fallen from grace had been disciplined.[160] Again White reported about the same time from Kadavu that during the singing of the first verse of the ninth hymn, while they were on their knees, "the Lord opened heaven

---

158 Journal of Hazlewood, 25 December 1848 (Williams and Calvert 1884, 289).
159 Journal of Wesley, 4 June 1772.
160 Langham to LC, 9 December 1864, WMN, April 1865, 493.

and literally poured the Holy Spirit down upon us ... There were more than 300 praying and praising God all at once," upon which Paula Vea, standing up, shouted and took possession of the meeting, as we have seen Noah did in Watsford's narrative of the Viwa revival.[161] The ninth hymn in the third Bauan edition, which would be the one in use, was a hymn of Dr. Lyth, not from the Wesley Collection, but placed among the "Repentance" hymns. It could be translated thus:

> It is good and right
> That I should give
> My heart to God:
> My body also
> It is right
> That I should give to Him.[162]

In their own time, these Kadavan movements were quite as dramatic as those twenty years before in Viwa. Let Nettleton, who witnessed some of them, speak for himself:

> On Kadavu, when such a revival was going on, thirty young chiefs banded themselves together to put a stop to it. Some of the young women to whom they were betrothed were among the penitents. They feared that their conversion and confession of Christianity might make difficulties about their marriage with them as heathen. With uplifted clubs they marched round the chapel, threatening death to those within, who were in earnest prayer with several penitents. They called some by name to come out or be killed. No notice was taken of their savage yells or threats. At length one ventured inside the church, and fell immediately on the floor in a swoon. The others followed, greatly excited, till one by one they were all prostrate, every nerve quivering convulsively, and the perspiration running from their bodies. Their veins stood out like whipcord and they moaned as if in agony. (1906, 81–82)

Twenty years had passed since those Viwa and Ono revivals, but the native missionary present on that occasion well remembered the earlier occasions and wisely sent the younger white man home to bed. He rose at six the next morning to see the old man just leaving the chapel—"The last penitent," he said, "has just come out of his third faint, and is now shouting for joy." After witnessing the struggles and contortions of the young chiefs all night, they were all converted, and Nettleton testifies that "the fruits of their repentance were abiding and goodly" (ibid., 83).

Though Wesley does not appear to have sought for these experiences, it is quite apparent that he did not stop them, and that he thanked God for them.[163] However, he was cautious—he did put some down to hysteria and some to lunacy, and some to the deliberate influence of the devil to discredit God's work.[164] Yet he thoroughly believed that people

---

161 White to LC, 4 October 1864, from Tavuki, *WMN*, January 1865.
162 Journal of Lyth (index).
163 Journal entries (Knox 1950, 531).
164 Journal of Wesley, 25 November 1759.

suddenly convinced of sin by the work of the Spirit were led to cry out or have convulsions, and he also believed that sometimes trances, visions, and dreams were divinely sent to encourage believers.[165] Unless I am much mistaken, I feel that Hunt and Watsford would have taken much the same view. Remembering that the mission to Fiji from Tonga was itself the fruit of a similar revival over there (1833–44), after the events at Ono and Viwa, Hunt wrote to Watkin in New Zealand, "I am persuaded that this is the blessed means which God has chosen for converting the world."[166]

Why did Hunt so approve this somewhat vigorous form of evangelism? "It is," he goes on, "a way of saving souls, which lays the pride of man in the dust." Hunt knew that the bar which prevented many a big chief from fellowship in the church was arrogance. The Christianity of some of the mere political conversions had convinced Hunt of this—even at that early date. The experiences of Namosimalua and Varani stood out in contrast, and very few of the missionaries of the period, if any, failed to comment upon it.

Fison, sometime later (1864), tells of a chief who had become a Christian, and when asked the name he chose at baptism he said, "Goliath." What happened to the giant of Philistia mattered not to the Fijian chief concerned, and on his own word he chose the name because he "was such a big fellow."[167] Hunt saw this idea of being the big fellow was a hindrance to spiritual experience. One had to feel one's sense of need and throw oneself on God as the only hope. No man was big enough to save himself, and a form of evangelism which really laid pride in the dust met with Hunt's hearty approval. So he writes:

> We like to have souls saved in connexion with the gradual of means, so that we can philosophically trace the event to its cause, but the blessed God, goes out of our ordinary way, pours contempt on our philosophy, and by the means we should never have thought of, accomplishes His own purposes.[168]

So the first reason for His approval is that humility replaces arrogance, and the self-satisfied learned their utter dependence on God.

In a letter to Dr. Hannah, his old theological tutor at Hoxton, he wrote, "The natives require much Divine influence as well as much Divine truth."[169] Here again is Hunt's doctrine of the power of God. Truth alone is not enough. It must be amplified by a spiritual force; Bible study requires a feeling of guidance; personal zeal requires a consciousness of direction from above. Translate, teach, preach, nurse—all these things he can do to help the heathen—but without some demonstration of divine power and approval, it is all incomplete. There must be something beyond philosophy, beyond theology. "Conversion," he

---

165   Ibid.
166   Hunt to Watkin, 1846, on revivals (Rowe 1860, 185).
167   Journal of Fison, 8 August 1840.
168   Hunt to Watkin (Rowe 1860, 185–86).
169   Hunt to Hannah, 1 December 1847, from Viwa (Rowe 1860, 237).

wrote after witnessing a year of it at Viwa, "Conversion to God is the only proper means for making theological knowledge practically useful."[170]

We have already seen in the earlier part of this study that the missionaries spoke of a twofold conversion. Hunt, writing to his friends at home, said:

> The work of conversion has been going on among our people gradually during the last three years. [Written 1847. A.R.T.] You are aware that here there are generally two conversions—one from heathenism to Christianity as a system, and the second from sin to God. Both these are of greatest importance. Without the first there is no hope of the second. We seldom witness anything like penitence in a heathen. Generally it is not until they have professed Christianity for some time, that they sincerely seek the Lord.[171]

At this time there were about three thousand professing Christians, and the revivals were taking place within this group. This was still two years before the conversion of Tui Nayau and seven before that of Cakobau.

These revivals revealed that Christians were indeed at various stages of religious experience, and though Hunt does not seem to comment much on this, it is quite apparent that he realised it was a fact. One person might be convinced of sin, and another, having felt this for some time, might now find peace with God, at the same moment of time. Another, of sound experience already, might be challenged to undertake further responsibility. Wesley admitted it was possible for people to be convicted of sin and not yet converted to God (Knox 1950, 534). Hunt actually places Cross in this position in his biography (1846, 1–6). Joeli Bulu (Fison 1873, 15),[172] James Havea (n.d.),[173] Bilivucu (Fison n.d., 13–14),[174] Varani,[175] Mateinaniu,[176] and many others admit it of themselves in their testimonies. It is therefore essential to realise that one of these revivals might help scores of people on to the "next base" as it were. This became a characteristic of Fijian evangelism and remains so unto this day. It has continually been my own experience.

This raises another question. I believe the strength of such evangelism can only be really known when a church provides a new opening for service or responsibility with each advancing religious experience. In the early days the Fijian church appreciated this. There was always some way in which a man could demonstrate his new experience in service. The follow-up work was good. Much of the fruit of revival is lost at this point. Wesley saw this. The great display of emotion among the Kingswood schoolboys, he found later, had

---

170 Hunt to LC, 6 November 1846, WM, 1847, 2:931.
171 Hunt to Lincolnshire friends (Rowe 1860, 240–41).
172 On his own testimony.
173 Own testimony.
174 For which reason he went to Cargill.
175 Often testified; e.g., Viwa (Lawry and Hoole 1850, 60).
176 Same occasion (ibid., 61).

not lasted.[177] Again at Newcastle, where there was little to show after a couple of years, Wesley put it down to "nothing but the want of visiting from house to house, without which people will hardly increase, either in number or grace,"[178] which Tyerman says was a "thrust at some of the most distinguished preachers of the day" (1870-71, 3:125). The Everton experiences did not last, and the reason given was the inexperience of the workers, and this is contrasted with Weardale (ibid., 3:124-25).[179] In Tonga, Cargill, who had witnessed the revival of 1833-44, was disappointed on his return there in 1843. He found the number of sincere believers small, their class statements superficial and monotonous; and their religious knowledge had declined, heathen customs had revived; and he felt "much time must elapse, much labour must be performed and much faith exercised, before the people recover their former tone of religious experience." He felt the main reason for this was the "pernicious influence of the distracting civil wars."[180] Wars did interfere with evangelism (the missionaries in Fiji all said that at one time or another); but though Christianity did not terminate war—not for many, many years—it did, however, make an impact on war even greater than war had made on her. It changed the whole nature of war, and particularly what happened after war, which previously had been worse than the war itself.

But in Viwa and Ono we are dealing with growing, not declining, causes. The personal follow-up of evangelism was excellent, and without doubt here is the reason for the enduring nature of the revival fruits. In one short, modest sentence, Hunt admits, "At the end of five or six days we visited the whole of the people for the purpose of learning their state."[181] In Fiji there was abundant opportunity for expressing one's new faith, the church was well organised, and responsibility was handed out to all who showed willingness to accept it, provided only that they could give a good account of their experience and were willing to accept the standards of the church required for their respective offices. This led to a definite growth—both individuals and the fellowship grew.

So we must admit that the church did gain strength from these revivals. Did the experience last in the minds of the people who felt them? In 1848 Lawry attended a love feast at Viwa and made notes of the testimonies (Lawry and Hoole 1850, 58-61). Quite a number of these were among the 1844 and 1845 converts of these revivals. In the same way Hazlewood records the testimonies of some of the Ono revival converts some time later (Williams and Calvert 1884, 288-92). From these it may be observed that they have growing experiences, that they had received something quite definite on that primary occasion, but that more had been added to it afterwards. A number of them went on to become native ministers later, and several of them laid down their lives preaching the gospel on the "front line."

---

177 Relevant passages from Journal of Wesley (Knox 1950, 535).
178 From 5 June for ten days in 1772. See Journal of Wesley.
179 Quoting Journal of Wesley, 1772.
180 Last Journal of Cargill, 12 and 28 March 1843.
181 Hunt to LC, 6 November 1846, WM, 1847, 2:931.

Of the eighty-one to whom Silas Faone had given some responsibility before the arrival of Calvert in 1845, Calvert himself selected ten to take the gospel into the unevangelised regions (ibid., 283). It lasted all right—but I feel we must admit also that it lasted because each case was personally dealt with and opportunity was provided for growth and action. They were occupied in many ways—preaching and teaching as prayer leaders and class leaders, building chapels, learning to read and write and teaching others to do so, school, sewing, craftwork, improving gardens and homes, folding and binding their own books, Bible classes, family devotions, and other church activities—and for the more venturesome spirits there were still scores of cannibal tribes awaiting the gospel. It should ever go down to the credit of the early missionaries in Fiji that they never allowed these revivals to become mere ends in themselves, but rather a gateway into a new life in every sense of the word. The converts received a new sense of living—new sense of work, of social responsibility, of home development, of education, and agriculture, as well as of religion. So Hazlewood got his converts folding pages of the New Testaments for binding,[182] and Williams offered prizes for the best gardens,[183] and men with authority—like Tui Nayau[184] and Ra Esekaia[185]—set about chapel building. Before long the heathen came to see what was going on. At Bua there was a Christian town on one side of the river and the heathen on the other. They stood out in contrast.[186] Joeli Bulu said the same thing of Rewa (Fison 1873, 21). Cakobau was astonished at the change that took place in Lakeba after it became Christian (AR Viwa Circuit 1852). Travellers talked of the church at Bua as one of the best in all the islands.[187]

These social and group changes were by no means more remarkable than the individual changes of the people themselves. Some of the earlier teachers and leaders lived still on into the sixties, and Nettleton says of them that they would "never be surpassed for self-sacrifice, religious power and unselfishness." On one occasion he was distressed that something more could not be done for them and got the following reply from one, Filimoni:

> Was it to seek their property, Sir, that we came among these people? No, but to seek their souls; and if we turn many to righteousness, we shall shine as the stars for ever and ever. I am old and feeble now, Sir, and I only wish to be young again, that I might spend my life over again in God's work.[188]

There was a Fijian who with his own hand had murdered all the Christians of rank in Lomaloma by creeping into their houses after dark, one after another on one eventful night. Within a couple of years he was converted himself, and his zeal for persecution became

---

182 Journal of Hazlewood, 1 November 1848 (Williams and Calvert 1884, 288).
183 Williams to LC (Williams and Calvert 1884, 513).
184 His experience grew. Tait to Moore, 14 October 1864, from Bucainabua, *WMN*, January 1865, 474.
185 Journal of Williams. See entries April 1850. Also Williams and Calvert (1884, 520–21).
186 Many references in Williams' letters and Journal (Williams and Calvert 1884, 512, 513, 516); Journal, 12 November 1848, etc.
187 Henderson note in Journal of Williams (2:519). For opinions of Varani and Lawry, see Williams and Calvert (1884, 521).
188 *WJO*, 1869, 108.

zeal under persecution, and he passed through the stages of Christian advancement, and before long was out in an appointment as a Christian evangelist. He now called himself Josiah—but it might well have been Paul.[189]

There is no end to such stories. Practically every man converted from cannibalism had a story to tell and a changed life to prove it. The records show that a very good percentage of those who passed through these revival experiences found themselves stronger in faith and stood the test in years to come. If there is any truth in the words, "By their fruit ye shall know them," (Matt 7:20, paraphrase) then there would appear to be also every justification for the Fijian Christian claiming that these revivals were of God in spite of their unusual and enthusiastic nature.

Recapitulation: To what extent may the remarkable revivals of Viwa, Ono, Kadavu, and other places in Fiji be compared with those of England, Scotland, and America a century earlier? To what extent were they mere enthusiasm, and to what extent of God? From what type of preaching (or other exercises) did they spring? What type of people were concerned? What did they reveal of the spiritual experience of the early Fijian Christians?

1. When journal extracts of Fiji and overseas revivals are set side by side, their similarities are seen to be remarkable, and it could well be that the Fiji revivals were but a projection of those a century earlier in Britain and America. Hunt, Watsford, Bulu, Vea, and company are in direct spiritual succession to Wesley, Berridge, Hicks, Kobe, and Edwards.

2. These revivals are found to have sprung from preaching, prayer, or hymn singing, which was soteriological in nature. This applies both in and out of Fiji. The only difference noted in Fiji is its common association with baptism.

3. The revivals are found to have been of value to people at all stages of religious development, but usually to those who have been some time under instruction. Both children and adults were affected.

4. Effects are found to have been generally lasting. Many testimonies exist showing this. They show also that those concerned continued growing in experience after the revivals had passed.

5. The Fijian evangelists excelled in follow-up work, visited, instructed, provided opportunity for service and responsibility, etc. It was a period of definite growth, both in the individual and in the fellowship.

6. Hunt considered these revivals the demonstration of God's power, needed to make divine teaching practical and understandable, and to reduce the arrogant to humility, and to inspire Christians to advance a stage in their church life. As such he considered it a definite act of God.

---

189 WJO, 1871, 17–18.

The theocratic historian has no trouble with these findings; but the determinist has still to account for a number of astonishing facts, such as, for example, the adventures of the thirty young Kadavan chiefs, the facts of which are verified by corroborative evidence. While leaving the reader to judge these things for himself, the research student must, in simple honesty, point out that the missionaries and native preachers had no doubt in their minds that the whole movement was of God. In the same way, the historian is honour-bound to place the study of these revivals side by side with those issues discussed in part 1 of this monograph; for to say that Fiji became Christian because of the conversion of a few big chiefs, and the result of Kaba and the wars of Ma'afu, and to leave it there, is just plainly to refuse to face the facts in the documents.

9

THE CHRISTIAN UNDER PERSECUTION

To this point we have attempted to assess the nature of the personal faith of the Fijian evangelical and the place of revivalist phenomena. In reality, of course, things could not be so separated from life. It was more or less a literary device for purpose of investigation, and so the study needs a corrective of some sort, to show what this faith meant when thrown into the pagan realities that surrounded these Christians. We have already seen its uplifting influence—better gardens, better homes, better health, better industry, and so on. But this is still only part of the picture. What did it mean to this household to maintain their Christianity in a pagan village? Obviously some degree of persecution was inevitable. How did these people stand up to persecution? No study of faith is complete without examination of its strength or otherwise in adversity.

This could, if I allowed it, become a subject for the whole monograph. I want to give concrete examples in detail, so must confine myself to a limited period and area, but I qualify my action by saying it is typical. It should be clearly understood from the start that there was practically no part of Fiji where the Christians escaped persecution. There was continual petty persecution and, more often than not, something serious—firing houses, murder, torture, and massacre. Nor did this by any means end with the conversion of the big chiefs. The conversion of Cakobau only increased his own enemies.[190] More than a decade after this Langham described the death drum only so many miles from Bau—"a hundred slain and eaten."[191] Very shortly after this, in the same part of Fiji, a Christian congregation is attacked as it leaves the church, and massacred[192]; and the same document tells of fifty more eaten, a little farther away, but still in the Bau Circuit.[193] The Christian cause in Kadavu was commenced three times, and completely wiped out by the heathen[194]

---

190 Many rebelled because of it (AR Bau Circuit 1854).
191 Moore to AC, quoting Langham to Moore, 11 October 1864. Also confirmed in Journal of Fison, 8 October 1864.
192 Koroveitoga Massacre, Journal of Fison. Also Fison to AC, 16 March 1865, in *WMN*, July 1865.
193 Nabeka Massacre, Journal of Fison, January 1865. Also Fison to AC, 16 March 1865, *WMN*, July 1865.
194 Locality of one unknown. One at Suesue (Naikorokoro) (Fison 1873, 24ff.). Another at Matanivanua and Lawanidoko (Naceva), Journal of Lyth (5:16–20); also Rewa Baptismal Records.

before the arrival of Paula Vea in Yale.[195] Many a time when working or sailing with heathens, Christians were murdered for no other reason than that they were Christians (AR Viwa Circuit 1852).[196] In many places they were unable to go out after dark, and even in the daylight they would never go from village to village except in large groups (Fison 1873, 54–55).[197] There were times when whole villages were suddenly attacked and destroyed,[198] the men killed and eaten, and the women and children carried off as slaves (Fison 1873, 57). Their houses were fired (ibid., 56),[199] the gardens and property robbed (ibid., 62; Hunt 1846, 109; Cargill 1841, 139–45, etc.),[200] their foodpits dug up (Fison 1873, 34), and they were subject to all sorts of insults (ibid., 35, 57–58, 66; Havea n.d.; Fison n.d.).[201] At times they were forced to take refuge in the mountain forts; indeed, if ever a military history of Fiji is written, some of the Christian defenses of these forts will be found among the epics (especially in Vanua Levu).[202] Two faithful teachers were murdered and eaten, the Christian town of Nasavu destroyed, five young women brought up by the missionaries offered abuse or martyrdom, and other villages burned,[203] and about one hundred killed in Nadi area alone in twelve months (Williams and Calvert 1884, 551). Many Christian towns in Viti Levu, in Ra and Ba, and in the mountains suffered similar fate. The Naloto branch of the Viwa Circuit was cut off after Baker's murder. One village was attacked and twenty-eight Christians murdered. One hundred and fifty Christians were killed in the Viwa Circuit alone that year (ibid., 568). One could go on like this for twenty pages; to give detail would require a whole book—and what a terrible book it would be. From this mere catalogue the reader will have some idea of what it meant for a Fijian to become a Christian at any time up to the end of the sixties, and in some parts till after Cession. No estimate could possibly be made of the numbers of Christians massacred, eaten, enslaved, or killed in one of the many unpleasant ways that the heathen devised, and in my own reading I have known the figure to stand at many thousands.[204] The massacre of parties of from ten to twenty was regular news throughout the sixties and even after that of Baker and his team.[205]

---

195 Kadava Circuit Register, etc.
196 All male Christians massacred sailing to Rewa from Kadavu.
197 For instances of small groups murdered, see Journal of Williams, 23 April 1850; 22 February 1851; 15, 22, and 23 March 1851; 24 May 1851; etc.
198 Wilson to Calvert, April 1858 (Williams and Calvert 1884, 540–41).
199 Also, Journal of Williams, 11 May 1852.
200 Also, Journal of Williams, 29 March 1848, 9 October 1848, 20 February 1849.
201 Scores of references in Journal of Williams, especially to suffering of teachers—20 January 1848, 28 August 1848, 20 February 1849, 4 February 1850, 7 June 1850—others in exile, 1 and 10 July 1850, 17 November 1850; Hunt (1846, 99, 109).
202 Annual Reports, Bua Circuit and Nadi Circuit, over period.
203 Wilson to Calvert, April 1858 (Williams and Calvert 1884, 541).
204 Large massacres of whole Christian settlements were common in Vanua Levu, Kadavu, Viti Levu Interior, Ba, and Ra.
205 See Langham to AC, 20 June 1865, *WMN*, 577, and *WMN*, October 1867, for detail of Baker's death.

That figure in itself is evidence of the strength of their faith. Usually plenty of opportunity was given to apostatize, and from time to time some took advantage of it. But there was a great solidity of faith on the whole. There was one occasion when Cakobau sent a message to a Christian community, to reject their new faith or to prepare themselves for the ovens, and they replied that they were ready—it was easier to be killed than to reject Christ (Rowe 1860, 187). More often the Christian resistance was more passive than active, but cases of tactical anticipation were not unknown. Solomoni Raduva, of Viwa, Christian teacher at Bua, saved a village by a bold tactical action, which fooled the enemy and caused their flight (Lawry and Hoole 1850, 83). When the Christians had time to erect their defenses or to establish themselves in the mountains, the best heathen armies of Fiji could not dislodge them. This happened on numerous occasions, and their powers of endurance under siege were phenomenal. On one occasion Tui Bua called it off after many unsuccessful attempts and sent a message to Williams, the missionary, that the Christians' prayers were stronger than his muskets.[206] In all forms of persecution, under siege, in flight, in dangerous journeys, in Christian living, they clung to their faith—generally that was so. When their houses were set on fire, if nothing else could be saved, it had to be their copies of whatever Scriptures they had (Lelean 1940). The faith that stood the fears of danger at sea (Bulu n.d.; Havea n.d.) also stood by them as they ventured on peace missions in cannibal regions, and not a few lost their lives that way, among them Ilaija Varani (AR Viwa Circuit 1854; Williams and Calvert 1884, 486; Young 1858, 303–4, 322) and Ratu George of Dama.[207]

One of the best examples of pure passive resistance I give here just as it was told by Joeli Bulu to Lorimer Fison some years later—but with some abbreviation. The heathen towns had decided to wipe out a Christian settlement. It was well known, and trader Whippy had offered Joeli and the Christians a supply of arms and ammunition, but these had been declined. Joeli explained this refusal as mainly because he did not want to create any impression that the Christian party was defying the heathen chief.

> In the early morning we heard the war trumpets sounding from three different points, and our people gathered together in the open space in front of my house, waiting for the battle. I cried with a loud voice, "Let every man sit down. Let them see that we do not want to fight. Sit down and wait for the will of God. Then, if they fire upon us, let us spring to our feet and fight for the lives He has given us." So they all sat down in silence, each man with his weapon lying across his knees; and the blast of the war trumpets sounded nearer and nearer, louder and ever louder, until the enemy appeared in sight on the edge of the forest—a great multitude of heathen warriors, all painted and armed for war. When they saw us they set up a shrill cry, and with confused noise came rushing towards us. "Sit still," said I, "the Lord will fight for us." The heathen came up to where

---

206 Defense of Nakorbase (Williams and Calvert 1884, 522); also AR Bua Circuit and AR Nadi Circuit.
207 Journal of Williams, 13 December 1850. Setareki, pioneer of work in Yasawas, perished also.

we were sitting. Those who had guns pointed them at us; those who were armed with clubs raised them to strike; the spearmen poised their spears, making them quiver before our eyes; and the bowmen bent their bows: but no shot was fired, no blow was struck, no spear was thrown, and no arrow flew in our midst. What held them back I cannot say; only this I know, that for a long while they stood there threatening us with their weapons of war, while we sat in silence, speaking never a word; but our hearts were crying to the Lord for help, and He heard our cry. At length a chief came towards us with a whale's tooth in his hand, and presented it to them, begging that we might live and that there might be no fighting, and they drew off to hold council. Presently Mr. Whippy came in leading a party with guns and bayonets fixed. After a while two chiefs from the heathen war-party came to me, bringing with them a whale's tooth as a token of peace. "Joeli," they said, "we know this day that you are a true man, and that your God is a great God. Wonderful are the things we have seen today, for there was rage in our hearts and it was in our minds to kill you all; but when we came to where you were sitting in silence, all the strength departed from our hands, and we could do nothing against you. We ask your pardon for our anger, and thank you for your long-suffering. Let this tooth be the burying of ill-will between us." Thus did the Lord deliver us on that fearful day. Not once or twice, but many times, when there was none to help, He has delivered me. (Fison 1873, 37–42)

Let us not be sidetracked at this point by other elements in that story. We are considering the religious experience of the early Christians in Fiji—what sort of faith did they have? How did it stand up to danger and persecution? How did a people, once so treacherous and untrusting, learn so suddenly to commit themselves like this into the hands of God? Taking a purely critical view of these narratives, how can we account for this dramatic change in character?

Recapitulation: How did the Christian's faith stand up to the fire of persecution?

1. Generally speaking, it stood up to every form of persecution. Especially may this be said of those who had reached any degree of religious experience in their Christianity.
2. True, some fell from grace and were disciplined, but virtually none of these did so on account of persecution.
3. Some did apostatize, but these were usually small groups, or perhaps a village, whose previous conversion had been merely nominal or political. But these were not common.
4. Persecution threw into bold relief the Christian character and revealed a faith that was prepared to trust God, even when death threatened on every side.
5. Patient endurance under persecution invariably worked out for the spread of the gospel. Christianity grew, in spite of persecution.

10
COMPARATIVE MERITS OF FACTORS EXAMINED

It appears then that the story of the conversion of Fiji is a two-sided affair. We have admitted there were political conversions, and conversions of convenience, such as following a chief. We have observed also that some large groups indicated their willingness to receive a teacher, mainly because of the result of wars. But having admitted that, the question still has to be asked, "Where did the teachers come from?" Most of them came from the revivals of Viwa, Lakeba, Ono, and Kadavu. At once we become aware of a much greater force at work—but a force which produced not just political or convenience Christians, but men fired with some inexplicable power, a fearlessness and a faith from which even persecution and death could not shift them.

Furthermore, a thorough examination of the statistics indicates that the great periods of expansion did not always coincide with the conversions of chiefs, or with wars, and the historian is compelled to seek other causes. Once again he meets these intrepid preachers, and he finds the growth not on the battlefield, but in a class meeting.

This study makes an attempt to throw all these factors into a better perspective than they have been hitherto viewed. The conversion of Cakobau was a far more important event than that of Tui Nayau, because Bau was still dominantly pagan when Cakobau "bent the knee," but most of Tui Nayau's people had accepted the gospel before their chief. Many who followed Cakobau were mere nominal converts—others, like Cakobau himself, had a spiritual experience of some sort. (The great complication of factors involved makes it difficult to evaluate Cakobau's experience.) We must also admit that Ma'afu played his part—but much less than imagined. Tui Bua also took a page from his book. But having admitted all this, it is still quite apparent that had it been only that, there would have been no Methodist Church in Fiji today.

The Methodist struggle for Fiji was fought and won on a spiritual plane. The great period was the forties, before the conversion of either Cakobau or Tui Nayau, and the places of greatest victories were Viwa, Ono, Tiliva, Nadi, and Lakeba. Methodism came out of that decade in possession of Lau and with a powerful base at Viwa, with a-first class training system for native agents and an excellent translation of the whole New Testament and certain books from the Old, including the Psalms. These had been printed in thousands within the Group and distributed by the native agents, who were also armed with teaching aids, catechisms, hymnbooks, and model sermons. But beyond all these things there was that band of men, fired with spirit and fearlessness and faith, to whom death meant nothing but victory and glory. By Cession some thirty thousand had been received into the inner fellowship—and no war, nor the conversion of any chief, ever got a single man into that inner fellowship of membership. After twelve years of combing the records, I have not found one single case. They may have won adherents but not members, and without members there could be no Methodist Church. True, those other events did bring many under the influence of Christian teaching, and they helped bind the church to the native culture, and may even have opened new fields for evangelism—but the winning of those fields was the work of "men whose hearts God had touched."

But here I must safeguard a point, lest I have created an impression that this work was done by the employed agents only. Let it not be thought that there were not hundreds of ordinary members, just as strong in the faith. It would be difficult at any period, or in any part of Fiji, to find characters who did a better job or manifested greater zeal than Ra Esekaia of Tiliva, Ratu George of Dama, Ilaija Varani of Viwa, to name three obvious examples. These were free citizens, none of them employed agents. These were men of some rank, but they were men who believed that there was a place and work for good Christian chiefs in Fiji—men who were prepared to maintain their civil responsibilities with an applied Christianity. Two of these men died because of these convictions. Their religious experiences were real and in advance of their day.

> These were men of piety,
> Whose righteousness hath not been forgotten;
> With their seed their goodness remaineth sure;
> And their inheritance with their children's children.[208]

When in 1948 the Lelean Memorial School at Davuilevu determined to honour Fiji's pioneers in the names of the school houses; the four names chosen were Bulu, Naucukidi, Mateinaniu, and Varani. They were chosen as types of Christian pioneering, Christian responsibility beyond one's homeland, Christian service within one's country, and practical Christian leadership.[209]

Yet all these men paid a price for this vision of Christian leadership. Ra Esekaia was born to be Tui Bua, but knowing his people would not accept him on account of his Christianity and not wanting to divide them with Ritova always on the frontier, he let title and rank pass to his brother, a generous act which showed him as fine a statesman as Christian.[210]

---

208 Ecclesiasticus 44:10,11.
209 Lelean Review Supplement, 1948.
210 These references in Journal of Williams show the part played by Ra Esekaia in building the church in Bua: 3 and 4 March 1849, 5 May 1849, 11 July 1849, 11 September 1849, 15 and 22 November 1849, 24 April 1850, 30 August 1850, 13 December 1850.

Meantime he gave guidance and protection to the little Christian community at Bua. Josaia Raitono of Bua had carried the stigma of humiliation and persecution for the sake of his Master. His was the initial drive that first sought the gospel for Bua (Lawry and Hoole 1850, 83; AR Bua Circuit 1848; AR Viwa Circuit 1842-43),[211] but he lived to see himself deprived of office because of it (Williams and Calvert 1884, 510), and his faithfulness in persecution was even unto death in the presence of his people.[212] Both Ratu George[213] and Ilaija Varani (Williams and Calvert 1884, 485-87) were treacherously murdered when engaged on peace missions, seeking "the better way."

Both Mateinaniu and Varani admitted later that their experience upon conversion had been very rudimentary (Lawry and Hoole 1850, 60-61), yet both had been real conversions of religious value, and both grew greatly later on. Mateinaniu, though a Fijian, was the fruit of the Tonga revival (Cargill 1841, 82, 110-13; Williams and Calvert 1884, 232) and had no illusions about what it meant to be going with Cross and Cargill to his own land (Williams and Calvert 1884, 232). He pioneered the missions in Somosomo (Cargill 1841, 110-13), Rewa,[214] and Bua (Lawry and Hoole 1850, 83). Varani's conversion was long delayed. Everything was against it, as Varani was Cakobau's right hand, and the chief was in strong opposition (Williams and Calvert 1884, 411). Yet for long he had investigated the *lotu* and had even learned to read (ibid., 428) (one of the few cases of a Fijian learning to read before conversion), and the carefully selected passages Hunt gave him to read played their part in breaking down his resistance to the light (ibid.), and then he took to forest prayers (ibid.), and finally on Good Friday 1845 he "bent the knee" (ibid., 429).[215] Immediately a terrific test was thrown on his new faith, the insult of the murder of one under his protection. Varani's refusal to retaliate astonished Viwa and Bau (ibid.). I have read the records and am convinced it was a spiritual conversion. Then as he went on trying to be a good Christian and a leader of his people at the same time, his leadership assumed a new quality and his experience grew and grew (Lawry and Hoole 1850, 60, 80), and even in his death he was "not disobedient to the heavenly vision" (Williams and Calvert 1884, 485-87).

I should like to add many other names to the list. There was Isireli Takai, who brought the first Christian preachers to Fiji (ibid., 231) and protected them at Oneata (ibid., 230), when they found none at Lakeba. And there was Lua, who faithfully ploughed his lonely furrow in Nadroga and could exclaim when Lyth called unexpectedly, "My mind is high like Nabukelevu or Ovalau."[216] And there was that intrepid teacher, Malakai Butuki, and Tepora his wife, who endured more than their share of persecution, were plundered of their

---

211 Also Hunt to LC (Williams and Calvert 1884, 419).
212 Journal of Williams, 25 June 1848.
213 Ibid., 13 December 1850.
214 Cross and Cargill to LC, 15 September 1836, *WM*, 1838, 227.
215 21 March 1845.
216 Journal of Lyth, 6 November 1848 (5:20).

possessions, and would stop at nothing to rescue a kidnapped Christian,[217] and Iliesa Takelo, who translated Matthew's Gospel into Rotuman (Churchward 1939, 2); and Zerubbabel, who despite opposition got it into the hands of the people (ibid., 3). The line is endless. There were chiefs and preachers and ordinary people also—thousands of them who had real experiences and who grew as they went on, under instruction, and in applying their faith to life. The evidence is all in the records.

The growth was itself evidence of the reality of the religious experience. "The conversion experience" writes Rattenbury,

> was the experience of a discovery . . . a communicable experience, which they communicated to others, who made a like discovery . . . They sought God and they found Him. And it was because they discovered for themselves His grace and mercy in the cross of His Son, and for no other reason, that a fire was kindled that set the world aflame. (1928, 80–81)

Those words were not written of Fiji, but they perfectly fit the Fijian religious scene. Thus Rattenbury concluded his study on the validity of evangelical experience—a discovery, a communicable discovery, a discovery of grace, a fire, a world aflame. So Methodist people put it. The non-Methodist put it thus—"England . . . was committed to a religion of experience; you did not base your hope on this or that doctrinal calculation; you knew" (Knox 1950, 547).

Neither the historian nor the general reader will ever appreciate the real reasons for the growth of Wesleyanism in Fiji without first recognising this basic truth and seeing the conversion of Fiji as a projection of the Wesleyan revival at home. In many ways the despair and desperation of Britain in the eighteenth century and of Fiji in the nineteenth compare. The preachers compare—Vea, Bulu, Havea, Lagi (and the other Tongans); and Mateinaniu, Bilivucu, Ravuata, Varani, Butuki, Raduva, and hundreds of other Fijians like them—but for their appearance and tongue might well have been found among the "early Methodist preachers." Never was there a better mission team of thoroughly Wesleyan preachers than that which pioneered Fiji. They consolidated their gains. Their organisation was excellent, and likewise the follow-up after revivals. Head and shoulders above them all, their father and leader was John Hunt—a saint who got so very near to the perfection he preached.

This is the key to the spread of the gospel in Fiji—not the conversion of a big chief or the result of a battle. Wars did remove some obstacles and open up new areas for evangelism, but they created quite as many problems as they solved. The conversion of a chief always had some influence in the immediate vicinity of his stronghold, but it did no more than bring people under instruction; it terminated inhuman practices but brought none into the fellowship of members.

---

217 Ibid., 5:57–58.

There is one thing in which the Wesleyanism of Britain and Fiji greatly differ. Wesley and his followers had to deal with no chiefly system. It is due to the conversion of Ratu Cakobau that the church in Fiji permitted itself to be tied to this system. It is a Fijian not a foreign church. Its present constitution has evolved within itself. It suits the people and up to date has suited the times. Tradition is still cherished, but change is not impossible, for the church is geared not fixed. The colony for some time has been facing a rapid influx of highly foreign elements. Had it not been for this, the white missionaries might well have been dispensed with. Actually there are only two positions held by ministerial missionaries a decade ago that are not today occupied by Fijians. Increased foreign life has demanded the creation of some new positions for white men, but the fieldwork of the church today is virtually carried by the Fijians themselves.

The greatest internal problems of the church today, as of old, arise from the existence in our midst of people whose Christianity is merely nominal. But the church now, as then, is not blind to this, and her programme is essentially evangelistic. I myself have witnessed over two thousand responses to evangelistic appeal in twelve months, and the messages from which these have come have as a rule had the same theological bent as those of Wesley's day and Hunt's. And again they have come mainly from folk who have received some degree of instruction or introduction to Christianity—generally it is so, but not entirely. At heart the Fijian church today bears the impress of Wesley, Hunt, Bulu, Varani, and Cakobau. Not even the rapid changes of the last decade have removed this in any way.

But though "no age can live on the hoarded gleanings of the past," as Elliott-Binns put it, "it must earn the right to live under its own vine and fig-tree; none the less that past has abundant lessons for those who have the insight and power of imagination to receive them" (1946, 9). A glance at the present youth department will show how methods change, but not the heart. Each generation has to be evangelised for itself, and each generation of church folk has to learn this. And still today as we have seen of old, the success or failure is not determined only by the evangelism, but more by the follow-up. And evangelists of each generation have to relearn this truth.

The peculiar genius of Cakobau's Christian days was evidenced in the manner in which he made the church in Fiji so very Fijian. It suited the times, and it met the spiritual and social needs of the people. This next century will meet different problems. The Fijian now has to adapt himself to new neighbours and new social conditions; problems of town and country, not known before, are new upon him. I believe there is no doubt that the church of the Fijian people will move with the times, but her success or failure will largely depend on whether or not her sons and daughters can produce a faith as equal to the new day, as that of their fathers was to the times in which they lived. And if the past has any lesson for the young Fijian of today, it is surely that they are committed to a religion of experience. We live in dangerous days, but no more dangerous, surely, than those we have been studying. They were men and women who, with less learning than ours, cultivated companionship with God. They grew. They wrestled and they grew.

It is fitting that this monograph should terminate with a closing thought of Cakobau, for what better example could one want of the struggling pilgrim? True there were, and are, many who doubted the genuineness of his conversion, but as I have pointed out, it was not without its religious content.

When he died, the *Sydney Morning Herald* looked back to that conversion and the difference it made at Kaba:

> It is easy enough to sneer at the missionaries and mission work, and to laugh at the notion of a cannibal chief understanding the principles of Christianity; but the fact remains that Cakobau, during his triumph after the Battle of Kaba, acted according to those principles, whether he understood them or not. One great lesson the chief had certainly learned, that mercy is better than revenge.[218]

The slowness with which Cakobau moved from step to step in the Christian way but indicates the struggle he had and the sincerity with which he considered each step before he took it. Nearly three years he waited before presenting himself for baptism, and he did not accept Christian marriage until that time. But that was not the main reason for his delay. I say—nothing Christian came easily in those early days, nothing without cost, nothing without mental and spiritual struggle. But when it came—it was clear.

What it must have cost him to stand on the occasion of his baptism before a congregation, which knew him in all his cannibal ferocity, many of them children of men he had clubbed, and relatives of women he had strangled, and make his confession to them—I say, what it cost him, who can tell. Slowly from his heart and soul came the words of confession:

> I have been a bad man. I have disturbed the country. The missionaries invited me to embrace Christianity, but I said I will continue to fight. God singularly preserved my life. At one time I thought that I had myself been the instrument of my own preservation, but now I know it was the Lord's doing. I desire to acknowledge Him as the only true God. I have scourged the world.[219]

That in less than three years this king of the cannibals could formulate in his heart such a confession is to me a truly remarkable thing. Look at the words. In the first place, there is a personal God acting in his daily life—not an impersonal deity to be fearfully approached with requests for favourable winds, for plentiful harvests, or victory in war and an offering commensurate with the request. This is a belief in a God who has preserved his life to a purpose, who "girded him though he knew Him not" (Isa 45:5, paraphrase). Do we then wonder that he took upon himself that day the name Ebenezer, saying, "Hitherto hath the Lord helped us." Cakobau's was a growing faith. As he wrestled, it grew.

---

218 February 1883, on the occasion of his death.
219 A Waterhouse source in a Melbourne church paper, 1883.

In his old age, disillusioned by his many political failures in a rapidly changing world, relieved that Britain had taken over and given assurance that she would preserve the country for his people, he gave more and more of his thoughts to this God he had come to know and trust.

Not long before his death, he said to one of his attendants (not a missionary or one connected with them), "Faith is a good thing; it is a great thing for it is by faith we are saved. Saved! Ah! Salvation is a great thing; it is the one thing."

Then he repeated a verse which, when translated, begins:

> We who are one with Jesus,
> What gladness do we feel!

In his last sickness he prayed thus, "Lord! Be gracious unto me. Here I lie in obedience to Thy will. Life and death are in Thy hands. Thou alone rulest." It is interesting to know he had reached that point; he, who styled himself Tui Viti—King of Fiji—and sought so long to bring all Fiji under his rule. He had accepted that theologians call the doctrine of the "sovereignty of God."

As death was about to fall about him as a mist, he breathed his last audible prayer: "Hold me Jesus! My faith in Thee is firm."

How far he had now gone beyond that rudimentary faith in the "God of Battles"! That one whose childhood even was bathed in blood should die clinging to no name but the Saviour's was to all who gathered round him evidence of the power of a gospel that "saves to the uttermost."[220] His death was clear and sure. Several times in that last day he breathed the word, "Heaven!" Here is the Cakobau of whom the world has heard but little. Whether he understood what the doctrine of assurance was or not, he knew the experience. However long and difficult his pilgrimage, he found his haven of rest.

The Methodist Church that stands in Fiji today was founded not on a principle of "following the leader," nor by a "God of Battles." It has been, and is, a religion of experience that lies at its foundations.

This is meant to be a historical rather than a religious study. We are dealing with facts about the experiences of men. I have tried to document every statement I have made, and I have done this that the reader may see I am trying to present a real study of what the early Christians did and thought, without reading my own mind back into it. I have aimed also at presenting an assemblage of facts, gleaned from private and mission archival sources, not open to all, and because of this, the secular historian can no more bypass this evidence. He must at least recognise the religious evidence and make some attempt at evaluating it. Be he a theocratic or determinate historian, the facts must be faced.

---

220 Quotations from Cakobau obituary, written by Langham from Bau, 5 February 1883.

KEY TO ABBREVIATIONS

AC: Australian Committee
AR: Annual Report
CB: Cuttings Book, Mission Archives
LC: London Committee
WJO: *Wesleyan Juvenile Offering*
WM: *Wesleyan Magazine* (Britain)
WMN: *Wesleyan Missionary Notices* (Australia)

REFERENCES CITED

Manuscripts and Journals

Bulu, Joeli. n.d. Manuscripts.
Cargill, David. n.d. Journal of Cargill.
Fison, Lorimer. n.d. Journal of Fison.
Havea, James. n.d. Manuscripts.
Lockerby. n.d. Journal of Lockerby.
Lyth, Richard Bursdall. n.d. Journals and note books of Richard Bursdall Lyth. Mitchell Library, Sydney.
Wesley, Charles, II. n.d. Journals of Charles Wesley II.
Williams, Thomas. n.d. Journals of Thomas Williams. Mitchell Library, Sydney.

Material from Archives of the Methodist Church in Fiji

Annual reports:
    Bau Circuit. 1854–60.
    Bua Circuit. 1848–60.
    Cakaudrove Circuit. 1860.
    Kadavu Circuit. 1862.
    Nadi Circuit. 1847–60.
    Viwa Circuit. 1842–54.

General Works

Blacket, John. 1914. *Missionary Triumphs among the Settlers in Australia and the Savages of the South Seas.* London: C. H. Kelly.
Brewster, A. B. 1937. *King of the Cannibal Isles.* London: R. Hale.
Burton, John W., and Wallace Deane. 1936. *A Hundred Years in Fiji.* London: Epworth Press.
Carey, Jesse. 1891. *The Kings of the Reefs.* Melbourne: Spectator.
Cargill, David. 1841. *Memoirs of Mrs. Margaret Cargill.* London: John Mason.
Carter, Henry. 1851. *The Methodist Heritage.* Nashville: Abingdon.

Churchward, C. M. 1939. One Hundred Years of Christian Work in Rotuma. *Missionary Review* 48, no. 2 (August): 1–5.

Colwell, James. 1914. *A Century in the Pacific.* London: C. H. Kelly.

Cooper, H. S. 1888. *The Islands of the Pacific.* London: R. Bentley & Son.

Cumming, Gordon. 1881. *At Home in Fiji.* London: W. Blackwood.

Dimond, Sydney George. 1932. *The Psychology of Methodism.* London: Epworth.

Elliot-Binns, Leonard. 1946. *Religion in the Victorian Era.* London: Lutterworth.

Ellis, William. 1830. *Polynesian Researches,* vol. 1. London: Fisher, Son & Jackson.

Erskine, John E. 1853. *Journal of a Cruise among the Islands of the Western Pacific.* London: J. Murray.

Fison, Lorimer, trans. 1873. *Autobiography of Joeli Bulu.* London: Wesleyan Mission House.

———, trans. n.d. *Old Sefanaia: The Fijian Herald.* London: C. H. Kelly.

Gill, William. 1856. *Gems from the Coral Islands.* Vol. 2, *Eastern Polynesia.* London: Ward.

Hazlewood, David. 1850. *A Compendious Grammar of the Feejeean Language.* Vewa, Fiji: Wesleyan Mission Press.

Henderson, G. C. 1931. *Fiji and the Fijians 1835–1856.* Sydney: Angus & Robertson.

Hunt, John. 1846. *Memoir of the Rev. William Cross.* London: John Mason.

Knox, Ronald A. 1950. *Enthusiasm: A Chapter in the History of Religion.* New York: Oxford University Press.

Lapthorne, Ivy S. 1935. *Fiji 1835–1935: Three Missionary Studies.* Melbourne: Methodist Young Women's Missionary Movement.

Lawry, Walter, and Elijah Hoole. 1850. *Friendly and Feejee Islands.* London: John Mason.

Lelean, C. O. 1940. *The Story of an Old Fijian Bible.* London: British & Foreign Bible Society.

McGavran, Donald. 1955. *The Bridges of God.* New York: Friendship Press.

Nettleton, Joseph. 1906. *John Hunt: Missionary Pioneer and Saint.* London: Charles H. Kelly.

Pickett, J. Waskom. 1933. *Christian Mass Movements in India.* New York: Abingdon.

Pritchard, W. T. 1866. *Polynesian Reminisences.* London: Chapman & Hall.

Rattenbury, J. Ernest. 1928. *Wesley's Legacy to the World.* Nashville: Cokesbury.

Rowe, George Stringer. 1860. *The Life of John Hunt: Missionary to the Cannibals.* London: Hamilton, Adams & Co.

———. 1882. *Memoir of Mary Calvert.* London: T. Woolmer.

Seemann, Berthold. 1862. *Viti: An Account of a Government Mission to the Vitian or Fijian Islands.* Cambridge: Macmillan.

Tippett, Alan R. 2013a. *The Road to Bau.* The Missiology of Alan Tippett Series. Pasadena: William Carey Library.

———, and Tomasi Kanailagi. 2013b. *The Autobiography of Joeli Bulu.* The Missiology of Alan Tippett Series. Pasadena: William Carey Library.

Tyerman, Luke. 1870–71. *The Life and Times of Rev. John Wesley*, 3 vols. London: Hodder & Stoughton.

Wallis, Mary. 1851. *Life in Feejee*. Boston: William Heath.

Waterhouse, Joseph. 1866. *The King and People of Fiji*. London: Wesleyan Conference Office. Reprint, 1997, Honolulu: University of Hawaii Press.

Watsford, John. 1900. *Glorious Gospel Triumphs.* London: C. H. Kelly.

Wilkies, Charles. 1944. *Record of the United States Expedition under the Command of Lieutenant Charles Wilkies 1838-42.* Washington, DC: National Archives.

Williams, Thomas, and James Calvert. 1884. *Fiji and the Fijians.* 2 vols. London: Charles H. Kelly.

Young, Robert. 1858. *The Southern World.* London: John Mason.

INDEX

The Integrating Gospel

A

Abel, 63, 118–19, 123
Abraham, 79, 86, 109, 121–22, 124, 140
Achan, 125
Africa, 51, 82–83, 86–87
Age of Reason, 105
America(n). *See* United States of America.
animism, 66
apostolic, 17, 27, 30, 64, 131, 139–42
   church, 30, 45, 97, 140–42
   movement, 17
Arabia, 136
   Arabs, 136
architecture
   church, 19, 46–47
   Gothic, 146
atonement, 14–15, 63–64, 92, 94, 101, 138–39
Augustine, 6, 29, 31
Australia, 46, 90, 143

B

Baker, Thomas, 111
baptism, 9, 41, 115, 140–41
Battle of Kaba, 147
Bau, 46, 117, 146–47
   Bauan, 58, 147
Benedict, Ruth, 146, 148
Bethel, 108
Bethlehem, 100
Bible, 5–7, 9, 14, 17, 42, 48, 50, 75–77, 79, 86, 93, 96, 99, 108, 121, 123–25, 127, 143
   See also Scripture; gospel.
biblical, 9, 29, 50, 66, 82, 107–08, 119
   history, 3
   languages, 73
   narrative, 61, 76, 116
   studies, 6, 29
   times, 6
   translation, 8, 12, 14–19, 26–27, 36, 61–63, 71, 76, 93, 96–97
birthright, 85, 125–26
Bishop Moore, 5
Bowman, John W., 151
Bromilow, 24, 111
Bua, 13, 69, 111
Buadromo, Inoke, 91–92
Buddhism, 51
Bultmann, 107
Bulu, Joeli, 40, 79, 113

C

Caesarea Philippi, 5, 29
Cain, 63, 118, 123
Cakobau, Ratu Seru, 16, 50, 111, 117, 146–48
Calvin, John, 6, 31
Canaan, 80, 122
   Canaanite, 58, 60, 143
cannibalism, 21, 30, 79, 94, 111, 113, 148

catechism, 8, 21, 27, 46, 50, 69, 71–72
Cession, 14, 86, 99, 111, 115, 117
Chao, T. C., 52
children, 24, 46, 49, 76–77, 88, 98, 100, 121, 125, 138
China, 51–52, 108, 134
  Chinese, 51, 134, 136
church
  early, 5, 114, 140
  history, 5–6, 58, 79
  home/household, 4, 30, 140
  local, 4
  membership, 46, 141
colonialism, 149
commercialism, 30, 47, 114, 117, 148–49
communalism, 39, 66–70, 72, 92, 98–99, 123, 126–27, 130, 135, 145
communication, 7, 24, 36, 40, 51, 59, 60, 64, 69, 83, 85, 88, 106–07, 128, 138, 140
communism, 30
conversion, 13, 50, 105, 111–13, 136, 141, 147
  convert, 8, 10, 30, 41, 99, 112, 121, 133–34, 137, 140–41
Coverdale, 17, 31
Cross, William, 76
cult, 20, 59–60, 114–16
culture, 8, 19, 35, 39–40, 47–48, 61, 66, 71, 74, 78–79, 93, 105–06, 109, 111, 124, 128–29, 131, 133, 135–36, 138–39, 143–46, 149–50
  clash, 111, 122, 130, 135
  cultural
    background, 36, 73
    barriers, 54, 65, 70, 78, 105–06, 133–34, 151
    conditioning, 66–67, 80, 121, 124, 127, 131, 138, 141
    custom, 3

development, 36, 105
elements, 3, 9, 29, 35, 46–47, 54, 72, 77, 124, 126, 131
ethos, 4–5, 15, 57
impact, 26, 41, 44, 78, 86, 93
pattern, 5, 11, 94, 110
setting, 4, 152
studies, 3
Fijian, 12, 81
Hebrew, 121
local, 51, 132
pattern, 5, 13–14, 35–37, 48–49, 51, 60, 66, 70, 77, 93, 96, 105, 120–23, 127–29, 131–32, 134–36, 138–39, 142–44, 147–48
Western, 9, 35, 140
cumulative heritage, 5–6, 30

D

Damascus, 50
David, 121–22
Davies, W. H., 146
Davuilevu, 101, 118
Degei, 20, 72, 87
demonopathy, 115
demons, 135
devil, 10–11, 20, 43, 74, 80, 94, 99
Dispersion, 4
Dobu, 25
  Dobuan, 24–25
Dreketirua, Opetaia, 43–44, 60, 82–83, 86–87, 97, 110–111
Druidism, 30

E

ethic(s), 5, 16, 18, 21, 23–27, 29–30, 43, 77, 85, 120–28, 136, 138
  new, 8, 21–23
ethnocentric, 77, 135, 144

ethnolinguistics, 3–4, 29, 74, 85
evangelism, 30, 40, 42, 83, 85, 110, 113, 131, 137, 141
evangelist, 7, 44, 61, 76, 113, 132, 134, 137, 141

F

Father Mapple, 132
Fison, Lorimer, 68, 81
foreign borrowings, 8–10, 26
Frum, John, 114

G

gospel, 8, 14, 17, 21–24, 35–36, 40, 42, 47–48, 53–54, 57–60, 65, 69–71, 76–80, 83, 85, 89, 91–92, 94, 105–06, 110, 112–13, 120–21, 128, 132–33, 136, 138–41, 143–46, 148–52
Graeco-Roman world, 4, 35, 57, 77, 96, 124
Greece
    Greek, 4, 9, 43, 62–63, 77, 124, 139

H

Harvest Festival, 57–58
Havea, Jemesa, 79
Havergal, Francis Ridley, 70
Hazlewood, David, 31, 51, 69, 76, 112–13
Hebrew, 4, 9, 53, 57–58, 77, 80, 121, 124–25, 127, 131, 143
Hill, David, 134
Hinduism, 83, 140, 150
Hodges, H. A., 121
Horton, Walter Marshall, 151
Hunt, John, 31, 65, 76, 112–13
hymn(s), 19, 21, 26–27, 37, 50–53, 69, 86–93, 98–101, 113, 115, 136, 140, 145

I

incarnation, 71, 73–74, 98, 100, 151
India, 145, 150

indigenous, 7–9, 26–27, 31, 36–37, 39, 47, 51, 53, 72, 77, 82, 86, 92–93, 98, 105, 117, 131, 136, 141–42, 146
individualism, 39, 123–24, 135–36
Israel, 49, 82–83, 86, 110, 113, 151

J

Jacob, 61, 125
Jerusalem, 82, 151
    new, 50, 79, 89
Jewish, 5, 57, 121, 124–25, 139
    priesthood, 17
Joseph, 49
Joshua, 50
justice, 3

K

Kadavu, 13, 114, 116
Kahn, Robert I., 3
Kikuyu, 80–81
Kluckhohn, Clyde, 129, 135
Koro, 77

L

Lakeba, 111
Langham, 117
language, 8, 14, 18–19, 21, 23–27, 36, 48, 53, 57, 63, 71, 73, 75, 92, 96, 108, 130–31, 135–36, 144
    foreign, 136
    primitive, 24
linguistics, 7, 9–10, 14, 19, 24–26, 30, 36–37, 54, 62, 71, 102, 108, 134
Luther, Martin, 6, 29, 31, 79

M

Mackenzie, John, 59
magic, 11, 93, 95, 116
    black, 11, 75, 94–95, 102
marriage, 18, 60, 81, 126
materialism, 47–48, 133

Melbourne, 138
Methodist, 6, 46, 115
Middle Ages, 105, 122
ministry, 27, 42, 61, 64–65, 84, 137, 151
missionary, 7–8, 12, 14, 17, 19–20, 23, 25, 36–37, 39–44, 46–48, 51, 54, 59–60, 67–68, 71–73, 75–76, 93–94, 96, 99, 106–10, 113, 126, 128, 131, 134, 136–37, 147
missions, 47, 68, 130
Moses, 64, 76, 113, 121–22
Muanaicake, 41, 111
Mulholland, 127
mythical approach, 107–08, 118
mythology, 17, 48, 86, 107, 114

N

narrative, 31, 48–50, 71–72, 76–77, 79, 99–100, 108, 118, 120, 122–27, 147, 149, 151
  biblical, 61, 76, 116
  gospel, 5, 22, 71
  Scripture, 27, 76–77, 140
native, 10, 20, 26, 36, 41, 51, 53–54, 61, 65–66, 68, 73, 76, 78, 81, 85–88, 109, 111, 135, 138, 146
  nativistic, 36, 82, 114–15, 136, 148, 150
    thought forms, 7–8, 71
Nazareth, 74
Nettleton, Joseph, 53
New Testament, 12, 44–45, 57, 59–62, 65–66, 112, 124, 127, 143
New Zealand, 69

O

Old Testament, 48, 57–60, 66, 76, 118, 121–22, 125, 127, 143
oral tradition, 17, 48, 51, 75–76, 78–79, 98, 123

P

pagan, 8, 10, 16, 23, 58–60, 71–72, 80, 93, 112, 148
Palestine, 91, 124
  Palestinian, 57, 127
Papua New Guinea, 86–87
Paul, 5, 31, 42, 45, 50, 63, 77, 101, 107, 121–24, 151
peacemaking, 60
Pentecost, 57–58, 114
prayer, 12–14, 16, 20, 22, 40–41, 46, 61, 68, 74–75, 82, 91, 97, 99, 115, 132, 134, 140
preaching, 6, 15, 18–21, 36, 41, 46, 57–58, 61, 65, 74, 76, 78–79, 82, 86, 89, 91, 93, 97–98, 101, 107, 109–10, 113, 115, 122, 125, 139, 145, 148, 151

Q

Quran, 150

R

Rahab, 49, 124–25, 127
Ramasi, Conilio, 111
Reformation, 105
religion, 26–27, 36, 39, 60, 66–67, 82, 113–16, 121–22, 126–27, 129–31, 137, 139, 143–44, 146–47, 149–50
  apostolic, 30
  Christian, 9–10
  Hebrew, 80
  imposed, 133
  pagan, 8
  pre-Christian, 12, 14, 41, 65, 73
  religious, 37, 40, 42–43, 57, 65–66, 68, 71, 78–80, 82, 89, 93, 98, 105, 112, 114, 122, 129, 133–34, 136, 141, 144, 147, 150
    affiliations/associations, 72, 117
    background, 6
    belief, 86

concepts, 3
experience, 21–22, 27, 48, 74, 90–91, 98, 102, 109, 137, 143, 146
knowledge, 75
meaning/significance, 15, 72
practices, 12, 147
ritual, 59, 64, 114, 139
system, 14
work, 19
Rika, Setareki, 61
ritual, 10, 12, 14, 20, 26, 40, 48, 59, 64, 66, 80, 94–95, 97, 110–11, 114, 116, 122, 127, 129–31, 136, 139
Rokowaqa, Epeli, 45, 55–57, 73, 86–87, 114
Roman Catholic, 6, 17
Rome, 29–30
  Roman, 30, 124
Rudra, Shushil Kumar, 150

S

salvation, 71, 74, 78, 91–92, 101–02, 113, 121, 132, 138–41, 144
Samaria, 131
Samoa, 24, 88
  Samoan, 25
Sapir, Edward, 36, 134, 136
Satan. *See* devil.
Scripture, 3, 5, 8, 11–12, 17, 21, 24, 26–27, 46, 73, 76–77, 89, 92–93, 101, 107, 115, 121, 140, 143
  See under narrative; *See also* Bible.
secular, 9–10, 14–15, 27, 47, 72, 148
semantic change, 5–6, 8, 15, 17, 26, 29
Seru, Rev. Paula, 13
Smith, Ryder, 48
Snaith, 60
spiritual, 15, 23, 30, 48, 62, 93, 96, 113, 116, 121, 139, 144
  experience, 8, 70, 112–13, 122, 137

growth, 31
need, 60
power, 94, 96–98
significance, 12–13, 27
Suva, 46, 55, 61, 88

T

Talmud, 3
Tanna, 114
terminology, 8, 12, 15, 21–22, 26–27, 30–31, 59, 71, 73–76, 82, 99, 100–101, 112, 123
theology, 6, 23, 26–27, 30, 46, 73, 88, 90, 92–94, 98, 127, 136
  theological, 3, 7, 9, 17–19, 26, 30, 74, 85, 87, 93, 101–02, 106, 118, 137–38, 144, 151
  colleges, 5
  concepts, 3, 5, 29, 151
  courses, 7
  potential, 18, 30, 74, 97
  students, 83–85, 101, 118
  terms, 6, 73
Tonga, 10, 24, 54, 64, 88
  Tongan, 10, 24, 54, 69
Tora, Maika, 101–02
translation, 4, 7, 22–23, 40, 49, 51–53, 56, 72–73, 87–89, 99, 136–37, 152
  See under Bible
tribal, 11, 69, 81, 84, 95, 98, 110, 119, 123, 125–26, 149
Tuilovoni, S. A., 61
Turkestan, 86
Tyndale, 31

U

United States of America
  American, 127, 136

V

Varani, 112

Vasili, 82
Vatanitawaita, Iliesa, 64
Vea, Paula, 113
Viwa, 13, 22, 40, 53, 69, 76, 112

W

Wainimala, 116
Wanderobo, 80–82
Wesley, John, 31, 79, 91–94
Western, 6–7, 11–12, 30, 35–37, 42–43, 46, 51, 59, 63, 66, 72, 77, 88, 93, 98, 122–23, 125–26, 128, 131, 135–37, 139–40, 143, 149
   Christianity, 7, 35–36, 42, 105, 120
   culture, 9, 35
   influence, 11, 96
Wiant, Bliss, 52
Williams, Thomas, 66, 69
worship, 12–14, 20, 26, 30, 39–42, 47–48, 50–51, 57, 75, 88, 93, 111, 113, 115–16, 119–22, 130, 144–45, 147–49
   act of, 10, 57, 59, 63, 66–70, 76, 97, 147
   corporate, 14, 72
   liturgy, 40, 72, 115
   offerings, 66–68

Y

Yala, 82
Yang, Y. L., 52
youth, 39–40, 58, 118, 124–25, 130, 137–38
   camp, 39–40, 101

INDEX

The Christian: Fiji

A

Abraham, 180–81
America(n). *See* United States of America.
atonement, 227, 235
Australia, 191, 211

B

Baal, 197–98, 206
Baker, Thomas, 189, 191–92, 194, 199, 232, 254
baptism, 183, 213, 221, 241, 244, 247, 251, 262
Batiki, 174–75, 180
Batinamu, 192
Battle of Kaba, 181, 184, 188, 262
Bau, 173–74, 177–78, 180–83, 187–91, 194–99, 205, 209–10, 212–13, 215, 224–25, 235, 253, 257, 259
    Bauan, 180–81, 185, 191, 195, 197, 224, 235, 246
Bau Circuit, 187, 190, 253
Berridge, 240, 251
Bible, 202, 228, 233, 247, 250
    gospel, 179–80, 187, 199, 205, 224, 229, 249–50, 256–57, 259–60, 263
    See also Scripture(s)
Bua, 182, 188, 190, 192–94, 196, 250, 255, 259
Bulu, Joeli, 175, 203–04, 211, 223–24, 226, 228–30, 232, 234, 245, 248, 250–51, 255, 258, 260–61

Bunauia, 187
Buretu, 190
Butuki, Malakai, 228, 259–60

C

Cakaudrove, 182, 192, 194
Cakobau, Ratu, 173–75, 177–85, 187, 189, 195, 197, 209–15, 219, 225, 228, 235–36, 241, 243, 248, 250, 253, 255, 257, 259, 261–63
Calvert, 177–78, 183–84, 191, 194, 202, 209–11, 223, 230–31, 244–45, 250
cannibalism, 175, 177, 180, 185, 190, 196, 198, 206, 211, 221, 242–43, 250–51, 255, 262
Carey, Jesse, 190–91
Cargill, 203, 230, 236, 249, 259
Cataki, Necani, 224, 235, 244
Cession, 189, 194, 196, 254, 258
Chief Wetasau, 174, 183, 245
church, 173–74, 177, 181–82, 184–85, 187, 189, 191–94, 196–97, 199–204, 206, 209, 213–16, 219, 224, 227–29, 236, 240–41, 244–51, 253, 257–58, 261
    membership, 185, 196, 200–01, 204
Collis, 188
Cross, William, 199, 203, 220, 224, 228, 236, 241, 248, 259
culture, 197, 200–07, 216, 258

barrier, 204
clash, 183, 197–98, 200, 203–04, 206
customs, 177, 202–03, 211, 231, 233, 249
elements, 204

D

Dama, 193, 228, 255, 258
Davuilevu, 163, 191, 258
devil, 246
Dreketi, Tui, 192, 214

E

Ebenezer, 184, 262
Edwards, Jonathan, 220, 239, 251
Egypt, 178
Elliott-Binns, 261
England, 174, 221, 240–41, 245, 251, 260
English, 203, 235, 242
Erskine, John, 179, 202, 211
Esekaia, Ra, 228–29, 250, 258
Europe
  European, 204, 235
evangelical, 219–21, 253, 260
evangelism, 188, 229–30, 237, 247–49, 258, 260–61
evangelist, 192, 224, 243, 251, 261

F

Filimoni, 250
Fison, Lorimer, 190–91, 203–04, 247, 255
Fordham, John Smith, 188, 201

G

Gagavoka, Ra, 192
Galilee, 226
Gau, 174–75, 180–81, 184
Great Britain, 220, 239, 251, 260–61, 263
  British, 174, 204

H

Havea, James, 219, 223–26, 228–29, 248, 260
Hazlewood, 202, 205, 245, 249–50

heathenism, 173, 177, 181–83, 185, 187–88, 190–92, 194–206, 212–13, 220–21, 223–25, 227–31, 243, 246–50, 253–56
Hebrew, 203, 228, 235
Henderson, G. C., 198
Hunt, John, 189–90, 198–99, 202–03, 205, 209–10, 219–20, 229–33, 241–44, 247–49, 251, 259–61
hymn(s), 177, 205–6, 221, 232, 240, 245–6, 251, 258

I

iconoclasm, 178–80

J

Jerusalem
  new, 240
justification, 199, 220, 251

K

Kaba, 175, 180–81, 185, 187–92, 194–97, 201, 210, 215, 252, 262
Kadavu, 184–85, 188–89, 193, 220, 236, 239, 245–46, 251, 253, 257
Keteca, Joeli, 224, 228
Kipa, Taniela, 228
Kiuva, 175
Koro, 174–75, 180, 184, 195
Koroveitoga, 190

L

Lakeba, 175, 182, 210, 219, 226, 235–36, 245, 250, 257, 259
Langham, 190, 192, 245, 253
Lau, 181, 188–89, 192–93, 225, 230, 244, 257
  Lauan, 188–89, 236
Lawry, Walter, 203, 231, 249
Levuka, Mara, 193
Levuka, Tui, 193
linguistics, 173, 202
Lockerby, 204

Lomaiviti Islands, 174, 180, 183, 188, 209
Lomaivuna, 191
London Committee, 175, 203, 243
lotu, 174-75, 180, 184, 190-91, 193-96, 198, 203, 225-28, 230-33, 259
Lyth, 190, 205, 230, 246, 259

M

Ma'afu, 187, 192-94, 196, 252, 257
Macuata, 190, 192, 194, 196
marriage, 182-84, 246, 262
Masima, Ra, 193
massacre, 190, 253-54
Mateinaniu, Josua, 202, 228, 248, 258-60
Matuku, 189
membership, 181-83, 200-02, 204, 206, 258
    church. *See* church.
Methodist, 189, 205, 219, 230-31, 257-58, 260, 263
ministry, 174, 240
missionary, 173, 175, 177-79, 182-85, 188-89, 191-94, 201-06, 209-13, 215, 219-20, 223-25, 230-32, 243-44, 247-50, 252, 254-55, 261-63
missions, 189, 200, 255, 259
Moore, William, 189, 194
Moto, Joeli, 225
Moturiki, 181

N

Nabeka, 190
Nadi, 173, 202, 243, 254, 257
Nadroga, 184, 189-90, 259
Nairai, 175, 180-81, 226, 245
Naitasiri, 181
Nakelo, 181
Namata, 175, 181
Namosimalua, 178, 195, 247
narrative, 206, 220
biblical, 202
native, 182, 188, 199-202, 205-06, 214, 219, 223, 228, 230-33, 235-36, 243, 245-47, 249, 252, 257-58
Natutuniba, 191
Naulivou, Juliasa, 228
Navakadua, 191
Nayau, Tui, 173-75, 205, 214, 219, 228, 236, 241, 245, 248, 250, 257
Nettleton, Joseph, 244, 246, 250
New England, 220, 239-40
New Testament, 197, 205-06, 242-43, 250, 257
New Zealand, 247

O

Old Testament, 197, 206, 235
Oneata, 175, 259
Ono, 185, 189, 195, 205, 220, 225, 232, 234, 236, 239, 244-47, 249, 251, 257

P

pagan, 201, 203-04, 253, 257
Paul, 225-26, 229, 233, 242, 251
Pentecost, 220
persecution, 173, 190-92, 215, 219, 223, 225, 228, 250-51, 253, 255-57, 259
Pollard, 211
polygamy, 182-84, 200
Polynesia, 179
prayer, 177, 182, 197-98, 200-03, 205-06, 211, 220-21, 226-27, 229, 233-34, 236, 239, 241-46, 250-51, 255, 259, 263
preaching, 173, 180, 182-83, 189, 196, 199-200, 203, 206, 220-21, 224, 228-32, 236-37, 240, 242, 244-45, 247, 249-52, 257, 259-60

Q
Qaraniqio, 188–89

R
Raitono, Josaia, 228–29, 259
Rattenbury, J. Ernest, 260
Ravuata, Aiskae, 228, 260
Ravulo, Koroi, 195
religion, 174, 183, 187–90, 203, 205–06, 209–10, 212–15, 223, 225, 233–34, 236, 250, 260–61, 263
   religious, 179, 199, 206–07, 211–13, 215, 229, 236, 239, 241, 249–51, 259–60, 262–63
      experience, 182–83, 199–200, 209, 213–14, 220, 236, 239, 248–49, 256, 258, 260
      instruction, 173, 182, 199, 213
      significance, 185
      system, 198
revivals, 182–83, 189, 205, 219–21, 236, 239, 241, 243–53, 257, 259–60
Rewa, 173, 181, 187–90, 194, 196, 198, 210, 225, 244, 250, 259
Ritova, 192–93, 258
ritual, 180, 204, 213,
Robe, James, 220, 239
Rome, 226

S
salvation, 199, 209, 220, 233–34, 243, 263
Samununu, Adi, 211, 213
Savusavu, 193
Scotland, 239, 241, 245, 251
Scripture(s), 177, 202, 204, 226, 228, 233, 244, 255
   See also Bible
Seemann, Berthold, 179, 190, 192–93
Sefanaia, 226–28
Sikovi, 245
Silivanusi, 224–25
Soloira, 191–92, 199
Solomons, 229
Somosomo, 173, 205, 210, 259
spiritual, 185, 196, 199, 204, 214, 219–20, 228, 240, 242, 261–62
   conversion, 189, 206, 259
   experience, 181, 184, 199, 206, 219–20, 225, 236, 243, 247, 251, 257
   significance, 177
Suva, 181, 213

T
taboos, 198–99, 201, 206, 214
Tahiti, 173, 187
Tailevu, 188
Takelo, Iliesa, 228, 260
Taveuni, 188
temple, 178–79, 190, 198, 203, 205–06
terminology, 181, 203–04, 206, 220, 235
theology, 197, 203, 206, 247
   theological, 192, 206–07, 228, 231, 243, 247–48, 261
Tiliva, 203, 243, 257–58
Toki, Johi, 228
Tonga, 178, 189, 211–13, 225, 229, 247, 249, 259
   Tongan, 174–75, 178, 180, 187, 193, 196, 211, 219–20, 225, 228, 260
Tuikilakila, 210–11
Tukana, Ifereimi, 232
Tukana, Koroi, 224, 235

U
United States of America, 220, 239, 241, 245, 251

V
Vakatekau, Asefa, 232
Vanua Levu, 174, 187–88, 190, 192–93, 196, 202, 243, 254
Varani, Ilaija, 174, 189, 195, 210, 223, 225, 228–29, 235, 242, 247–48, 255, 258–61

Vea, Paula, 189, 223, 228, 246, 251, 254, 260
Viria, 191
Viwa, 178, 182, 185, 187–89, 199, 205, 210, 219–20, 225, 228, 233, 235–36, 239, 241–51, 254–55, 257–59
Vugalei, 191
Vunisa, Tamai, 192

W

Waidina, 191
Wakaya, 181
Waterhouse, Joseph, 178–79, 181, 184, 197, 199, 203–04, 210, 212–13, 230–31
Wesley, 205, 220, 229, 240–41, 245–46, 248–49, 251, 261
Wesleyan Missionary Society, 183
Wesleyanism, 204, 260–61
Wetasau, 174, 183, 245
widow strangling, 177, 194, 209, 211
Williams, 179, 203–04, 211, 213, 250, 255
worship, 173–74, 177, 179–82, 184, 187, 189, 194, 197–203, 205–06, 214, 225, 241, 244

Y

Yadrana, 174
Yale, 189, 254
Yasawa, 188, 190, 192
Young, Robert, 174, 231
    experience, 182–83, 199–200, 209, 213–14, 220, 236, 239, 248–49, 256, 258, 260

www.ingramcontent.com/pod-product-compliance
Ingram Content Group UK Ltd.
Pitfield, Milton Keynes, MK11 3LW, UK
UKHW050416240426
12048UKWH00021B/1533

9 780878 084807